WILLIAMSTON ANTHOLOGY

VOLUME II

This is a work of fiction. All of the characters, events, and organizations portrayed in this novel are either products of the authors' imaginations or used fictitiously.

Williamston Anthology - Volume 2

Copyright © Williamston Theatre 2016

Each play is the copyright of the playwright or adaptor.

All rights reserved. No part of this book may be reproduced in any form by any electronic or mechanical means including photocopying, recording, or information storage and retrieval without permission in writing from the authors.

ISBN-13: 978-1944540210
ISBN-10: 1944540210

Published by Sordelet Ink
www.sordeletink.com

WILLIAMSTON ANTHOLOGY

VOLUME II

AN ANTHOLOGY OF PLAYS
FROM 10 YEARS
OF GREAT THEATRE

Published by
Sordelet Ink

CONTENTS

INTRODUCTION

DEAD MAN'S SHOES
by Joseph Zettelmaier
1

THE USUAL - A Musical Love Story
Book & Lyrics by Alan Gordon
Music by Mark Sutton-Smith
63

EBENEZER
by Joseph Zettelmaier
119

10:53
by Annie Martin
165

THE GRAVEDIGGER
by Joseph Zettelmaier
219

THE DECADE DANCE
by Joseph Zettelmaier
273

SUMMER RETREAT
by Annie Martin
329

The Williamston Theatre Founders

John Lepard, Executive Director

Tony Caselli, Artistic Director

Chris Purchis, Managing Director

Emily Sutton-Smith, Development Director

Introduction
By Nan Barnett

New works in the American theater are as crucial to the future of our world as story-telling has been to our past.

Stories are vital to our ability to understand that which we have not directly experienced. We humans began to tell stories to allow others - an audience - to share activities witnessed and lessons learned: the glories of the hunt, the valor of death on the battlefield, the humor of water spilled at the well. We began to fill our stories with emotion, provoking in those listening and watching feelings similar to the ones experienced by the characters. Story-telling became instructive and manipulative and musings on power and the afterlife entered into our tales. Stories are told in order to share.

But why is it important to create new stories? We must communicate our evolving understanding of the current human condition because life's questions continue to be unanswered and what we do know morphs and changes with each passing year. And because there will always be new narratives, lives to be examined and insights to be shared.

Plays, specifically those by living writers, allow an essential insight into the now of who we are, and into the world that might yet come to be. Even currently written historical works are influenced by the lives led by the theater-makers responsible for their creation, putting the now on stage in spite of the setting.

And this is why the works being created all across America, in towns and cities and hamlets and metropolises big and small, rural and urban, considered hip or retro or dying or emerging, are so very important. Americans don't all live in (and therefore experiences don't all come from) New York or Los Angeles. The truths told in new plays by playwrights and producers in Iowa and Mississippi and Vermont and North Dakota and Williamston, Michigan – yes Williamston, Michigan – are as provocative and perceptive and important to the rest of the world's understanding of who we are as a species now as anything being created in the world's acknowledged cultural centers. Maybe even more so.

And this is why it is important that we stop and applaud the courage and tenacity and vision that it takes to bring these new American stories to life on stage in middle America, and why we celebrate these new works developed and produced by Williamston Theatre. These writers and theater-makers - all active in the here and now - share a passion for story-telling that has and will continue to impact those lucky enough to bear witness to the work. Thank you to the founders, supporters, artisans, artists, and audiences of Williamston for encouraging these story-tellers to bring to life the wonders of our time and place, and for allowing the rest of us to share in them.

Keep them coming!

– NAN BARNETT
EXECUTIVE DIRECTOR
NATIONAL NEW PLAY NETWORK

Nan Barnett is the Executive Director of National New Play Network, the country's theaters dedicated to the development, production, and continued life of new plays and pioneering programs for the new play sector. She helped create NNPN's acclaimed Rolling World Premieres and Residency programs, and led the organization through the development and launch of its field-altering database, the New Play Exchange. Nan also serves on the Artistic Council of the Eugene O'Neill Theater Center and was a Coordinating Producer for 2015's nationally acclaimed Women's Voices Theater Festival in the nation's capital region, where she currently resides.

Visit www.nnpn.org for more information about the National New Play Network.

Dead Man's Shoes

A PLAY BY
JOSEPH ZETTELMAIER

Cast of Characters

INJUN BILL PICOTE: 35, an outlaw
FROGGY: 30s, army cook
ACTOR 1: Sheriff, Madame Flora, Abel, Death
ACTOR 2: Sister Bernadette, Belle, Bjarma, Martha

Time and Place:
1883, Various locales in the Western United States

Dead Man's Shoes premiered as a co-production between Williamston Theatre (Williamston, MI) and the Performance Network Theatre (Ann Arbor, MI). It opened at Williamston Theatre on January 26, 2014. The production was directed by David Wolber. Set Design by Kirk Domer. Costume Design by Amber Marisa Cook. Lighting Design by Daniel C. Walker. Sound Design by Will Myers. Prop Design by Stefanie Din. Technical Direction by Ed Weingart. Stage Managed by Rochelle Clark.

The cast was as follows:

INJUN BILL PICOTE: Drew Parker
FROGGY: Aral Basil Gribble II
ACTOR 1: Paul Hopper
ACTOR 2: Maggie Meyer

"The Ballad of Injun Bill" - Lyrics by Joseph Zettelmaier. Original music by Rochelle Clark and John Natiw. *NB: It is the playwright's intention that each production can compose their own music around the lyrics, as best suits the production.*

Dead Man's Shoes was the recipient of an Edgerton Foundation New American Play Award in 2013.

For information about production rights, visit www.jzettelmaier.com.

Dead Man's Shoes

ACT I
SCENE ONE

(ACTORS 1 and 2 are illuminated. They speak the first part of the ballad out loud)

ACTOR 1
Gather 'round, all you sinners
And tall-tale spinners
Gather 'round, all you trav'lers
And sit for a spell

ACTOR 2
Let the fire here warm you
While we players inform you
Of a black-hearted scoundrel
Come straight out of Hell

ACTOR 1
T'was a murderous liar
Who ate coal and crapped fire

ACTOR 2
With a belly for vengeance
He never could fill

ACTOR 1
And he wandered the West
Doin' what he did best

ACTOR 2
The villainous outlaw
They called Injun Bill.

(The music plays. ACTOR 1 sings)

ACTOR 1
In a dark and run-down prison
In the heart of North Dakota
Sat the son of the Lakota
With the devil in his eyes
He spent two years in the saddle
Fightin' his own private battle
And it landed him in jail,
One step further from his prize

Injun Bill, Injun Bill
Think on this before you slaughter
Every girl is someone's daughter,
Every man is someone's son
Injun Bill, Injun Bill
Let your better Angels guide you
'Cause the Devil that's inside you
Wants his due before it's done

(Lights rise. A prison in North Dakota. It's dirty & dark. There are two cells, with bars separating them. In one sits INJUN BILL PICOTE, a hat over his face making it unclear if he's sleeping or not. In the other is FROGGY, playing a harmonica. He is a large man with a moustache wear-

ing a ragged shirt, a forage cap & military pants. FROGGY finishes his song. After a moment--)

INJUN BILL
Don't stop.

(Beat. FROGGY just stares at him)

INJUN BILL
I said don't stop. *(Beat)* You deaf and ugly, or just ugly?

(Beat. FROGGY laughs at that)

FROGGY
You a funny som'bitch, ain'tcha?

(INJUN BILL shrugs)

FROGGY
In there for two days, you ain't said one word. Hell, you farted in your sleep and I thought we was about to have a conversation. Sittin' there for two days and all you gots to say is "Don't stop?"

INJUN BILL
This isn't a social club.

FROGGY
Just a neighborly howdy-do is all I ask.

(INJUN BILL says nothing)

FROGGY
What'cha in for?

INJUN BILL
Being sloppy.

FROGGY
That's a crime? Shit, I been sloppy since I came outta my momma.

INJUN BILL
Got drunk. Got caught.

FROGGY
Gettin' tore up ain't a crime.

INJUN BILL
Cut a man up.

FROGGY
That a fact?

INJUN BILL
It is.

FROGGY
Yeah, I can see the law frownin' on that. What'd he do?

INJUN BILL
Wore the wrong shoes.

(Beat)

FROGGY
Huh. Wrong shoes?

INJUN BILL
That's right.

FROGGY
I reckon I don't follow.

INJUN BILL
Not my concern.

FROGGY
You carved some poor som'bitch up 'cause he was wearing the wrong shoes?

INJUN BILL
Would've been worse if he was wearin' the right ones.

FROGGY
Mister, I can't quite decide if you're crazy or just puttin' me on.

INJUN BILL
That's not my concern either.

FROGGY
My gut tells me "crazy". And I'm a man who goes with his gut.

INJUN BILL
Obviously.

(Beat)

FROGGY
You sayin' I'm fat?

INJUN BILL
You're saying you're fat. I'm just seeing it.

FROGGY
Why don't you smart-ass your way over here and say that to my face?

INJUN BILL
Nope.

FROGGY
You gutless?

INJUN BILL
I just wanted to hear more mouth-harp. You gonna play or not?

FROGGY
(Lifts his leg and farts) That's a song I wrote special, just for you.

(Beat. INJUN BILL gets deadly serious)

INJUN BILL
Where you get your shoes?

(Beat)

FROGGY
What?

INJUN BILL
See them things on your feet? Those are shoes. Where'd you get 'em?

FROGGY
(Crossing to the bars) Your mama give 'em to me for a job well-done.

(With surprising speed, INJUN BILL runs to the bars and grabs FROGGY's ankles, tips FROGGY over, and pulls off his shoes. FROGGY squeals with fear)

FROGGY
AH! AH! Save me, Jesus! This som'bitch gonna cut off my feet!

(The SHERIFF walks in as INJUN BILL examines the shoes)

SHERIFF
Hey! People are trying to sleep here!

FROGGY
Sheriff, that som'bitch stole my shoes and tried to....

SHERIFF
Oh fer... just give him his shoes back already.

INJUN BILL
Make me.

FROGGY
Yeah! Make him!

SHERIFF
(Lowering his head) I tell ya, after everything we've been through, havin' you as my guests these past days...I had hoped you'd find yourselves more agreeable.

FROGGY
I want another cell.

SHERIFF
Ain't got one. *(Sits)* "If you chase two rabbits, you shall catch neither." That's a Russian proverb, ladies. Means if you want too much, you wind up with nothin' at all.

FROGGY
You sure that's...?

SHERIFF
I'm a student of philosophy myself. Somethin' about swimmin' through the great minds of the past, seein' how they reflect upon these times we live in...makes me feel a certain... connectedness. For example... *(He rises, crosses towards them)* You men... you in dire circumstances.

FROGGY
We ain't even gone to trial yet!

SHERIFF
Surely, surely. But 'round here, not many do. Fella gets a drunk on, gets a lynch mob rollin'…and I'm just one man here, ladies. If they come to hang ya, I'm not likely to stop them.

FROGGY
WHAT?!

SHERIFF
This is my conundrum. For reasons passing all logic, I've taken something of a shine to you two butt-flaps. I look at you, and I see the failure of the human condition. And I'm reminded of something Hippocrates said. "Extreme remedies are appropriate for extreme diseases."

FROGGY
We ain't sick!

SHERIFF
A hangin' won't help you boys, so I ask myself…what would prove an effective remedy?

FROGGY
Lettin' us go?

SHERIFF
Nothing short of a sign from God would possess me to do that.

FROGGY
Then at least put me somewhere else! I don't wanna be next to this foot-cuttin' som'bitch.

SHERIFF
Pigs don't wanna sleep in shit, and yet they do. You think on that.

(A knock at the door)

MABEL
(offstage) Sheriff!

SHERIFF
Ladies, if you'll excuse me. What is it, Mabel? *(He leaves)*

FROGGY
You gonna try to kill me again?

INJUN BILL
Didn't try to kill you before.

FROGGY
I was just trying to make conversation before. You didn't have to get all surly.

INJUN BILL
I don't care.

FROGGY
I feel like we got off on the wrong foot. *(Beat)* Yep. The wrong foot. *(Beat)* Can I have my shoes back?

(INJUN BILL tosses him his shoes. FROGGY inspects them)

FROGGY
You sure these are my shoes?

INJUN BILL
Yep.

FROGGY
'Cause I can't see real good in the dark.

INJUN BILL
Yep.

FROGGY
I ain't so sure.

INJUN BILL
I don't care.

FROGGY
I'm real familiar with my odors. These don't smell right.

INJUN BILL
(Temper rising) Who's shoes you think they are, jackass? It's just you and me

here!

FROGGY
Coulda give me your shoes.

INJUN BILL
Why would I do that?

FROGGY
'Cause...um... 'cause my shoes are better?

(INJUN BILL *walks to the bars, puts his boot up*)

INJUN BILL
These are genuine shitkickers! What you got are two snot-rags tied 'round a sole! So why don't you shut the fuck up and...!

(FROGGY *runs over, grabs* INJUN BILL's *boot, and flips him over.* INJUN BILL *lies there for a long time saying nothing. Finally--*)

INJUN BILL
Reckon I had that coming.

FROGGY
Reckon you did.

INJUN BILL
Yep.

FROGGY
You ain't mad?

INJUN BILL
Should be. But I ain't.

FROGGY
Why not? *(He thinks about it)*

INJUN BILL
Hmmm.

(*The* SHERIFF *enters, excited and carrying a telegram*)

SHERIFF
Ladies...I...huh...I got a situation. This here telegram says...ah.... *(He drops the keys just out of the men's reach)* Best of luck! *(He giggles excitedly then bolts out the door)*

(FROGGY *and* INJUN BILL *stare at the keys*)

FROGGY
What the hell was that?

INJUN BILL
No idea.

FROGGY
Them the keys?

INJUN BILL
Looks like it.

FROGGY
All right then.

(*They both dive for them, but neither can quite reach*)

FROGGY
C'mere, you rat bastards.... *(Manages to grab them)* Yes! Oh sweet merciful Jesus yes!!

(*He frees himself. He then runs straight out the door.* INJUN BILL *just watches him, expressionless.* FROGGY *returns*)

FROGGY
Say you're sorry.

INJUN BILL
What?

FROGGY
Say you're sorry that you almost cut my feet off.

INJUN BILL
I didn't almost cut your feet off.

FROGGY
Just say it.

(INJUN BILL *says nothing*)

FROGGY
S-A-R-Y. Say it.

(INJUN BILL *says nothing*)

FROGGY
Som'bitch.

(FROGGY *opens his cell.* INJUN BILL *just stands there*)

FROGGY
I reckon we should leave before the Sheriff changes his mind.

INJUN BILL
I reckon.

(*They run out of the jail. Lights fade*)

SCENE TWO

ACTOR 2
(*singing*)
THE OUTLAW CAVES HE HID IN
HELD HIS TREASURE AND HIS MEM'RIES
OF DEAD FRIENDS AND DEADER ENEMIES,
AND THE TALES HIS KNIVES WOULD TELL
AND HE THOUGHT OF OLD GEORGE PARROT
'TIL HIS HEART JUST WOULDN'T BEAR IT
'CAUSE HE KNEW THEY'D NEVER MEET AGAIN,
'CEPT AT THE GATES OF HELL

(*A cave in Rattlesnake Butte, North Dakota.* FROGGY *inspects it while* INJUN BILL *goes through some supplies*)

FROGGY
Good lord, I coulda had a compass, two hounds, and a map tattooed to my hand, I still wouldn't have found this cave.

INJUN BILL
I been here before.

FROGGY
This a hide-out?

INJUN BILL
It is.

FROGGY
That make you some kinda outlaw, then?

INJUN BILL
It does.

FROGGY
No shit?

INJUN BILL
No shit.

FROGGY
What's your name?

(INJUN BILL *says nothing, inspecting a belt full of knives*)

FROGGY
We been on the road two hours now. Reckon I should know your name.

(INJUN BILL *finds a military saber, examines it*)

FROGGY
They call me Froggy.

INJUN BILL
That's fine.

FROGGY
On account of my Christian name.

INJUN BILL
Mm-hmm.

FROGGY
Jean-Phillipe DeLaRoux Baptiste.

(*Beat*)

INJUN BILL
I get it.

FROGGY
Born in Baton Rouge. Formerly of the 7th Cavalry, under General Custer hisself.

INJUN BILL
Mm-hmmm.

FROGGY
So…what do they call you, fella?

(Beat)

INJUN BILL
Bill.

FROGGY
Bill?

INJUN BILL
Bill.

FROGGY
That don't sound like no outlaw name.

INJUN BILL
That's not my concern.

FROGGY
You should be somethin' like "Bloody Bill" or "Bill the…Bloody" or somethin' like that.

INJUN BILL
Don't care what I should be.

FROGGY
Jesus, you a tight-lipped som'bitch. You got a last name, Unimpressive Bill?

(Beat)

INJUN BILL
Picote. (*Pronounced PEE-coat*)

FROGGY
(*That sinks in*) Smack my ass! You're Injun Bill Picote?!

INJUN BILL
Bill.

FROGGY
All this time, I've been talking to Injun Bill Picote?

INJUN BILL
I reckon.

FROGGY
Smack my ass!

INJUN BILL
No.

FROGGY
I heard you was in jail.

INJUN BILL
I was. With you.

FROGGY
No, no. I mean…didn't they catch you in Montana or somethin'?

INJUN BILL
Caught the gang I rode with. Didn't catch me. At least, not then.

FROGGY
Goddamn, son. You're famous.

INJUN BILL
I am?

FROGGY
Well, with some folks. I heard you was the deadliest man alive with a knife.

INJUN BILL
There's probably deadlier.

FROGGY
Heard you put a man's eye out at a hundred paces for calling your mama a bean-eater.

INJUN BILL
My mother was Lakota.

FROGGY
I figured it was something like that. What with you bein' Injun Bill and all. (*Beat*) Wait. You say "Lakota?"

INJUN BILL
Mm-hmm.

(Beat)

FROGGY
What you need to understand is...I was just Custer's cook, alright? I never went on no battlefield, and I never killed me no injun. Redskin. Lakota.

INJUN BILL
Fine.

FROGGY
So don't cut off my scalp or...

INJUN BILL
I ain't gonna kill you.

FROGGY
You sure about that?

INJUN BILL
You ain't wearin' the right shoes.

FROGGY
So I gotta ask. What's your hitch when it comes to a man's shoes?

INJUN BILL
Lemme ask you somethin'. Why are you still here?

FROGGY
Huh?

INJUN BILL
We busted out two hours back. Why ain't you shoved off?

FROGGY
Oh. I just...um...do you want me to go?

INJUN BILL
Yep.

FROGGY
Oh. OK. I understand.

INJUN BILL
Good.

FROGGY
You don't want me around.

INJUN BILL
Yep.

FROGGY
Fine! I don't need to follow around no half-injun foot-cutter!

INJUN BILL
Good. Go back to Louisiana.

FROGGY
Like this? Nossir. I gotta make my way. Then I'll send for my momma and my sister.

INJUN BILL
You about as far from makin' your way as one man can get.

FROGGY
Do not mistake my current...sloppiness...for being a bum. I ain't a bum.

(INJUN BILL starts packing up)

FROGGY
Look. When I got kicked out of the army, I...fell on hard times. I'm a big enough man to admit it.

INJUN BILL
Yes you are.

FROGGY
And so I...hey! Was you callin' me fat again?

INJUN BILL
Just go on.

FROGGY
No! I wanna know if you was...

INJUN BILL
GO ON!

FROGGY
So alls I need is some direction. I'm a hell of a cook. Best you ever seen.

I'm gonna head to Billings, and set me up a restaurant. Then, I send for my kin. Ain't seen 'em in ten years. *(He pulls a photo out of his pocket)* See there? That's my momma. And that little darlin' is my sister Annabelle. Well, ain't so little now, I guess. Be eighteen if I got my numbers right.

(INJUN BILL starts to leave)

FROGGY
Where you goin'?

INJUN BILL
I gotta see a man about some shoes.

FROGGY
Right. But where's that?

INJUN BILL
It don't matter.

FROGGY
If it don't matter, then tell me.

INJUN BILL
Fuck off, fat man! I don't gotta tell you nothin'!

FROGGY
Oh! I'm sorry! I figured what with me bein' responsible for bustin' you outta jail, you might treat me with certain…hospitalitude!

(Beat)

INJUN BILL
Goddammit. I'm going to Billings.

FROGGY
Billings? Billings, Montana?

INJUN BILL
Yeah.

FROGGY
Smack my ass! That's where I'm goin'.

INJUN BILL
I caught that.

FROGGY
Let me go with you.

INJUN BILL
No.

FROGGY
Please?

INJUN BILL
You just slow me down.

FROGGY
I won't bother you. Hand to god.

INJUN BILL
No.

FROGGY
I'll cook for you! Gimme the right spices, and I can make a buzzard taste like sirloin steak.

INJUN BILL
No.

FROGGY
I'll play my harmonica.

(That makes INJUN BILL stop)

FROGGY
Yessir. Whenever you want. I know lots of songs, too. Clementine and Dog Spit Blues and…

INJUN BILL
You know Let the Circle Be Unbroken?

FROGGY
Yes. Yes I do.

INJUN BILL
I like that one. Makes me feel…something.

FROGGY
So I can come with ya?

INJUN BILL
'Til I get sick of ya.

FROGGY
(shaking BILL's hand roughly) Thank you, Mr. Injun Bill. You will not regret it.

INJUN BILL
I gotta make one thing clear. We ain't friends. You get me?

FROGGY
I get you.

INJUN BILL
You can follow me. You can play the mouth harp. But we ain't friends.

FROGGY
I can live with that.

INJUN BILL
All right then.

(FROGGY looks at INJUN BILL)

FROGGY
Wait. You forgot your…I'll get it. *(Goes through the supplies)* Where the hell's your gun?

INJUN BILL
I ain't got one.

FROGGY
You ain't got a gun?

INJUN BILL
No.

FROGGY
What the hell kind of outlaw gots no gun?

INJUN BILL
I don't use guns. Not anymore.

FROGGY
What? Guns are great! They take all the diffi… difcult… trouble out of killin' a man.

INJUN BILL
That's why I don't like 'em. You kill a man with a gun… don't take no more skill than pointing a finger. But a knife…*(Closes on FROGGY)* With a knife, you gotta get in close. You gotta know how to fight, gotta be quick. That's how a man fights. How a man kills. You get me?

FROGGY
I feel I gotta be honest with you. I'm one scary sentence away from pissing myself. I bring this up on account of I got no other pants.

(Beat. INJUN BILL slaps FROGGY on the shoulder and laughs)

INJUN BILL
Come on. We're killin' daylight.

FROGGY
Where we goin'?

INJUN BILL
Like any good sinner, we're headin' South.

(INJUN BILL leaves. FROGGY quickly checks the front of his pants)

FROGGY
Goddamn, that was a close one.

(Runs after INJUN BILL. Lights change)

SCENE THREE

ACTOR 1
(singing)
So Bill headed to Montana
With a partner that plain galled him
Froggy was the name they called him
When they got the chance to speak
But the city that they came to
Looked like God had set a flame to
None left there but cold dead corpses
'Round a chapel, burned and bleak

(An abandoned church in Northern

Montana. Night. The place looks ransacked. FROGGY pokes his head through the door. He has a broken chair leg for a club. He looks around, leaping between pews. Satisfied, he goes back to the door)

FROGGY
What the hell happened to this town?

INJUN BILL
Goddamn blood bath.

FROGGY
I ain't seen so many dead folks since Little Bighorn. *(He stops, stares at INJUN BILL)* Now remember - y'all won that one.

INJUN BILL
Grab that pew. We're gonna put it against the door.

FROGGY
How come?

INJUN BILL
If whoever killed this town is out there, I don't want him gettin' in here.

FROGGY
That is solid thinking.

(They grab the pew and move it to the door. FROGGY plops down on a different pew while INJUN BILL searches the room)

INJUN BILL
We shouldn't have stopped here.

FROGGY
Bill, we been on the road all day and damn near all night. When my sweaty balls stick to my leg for too long, I get irritable.

INJUN BILL
We shoulda camped outside of town.

FROGGY
Look. I didn't know this place had gone tits up when we got here, all right? I figured we'd hit the saloon, stake out a couple of rooms...

INJUN BILL
...whole place feels wrong...

FROGGY
...hook up a card game, maybe do a little alley-catin'...

(INJUN BILL stares at him)

FROGGY
I got needs, Bill. And I'm saying this for your benefit; you look like you could use a good...*(FROGGY's gesture indicates a blowjob)* That comes from a place of kindness.

(INJUN BILL sits, takes a whetstone to a knife)

FROGGY
Well, I'm out. See ya in the morning.

(FROGGY lies down, attempting to sleep. The sound of the whetstone makes it impossible. He tosses and turns, finally just stares at INJUN BILL. INJUN BILL speaks without even looking back)

INJUN BILL
Different knives got different functions. My big Bowie... that's if you wanna end it quick. They call it a knife, but it's damn near a sword. Now this sweet girl... *(Holds up the one he's sharpening)* I call her Quiet Annie. I keep her sharp as a scalpel. Small as she is, you can slide her right in and a fella won't even feel it. Not if you put her in the Sweet Spot. Might even pass out before he even sees the blood.

FROGGY
Bill. I can respect a man who's passionate about his work. But that little

speech don't help my restfulness at all.

(INJUN BILL *stares at him, confused*)

INJUN BILL
I say somethin'?

FROGGY
Hell yes! You just told me the fuckin' life and times of Quiet Annie!

INJUN BILL
No I didn't.

FROGGY
Then why am I scared for my life right this second? And how did I know her name?

INJUN BILL
I was just thinkin' 'bout her is all.

FROGGY
Well, then you were thinking real goddamn loud, 'cause I heard it all the way over here.

(INJUN BILL *sits, confused*)

INJUN BILL
Huh.

FROGGY
You talk to yourself. That's all.

INJUN BILL
I do?

FROGGY
Yeah. I'm guessin' you ain't had company for a while, so you don't notice it.

INJUN BILL
Huh.

FROGGY
And if I might hazard another word of advice…you need to talk more.

INJUN BILL
Hmm.

FROGGY
I'm basin' this on that completely mortifyin' bedtime story you just told me.

INJUN BILL
I like knives.

FROGGY
Fair enough. But can you see how maybe it's not somethin' I want to hear about as I sleep in the abandoned church of a town full of dead folk?

(INJUN BILL *puts his knife away*)

INJUN BILL
I don't like talkin'.

FROGGY
All's I'm sayin' is we all need a friendly ear sometimes.

(INJUN BILL *stares at him*)

FROGGY
Right, right. We ain't friends. But I'm close as you got now.

INJUN BILL
(*Gets up, wanders as he speaks*) I had a friend once. George Parrot. Ever heard of him?

FROGGY
Yeah, yeah. But they called him something else…

INJUN BILL
Big Nose George.

FROGGY
That's it.

INJUN BILL
Only friend I ever had. He's dead now.

FROGGY
Sorry to hear that.

INJUN BILL
Bein' only a half-breed…I never fit

in nowhere. The Lakotas hated me. My pa's people hated me. But George liked me. Said I was funny.

FROGGY
Yeah, you're a real gut-buster. *(Beat)* Go on.

INJUN BILL
I joined up with him when I was 14. Stealin' cattle mostly. Robbin' coaches and banks, too. George was the one who taught me how to kill. He saw how much hate I had inside me and said "Billy-boy"... he called me "Billy Boy"...

FROGGY
All right.

INJUN BILL
He said "Hate's a good thing. Makes the world go 'round, and murder keeps it interesting."

FROGGY
Jesus Christ.

INJUN BILL
Pretty smart, huh?

FROGGY
That ain't smart! It's batshit crazy!

(INJUN BILL glares at him)

FROGGY
You know what? I was speakin' in haste.

INJUN BILL
What do you know about it? Only thing you ever killed was peace and quiet!

FROGGY
How's that?

INJUN BILL
I gotta wonder.... did your ass get big 'cause it was jealous of how big your mouth was?

FROGGY
You sayin' I'm fat?!

INJUN BILL
Yes! Yes, goddammit! That is exactly what I'm sayin!!!

(Beat. Instead of being angry, FROGGY is genuinely hurt)

FROGGY
I know about killin', Bill. Custer told me all about it.

INJUN BILL
I don't care.

FROGGY
He said "Son, you kill for two reasons only: If your life is in danger, or if the life of someone you care about's in danger. Those are the kills Jesus doesn't give two shits about."

(They sit in uncomfortable silence for a bit)

FROGGY
What happened to him? Big Nose George, I mean.

(INJUN BILL falls silent)

FROGGY
Just... 'cause you said he was dead, and I figured...

(INJUN BILL bursts into action, shouting & knocking things over. After a bit, he hangs his head in despair)

INJUN BILL
He's shoes, Froggy.

(Beat)

FROGGY
What?

INJUN BILL
Two years back, they caught George

and the rest of the gang back in Wyoming. Twenty-thousand dollar bounty on his head.

FROGGY
Damn.

INJUN BILL
Before he even got his trial, lynch mob got him. Strung him up on a goddamn telegraph pole. If it had ended there... shit, that would've been bad enough but... *(He stops to collect himself)* Some rich asshole doctor bought George's body.

FROGGY
Oh lord...

INJUN BILL
Cut up his skull. Said he wanted to study his brain. But then why'd he skin his chest, huh? Why'd he skin his legs?

FROGGY
I don't...

INJUN BILL
So he could make ruttin' shoes out of my dead friend George! That's why!

(Beat)

FROGGY
I feel like maybe you ain't got your facts right.

INJUN BILL
Oh, I ain't done.

FROGGY
That's fine, but...

INJUN BILL
That self-same bastard...he's governor of Wyoming now. A corpse-cuttin' son of a bitch, and he's a governor! And...AND...he wore them shoes to his inauguration! Walkin' 'round, shakin' hands and kissin' babies...with my dead friend on his feet!

FROGGY
Just calm down there...

INJUN BILL
John Eugene Osborne! That's the bastard's name, and I curse it to Hell! Damn you, John Osborne! And damn your god-forsaken footwear!

(Beat)

FROGGY
Now I want you to know right off that I'm not callin' you a liar...

INJUN BILL
You don't believe me?!

FROGGY
Men don't make other men into shoes.

INJUN BILL
I was like you once. Naïve.

FROGGY
Lord...

INJUN BILL
I gotta hunt down the shoes, Froggy. I gotta hunt them down, and kill the no-good, stinkin', ruttin' bastard is wearin' 'em.

(Beat)

FROGGY
See? Don't that feel better?

INJUN BILL
You don't know. I've been hunting Osborne for 2 damn years...it takes its toll. Ain't easy getting' to a Governor. I gotta get him this time. I gotta. This time, either he ends up dead or I do.

FROGGY
You want I should find a confes-

sional?

(INJUN BILL stares at him, almost amused)

FROGGY
What?

INJUN BILL
I only ever told that story once before. To a priest.

FROGGY
You don't strike me as the church-going type.

INJUN BILL
Poor bastard was in the cell next to me, year or two back.

FROGGY
They put priests in jail now?

INJUN BILL
Ain't thought about him in a long time. Must be all this…churchiness.

FROGGY
I don't know. I like church folk. Always got a…calmness to 'em, you know?

(Suddenly, a figure lurches out of the dark. It is a nun, her clothes stained and her demeanor crazed)

SISTER BERNADETTE
And when he had opened the fourth seal…!

FROGGY/INJUN BILL
AAAAAH!

SISTER BERNADETTE
…I heard the voice of the fourth beast say…Come and see! *(She staggers to FROGGY, grabbing him by the shoulders)* Come and see!

FROGGY
Get this crazy bitch off me!

SISTER BERNADETTE
COME AND SEE!

(INJUN BILL pulls his sword, as SISTER BERNADETTE staggers to the pulpit)

SISTER BERNADETTE
And I looked, and BEHOLD! A pale horse! And his name that sat on him was Death, and Hell followed with him!

(She slams her head on the pulpit, perhaps having passed out. FROGGY & INJUN BILL just stare at each other for a bit)

FROGGY
Bill?

INJUN BILL
Yeah?

FROGGY
I'm feelin' a mite unnerved right now.

INJUN BILL
Yeah.

(SISTER BERNADETTE quickly raises her head, launching back into her sermon. FROGGY & INJUN BILL leap in surprise)

SISTER BERNADETTE
Death has come to Garden Ridge, sisters! And he has left naught but damnation is his wake!

(BILL & FROGGY bolt for the door. In attempting to remove the pew, they get in each other's way and achieve nothing)

SISTER BERNADETTE
Prepare to render your souls unto God our deliverer! None shall be spared, for this is the hour of his righteous judgment! *(She points at people who aren't there)* Guilty! *(She points*

again) Guilty! *(She points at FROGGY & BILL, her eyes growing wide, her voice deadly serious)* Guilty!

FROGGY
Ma'am, that's the sort of behavior what keeps people from going to Church.

(She staggers towards them. They redouble their efforts to get out, but fail)

SISTER BERNADETTE
You must flee this place!

INJUN BILL
We're tryin'!

SISTER BERNADETTE
The pale horseman has ridden through our city, and taken the lives of all!

FROGGY
Well, obviously not all…

SISTER BERNADETTE
He killed the father! He killed the Mother Superior! Only Bernadette was spared, that she may proclaim his coming to the world!

INJUN BILL
Good for you.

SISTER BERNADETTE
And the stars of Heaven fell unto the Earth, even as a fig tree ceaseth her untimely figs when she is shaken of a mighty wind!

FROGGY
Untimely figs?

SISTER BERNADETTE
And they cried with a loud voice, saying "O Lord, holy and true, dost thou not judge me and avenge our blood on them that dwell on Earth?!"

(INJUN BILL gives up on the door, grabbing SISTER BERNADETTE)

INJUN BILL
Ma'am! I need you to come to your goddamn senses!

SISTER BERNADETTE
(Grabbing INJUN BILL by the ear) This is still a church, young lady.

INJUN BILL
Sister, I would take it kindly if you would just tell me what the fuck happened here?

FROGGY
Or we could just leave. Yep. Let's do that.

SISTER BERNADETTE
Judgment Day, sisters! Revelation is upon us.

INJUN BILL
A man done this killing, didn't he?

SISTER BERNADETTE
Yes.

INJUN BILL
A man on a horse?

SISTER BERNADETTE
The pale horseman. And Hell followed with him. *(She staggers about, attempting to remember the events)* He appeared as a mortal man…rode into the square on a horse white as bleached bones…questions he had…answers he demanded…He spoke to Father Gregory…so much anger…he looked at all of us…looked into us, into our very souls, and judged us sinners all. Then with gun and sword, he cut us down. He left only me alive. I clutched his boot and cried out "What is your name? You who are the fire and fury of God…what is your name?"

FROGGY
What...what did he say?

SISTER BERNADETTE
"Death". He said his name...was Death.

(They stand there, terrified. FROGGY sees a collection plate. He picks it up, drops some coins in it)

FROGGY
The service has ended. May you go in peace to love and to serve the lord.

(He hurls the pew out of the way, opens the door and bolts. INJUN BILL follows. SISTER BERNADETTE sits on a pew)

SISTER BERNADETTE
Death has come for us all.

(Lights fade)

SCENE FOUR

ACTOR 2
(singing)
INJUN BILL, INJUN BILL
FLEE THE CHURCH BEFORE HE FINDS YOU
'CAUSE DEATH FOLLOWS RIGHT BEHIND YOU
AND YOUR JOURNEY'S FAR FROM DONE
INJUN BILL, INJUN BILL
RIDE TO BILLINGS AND TO GLORY
WELL, THIS AIN'T THAT KIND OF STORY
SO JUST WATCH THE SETTING SUN

(Billings, Montana. The next day. A large outdoor bathtub is onstage. INJUN BILL sits at the foot of it. FROGGY lifts head out of the water, sopping wet)

FROGGY
Goddamn! That is what the doctor ordered! *(He shakes his head vigorously, soaking INJUN BILL)*

INJUN BILL
Watch it!

FROGGY
Bill, you gotta get in one of these! Wash the stink right off ya.

INJUN BILL
I don't stink.

FROGGY
Well I did! And now I feel like a new man. Don't know what your business is in Billings, but hallelujah! Here we are!

INJUN BILL
Gotta talk to a man at the saloon.

FROGGY
WOO! Got my clothes warshed, got my body warshed. Next I'm gonna buy me some smell'um for my hair, some wax for my whiskers, and get me some tail.

INJUN BILL
You get yourself cleaned up, then you're gonna go balls-deep in some stinking whore?

FROGGY
No sir! I'm gonna get me the best... *(Reaches over, grabbing his wallet)* The best thirteen dollar-and-82-cent whore money can buy.

INJUN BILL
Where you get all that money?

(Beat. FROGGY has been caught, and can't think of a good lie to get out of it)

FROGGY
Distant relation?

(INJUN BILL grabs him and shoves his head under the water. FROGGY struggles, and BILL lets him up)

FROGGY
Jesus Christ!

INJUN BILL
You lie to me again, I'm holdin' you down there for ten minutes!

FROGGY
I took it off the dead folks! You happy now, you crazy som'bitch!?

INJUN BILL
You what?

FROGGY
Them dead folk in Garden Ridge! While you was inspecting the town, I was makin' donations to the Get-Froggy-Bathed-And-Humped fund.

INJUN BILL
That's low, Froggy. Stealin' from dead folks is low.

FROGGY
I don't need no moral condemnation from some half-Injun foot-cutter.

INJUN BILL
I'm on a quest for vengeance. I'm doin' what I gotta do. And I ain't gotta steal from dead folk.

FROGGY
...just mad that you didn't think of it first...

INJUN BILL
Now here's an interesting thought to throw at ya. What kind of man kills a whole damn town, but don't take their money?

FROGGY
That is an interesting thought. A rich man?

INJUN BILL
I never met a rich man wouldn't stop a train if he saw a nickel on the tracks.

FROGGY
Fair enough. So I guess you gotta ask yourself...what kind of man don't care about money?

INJUN BILL
A dangerous man.

FROGGY
Yes. Thank you for that, Bill. The fact that he killed fifty people didn't clue me in to his dangerous nature.

(MADAME FLORA enters. She is a large, heavily coifed & made-up woman)

MADAME FLORA
Howdy, boys. You new to these parts?

FROGGY
That we are, ma'am.

MADAME FLORA
Madame, sugar. Madame Flora, at yer service.

FROGGY
Hot damn. I think you might be just what I'm lookin' for.

MADAME FLORA
(Leans in close, hand in the water) Is that a fact?

(FROGGY jumps)

FROGGY
I... that is to say... you run the local brothel?

MADAME FLORA
I cater to the needs of the menfolk, introducing them to ladies of my acquaintance for a small fee.

FROGGY
Madame Flora, I am in dire need of feminine companionship this night.

MADAME FLORA
Sugar, you came to the right town.

(INJUN BILL *rises, going to leave*)

MADAME FLORA
My my my my my. Who is this tall drink of handsome?

FROGGY
That's my friend Bill. Bill, say howdy to the lady.

(INJUN BILL *tips his hat*)

INJUN BILL
Miss. And we ain't friends.

(MADAME FLORA *moves in on* BILL)

MADAME FLORA
I am duty-bound to ask if you are also in need of companionship. And if you absolutely have to know, I'm very much hopin' that I'm just your type.

INJUN BILL
You ain't.

(*She slaps* BILL)

INJUN BILL
That is to say…I don't roll with trade that speaks English.

MADAME FLORA
I see. While I'm disappointed that I won't be riding you into the sunset, I can respect a man who knows what he wants and doesn't mince words about it.

INJUN BILL
That's fine, but I ain't lookin' to roll.

FROGGY
Madame Flora, he don't speak for the both of us.

MADAME FLORA
Not even for Bjarma?

(BILL *stops. The name is pronounced* BYAR-ma)

INJUN BILL
What kind of name is Bjarma?

MADAME FLORA
Faroese, and that's a fact.

INJUN BILL
Where she from?

MADAME FLORA
The Faroe Islands.

INJUN BILL
Where's that?

MADAME FLORA
Up north, by Denmark. Little island chain, not much on it but sheep and buxom ladies. And William… she doesn't speak a word of English. Not. One. Syllable.

FROGGY
Come on, Bill. That's gotta be some kind of sign.

(*Beat*)

INJUN BILL
How much?

MADAME FLORA
Specialty acts like Bjarma cost ten up front.

(BILL *hands her a ten dollar bill*)

FROGGY
Where you get that money?

INJUN BILL
Had a stash in the cave.

FROGGY
How much for a regular-speakin' whore, Miss?

MADAME FLORA
In the front, or 'round back?

FROGGY
In the front.

MADAME FLORA
Five dollars.

FROGGY
Sold!

(*FROGGY starts to rise, with BILL grabbing a towel to cover him at the last second*)

MADAME FLORA
I appreciate the gallantry, sir. But I'm sure this gentleman doesn't have anything I haven't seen…

(*She looks on the other side of the curtain, surprised by what she sees*)

MADAME FLORA
Oh my.

(*FROGGY smiles proudly*)

FROGGY
And that's why I wear my pants loose.

(*Lights fade*)

SCENE FIVE

(*The brothel, moments later. BELLE, a beautiful young prostitute sits on a bed. FROGGY enters. He is noticeably cleaner, with his hair and moustache styled*)

FROGGY
Oh my lord. Ain't you as sweet as cinnamon.

BELLE
Am I?

FROGGY
You are indeed. You are indeed.

BELLE
(*Offering her hand*) I'm Belle.

FROGGY
They call me Froggy. (*Kisses her hand*)

BELLE
Well. Most men shake my hand. Those who don't throw me to the bed, that is. You know your manners.

FROGGY
My mama raised me right.

BELLE
Clearly.

(*She pats the bed. He joins her. She rubs his shoulders. He moans in pleasure*)

FROGGY
Miss Belle, before tonight, I believed myself to be just about the unluckiest som'bitch walkin' the earth. I admit I may have been wrong on that subject.

BELLE
Am I your rabbit's foot then? (*She puts her foot on his lap*)

FROGGY
You just might be.

(*He moves in to kiss her. She moves him to her neck*)

BELLE
Not on the lips, dear. Never the lips.

FROGGY
Yes, ma'am. I was wonderin' if I could ask a favor of you.

BELLE
It's your dollar, darlin'.

FROGGY
Could you…just stand right there? (*He moves her in front of a lamp, so she is now silhouetted by the light*) That's it. Perfect. Now, could you undress for me?

BELLE
That is usually the preferred way to go.

FROGGY
I mean… slow. Undress slow.

BELLE
Your wish is my command. *(She slowly removes her clothing)* I like you, Froggy.

FROGGY
You do?

BELLE
Most men who come through these parts…they just throw my skirts up over my shoulders and get to it. I like a man who can enjoy the female form.

FROGGY
Oh. I'm enjoying it.

(She has removed her vest, and begins undoing her corset)

FROGGY
Slower.

BELLE
All right then. *(She slowly works on her corset)*

BELLE
You a soldier, Froggy? I'm guessing you are on account of your pants and your hat.

FROGGY
I was, ma'am. Dishonorably discharged on account of drunkenness, horse-thievery, and general ineptitude.

BELLE
You don't seem drunk now.

FROGGY
That's what I'm doin' after.

BELLE
And you certainly don't seem inept.

FROGGY
That's kind of you to say, but I'll tell you the truth.

BELLE
Please do.

FROGGY
Only thing I was ever good at was cookin'. That's why I come out this way.

BELLE
To be a cook?

FROGGY
Yes, ma'am. I mean to open a restaurant. I hear tell Billings done sprung up good, what with the new train runnin' through it. I figure, trains bring more people, and them people gotta eat.

BELLE
Aren't you enterprising?

FROGGY
My mama always told me "Be a cook or be an undertaker. People always gotta eat, and they always gotta die."

BELLE
So why not an undertaker?

FROGGY
Well, dead folks got an odor to 'em.

BELLE
I see. Well Froggy, do you have a specialty?

FROGGY
Um…well…I'm good South of the border, if you get my meaning…

BELLE
(Laughs, removing her corset) I mean with your cooking.

FROGGY
Oh! Right, I… You know what I really want to do is start up a Cajun restaurant somewhere 'round here.

BELLE
Really?

FROGGY
Oh yeah. I'm from Louisiana. Nothing better than that smell when you're lettin' the roux brown up, throwin' in some sassafras and some andouille…

BELLE
I'm from Louisiana myself.

FROGGY
No!

BELLE
God's honest truth. Left when I was just a girl.

FROGGY
Where abouts?

BELLE
Baton Rouge.

FROGGY
No kiddin'? I'm from Baton Rouge! Slower.

(BELLE slowly removes her stockings)

FROGGY
You don't have an accent.

BELLE
Worked hard to lose it. Some folks think it makes you sound ignorant.

FROGGY
Fellas in the army said the same thing. Turns out I sound ignorant with or without it.

(She laughs at that)

FROGGY
Goddamn! A fine lookin' Louisiana gal just like my momma would want me to marry.

BELLE
Oh hush.

FROGGY
You know Old Man Montpellier? Mixed fella that runs the bakery on Convention Street?

BELLE
Know him? Hell, we were practically neighbors!

FROGGY
I used to steal croissants from his window every morning when he was in the back! Well, me and the fellas I ran with.

BELLE
No!

FROGGY
I did!

BELLE
You must've known my brother then! I bet he was one of your gang!

FROGGY
Wouldn't that be just too much?

BELLE
You know Jean-Phillipe Baptiste?

(Long, awkward beat)

FROGGY
What?

BELLE
That was my brother's name. Sandy blonde hair, thin as a rail.

FROGGY
Oh sweet Jesus.

BELLE
He left…must've been ten years ago. Got killed fighting with General Custer. (She sees the look of utter horror on his face) Do you know him, Froggy?

(FROGGY says nothing, his expression frozen)

BELLE
Froggy?

FROGGY
Annabelle?

(Beat)

BELLE
Did Flora tell you my Christian name?

FROGGY
Annabelle, it's me!

BELLE
Me who?

FROGGY
Jean-Fucking-Philippe!

(Beat)

BELLE
That's not nice.

FROGGY
I know, but it's the goddamn truth!

(BELLE goes to him, places her hand on his face. She pushes his cheeks back, trying to picture him thinner. She sees it)

BELLE
Jean-Philippe?

FROGGY
Uh-huh.

(BELLE hugs him. FROGGY hesitantly hugs her back)

BELLE
Oh my god! You're alive! They told us you took two arrows to the face!

FROGGY
I imagine they was tryin' to be kind.

BELLE
Why didn't you come back to us?

FROGGY
I was ashamed. I wanted to hold to my word, build my restaurant.

BELLE
But ten years?! Seven of which I thought you were dead!

FROGGY
What about Mama? You gotta tell her...

BELLE
Jean-Philippe, Mama passed.

FROGGY
(Lowers his head, crushed) ...no...

BELLE
She got the TB in her lungs. It was quicker for her than it was for most. When she heard that Jesus had called you home... I think she just wanted to go.

(FROGGY sits on the bed, defeated)

BELLE
I'm so sorry. If I knew you were still with us, I'd have tracked you down.

FROGGY
I shoulda gone home. Instead, I shoved my head in a bottle and never come out.

BELLE
We still have each other. You're not alone. *(She touches his arm gently)*

FROGGY
I can't believe she's gone, Anna. All this time, I been holdin' on to this belief that... and lookit what I am now! A fat drunk in a whorehouse! Maybe that's what I should call my restaurant!

(He laughs at that. She does as well)

BELLE
And what about me? I've been roll-

ing with johns for the better part of a year. I think things went just ducky for the both of us!

(They laugh again)

FROGGY
I know! I was about to be one of those johns!

(They laugh again, then stare at each other. She goes to the window and vomits just as he grabs an empty chamber pot and vomits)

FROGGY
OH GOD! OH MY GOD! What have I done!?

BELLE
(Scrambling to dress herself) Unclean! I'm unclean!

FROGGY
Anna, I… I gotta go!

BELLE
I'm a monster!

FROGGY
I'll… visit or… something I… so long. *(He heads for the door, muttering as he goes)*…unluckiest som'bitch walkin' the earth…

(Lights fade)

SCENE SIX

(The brothel, but a different room, at the same time as Scene 5. INJUN BILL paces, waiting for BJARMA. He finds a tall mirror & inspects himself in it. He fiddles with his knives, then realizes he should remove his knife belt. He does so as BJARMA enters)

MADAME FLORA
Last chance to change your mind. *(Beat)* It could've been…magic. *(She exits)*

INJUN BILL
You're beautiful.

(She curtsies)

INJUN BILL
Do you…beautiful. Do you know that word?

(She smiles at him)

INJUN BILL
Beautiful? You are…forget it.

(She sits on the bed, motioning for him to join her)

BJARMA
Bola? (Sit?)

INJUN BILL
Is that…you want me to sit?

(He sits next to her. They share a moment of uncertainty. She then puts her hand high on his leg)

INJUN BILL
No. That's all right.

(She stares at him, confused. She then raises her arms in the air, wrists together, inquiring if he wants to tie her up)

INJUN BILL
No. No, nothing like that.

BJARMA
Als kyn? (No sex?)

INJUN BILL
You don't know what I'm saying, do you? No English?

BJARMA
Foroyskt. Als Enskt. (Faroese. No English)

INJUN BILL
Goddamn, you got a pretty way of talking. I'm…my name is Bill. *(He*

points to himself) Bill.

BJARMA
Beel.

INJUN BILL
Now say your name.

BJARMA
Beel?

INJUN BILL
No. I'm Bill. You are…?

BJARMA
Bjarma.

INJUN BILL
That's real pretty. Like you.

(They smile at each other, not talking)

BJARMA
Nuh i hafa kyn? (Now we have sex?)

INJUN BILL
(Taking her hands in his) Darlin', I know I might as well be speaking Chinee to ya, but I'm hoping you'll pick up my meaning none the less. It would mean an awful lot to me if I could just… here.

(He leans her back on the bed. She's confused but lets him)

INJUN BILL
And I'm gonna…

(He leans back against her, his head resting on her chest. She instinctively puts her arms around him)

INJUN BILL
That's it. Yes. That's exactly what I want. I just want to lie here like this.

(She strokes his hair)

INJUN BILL
Thank you.

(They lie there in silence for a bit)

INJUN BILL
I never knew my father. He was a cavalryman, stuck it to my mama and left. She had to leave her people, 'cause of the shame. She hated me. My whole life, she looked at me with nothin' but a wish that I was dead. One day, she just up and left. I was ten. Hell, I don't know why it took her so long to do it. Bjarma…

(She looks at him)

INJUN BILL
Used to be I'd hump a girl, pull up my pants and walk out the door. The first time a woman just…held me after… I cried. Cried like a damn baby. So if I end up doin' that again, I'm hopin' you'll be sympathetic to my situation. *(Beat)* Damn near all my life, I been hated. And the only folks that didn't hate me are dead now. Them bastards that caught George, they was after the bounty. Twenty-thousand dollars 'cause George shot a deputy in the face. 'Cept it wasn't George that shot the man. He told folks he did, 'cause he liked to brag. That was always his way. But George… he could shove a gun up a man's ass and he'd still miss. *(Beat)* They killed George 'cause of what I done. What I done, and what I let him say he did. 'Cause I thought it would make him happy. And now… I'm wantin' to make amends, but in my heart… I don't know why the hell I'm doing this. I'm doin' what George would've done…but is that a reason to do somethin'? The man's dead two years now, and he's still tellin' me what to do. I feel like I owe it to him, but all he ever give me was this… wreck of a life. Is that somethin' to be grateful for?

(He stares at her. She stares back, confused. She puts her mouth around his nose. Beat)

INJUN BILL
I don't know if this is stimulatin' where you come from, but it's doin' nothin' for me.

(Suddenly, a loud knock on the door)

FROGGY
(offstage) Injun Bill? We're goin'. Now!

INJUN BILL
Gimme a minute here.

FROGGY
(offstage) Now!

(BILL rises, grabs his belt, and kisses BJARMA sweetly)

INJUN BILL
Thanks for listenin', Bjarma. You're a peach.

(He leaves. BJARMA lies back in bed, holding her head)

BJARMA
Jesus Christ. Why do I always get the crazy ones?

(Lights fade)

SCENE SEVEN

ACTOR 1
(singing)
At a tavern name of Crossroads,
Bill & Froggy came a callin'
For a barkeep so appallin'
He had hellfire on the tap
But the man of whom I'm speakin'
Had the knowledge they were seekin'
So Bill never stopped to wonder
If the meeting was a trap

(Crossroads Saloon, later that night. The sound of a crowd talking, and old time piano music. ABEL WEXFORD is cleaning the bar. He's a rough looking Irishman w/ an eye patch. INJUN BILL & FROGGY enter. FROGGY already has a bottle & is fairly drunk. INJUN BILL smiles widely, throws his hands in the air and shouts his friend's name)

INJUN BILL
Abel Wexford!

(ABEL smiles wide, throws his hands up and responds in kind)

ABEL
Injun Bill Picote!

(Without changing his expression, he pulls a gun from beneath the bar and fires. INJUN BILL & FROGGY duck for cover. The crowd grows silent, and the music stops)

FROGGY
Jesus Christ!

INJUN BILL
Just calm down, Abel!

ABEL
How can I be calm when one of me favorite people just walked through me door? *(He fires again)* Come on over! Let me give ya a hug!

(He fires again, but the gun jams. INJUN BILL quickly runs over & wrestles the gun from him)

ABEL
Still pretty quick, are ya?

INJUN BILL
Quick enough.

ABEL
Think so? *(He pulls a derringer out of his jacket. INJUN BILL grabs it)*

ABEL
Damn!

FROGGY
Can I stand up now?

(ABEL hurls himself at INJUN BILL. They fall to the ground wrestling. As they do, FROGGY heads over to the bar and starts pouring himself drinks)

FROGGY
Get 'em, Bill.

(INJUN BILL ends up on top of ABEL, his Bowie knife to ABEL's throat)

INJUN BILL
You gonna settle down now, Abel?

ABEL
I'm half-deaf, Bill! I can't hear you!

INJUN BILL
I said…

(INJUN BILL leans in and ABEL head-butts him. INJUN BILL staggers back)

ABEL
I'm truly surprised you fell fer that.

(ABEL almost charges again, but FROGGY grabs him, putting him in a full-nelson)

FROGGY
That's enough, barkeep.

ABEL
Let me go!

FROGGY
Not a Chinaman's chance!

ABEL
I mean ta kill that redskin shitbird!

FROGGY
And that's why I'm not lettin' you go.

(INJUN BILL rises, crosses to them)

INJUN BILL
You still pissed off about the eye?

ABEL
No, it's a distant feckin' memory. What eye are you speakin' of?

INJUN BILL
It was an accident and you know it.

ABEL
Oh thank god! Now I can see outta my left side again.

INJUN BILL
Abel, I come here for answers. Once I get 'em, I'll leave. (Slams some bills on the table)

ABEL
What's that?

INJUN BILL
My appreciation for the answers.

ABEL
How much?

(FROGGY & ABEL hobble over to the table. ABEL counts the bills)

ABEL
Why don't I pour you fellas some drinks?

(FROGGY lets ABEL go)

ABEL
Name your firewater, redskin.

INJUN BILL
Bourbon if you got it.

ABEL
I do. What about you, tiny?

FROGGY
Gimme somethin' that'll knock me on my ass. I got some forgettin' to do.

ABEL
Comin' up. Franky! Get back ta that

piana or I'll box yer ears for ya!

(*The crowd starts talking again, and the music starts back up. He slides them their drinks. FROGGY downs his, then goes down to one knee*)

FROGGY
Good god.

ABEL
That's straight from the homeland, boyo. Now, onto our business.

INJUN BILL
You know where they are?

ABEL
What "they" would that be?

INJUN BILL
Don't bust my balls, Abel. That letter you sent said you knew.

ABEL
Ever think I sent that to get you here so I could put a bullet in yer brain?

INJUN BILL
(*Draws a knife*) That best be a lie. Otherwise, Quiet Annie might have to enter negotiations.

ABEL
All right, all right, all right. Jesus.

(*As they talk, FROGGY rises, signals for another drink. ABEL pours him another*)

ABEL
The Governor is headin' down to Denver this very week. Might already be there.

INJUN BILL
Why Denver?

ABEL
They say he's investin' in a gold mine. S'possed to be real hush-hush, so I figure he won't have his full entourage, if you get my meaning.

FROGGY
...can't believe I nearly ram-rodded my own sister...

(*ABEL & INJUN BILL stare at him*)

FROGGY
What? I didn't...nothin'.

INJUN BILL
How do I know he'll have the shoes?

ABEL
Way I hear tell, he don't go nowhere without 'em. It's a point of pride.

INJUN BILL
Pride is a deadly sin.

ABEL
Yes it is.

INJUN BILL
Reckon it's high-time he finds out how deadly. Come on, Froggy. (*Grabs FROGGY, mutters to himself*) I'm comin' for you, Osborne. You ain't slippin' away this time, you son of a whore.

ABEL
Hey! Come back here and I'll kill ya. You hear me? Don't let me see you again.

INJUN BILL
Then I guess I'll just stay to your left.

(*He and FROGGY head out. Lights fade*)

SCENE EIGHT

ACTOR 2
(*singing*)
INJUN BILL, INJUN BILL
THINK ON THIS BEFORE YOU SLAUGHTER
EVERY GIRL IS SOMEONE'S DAUGHTER,
EVERY MAN IS SOMEONE'S SON
INJUN BILL, INJUN BILL

Let your better Angels guide you
'Cause the Devil that's inside you
Wants his due before it's done

(Later. A train station. FROGGY's alone. INJUN BILL soon walks up, carrying a package)

FROGGY
What'cha got there?

INJUN BILL
Trail rations. It's 500 miles to Denver, and I reckon I gotta eat sometime in there.

FROGGY
Where's mine?

(Beat)

INJUN BILL
Where's your what?

FROGGY
Where's my food?

INJUN BILL
I think Abel's saloon has potatoes or some such.

FROGGY
I mean, my rations. I gotta eat too.

INJUN BILL
What the hell are you talkin' about? You're stayin' here.

FROGGY
Nope.

INJUN BILL
This was where you were going. Billings. Well, look around! You're here. I'm headin' out tonight, so don't get mushy on me.

FROGGY
I'm comin' with you.

INJUN BILL
The hell you say.

FROGGY
The hell I do say!

INJUN BILL
This is my mission, Froggy!

FROGGY
What if the Governor ain't even there? What if Abel just said that to…

INJUN BILL
Don't say that! Don't you even think it! The time has come for all debts to be paid. And you don't wanna be around when that bill comes due.

FROGGY
Please let me come with you. Never had me a Denver Omelet. Like to give that a try.

INJUN BILL
No.

FROGGY
I'm begging you.

INJUN BILL
This town ain't half bad. Set up your restaurant, send for your mama and…

FROGGY
I can't, dammit! I got nothin' left! In a thunderbolt, it all got took away from me! My momma's gone and I'll never be able to look my sister in the eye and…

INJUN BILL
I'm resolved, Froggy. You stay here.

FROGGY
Well then I'm gonna follow you whether you want me to or not. And I'd like to see you stop me.

(INJUN BILL gets deadly serious)

FROGGY
Wait. No. I don't wanna see that.

INJUN BILL
Lemme tell you something. I don't give two shits what happens to you, and I expect the same goddamn courtesy in return. You start followin' people around in this world, and they end up leading you straight to Hell.

FROGGY
I'd rather go to Hell with a friend then to Heaven by myself.

INJUN BILL
(Grabs FROGGY roughly) We ain't friends! How many times I gotta tell you? Say it again and I'll cut your damn tongue out! *(Collects himself)*

FROGGY
How you gettin' to Denver?

INJUN BILL
My own damn way.

FROGGY
All the way to Colorado? You best take the train.

INJUN BILL
Well, thank God Froggy's here to point out the goddamn obvious! I can't take the train 'cause I can't afford the train! Figure I'll steal a horse and…

(FROGGY walks off)

INJUN BILL
Well. There he goes.

(INJUN BILL opens his rations, eats some beef jerky)

INJUN BILL
Mm. Good jerky.

(FROGGY soon returns with two train tickets)

INJUN BILL
Aw, dammit all to hell…what're you doin' back?

FROGGY
Here. *(Gives him a ticket)*

INJUN BILL
What the hell is this?

FROGGY
Well, since clearly I'm just here to point out the obvious, them there's a train ticket.

INJUN BILL
Where'd you get it?

FROGGY
I said the magic words, reached right up my butthole and WOOP. Train tickets.

INJUN BILL
You steal these?

FROGGY
Of course I stole 'em. I'm good at stealin'.

INJUN BILL
You stole two of 'em.

FROGGY
Figure that out all by yourself.

INJUN BILL
Stop bustin' my balls, fat man!

(Beat. FROGGY smiles, laughs a little)

FROGGY
Bill, I don't know what happened your whole life. I'm guessin' you got kicked around more then's fair. But this is what people do.

INJUN BILL
They steal train tickets?

FROGGY
They help… sometimes for no good reason at all.

(INJUN BILL thinks on that)

FROGGY
What d'ya say? Am I in?

(Beat)

INJUN BILL
There's a crazy man out there killin' whole villages. I reckon I could use the backup.

FROGGY
Damn right.

(In the darkness, the sound of a hammer drawing back on a shotgun. The SHERIFF can be heard in the darkness)

SHERIFF
There's an old saying that goes "No snowflake falls in the wrong place."

(They turn, arms raised)

SHERIFF
And here are two snowflakes I thought I'd never see again, holdin' stolen tickets. (Steps into the light) Ladies, you just rolled snake-eyes.

(Lights fade)

END OF ACT ONE

ACT II
SCENE ONE

ACTOR 2
(singing)
BROKE AND SHACKLED IN A TRAIN CAR,
BILL AND FROGGY SEEMED DEFEATED
'CAUSE THE SHERIFF, HE HAD GREETED THEM
WITH SMILES AND A GUN
SO THEY RODE OFF WITHOUT KNOWIN'
WHERE THE GODDAMN TRAIN WAS GOIN'
AND THEY HAD THAT SINKIN' FEELING
LIKE THEIR RACE WAS ALL BUT RUN

(Lights up. FROGGY & INJUN BILL sit in a train car. Their hands are bound. They bounce occasionally to indicate motion. FROGGY whimpers occasionally. INJUN BILL ignores it initially, but finally--)

INJUN BILL
What? What is it?

FROGGY
You got a cup or somethin'?

INJUN BILL
What do you think?

FROGGY
Bill, it's an emergency!

INJUN BILL
I ain't got no goddamn cup, Froggy! Christ.

FROGGY
Well, then...I'm real sorry about this. (Dashes to BILL's side of the car and begins to undo his pants)

INJUN BILL
What the hell are you doin'?

FROGGY
I gotta piss, and I ain't gonna piss where I sit!

INJUN BILL
Don't.

FROGGY
I gotta!

INJUN BILL
I don't wanna smell your piss from here to wherever we're goin'!

FROGGY
Dammit! I can't get my damn pants off!

INJUN BILL
Just hold it!

FROGGY
No! That makes my pecker hurt!

(BILL gets up, grabs FROGGY and throws him back into his previous seat)

INJUN BILL
You're gonna hold it 'til the train stops. It ain't stopped yet today, so I reckon it's gonna soon.

FROGGY
Look, I'm not doin' this to spite you. This here's a bodily function with a will utterly independent of my wishes. *(He groans)* And I ain't about to ruin my one pair of pants.

INJUN BILL
You're thinkin' about it too much.

FROGGY
Well, Bill, it's like someone farting in Church. You can sit there, lookin' at your hymnal, singin' about The Virgin Jesus but all you're really thinkin' about is "Who the hell just farted in church?"

INJUN BILL
Pretty sure it was the Virgin Mary.

FROGGY
And I'm pretty sure I got a goddamn gorilla squeezin' my balls!

INJUN BILL
(Starts to rifle through FROGGY's pockets) Here.

FROGGY
Um... what... whatcha doin' there, Bill?

INJUN BILL
(Handing FROGGY his harmonica) Play somethin'.

FROGGY
Come on!

INJUN BILL
It'll take your mind off your piss-pipe. Do it!

(FROGGY half-heartedly plays Swanee River. He begins to get into it. BILL perhaps sings along. He finishes the song, then just lies there for a bit)

FROGGY
Injun Bill?

INJUN BILL
Yep.

FROGGY
I regret playing a song about a river.

INJUN BILL
You gotta hold it in, son.

FROGGY
I'm worried that I'm doin' irreparable damage to my nethers as we speak.

INJUN BILL
You ain't. I gone two days without pissin' once. I'm fine.

FROGGY
You lie.

INJUN BILL
Hand to god. Remember that preacher I was in jail with?

FROGGY
The fella you told about the shoes?

INJUN BILL
That's him. Well, he was a talker. Never shut up. Went on and on about his family gettin' burned up in Georgia, 'bout how God don't make no sense, bullshit like that. Problem was, he was sittin' on the pisspot the whole time. I was too damn drunk to knock him off it, so I just pinched it shut and waited.

FROGGY
How much time you spent in jail, Bill?

INJUN BILL
Enough.

FROGGY
That place where you and I met... that was my first time. Got me a drunk-on and tried to steal some horses.

INJUN BILL
While you was drunk?

FROGGY
Yep.

INJUN BILL
How many you try to steal?

(Beat)

FROGGY
The thing you gotta remember is rye whiskey can fuck a man up good.

INJUN BILL
How many?

FROGGY
It woulda been in the neighborhood of...fifteen. Twenty at the limit.

INJUN BILL
(chuckling) What did you do? Just open the gate at the corral?

FROGGY
(starting to chuckle too) I swear to god, I thought it would work.

(They laugh together)

FROGGY
You think the sheriff's takin' us to jail?

INJUN BILL
Naw. We been on this train all day. He coulda dropped us off at a half-dozen towns.

FROGGY
Guess you're right.

INJUN BILL
I don't trust a man what speaks philosophy.

FROGGY
I don't like that he called us snowflakes.

INJUN BILL
What the hell did that even mean?

FROGGY
Got me. For a second, I thought I must've heard him wrong. Like maybe he was callin' us... pancakes.

INJUN BILL
Froggy, that makes less sense than callin' us snowflakes.

FROGGY
I think it makes exactly as much sense. *(Beat)* Now I want pancakes.

INJUN BILL
Me too.

FROGGY
Drippin' with syrup.

INJUN BILL
And bacon.

FROGGY
Yes. Hell yes. A whole pigs-worth.

INJUN BILL
Nice and crispy.

FROGGY
But not burned.

INJUN BILL
Nope. Done up right so's they crunch, but they ain't burned.

(They lie back, enjoying the thought)

INJUN BILL
Hey, Froggy.

FROGGY
Yes'm?

INJUN BILL
What's it like to want somethin'?

(Beat)

FROGGY
Like bacon?

INJUN BILL
No, I mean…to want somethin' more than…essentials. Like…what's it like wantin' to start up a restaurant?

FROGGY
Bill, that particular dream's gone tits-up.

INJUN BILL
Before then. Before you let it go. What's it like?

FROGGY
(Thinking on that) Like fuel for the furnace of your heart.

INJUN BILL
(smiling a bit) That sounds nice.

FROGGY
Sure enough. Keeps you goin' when there ain't no reason to go on. Like you know that if you can just hang on a little longer, that your luck'll change. That you won't end up some fat drunk who damn-near ramrods his own sister.

(Beat)

INJUN BILL
What?

FROGGY
I'm just sayin'…havin' a dream matters. Matters more than anything. *(FROGGY looks at INJUN BILL)* Ain't you never had somethin' like that?

(Beat)

INJUN BILL
I'm gonna kill the man that wears my friend as shoes.

FROGGY
That ain't a dream. That's a mission. What do you dream about?

INJUN BILL
I don't know.

FROGGY
When you pray to God, "God, please gimme this one thing so that I got a reason to roll my ass outta bed"…what is it you pray for?

(INJUN BILL thinks on that)

FROGGY
OK. So let's say you kill this Osborne fella. What're you gonna do after that?

INJUN BILL
I ain't thought it out that far.

FROGGY
Bill, you gotta figure out what makes you happy.

INJUN BILL
Not sure I ever been happy.

FROGGY
I'm tellin' you. One day, something's gonna happen to you, somethin' so beautiful it's gonna take your breath away. Then you'll know what I'm talkin' about.

INJUN BILL
Pffft.

FROGGY
It ain't that hard. Just gotta take time to smell the flowers is all.

(INJUN BILL laughs a sad laugh)

FROGGY
What?

INJUN BILL
I ain't never even smelled a flower.

(The train stops. The SHERIFF walks over)

SHERIFF
Last stop, ladies! Don't make me get the railroad bulls!

(FROGGY jumps down and runs offstage. The SHERIFF goes for his gun)

INJUN BILL
He ain't runnin' off, Sheriff. He just has to piss somethin' awful.

SHERIFF
(calling off-stage) Piss where you stand, Baptiste. That way I can see ya.

FROGGY
(calling from off-stage) I can't do it if you're watchin'!

SHERIFF
Make fuckin' do! (To INJUN BILL) Injun Bill Picote.

(Beat)

INJUN BILL
I don't actually know your name.

SHERIFF
Sheriff J.B. Abernathy, at your service. Well, not Sheriff anymore. I resigned that lofty position when last we saw each other.

INJUN BILL
You mean when you left us for dead?

SHERIFF
No, what I give you was but one of many tests. Gettin' yourselves free? You passed that one. I'd hoped that your sudden liberty would have set you on a path to greatness. I cannot tell you the disappointment I felt seeing you and the Cajun back to your larcenous ways.

SHERIFF
(calling off-stage) You about done there, sport?

FROGGY
Don't rush me!

INJUN BILL
I never asked nothin' of you.

SHERIFF
True enough, true enough. But still, I gave it to you. And you know why? 'Cause you two butt-flaps are my lucky charms.

(FROGGY returns)

FROGGY
Oh sweet merciful Christ. I think I coulda filled the Grand Canyon.

SHERIFF
C'mon over here, Froggy.

(FROGGY crosses to him. SHERIFF puts his arms around the two prisoners)

SHERIFF
Ladies, it wasn't so long ago that I was just some sheriff in a pisspot town, and you was my prisoners. I have since then elevated my station, and you, sadly, have not.

FROGGY
Ain't life a kick in the nuts.

SHERIFF
Oh, it can be. No denying that. But not if you hang on to hope. My hope was sending my wife and son down here to run my brother's claim. Poor Jeremiah got himself the small pox and passed, so the mine went to me. That telegram I got? Turns out my boy struck gold. *(throws his arms wide)* Welcome to Denver, city of dreams!

INJUN BILL
Wait, what?

SHERIFF
We have arrived at the land of my fortune.

INJUN BILL
Denver? We're in Denver?!

FROGGY
I'll be damned.

SHERIFF
That's right. Can't you smell the gold in the air? *(He breathes deeply)* That's the smell of a new life! Like the mighty phoenix, I am reborn!

FROGGY
Wait. Are we in Denver or Phoenix?

SHERIFF
Now, I reckon you're wondering why I dragged you all the way to Colorado. Well... I'm here to offer you another kindness. I'm puttin' you two buttflaps to work in my mine!

INJUN BILL
Now hold on...

SHERIFF
I figured you'd probably try to run off if I didn't drag you down here by force. But this... this is your chance to make a real life for yourself. Honest work at an honest wage. No more thieving and drinking and whoring... boys, you don't have to thank me.

(Beat)

FROGGY
Thank you?

SHERIFF
Oh, it's the least I could do.

INJUN BILL
Sheriff, you gotta let us go.

(Beat. The SHERIFF looks at him)

SHERIFF
Is that a fact?

INJUN BILL
You got us in the crosshairs, and I ain't about to argue it. But the hand of destiny is at work here. I can feel it.

SHERIFF
Can you?

INJUN BILL
When you caught us pick-pocketin'...

FROGGY
Allegedly pick-pocketin'...

INJUN BILL
...it was so we could make it to Denver. And now... here we are. That's gotta mean something.

SHERIFF
And what is it you seek to do here in Denver?

INJUN BILL
I'm gonna find my destiny! I been chasin' it for two long years and...

SHERIFF
Now, son. You're speakin' in vagaries.

INJUN BILL
I mean to settle a great injustice.

SHERIFF
That don't strike me as your long suit.

INJUN BILL
I'm a bad man, sir. I admit that with no hesitation. But a horrible thing been done to the last man on Earth I called "friend."

SHERIFF
Froggy?

INJUN BILL
No.

FROGGY
Thanks.

INJUN BILL
And the man what done this wrong is coming to Denver. Here is where we shall finally meet, face to face.

SHERIFF
Yeah? And what are you gonna do then?

INJUN BILL
I mean to kill him, if that's what you're asking.

SHERIFF
In so many words.

INJUN BILL
I need this, sir. I need it like a fish needs water and a fat man needs cake.

FROGGY
Hey! Are you...?

INJUN BILL
But you have my word on this, Sheriff. Once I see this man dead, my killin' days are over. I'll find somethin' else to do with my life. Somethin'...decent. But this vengeance needs doin' first.

(The SHERIFF stares hard at INJUN BILL)

FROGGY
I'd like to go on record as mostly just bein' in the wrong place at the wrong time.

SHERIFF
This man you mean to kill... what'd he do exactly?

INJUN BILL
He took my dead friend, skinned him, and turned him into shoes.

FROGGY
And now he's Governor of Wyoming.

SHERIFF
Sweet Jesus. I don't know which is worse. *(He uncuffs BILL & FROGGY)* If the devil were to open his eyes slowly enough, no one would even notice he'd awakened.

FROGGY
Come again?

SHERIFF
That's a bit of J.B.'s own personal philosophy. Fact is, the world we live in gets worse every single day, but it does it little by little so most don't notice. I do my part to correct the growing wickedness in the world with small acts of goodness.

FROGGY
That's right kind of you, but...

SHERIFF
I see before me a wicked man who may just recant if he can right this single injustice. Tell me, Injun Bill. Do I assess this correctly?

(Beat)

INJUN BILL
Yuh-huh.

SHERIFF
Then who am I to stand in the way of redemption?

(Both men are now free)

FROGGY
You lettin' us go?

SHERIFF
You must be the brains of the operation. *(Digs into his wallet, gives them some money)* Here's the bills we took off of you back in Montana, minus my fee for haulin' you here. Not much, but I reckon two resourceful buttflaps like yourselves will find a way.

(INJUN BILL looks at the money, then offers the SHERIFF his hand)

INJUN BILL
Thank you, Sheriff.

SHERIFF
It's just J.B. now, son.

FROGGY
(Shaking his other hand) Sir, if you was a woman, I reckon I'd kiss you full on the mouth.

SHERIFF
Then praise Jesus for my cock and balls.

INJUN BILL
C'mon, Froggy. *(Grabs him and starts to head off)*

SHERIFF
Swing on over to my claim, let me know how things turn out!

INJUN BILL
Yessir!

FROGGY
Full on the mouth!

(SHERIFF watches them leave, then takes another deep breath of the air and smiles)

SHERIFF
"Gold is tried by fire, brave men by adversity." I believe a Greek fella said that.

(He exits. Lights fade)

SCENE TWO

ACTOR 1
(singing)
INJUN BILL, INJUN BILL
AS YOUR PREY GROWS EVER NEARER,
IS YOUR VISION GETTING CLEARER,
OR DOES HATE STILL CLOUD YOUR EYES?
INJUN BILL, REST YOUR BONES
AT THE FIRST FLOPHOUSE YOU COME TO
'CAUSE THERE'S NOWHERE LEFT TO RUN TO
AS YOU CLOSE IN ON YOUR PRIZE

(The interior of the 4-Room Hotel. It is a cramped, decrepit place. A check-in desk stands at one side, a small table w/ two chairs stands in the other. FROGGY & INJUN BILL enter. FROGGY has an apple. A white hat hangs on a post)

INJUN BILL
Christ, what a shithole.

FROGGY
You said you wanted the cheapest hotel in town. This is it.

INJUN BILL
I seen bigger closets.

FROGGY
I'll bring it up with the management. *(looks around)* Where the hell's the management?

INJUN BILL
Place looks deserted.

FROGGY
Well, it's on the outskirts.

INJUN BILL
I don't know. Rest of the town seems full to overflowin'.

(Beat)

FROGGY
Bill. I'm havin' a bad thought.

INJUN BILL
Yeah?

FROGGY
What if that Death fella was here? What if he killed all that was in it, and ain't no one noticed yet?

INJUN BILL
Quit jumpin' at shadows.

FROGGY
The man what sold me this apple… he said a pale rider's been seen 'round these parts. Sometimes he wipes out a whole village, sometimes just a few people. And no one's been able to catch him.

INJUN BILL
Not my concern.

FROGGY
Gimme a knife.

INJUN BILL
No.

FROGGY
I need to defend myself.

INJUN BILL
You got that apple.

FROGGY
I got…?! What the hell am I supposed to do with this? Spit seeds at him?!

INJUN BILL
I killed a man with a plum once. I reckon the principle's pretty much the same.

FROGGY
You're a lyin' sack of crap.

(INJUN BILL glares at him)

FROGGY
You know what? I didn't… you're not a sack. *(Grabs the chairs and uses them to pin the door shut)*

INJUN BILL
For Christ's sake…

FROGGY
I'm tellin' you, Death is comin'. I feel it in my bones. We gotta be ready.

INJUN BILL
I'm always ready.

FROGGY
Well, I ain't. C'mon, give me a knife.

INJUN BILL
No.

FROGGY
Just a little one.

INJUN BILL
No.

FROGGY
How's about Quiet Annie? She ain't no bigger than…

INJUN BILL
Listen up. My knives are precious to me. Especially Annie. If someone comes for ya, I'll take care of him.

FROGGY
You'd do that for me?

INJUN BILL
A dog defends the fleas on him, even if he don't mean to.

FROGGY
Thank you, Bill.

INJUN BILL
De nada. *(He sits down, smiling)*

FROGGY
Ain't you the cat that ate the canary.

INJUN BILL
Osbourne's here, Froggy. I know it. I know it more than I ever knew anything else. Two years of hunting…. livin' in caves and hidin' in alleys and followin' every trail, even if… it don't matter. None of it matters no more, 'cause he's here. My quest is all but over. Death himself couldn't stop me.

(The back door shakes. FROGGY lets out a girlish scream. INJUN BILL draws his saber)

FROGGY
Save me, Jesus!

(The back door opens. MARTHA enters with a mop and bucket. She sees them and lets out a startled cry)

MARTHA
Oh my goodness!

FROGGY
DEAAAAAATH!

(INJUN BILL sheathes his blade quickly. MARTHA pulls a gun on them)

MARTHA
What do you want?!

INJUN BILL
Beggin' your pardon, Miss. We didn't mean to startle you.

(FROGGY checks the front of his pants for wetness. There is none)

FROGGY
…oh, thank god…

INJUN BILL
We're just arrived in town, and lookin' for accommodations.

MARTHA
With a saber drawn?

INJUN BILL
There's bad folks around, Miss. We was afraid you was one of 'em.

(She examines them for a bit, then lowers the gun)

MARTHA
All right then.

INJUN BILL
Again, real sorry about the fright.

MARTHA
Quite all right. I'm fine.

INJUN BILL
Is your husband around? Mayhap we should…

MARTHA
My husband passed five years ago. This is my place now.

(Beat. FROGGY looks around, taking in the disheveled décor)

FROGGY
And a fine establishment it is.

MARTHA
You say you're looking for a room?

INJUN BILL
Two rooms, miss. I can't emphasize that enough.

MARTHA
Just…here it is… (She pulls out a ledger) Please sign your name here.

(INJUN BILL looks at it, then to FROGGY)

INJUN BILL
I… um… Froggy, could you…?

FROGGY
Yessir. (signs them in)

MARTHA
Froggy? Your name is Froggy?

FROGGY
It's what ya call a pseudo... pseudo... psu...nickname.

MARTHA
I should hope so, Mr... *(checks the ledger)* Baptiste?

FROGGY
C'est vrais.

MARTHA
So that must make you... *(checks the ledger again)* Mr. Custer?

INJUN BILL
(glaring at FROGGY) I guess it must.

MARTHA
Well, you're in luck. I'm sorry to say we have many vacancies at the moment. In so much as you two would be my first real guests in three weeks.

FROGGY
Well, you got someone signed up here. Ber-Tram Shaw.

MARTHA
I'd hardly call him a real guest. He checked in last night and paid me in fool's gold. As soon as he returns, I'm tossing him out on his ear.

FROGGY
Sounds like you've had a bad run of things.

MARTHA
Yes. My husband built this hotel ten years ago. When the bigger, fancier ones popped up in the center of town, we couldn't compete. We also couldn't afford to renovate, so...here I am.

FROGGY
I'm real sorry to hear that, miss.

MARTHA
Oh, I make do somehow. The rates are five dollars a night, with two upfront.

(FROGGY gets the money)

MARTHA
And just how long will you gentlemen be staying with us?

INJUN BILL
Well, ma'am, that all depends. We're waitin' for someone. So we're here until he arrives.

MARTHA
Really?

INJUN BILL
Yes, ma'am.

MARTHA
I hope you don't mind my saying I'll pray for a delay in his arrival.

(INJUN BILL just stares at her)

MARTHA
Because... then you'll have to stay here longer. And I'd make more money.

(INJUN BILL continues staring)

MARTHA
It...it was a joke.

FROGGY
Sorry, miss. Mr. Custer here was born without a sense of humor.

MARTHA
I see. I hope you don't mind my asking, but are you by chance related to the great General Custer?

(Beat)

INJUN BILL
Distantly.

MARTHA
Isn't that remarkable? *(She produces two keys)* I'll give you gentlemen rooms 1 and 2. The small dining area there is open to you. I'm sorry to say I have no food, but there's plenty of liquor.

If I may be of further service, within the limits of Christian decency, please let me know.

INJUN BILL
Well, since you brung it up... You ever hear the name Dr. John Eugene Osborne?

MARTHA
I can't say that I have. Is he the gentleman you're waiting on?

INJUN BILL
And that's a fact.

MARTHA
Well, I'll certainly keep my ears open for his arrival. And please know that I was only joking about the...

FROGGY
He knows...don't you...um... Filbert?

(INJUN BILL glares at him again)

INJUN BILL
I reckon I do.

FROGGY
Well, I'm headin' on up. I feel like I ain't slept on a real bed since never.

INJUN BILL
You're in #2.

FROGGY
How's that?

INJUN BILL
I'm in charge, so I'm in #1. Got it?

FROGGY
...don't make no difference which...

MARTHA
Oh! Mr. Custer!

(INJUN BILL continues upstairs)

MARTHA
Mr. Custer!

(FROGGY turns him around)

FROGGY
I believe the young lady is addressing you, Filbert. You must forgive him. He's...um...he's deaf in one ear.

MARTHA
Oh. I'm sorry. *(Raises her voice to an uncomfortable level)* The gentleman you were referring to - John Eugene Osborne?

INJUN BILL
Yeah.

MARTHA
Is he some sort of politician? From Wyoming? Thick moustache, glasses...?

INJUN BILL
(lighting up) Yes! Oh god yes! Is he here?! Where's he stayin'?

MARTHA
Mr. Custer...Doctor Osborne came and went a week ago.

(INJUN BILL freezes. He remains immobile except for a twitching eye. He then turns & walks into the other room. He then screams loudly in unbridled rage. MARTHA jumps. FROGGY desperately tries to cover)

FROGGY
He...um...ah...kidney stone.

(Lights fade)

SCENE THREE

(The next day, still at the hotel. INJUN BILL is in the dining area, his head on the table. A variety of bottles are around him. FROGGY enters from his room)

FROGGY
Lord, Bill. How much can a man drink

in one night?

(FROGGY shakes him. BILL mumbles something incomprehensible and pushes FROGGY away)

FROGGY
C'mon, partner. Let's....

(FROGGY tries to lift BILL. BILL again mumbles and punches FROGGY in the gut. FROGGY stumbles back, more shocked than hurt)

FROGGY
Fine! Just sit there and pickle in your own juices for all I care!

(Beat. FROGGY sits down with him)

FROGGY
I didn't mean that. I was speakin' out of hurt.

(INJUN BILL mumbles)

FROGGY
Here's the thing, Bill. Time's come where we gotta figure out our next move. I figure you wanna get back on the hunt, but I don't wanna do nothin' without your say-so. 'Cause.... I gotta say, there are reasons to stay put. We got a real job with the Sheriff. Got a roof over our head, for a little while anyways. Now I know Big Nose George was your friend, but...

INJUN BILL
(Suddenly sitting straight up) You know what?! George Parrot was a son of a bitch! *(He takes a long drink out of a bottle, then slams his head back on the table)*

FROGGY
Well. Guess I'll try again tomorrow.

(MARTHA enters from the back room, and starts dusting the desk)

MARTHA
Good morning, Mr. Baptiste.

FROGGY
Mornin', Ms. Barnes. And please, it's Froggy.

MARTHA
Then I must insist you call me Martha. How fares your friend?

FROGGY
Less than sober.

MARTHA
I understand. My Walter had a kidney stone once. Liquor was the only thing that kept the pain at bay. In the end, it took his life.

FROGGY
Oh. I'm sorry. I...

MARTHA
It's quite all right. Ours was a marriage of convenience.

FROGGY
My momma said weren't nothin' convenient about marriage. 'Course my papa was a gator farmer, so...

MARTHA
My people were farmers too, but our crops withered in a drought, like a biblical famine of old. Walter was a family friend, and he took me in.

FROGGY
Don't sound real romantic, if you pardon my sayin'.

MARTHA
As I said, convenience, not romance. I was sixteen when I married. Walter was...much older.

FROGGY
Yeah, it's a bitch, but... Oh, I'm sorry.

MARTHA
It's quite all right. I'm no stranger to salty language, though I may not speak it myself.

FROGGY
You're a real proper lady.

MARTHA
I am what I was raised to be.

(FROGGY *has gone back to* BILL. *He tries to remove a bottle from* BILL's *hand, but fails*)

MARTHA
You're very loyal to your friend.

FROGGY
I suppose.

MARTHA
Do you mind if I ask why?

FROGGY
Filbert here...Life's dealt him every shit card in the deck. So I figure, give the poor som'bitch a hand when I can.

MARTHA
That's very big of you.

FROGGY
You callin' me fat?

MARTHA
What? No, not at all.

FROGGY
Oh. Sorry, I...it's a sore subject.

(*She just stares at him. He grows a bit uncomfortable*)

FROGGY
I... do I have something on my face?

MARTHA
I was just... if you're going to say here another night, I'll need another five dollars. From each of you.

FROGGY
Oh...ah, shit...I mean, shoot...I mean...

MARTHA
You're financial state is...?

FROGGY
To be honest, Miss, it's...bleak.

MARTHA
I see.

FROGGY
Me and Bill...

MARTHA
Bill?

FROGGY
Filbert...we're not men of means, if you gather my meaning.

MARTHA
I believe I do.

FROGGY
Well....all right then.

(FROGGY *tries to lift* INJUN BILL, *who leaps up and shouts a string of nonsense at him*)

INJUN BILL
Fuck off you cocksucking motherfucker touch me again and I won't but you will so stop all you're you know what I don't have to take this from mommy doesn't...!!! (*Collapses, unconscious*)

MARTHA
Oh my.

FROGGY
Sorry. He's an...interesting drunk.

MARTHA
Mr. Ba...Froggy, might I make a suggestion?

FROGGY
Sure enough.

MARTHA
I just...it's been nice having a masculine presence here. You, I mean. It's been nice having you here.

FROGGY
Thank you, miss.

MARTHA
And as you've likely noticed, my hotel is...in need of repair.

FROGGY
I've seen worse.

MARTHA
Really?

FROGGY
Well, not much worse.

MARTHA
So perhaps we can come to an... arrangement?

FROGGY
Um...I can play the harmonica.

MARTHA
Can you swing a hammer?

FROGGY
Sure.

MARTHA
Do you know anything about roofs?

FROGGY
Not really, but I'm a fast learner! *(Beat)* That's not true. I ain't real bright. But...

MARTHA
What I'm proposing, Froggy, is that... perhaps if you and your friend would agree to some manual labor, then I could forgo your payment for a short time.

FROGGY
Ma'am...I don't know what to say. That's about the kindest offer I've gotten since the Army kicked me out.

MARTHA
Then you agree?

FROGGY
It would be my pleasure.

MARTHA
Good.

FROGGY
And if you'd like...I used to be a cook. I can make shoe leather taste like sirloin.

MARTHA
Really?

FROGGY
Yes, ma'am. You like shrimp? Or crawdads?

MARTHA
Oh! Very much!

FROGGY
Martha, you give me ten minutes with your kitchen and you'll think you're in the French Quarter!

MARTHA
Oh, Froggy! That sounds lovely! *(She touches his hand)* Thank you.

(They realize their hands are touching, and she removes her hand quickly. FROGGY finally realizes her intent)

FROGGY
Oh. My.

MARTHA
I'm sorry. I didn't mean to be so forward.

FROGGY
Shucks, Martha. It's all right.

MARTHA
My mother would be mortified.

FROGGY
Ain't no reason.

MARTHA
I'll just get to my cleaning and...

(She starts to go. FROGGY takes her hand and holds it. They smile at each other)

FROGGY
See? Ain't no harm in this, is there?

MARTHA
No. I suppose not.

FROGGY
Now, I'm gonna head to the market square real quick like. See if I can wrangle up some food.

MARTHA
I thought you had no money.

(FROGGY grabs the white hat)

FROGGY
This belong to that Bertram fella?

MARTHA
Yes.

FROGGY
Well, since he played you rotten with that fool's gold, maybe I'll sell this. Bet I can get a half-decent price for it.

MARTHA
But it's not yours.

FROGGY
I won't tell if you don't. *(He puts it on, then tips it to her)* Ma'am.

(He leaves. She stands there for a bit, smiling)

MARTHA
Oh, Martha. Why do you always fall for the dangerous ones?

(Lights fade)

SCENE FOUR

ACTOR 2
(singing)
IN THE THOROUGHFARE OF DENVER,
FROGGY WALKED & FROGGY PONDERED
AND THE MORE THAT HIS MIND WANDERED,
THE MORE QUESTIONS WOULD ARISE
BUT THE ANSWERS KEPT REFUSIN'
TO GIVE HIM JUST ONE CONCLUSION
'TIL A FRIEND INSIDE A PLAGUE TENT
OFFERED TO PHILOSOPHIZE

(A plague tent in the Denver Thoroughfare. The SHERIFF lies inside, moaning. His face is pock marked. FROGGY walks by, still wearing the hat. He soon comes back and looks in)

FROGGY
Sheriff Abernathy?

SHERIFF
(Seeing him) Stay away, son. I've got the pox.

FROGGY
I ain't worried. I got the shot when I was in the Army.

SHERIFF
Then you're a luckier soul than I.

FROGGY
Sweet Jesus. What happened to you?

(Beat)

SHERIFF
Remember ten seconds ago, when I told you I got the pox?

FROGGY
Right. Sorry, I...right.

(The sound of coughing/moaning from elsewhere)

FROGGY
This is a hell of a place for a rich man to end up.

SHERIFF
That's the one admirable trait of Pestilence. It can't be bought off.

FROGGY
You don't look so bad.

SHERIFF
Then my external appearance does not reflect my internal concerns. My back hurts so much I can barely breathe. Can't seem to stop sweatin', even though I'm cold as a…as a… Jesus Christ. I can't even think of a fuckin' simile.

FROGGY
Hold up a second. *(FROGGY exits, then soon returns with a cup of water)* Here you go. Drink up.

(The SHERIFF drinks a little, but starts coughing)

FROGGY
You just hang in there, Sheriff. I seen men beat the pox before.

SHERIFF
I am nothing if not an optimist.

FROGGY
I don't know what to say, sir. I'm sorry as hell.

SHERIFF
No, no, no. Don't you be feelin' sorry for me. I'm still basking in good luck's graces.

(Beat)

FROGGY
I…think that maybe what you think is lucky and what I think is lucky ain't the same thing.

SHERIFF
You can't let a thing like the pox get you down. Beyond the literal inability to get up, that is.

FROGGY
I can't tell if you're really this cheerful, or if the fever's cooked your brains.

SHERIFF
Somethin' stuck in your craw, son?

FROGGY
Ah, just thinkin' is all.

SHERIFF
Hell, son! That's ol' J.B.'s favorite pastime!

(The SHERIFF sits up, puts his arm around FROGGY, who is clearly uncomfortable)

SHERIFF
Tell me what's on your mind, Froggy.

FROGGY
Well, sir. I feel like maybe I'm at one of them road-forks.

SHERIFF
Mm-hmm.

FROGGY
On one side, I got Bill. That fella he's after….som'bitch got away from us.

SHERIFF
Lord, lord.

FROGGY
So I reckon we'll be hittin' the road soon, back on the trail. And I know it ain't my mission, but… Bill needs someone to watch his back. There's some crazy bastard out there burnin' through the West like a brushfire.

SHERIFF
So you want to protect your friend. A noble motivation. So what's on the other side of the fork?

(FROGGY mumbles & blushes, embarrassed)

SHERIFF
Is it a woman?

(FROGGY *mumbles again*)

SHERIFF
Hot damn, son! In Denver for all of two days, and you got yourself a sweetheart!

FROGGY
Oh, it ain't all that. It's the Widow Barnes, over to the 4-Room Hotel.

SHERIFF
But you're sweet on her?

FROGGY
I reckon.

SHERIFF
And is the Widow equally enamored?

FROGGY
Well, we spent all last night just talkin', while Bill tore through the liquor. It was real…nice.

SHERIFF
Makes ya feel like stayin' put, don't it?

(FROGGY *nods*)

SHERIFF
How long's it been since you been with a woman?

FROGGY
Over a year now. Less'n you count when I damn near ram-rodded my own sister.

(*Beat.* SHERIFF *removes his arm*)

SHERIFF
Maybe you don't mention that to the Widow.

FROGGY
So now I'm feelin' kinda…split in two.

SHERIFF
Remember when I told you before about the rabbits? That's where you are again…chasin' two and catching neither. I reckon what you need to do is decide which one's the one you really wanna sink your teeth into.

FROGGY
Huh. I just now figured out what that meant.

SHERIFF
The best philosophy is like real good chaw. You gotta chew on it for a while to really appreciate the flavor.

(FROGGY *laughs. The* SHERIFF *pulls a gold rock out of his pocket & hands it to* FROGGY)

FROGGY
Hot damn!

SHERIFF
You take that rock, and you cash it out. Buy your lady some flowers and a nice meal. All I ask is that you have yourself one romantic evening before you make your decision.

FROGGY
I can't take this, sir. It's too much.

SHERIFF
I got a mine full of 'em. Take it with my blessing.

FROGGY
I gotta be honest. I don't know why you keep helping me out, but…

SHERIFF
A smarter feller than me once said "Be kind, for everyone you meet is fighting a harder battle." (*He claps* FROGGY *shoulder, then coughs*)

FROGGY
Ah, I'm an ass. Pissin' in your ear while

you're the one in the plague tent.

SHERIFF
You gave me a chance to philosophize, Froggy. That's a fine gift.

FROGGY
Is there anything I can do for you?

SHERIFF
Well, you got a little time?

FROGGY
Yessir.

SHERIFF
I'd sure take it kindly if you played on that mouth harp. I find it... soothing.

FROGGY
That I can do. You wanna hear anything in particular?

SHERIFF
Something...felicitous.

(Beat. FROGGY has no idea what that word means)

FROGGY
Okie-doke.

(FROGGY plays. The SHERIFF lays back down and smiles. Lights fade)

SCENE FIVE

ACTOR 1
(singing)
INJUN BILL, INJUN BILL
SING THE DARKEST HALLELUJAH
LET THE KNIVES THAT WHISPER TO YA
KEEP THE PROMISE OF THE PAST
INJUN BILL, INJUN BILL
FEEL THE CHILL OF THE SHADOW
ON YOUR SHOULDER
'CAUSE THE NIGHT GROWS EVER COLDER,
AND THE DEVIL'S COME AT LAST

(Back at the hotel, early evening of the same day. INJUN BILL is exactly where he was before. He's asleep, clearly having a bad dream. After a bit of twitching & mumbling, he bolts straight up)

INJUN BILL
Oh god! M'face is melting! (Looks around, coming to his senses. Rubs his face) Christ, my head...

(MARTHA enters. She is slightly more made up, with a flower in her hair)

MARTHA
Froggy? I... oh.

INJUN BILL
Miss...Miss...dammit. I forgot your name.

MARTHA
Ms. Barnes.

BILL
(He tips his hat) Ma'am.

MARTHA
I see you've come to.

INJUN BILL
That matter's up for debate.

MARTHA
You must have come down here last night. With the exception of some explosive profanity, you've been unconscious for the better part of a day.

(INJUN BILL sits down, drinks from a bottle)

MARTHA
I'm not sure more alcohol is the appropriate remedy.

INJUN BILL
I'll take that into consideration, doctor.

MARTHA
I'm not a doctor.

INJUN BILL
Then I guessed it. *(He rises, still a bit shaky and hung-over)* You took my reason for living.

MARTHA
I'm sorry?

INJUN BILL
No need. I ain't blamin' you. Just a messenger. But now... *(He laughs a bit)* How many times you gotta get your jaw broke before you walk out of the fight?

MARTHA
I'm not sure I...

INJUN BILL
I just...this thing's been eatin' up my life for two years. Time's come to let it go, but I don't know how. Part of me wants to be free of it worse'n anything, but the other part...You think I got one more punch in me, lady?

MARTHA
I'm afraid I don't really follow, Mr. Custer.

INJUN BILL
No. I reckon you don't.

(He tries to sit down, but slams into the table. MARTHA rushes forward to stable him and to rescue the bottles. This is the first time we've seen her out from behind the counter BILL stumbles, falls to her feet. He realizes that she's wearing a pair of men's shoes)

MARTHA
Oh my. Look at this mess.

INJUN BILL
Where you get them shoes?

MARTHA
I beg your...?

(He grabs her ankles)

MARTHA
Oh!

INJUN BILL
These....oh my god...these are...

MARTHA
Unhand me!

(INJUN BILL rises. He is now very sober and grim)

INJUN BILL
Them shoes don't seem real ladylike.

MARTHA
That isn't any of....

INJUN BILL
If you tell me this ain't my concern, I will cut your throat, I swear to Christ.

(MARTHA backs away from him, terrified. She bumps into the desk)

INJUN BILL
I ain't gonna ask again. Where you get them shoes?

MARTHA
Please...please don't...

INJUN BILL
Them's the governor's shoes, ain't they? The man from Wyoming?

(She doesn't answer)

INJUN BILL
AIN'T THEY!?

(She nods, trying to keep from crying)

INJUN BILL
Good. You keep your mouth shut. Good. *(He rubs his eyes, trying to decide what to do)* I made a promise, woman. I swore I'd kill the man wearing those

shoes. And now... here they are. And here you are. *(He draws his saber. She is about to scream)* Don't scream. You hear me? Screamin' is gonna force my hand.

MARTHA
Then...then you might not kill me?

(INJUN BILL *has no response*)

MARTHA
If you want the shoes, they're yours. Please, just take them.

INJUN BILL
It's bigger than that. Bigger than you or me or...*(Beat)* Them shoes is a friend of mine.

MARTHA
They belong to a friend of yours?

INJUN BILL
They don't belong to him. They are him.

(MARTHA *sits there, confused*)

INJUN BILL
You're wearin' shoes made from a dead man. My friend. They tore the skin off of his corpse and stitched him into... those things.

MARTHA
That's impossible.

INJUN BILL
You're wearin' my dead friend George on your goddamn feet!

MARTHA
(Removing the shoes) Please. Just take them. Here.

INJUN BILL
That ain't enough, woman! It ain't enough just to have 'em! A wrong has got to be righted!

MARTHA
I've done nothing!

INJUN BILL
Then why you got the shoes!?

(Beat. MARTHA slowly rises)

MARTHA
A week ago...when Dr. Osborne's coach was leaving. It rode past my hotel. One of his suitcases fell off and...I have nothing. Do you understand that? No food, no money... all my clothes were moth-eaten and... The day before, I had boiled and eaten my own shoes. I'd had no food for days and...when I found the Governor's bag, I knew it was a gift from God. I used his suits to mend my dresses. I used his stockings to warm my feet. And yes, I took his shoes and made them my own. I am not proud of these actions, Mr. Custer, but I'd do them again.

INJUN BILL
Picote. My name ain't Custer. It's Bill Picote.

MARTHA
Injun Bill Picote?

(He nods)

MARTHA
I've heard of you. You rob stagecoaches.

INJUN BILL
I do.

MARTHA
And you're a killer.

INJUN BILL
I am.

MARTHA
But...I'm a woman.

INJUN BILL
I killed women before.

MARTHA
For stealing a suitcase? For taking shoes to cover her bloody feet?

INJUN BILL
It's bigger than that, goddammit! *(He takes a beat to collect himself)* I'll do it gentle, I promise. I'll put the knife in the Sweet Spot. You won't even feel it go in. You'll just bleed out nice and easy. It's like fallin' asleep.

MARTHA
(Starting to weep) You don't have to! You can just walk away.

INJUN BILL
I can't.

MARTHA
Please!

INJUN BILL
No. I've been on this path for two years. This is where it has led me. God help me, I gotta end this.

(He closes on her. She tries to fight him off)

MARTHA
Stop!

INJUN BILL
NO! Stop telling me to…Just lie down and make this easy on yourself!

(She strikes him hard. He staggers back)

MARTHA
Don't you see how ridiculous this is?! I didn't do this to your friend! I gave you the shoes! Just leave!

INJUN BILL
I can't, goddammit! I made a promise, and the only way it ends is bloody! You set a date with my knives the minute you laced them shoes up.

MARTHA
Take the shoes, give them a proper burial, and this will be over and done.

INJUN BILL
It'll never be done. Not unless I spill blood. Don't you understand that?

MARTHA
I am innocent!

INJUN BILL
Ain't no one innocent! Not here, not now, not ever! We're all of us up to our knees in blood and filth and…and…A MAN IS NOT SHOES!!!

(MARTHA clings to the wall in fear)

INJUN BILL
Do you hear me, you miserable shit-pile of a world?! A Man! IS NOT! SHOES!!!

(He collapses, overwhelmed by his own emotion. MARTHA stands there frozen. After a long beat she rises, taking him the shoes)

MARTHA
I'm sorry for your loss. I am. But don't let it turn you into someone you're not.

INJUN BILL
You don't know who I am.

MARTHA
I know who Froggy is. And I know he stands by you no matter how roughly you treat him. That makes me think perhaps there's something better to you than the life you've lived.

(She hands the shoes to INJUN BILL. As soon as he touches them, a change comes over him. He stares at the shoes)

INJUN BILL
George? *(He looks at the shoes, then to MARTHA)* This is my friend. This is George.

MARTHA
I know.

INJUN BILL
He...used to be a lot bigger.

MARTHA
I can imagine.

INJUN BILL
I think...I think part of me never thought I'd see him again. But here he is and...*(He looks at the shoes again)* I'm sorry, George. I'm sorry you got killed on account of somethin' I did. And that some bastard doctor turned you into this. You were a shitheel, a loudmouth and a liar, but didn't deserve this. *(The truth of that hits him. He looks up at her)* You don't deserve this neither.

MARTHA
(Nearly collapsing with relief) Thank you.

INJUN BILL
Could you...I'm sorry to ask, but did I leave any liquor left?

MARTHA
One bottle. *(She gives him the bottle)* You wish to say goodbye to your friend.

(He nods)

MARTHA
Then I'll leave you to it. I find I could use some fresher air. *(Before she heads off--)* Froggy said that life has been less than kind to you. I know what that's like.

INJUN BILL
Froggy's an all right sort.

MARTHA
Yes. He is.

(She exits to the back room. INJUN BILL sits, putting the shoes next to him. He takes the bottle and drinks, then pours some into the shoe)

INJUN BILL
I gotta tell ya, George. You've looked better. *(He thinks on this, then starts to laugh. His laugh grows louder and longer)* I'm talking to shoes. I'm talking to a damn pair of shoes! I half expected you to chime right in! *(He laughs more)* George, George, George...I think I gotta get out of this business. I mean...shit, look what it did for you. I reckon I should do like Froggy said...take time to sm...*(He notices the flower from MARTHA's hair on the floor. He picks it up & stares at it for a bit. Finally--)* Ah, what the hell. *(Takes the flower, stares at it for a second, then smells it. It is an overwhelming experience)* Oh my god.

(FROGGY enters)

FROGGY
Bill! You're up on two feet again.

INJUN BILL
Looks like it.

FROGGY
Looky who I found! Bertram Shaw, this here's my good friend...um... Private Filbert Custer.

(DEATH comes to him, shakes his hand)

DEATH
Private Custer, is it?

INJUN BILL
Looks like it.

DEATH
A pleasure.

FROGGY
I was just on my way back when Mr. Shaw here spotted me.

DEATH
He was wearing my hat.

FROGGY
I sure was, I sure was. 'Course I didn't know it was yours at the time, but...

INJUN BILL
Hold up. Do I...were you gonna sell it or some such?

FROGGY
Hey, Martha! I'm back! Bill, you seen Martha?

INJUN BILL
She took some air couple minutes gone. I reckon she'll be back in two ticks.

FROGGY
Well, lemme just pack these eats away. You two get cozy.

(FROGGY *heads offstage. DEATH sits*)

DEATH
He's a hoot, that one.

INJUN BILL
Froggy? Yeah, he's a kick in the pants all right.

DEATH
He'll talk your ear off though, won't he?

INJUN BILL
That, sir, is a fact.

DEATH
He was telling me a story about a friend of his who killed a man with an apple. An apple, of all things! Can you believe it?

INJUN BILL
Yes. Yes, I can. (*Rises*)

DEATH
Oh. My. What a lovely pair of shoes.

INJUN BILL
Yeah, they're...somethin'.

DEATH
Might I see them?

(BILL *just stares at him*)

DEATH
I'll give them right back. I promise.

INJUN BILL
Not to piss on your boots, but I went through hell and back to get these. I ain't of a mind to hand 'em over, to you or anyone.

DEATH
I see. I meant no disrespect.

(BILL *tips his hat, then turns to go.* FROGGY *returns*)

FROGGY
C'mon over, Bill! Bought me a bottle of Sarsaparilla and I found me three glasses. How's about a snort?

INJUN BILL
I'm 'bout to call it a night.

FROGGY
Come on! This here's the good stuff! Let's... (*sees the shoes*) Smack my ass. Is them what I think them is?

INJUN BILL
Yep.

FROGGY
You did it. You did it, Bill!

INJUN BILL
Well, sorta....

(FROGGY *grabs* BILL, *sits him at the*

table)

FROGGY
Then we're havin' ourselves a goddamn drink, son! This is...I mean...HOT DAMN!

DEATH
Well, I'm not sure what we're celebrating, but by golly, sometimes it's enough to just celebrate being alive!

FROGGY
Now see! Bert-Ram here gots the right idea! *(FROGGY pours them all sarsaparilla)* Now I should warn ya. Sarsaparilla gives me the butt-trumpets somethin' fierce, but...

INJUN BILL
Jesus, Froggy...

DEATH
Bottoms-Up! And I'm referring to the drinks.

(They laugh, then drink)

FROGGY
Woo! Ain't that sweet.

INJUN BILL
Not bad.

DEATH
Just lovely. So tell me...how did you lads end up in Denver?

FROGGY
Well you might not know it to look at us, Mr. Shaw. But Bill and I met in jail.

DEATH
Is that a fact?

INJUN BILL
Froggy....

FROGGY
Naw, naw. He's all right. Ain't you, Mr. Shaw?

DEATH
I've actually been incarcerated myself.

FROGGY
What?! A nice feller like you?

DEATH
Oh, it's true. You see, I...oh, you don't want to hear that old story.

FROGGY
Sure we do! Don't we, Bill?

INJUN BILL
Honestly, I got no stake in it.

FROGGY
Don't listen to him. He's half-Lakota, half-rattlesnake and half-grizzly bear.

DEATH
Well let's see...this would've been about two years ago. I was in Rawlins... Rawlins, Montana.

FROGGY
Yuh-huh.

DEATH
This was after God burned my family in Atlanta's flames but before I began my bloody march toward the end of days.

FROGGY
Huh. Yeah. You know what, maybe...

DEATH
So there I was in Rawlins and this soldier walks by. A Union Soldier. Now there are few things I hate as much as a Billy Yank, so I...well, I'm not proud of this, but I thumped him. With my bible. Caught him unawares and just....

(DEATH pounds on the table hard. BILL and FROGGY jump)

DEATH
I kept hitting him and hitting him until my precious gospel was covered in his blood. The next thing I know, the constabulary have grabbed me and tossed me in a jail cell. Just me and my blood-soaked bible and...now come to think of it, there was a man in there with me.

FROGGY
Know what? I gotta get supper goin', so... *(FROGGY tries to leave, but DEATH pushes him back into his seat)*

DEATH
Well, I'm a chatty fellow. Always have been. I just started to tell this lout my whole story. And do you know what he did, Froggy?

FROGGY
...nope...?

DEATH
He told me his story in return. It turns out this poor man had lost everything too. His one and only friend had been strung up from a pole. And then skinned! And then...now, I know this may be hard to believe, but this man's friend had actually been turned into a pair of shoes! Can you believe it?

INJUN BILL
I know you. You're that crazy priest that....

DEATH
And as he's telling me this story... do you know what happened? *(claps his hands loudly)* Revelation! The truth of God's word made known to me! We two men had been washed in the bloody violence of the world that we might serve the Lord! That, THAT, was the reason why we'd suffered so! Well, as soon as I was released, I set myself to His service. Boys, there's nothing like the feeling of putting a bullet into some hick, and his wife, and his children. Watching them bleed out, then going to their neighbors and doing it again and again. I tell you, there's nothing like it. Nothing in the world.

INJUN BILL
Jesus Christ...you're Death.

DEATH
And you're Injun Bill Picote.

(DEATH quickly grabs FROGGY and slams his head into the table. FROGGY drops)

DEATH
Been a long time.

INJUN BILL
Froggy!

(BILL pulls his knife. DEATH points a gun at him)

DEATH
I hate to ask it, but would you be so kind as to remove your weapons?

(BILL slowly disarms himself)

INJUN BILL
What the hell do you want?

DEATH
Why, to kill every last soul in Denver.

INJUN BILL
What?

DEATH
I've never tried to slaughter a town this big. I don't mind saying, it's taking some doing!

(FROGGY moans. BILL goes to him)

INJUN BIL
Hang in there, son.

FROGGY
....he damn near...cracked my coconut...

INJUN BILL
You're gonna be all right.

DEATH
Well, that's not entirely true.

INJUN BILL
You ain't touchin' him again.

DEATH
William...may I call you William? Surely you can see what this is.

INJUN BILL
Just back off.

DEATH
Providence! God has brought us together for a reason! I mean, to end up in the same place at the same time after all these years...what else could it be?

INJUN BILL
It's just chance, preacher. Dumb, stinkin' chance.

DEATH
Oh, there is no "chance." There is no luck, or coincidence. Everything that has led us to this has been... little miracles in disguise.

INJUN BILL
All right, all right. Don't do nothing crazy.

FROGGY
...too fuckin' late....

INJUN BILL
What exactly is the plan here?

DEATH
The plan? William, the world is ending. There's only one plan. Set it all ablaze, and send the righteous to Heaven. Sing Hallelujah!

(No one says anything. He points his gun at FROGGY)

FROGGY
Hallelujah.

(INJUN BILL gets between them)

INJUN BILL
You got no call to kill this man.

DEATH
You may not know this, William, but every time I look into another man's soul, I see his sins manifest. Your friend there is a liar, a glutton and a thief. And you... *(He grabs BILL, staring into his face)* I see every life you've taken. Every lie you've told, and every penny you've stolen. I am the Lord's judgment and I name you guilty.

INJUN BILL
Preacher, I've been a killer damn near all my life, and I can tell you this for free; there ain't no answers in it. Just a long line of people that never got the chance to be something better. I can't never atone for that. Only thing I can do is stop. So I'm asking you, please, put the gun down. Don't make me stop you.

(DEATH shoots INJUN BILL. INJUN BILL stands there for a moment, then drops)

FROGGY
BILL!

(DEATH kicks FROGGY, then goes to BILL)

DEATH
Cursed be he who does the Lord's work remissly; cursed he who holds back his sword from blood - Jeremiah 48:10. *(He points the gun at FROGGY)*

INJUN BILL
...Preacher...

DEATH
Yes?

INJUN BILL
...hey, Preacher...

DEATH
Yes, William? What is it?

INJUN BILL
...you got somethin' on your shirt.

(Beat. DEATH checks his shirt. A large blood stain has formed. He reaches under his jacket and pulls out Quiet Annie)

DEATH
What on Earth?

INJUN BILL
Right in the sweet spot.

(DEATH begins to wobble, and drops his gun)

DEATH
I didn't even feel it.

INJUN BILL
I know. I'm that good.

(DEATH drops to his knees)

DEATH
So...this is what it feels like.

INJUN BILL
Yeah.

DEATH
I didn't think it would be so soon.

INJUN BILL
Hell, I thought it would be sooner.

DEATH
Do you think...everything that's happened to us...was there a reason for it all?

INJUN BILL
Maybe. Don't mean we're meant to know it.

DEATH
Well...I think we're about to find out.

(He falls over dead. FROGGY goes to BILL)

FROGGY
Aw Jesus, Bill....you hang in there...

INJUN BILL
...don't tell me what to do, ya bastard...

FROGGY
This is a lot of blood.

INJUN BILL
You're tellin' me.

FROGGY
Just keep breathing. I'm gonna get a doctor.

INJUN BILL
Won't do no good. I'm wormfood.

FROGGY
I'll think of something! Just...

(FROGGY rises to leave. INJUN BILL grabs his arm)

FROGGY
You gotta let me do this. I can save you!

INJUN BILL
I think I'm as close to saved as I'm gettin'.

FROGGY
Just stay awake, buddy. Froggy's here.

INJUN BILL
I smelled a flower today, Froggy.

FROGGY
That's real good. Just...

INJUN BILL
It was a hell of a thing. A hell of a thing.

(BILL is fading fast)

FROGGY
You saved me.

INJUN BILL
What're friends for?

FROGGY
C'mon, Bill. You gotta keep your eyes open.

INJUN BILL
Hey. Hey. Froggy?

FROGGY
Yeah?

INJUN BILL
Don't feel bad for me, all right?

FROGGY
…no, no. no….

INJUN BILL
This was a good day.

FROGGY
Bill!

INJUN BILL
This was the best day of my life.

(INJUN BILL dies. FROGGY holds his body and weeps. Lights fade)

SCENE SIX

MARTHA
(singing)
LET US PAUSE IN LIFE'S PLEASURES
AND COUNT ITS MANY TEARS,
WHILE WE ALL SUP SORROW
WITH THE POOR;
THERE'S A SONG THAT WILL LINGER
FOREVER IN OUR EARS;
OH HARD TIMES COME AGAIN NO MORE.
TIS THE SONG, THE SIGH OF THE WEARY,
HARD TIMES, HARD TIMES,
COME AGAIN NO MORE
MANY DAYS YOU HAVE LINGERED
AROUND MY CABIN DOOR;
OH HARD TIMES COME AGAIN NO MORE.

(Lights rise. MARTHA & FROGGY at the cemetery. Both are dressed in black)

FROGGY
Thank you for singin' that.

MARTHA
Of course.

FROGGY
Bill liked that song. At least, he told me he liked it. I don't know.

(Beat)

MARTHA
Would you like to keep waiting?

FROGGY
I guess not. Don't know who I thought would show up.

MARTHA
Did he have many friends here?

FROGGY
I don't think he had many friends anywhere.

MARTHA
Oh. *(Beat)* He saved my life, you know. Or rather…he didn't take my life when he could have. It's not exactly the same thing, I suppose, but…

FROGGY
He saved my life too.

MARTHA
Then I guess one might say he was a good man.

FROGGY
I think…for most of his life, he

didn't know that was even an option. His conscience came up on him real sudden like.

MARTHA
Then why did you follow him?

FROGGY
I don't know. I liked him.

MARTHA
He liked you too.

FROGGY
Really?

MARTHA
One of the last things he said to me. "Froggy's an all right sort."

FROGGY
He said that?

(She nods. FROGGY is deeply moved by the sentiment)

FROGGY
He was an all right sort too.

(They stand in silence for a bit)

FROGGY
You can go if you want to. You don't have to stay here with me.

MARTHA
I'd like to stay. If you'll have my company.

FROGGY
All right.

MARTHA
Would you like to say something? It might make you feel better.

FROGGY
Well, I wrote out this thing…whaddya call it…a eogo…eulio…

MARTHA
A eulogy?

FROGGY
That's it.

MARTHA
If you'd like to read it, I'll listen.

(He thinks about it)

FROGGY
Naw. It's stupid. And it's real short. Bill wouldn't want me to…

(MARTHA takes his hand)

MARTHA
Jean Phillipe, whatever you have to say, I think he'd want to hear it.

(Beat. FROGGY takes a small piece of paper out of his pocket)

FROGGY
Is there…am I supposed to do something first, or…?

MARTHA
You just have to read it.

FROGGY
All right. (He reads the paper. As he does, he fights back his own sorrow) Injun Bill….Injun Bill Picote… was my friend.

(He puts the paper in his pocket. MARTHA holds him. Lights fade to black)

END OF PLAY

THE USUAL
A Musical Love Story

Lyrics and book by
Alan Gordon

Music by
Mark Sutton-Smith

CAST OF CHARACTERS

KIP (also Troll, Witch, Imp and Wizard) -- Male, 41, bari/tenor. A computer geek, socially inept, but willing to learn.

VALERIE (also Kelly) -- Female, 33, soprano. A hacker, the leading character in her one-woman screwball comedy, with a shell that's not quite thick enough.

SAM (also Karen, Nancy and Valkyrie) -- Female, 28, soprano with some rock belt. A bartender, all-seeing and all-knowing.

THE USUAL received its world premiere on March 22nd, 2012 at Williamston Theatre. It was directed by Tony Caselli. Music Direction by Jeff English, Choreography by Dana Brazil, Set Design by Daniel C. Walker, Lighting Design by Ryan Davies, Costume Design by Holly Iler, Prop Design by Lynn Lammers, Stage Managed by Stefanie Din.

The cast was as follows:

Sam – Leslie Hull
Valerie – Emily Sutton-Smith
Kip – Joseph Zettelmaier

THE USUAL WAS THE RECIPIENT OF THE 2013 KLEBAN PRIZE FOR LIBRETTO.

For information about production rights, visit www.alan-gordon.com.

THE USUAL

ACT I

KIP
Okay, I've got one. This guy walks into a bar with an ugly, little, yellow dog. And when I say an ugly, little, yellow dog, I mean it was the ugliest *(VALERIE starts overlapping him)*, the littlest, and most definitely the yellowest dog you have ever seen in your life. So the guy is having a beer, and the dog is curled up by the foot of the barstool, and everyone is staring at it, thinking, "What the hell kind of dog is that?" So finally, another guy goes up to him and says, "Hey, buddy. Can't help but noticing that that there is one ugly little yellow dog." And the first guy says...

VALERIE
A duck waddles into a bar, hops up onto the barstool, and says to the bartender, "Got any gwapes?" The bartender says, "No, we do not have any gwapes. This is a bar, and you are a weird, creepy little duck, so get out of here." *(SAM starts overlapping both)* The duck hops down and walks out. The next day, the duck waddles back into the bar, hops up onto the barstool, and says, "Got any gwapes?" The bartender says, "I told you yesterday, and I'll tell you again. We do not have gwapes. You are a freaky, stupid duck, and I want you out of here, and if you come back in here and ask for gwapes again ...

SAM
A kangaroo hops into a bar and orders a martini. The bartender serves it to him and the kangaroo gulps it down. So the bartender ... *[KIP and VALERIE cut out here, leaving only SAM's voice]* Oh, wait. I'm telling it wrong. Let me start over.

SONG: THESE TWO WALK INTO A BAR

KIP
SO THIS GUY WALKS INTO A BAR.

Stop me if you heard this one.

HE'S GOT NO DOG, NO TALKING DUCK.
HE'S GOT NO HORSE, HE'S GOT NO LUCK.
HE NEEDS SOME LUBRICATION
SO HE'LL GET UNSTUCK.
SO THIS GUY WALKS INTO A BAR.

(VALERIE enters)

VALERIE
So this gal walks into a bar.
She's sometimes blonde. She isn't dumb.
She likes the wine, and loves the rum.
She likes to go in feeling,
and then come out numb,
So this gal walks into a bar.

KIP
I hear some folks like
to ride a bike
or go spelunk in caverns.

VALERIE
But when I want peace,
I seek release
by getting drunk in taverns.

BOTH
(overlapping clumsily)
So this guy/gal --
(They glare at each other)
These two walk into a bar.

KIP
He's got no fish.

VALERIE
She's got no bears.

KIP
He got divorced.

VALERIE
She's had affairs.

KIP
He gets morose and sullen.

VALERIE
And she overshares,

BOTH
When these two walk into a bar.

VALERIE
Stop me if you've heard this one.

This gal walks into a bar.
She's got no chimps; no kangaroos,
She's got no man. She's got the blues.
She thinks that all her problems
can be drowned in booze.

KIP
So this guy walks into a bar.
He's not a rabbi, he's not a priest.
He's not a cowboy,

VALERIE
To say the least.

BOTH
His prospects for salvation
have, I'm sure, decreased,

KIP
since this guy walked into a bar.

VALERIE
A gal walked into a bar.

KIP
Now the world can
Sure confuse a man.

VALERIE
A gal might let life trick her.

BOTH
And the sober kind
are too inclined
to grumble, whine, and bicker.
But in bars you'll find
some peace of mind.
'Cause that's what comes with liquor.

So these two walked into a bar.

VALERIE
She's thirty-three.

KIP
He's forty-one.

VALERIE
She's got no life.

KIP
He's got no fun.

BOTH
THEIR CHANCES OF CONNECTING
RANGE FROM SLIM TO NONE,
BUT WE HAVEN'T GONE VERY FAR.
THE JOKE GOES LIKE THIS:

KIP
THIS GUY

VALERIE
THIS GAL

BOTH
THESE TWO
WALK INTO A...
WALK INTO A BAR.
(They look at each other)
Stop me if you've heard this one.

SCENE ONE

(A bar in a city. Four p.m. SAM, the bartender, is a young woman with short hair and tattoos on her biceps. KIP, a man in his early forties, walks in)

KIP
Sam. Right? It's Sam?

SAM
I am Sam, Sam I am. How are you today, Kip?

KIP
You remembered my name. I'm impressed.

SAM
Don't meet many Kips.

KIP
How many have you met?

SAM
Besides you?

KIP
Yes.

SAM
None.

KIP
Still, it's amazing that you remembered at all, considering I've only been here once. You must be a very good bartender.

SAM
I am. Watch what I do next. What'll you have, Kip?

KIP
Very professional.

SAM
Thanks.

KIP
Sam, I've decided that if I'm going to keep coming here, I'm going to need a usual.

SAM
Okay.

KIP
I want to be able to walk in here, have the standard, customary pleasant exchanges, and then say, with complete confidence, "The usual, Sam."

SAM
I like it so far. I do see one problem.

KIP
What?

SAM
You haven't told me what your usual is yet.

KIP
You see, that's the problem from my end. I don't have a usual. I never drank much before.

SAM
But you're taking it up.

KIP
Yes.

SAM
As a hobby?

KIP
I don't think I'm ready to turn pro yet.

SAM
All right. What would you like your usual to be?

KIP
I want to try new things, Sam. I want to experience alcohol in all its many forms. I want to know about liqueurs and single malts, the difference between lager and porter, how many ingredients go into a Long Island Ice Tea, and why they started putting flavors in vodka. Didn't it have a flavor already?

SAM
It's not what people drank it for. So, I'm still trying to grasp the concept. You walk in here, I say --

KIP
Something convivial. Something welcoming.

SAM
"Hello, Kip."

KIP
That works. And then I say, "Hello, Sam. I'll have the usual, please."

(There's a pause as they look at each other)

SAM
And I do what exactly?

KIP
You give me a drink. You make a random selection from one of those hundred bottles or those six taps or those thousand recipes you have, and you give it to me. And I will try that drink, and then compensate you for the experience.

SAM
So the "usual" will be different every time.

KIP
Yes.

SAM
That actually is the exact opposite of a "usual."

KIP
Au contraire, Sam. The experience, the moment of trying something new -- that's what the usual will be.

SAM
Ahh. Now I get it.

KIP
You will be a Scheherezade of mixology.

SAM
Only without the threat of beheading after.

KIP
Is that what he did to her?

SAM
He married her instead. It's a fine line, as far as I'm concerned.

KIP
I'm not gonna marry you, Sam.

SAM
I'd like your assurance on the beheading, too, if you don't mind.

KIP
I won't do that either.

SAM
Thank you. What got you into this adventure in drinking?

KIP
My colleagues suggested I start.

SAM
I can't help noticing that they aren't joining you.

KIP
I have been sent as an advance scout from the Kingdom of The Nerds. I have emerged from our crenellated cluster of cubicles to seek out a bar where the women are single, beautiful, and not too discriminating, and the men aren't going to beat us up on a regular basis like they did in junior high.

SAM
What kind of nerds are these?

KIP
Computer geeks, Sam. Their idea of wild and crazy is watching "Doctor Who" marathons and doing shots of Jager whenever the Tardis materializes.

SAM
Thank you. I needed a new definition of hell. Why did they pick you when you don't know anything about drinking?

KIP
They thought it might cheer me up. My divorce was finalized this week.

SAM
I'm sorry. Or, congratulations. Which is it?

KIP
A mix. Speaking of which, how about that ---

(VALERIE, a woman in her 30's, enters rapidly, looking behind her)

VALERIE
Excuse me, is this a good place to hide?

SAM
Unfortunately, yes. Almost nobody finds it. Who are you hiding from?

VALERIE
I'm ducking a blind date. Shoot! He's walking this way! Mister, could you take pity on a fellow human being for a moment and pretend you're talking to me?

KIP
No problem.

(VALERIE sits next to KIP, and they lean toward each other, pretending to talk)

KIP
What shall we pretend to talk about?

VALERIE
We need a topic?

KIP
It makes it look real. Shall we pretend to talk about sports?

VALERIE
Not a fan. Movies? I could fake that conversation.

KIP
Haven't seen anything in a while. How about...

SAM
He's gone.

VALERIE
Thank you so much.

KIP
What was wrong with him? He didn't look like his picture?

VALERIE
I'm sure he did look like his picture

-- in 1982. God, these Internet dates. Do you do those?

KIP
No.

VALERIE
I always figured, well, at least you could tell if they could spell or not.

SAM
I like good spellers.

KIP
They have spell-checkers for that.

VALERIE
Well, that takes all the romance out of it. Hey, listen, thanks for bailing me out there. Let me buy you a drink. What'll you have?

KIP
The usual, Sam.

SAM
One mojito coming right up.

VALERIE
That's an unusual usual.

KIP
Is it?

VALERIE
What the hell, make it two. Hello, I'm Valerie.

KIP
My name's Kip.

VALERIE
No, it isn't.

KIP
Yes, it is.

VALERIE
Nobody outside of a Dickens novel is named Kip.

KIP
I am here to prove you wrong.

VALERIE
Is it short for anything?

KIP
Do you know any long names that start with Kip?

VALERIE
Uh, you got me. Is there a Mrs. Kip?

KIP
No.

VALERIE
Any little Kiplings?

KIP
No. *(Pause)* Are you hitting on me?

VALERIE
No.

KIP
Because that's not why I came here.

VALERIE
I know why you're here.

KIP
You do?

VALERIE
Sure. I mean, come on. It's four o'clock in the afternoon, you're the only one here, and you have a usual. I may go on Internet dates, but believe me, I draw the line on guys like you.

KIP
It's not really like --

(SAM *places the mojitos in front of them*)

SAM
Your usual, Kip. Enjoy.

VALERIE
What shall we drink to?

KIP
To your next date, whoever he is. God help him.

VALERIE
God help him.

(They clink glasses and drink)

VALERIE
I thought the Internet was going to make dating better. I mean, two hundred years ago, you lived in a village and found your mate within walking distance.

KIP
Then came the steam engine. I wonder if people sat around in saloons in the 1850's and said, Gee, dating was so much simpler before that damn railroad came along. And don't even get me started on that telegraph.

VALERIE
And now, thanks to the Internet, you can be rejected by millions of people on a global scale. Isn't technology wonderful?

KIP
Are you going to try again?

VALERIE
It's still better than being picked up in bars.

KIP
At least I look like my current picture.

VALERIE
Now, you're hitting on me.

KIP
No, I'm not. You're hiding from a blind date, I've only had one drink, and I still have enough self-control to avoid hitting on a crazy person.

VALERIE
Fair enough. Tell you what, let's just keep things friendly, nothing more.

KIP
We're friends now?

VALERIE
We are friends. Not Capital F trademarked computer friends, but actual live friends.

KIP
All right.

VALERIE
And friends don't hit on friends. That's a rule.

KIP
What if the friends become attracted to each other?

VALERIE
We won't let that happen. From now on, this bar is the Neutral Zone. No excessive emotions, no hormonally-driven behavior, nobody hits on anybody.

Song: *Welcome to Switzerland*

VALERIE
My life is rife with dating disorder.
I need an escape from reality.
Come flee with me, we'll run for the border,
and find us a state of neutrality.

We need some space.

KIP
Some peaceful base.

SAM
Hold on a sec, I know a place.

Welcome to Switzerland!
Here, ev'ry moment's planned.
Come exist
as a pacifist
where mountains are high
but emotions are bland.

Live life without a care.
Suck down that cold, thin air.
Feel the breeze

BLOWING THROUGH THE CHEESE.
WELCOME TO SWITZERLAND.

COME TREKKING THROUGH OUR VALLEYS,
WHERE THE LEDERHOSENED YOKELS YODEL YOOHOO!
PLEASE MARVEL AT OUR TUNNELS.
WAS THERE EVER ENGINEERING SO PRECISE?
THE PEOPLE ARE SO CALM HERE.
IT'S A PLACID PLACE WHERE ONLY CLOCKS ARE CUCKOO.
YOU CAN'T GET OVERHEATED WHEN YOU SPEND SO MUCH OF EACH DAY COVERED WITH SNOW AND ICE.

KIP AND VALERIE
HOW NICE!

SAM
HIDE YOUR HEAD IN THE SAND.
DON'T EVER TAKE A STAND.
YOU CAN'T WIN
WITH NO OXYGEN.
WELCOME TO SWITZERLAND!

[Note: If the set provides for no exterior to the bar, then SAM will during the next section draw a Swiss flag on a chalkboard hanging behind the bar, where it will remain until the last scene]

KIP
I'VE LEARNED I'M BURNED WHENEVER THERE'S FEELING,
SO PLEASE BE ASSURED I WON'T HIT ON YOU.
WHAT'S MORE, IGNORE THAT YOU SENT ME REELING,
THE VERY FIRST TIME MY EYES LIT ON YOU.
I'LL MAKE A PACT. I WON'T REACT,
NO MATTER HOW MUCH YOU ATTRACT.

VALERIE
WELCOME TO SWITZERLAND.

KIP
TRANQUILITY'S SURE GRAND.

KIP AND VALERIE
TOLERATE

ALL THE THINGS YOU HATE.

SAM
AND VALIUM PILLS ARE OUR NATIONAL BRAND.

KIP
IN HERE, WE'LL PLAY IT SAFE.

VALERIE
DON'T LET EMOTIONS CHAFE.

KIP AND VALERIE
HIDE YOUR FAULTS
IN OUR SECRET VAULTS.

ALL
WELCOME TO SWITZERLAND!
COME HIKING IN OUR MEADOWS,

SAM
WHERE THE PEASANTS WITH THEIR ALPHORNS SERENADE YOU.

ALL
COME SKIING ON OUR MOUNTAINS.

VALERIE
RISK YOUR LIFE AS YOU ENCOUNTER EACH ABYSS.

ALL
RECOVER IN OUR CHALETS,

KIP
DRINKING BRANDY TO FORGET THE GIRL WHO PLAYED YOU.

SAM AND VALERIE
AND IF YOU'RE VERY LUCKY,
YOU MIGHT GET AN OPPORTUNITY TO KISS THIS SWISS MISS.

KIP
WHAT BLISS!

ALL
COME JOIN OUR HAPPY BAND.
LOVE CAN'T GET OUT OF HAND.
BE REBORN
ON THE MATTERHORN.

*Sip your drugs
from our cocoa mugs.
Fix your life
with an army knife.
Welcome to Switzerland!*

VALERIE
Now, friend Kip, let us agree to meet again here in this Switzerland of bars, and I will tell you about my next dating disaster.

KIP
And Sam and I will judge you.

SAM
I don't judge. It's part of the Bartenders' Code.

VALERIE
You will sit on your regular bar stool like the king of mojitos on his throne, and I'll be like Scheherezade. A thousand and one regrettable dates.

KIP
Scheherezade.

VALERIE
Yeah. She was the one who--

KIP
I know who she was. But it's weird. I brought up Scheherezade right before you came in. Didn't I, Sam?

SAM
It's true. He did.

KIP
I've gone, I'm going to say my entire life without ever saying Scheherezade, and now she comes up twice in five minutes.

VALERIE
You've had a Cruikshank.

KIP
A what?

VALERIE
That's what I call it. A Cruikshank. I came across the name one day, thought to myself, what an odd name! Then I came across it again on the same day in something completely unrelated to the first thing. So, my word for a massive coincidence of something trivial is a Cruikshank.

KIP
So I could call the same thing a Scheherezade.

VALERIE
No, you can't.

KIP
Why not?

VALERIE
Because it's called a Cruikshank. I thought of it first, so I get to name it.

KIP
All right.

VALERIE
And I have finished my mojito, your majesty, and the streets are clear of deceptively decrepit blind dates, so I am going to make my getaway.

KIP
Wait. You need my number.

(He hands her a card. She looks at it)

VALERIE
It says Kip.

KIP
Yes.

VALERIE
You had cards made up with just the name Kip and your number.

KIP
Yes.

VALERIE
How will I know it's you?

KIP
Do you know any other Kips?

VALERIE
No.

KIP
Then it's me.

VALERIE
(Pausing) I'm not giving you my number.

KIP
Okay.

VALERIE
I mean, I may be a crazy person, but my mom always warned me about guys in bars, and you're just some guy in a bar, you know?

KIP
I know.

VALERIE
Line drawn. You're there, I'm here.

KIP
Makes sense.

VALERIE
I don't think you should know my number.

KIP
Got the idea by now.

VALERIE
I've got to go.

KIP
No, you don't.

VALERIE
What?

KIP
If you had gone on that date, you'd still be in opening discussions right now. You don't have to go.

VALERIE
No. I want to go.

KIP
It was nice talking to you. Call me when you're ready for the next post-mortem.

VALERIE
Okay. I will. Good-bye, Kip. Sam.

SAM
Bye.

(VALERIE exits)

SAM
What did you think?

KIP
Kind of sweet.

SAM
I was talking about the mojito.

KIP
So was I.

SAM
I'm confused. I don't know if that was the worst job I've ever seen of hitting on someone, or the worst job I've ever seen of not hitting on someone.

KIP
I wasn't hitting on her.

SAM
What are the mating practices like in the Kingdom of the Nerds?

KIP
Primitive and largely unsuccessful compared to your sophisticated world.

SAM
But you found a wife. For a while.

KIP
That's why they made me their king.

SAM
How did you meet her?

KIP
She was the girl next door.

SAM
Ah, a hometown sweetheart.

KIP
No. She worked at the corporation next door. Her office cluster was down the hall from mine.

    Song: The Geek Next Door

I always used to see her
Walking briskly past my doorway.
An MBA attired
In Armani business suits.

I'd wonder if she noticed
That I'd watch her pass my doorway.
The tee shirt-wearing techie
Who just daydreams and computes.

One day she said hello with her eyes locked on mine,
And could I fix her dedicated service line?
I said I'd dedicate my service if she'd dine
With the geek next door.

And so the geek next door surprised them both by speaking out.
He felt his courage soar,
He wooed her without freaking out.
He boldly went where no geek ever went before.
Let's hear it for the geek next door.

And so I started courting,
Never thinking I would win her.
But winning her was easy.
Turned out keeping her was hard.

Each morning we had breakfast.
Ev'ry evening we had dinner.
I'd play games in the basement,
While she sunbathed in the yard.
The chips kept getting smaller, the connections fast.
I burrowed into coding and I had a blast.
I never thought each day with her could be the last
For the geek next door.

And so the geek next door
Stopped reading in between the lines.
He managed to ignore
The growing list of warning signs.
Because she loved you doesn't mean forever more.
How foolish was the geek next door!

She got herself promoted.
Transferred to the corp'rate HQ.
I scored some big investors,
Staked my claim to cyberturf.

She couldn't meet at lunchtime.
I worked late into the evenings.
Sometimes she sent me e-mails.
I would read them, then go surf.

Then one day I came home and she had changed the locks.
I hid myself inside a box inside a box.
I measured my existence with irregular clocks.
Like a geek next door.

But then the geek next door decided to reboot his heart.
He finally knows the score
And is ready for the game to start.
He will listen for their signals.
If they're out there, he will greet them.
He won't wait for them to find him,
He will seek them out and meet them.
He has learned from his mistakes

AND HEREBY SWEARS HE WON'T REPEAT
THEM.
HE'S LEFT HIS HIDDEN FORTRESS.
NOW, LET'S GO EXPLORE!
LET'S HEAR IT FOR THE GEEK NEXT
DOOR!

SAM
Another mojito, Kip?

KIP
No, thanks. I'll stick to one usual at a time. My people need me. Good night, Sam.

SAM
Was the mission a success?

KIP
I made contact with live humans. Phase One is complete.

SAM
What's Phase Two?

KIP
I'm gonna listen to her, Sam. You just watch me.

SAM
Good night, Kip.

SCENE TWO

SAM
The earliest definition of cocktail appeared in the May 13, 1806 edition of the Balance and Columbian Repository. The article said that the drink "is supposed to be an excellent electioneering potion, inasmuch as it renders the heart stout and bold, at the same time that it fuddles the head. It is said also to be of great use to a Democratic candidate: because a person, having swallowed a glass of it, is ready to swallow anything else."

(Same setting. KIP and VALERIE enter from opposite sides)

VALERIE
You came.

KIP
You called. I said I'd come if you called.

VALERIE
I thought maybe with your work schedule--

KIP
My hours are flexible. Hello, Sam.

SAM
Hello, Kip. What'll it be?

KIP
The usual, please.

SAM
Coming right up. Valerie?

VALERIE
The same. *(They sit)* So his name was Cliff. Do you want the whole story?

KIP
Just the cliff notes.

VALERIE
From Ohio. Accountant. Nice-looking. Tall.

KIP
Is tall important?

VALERIE
Tall is better than short. Young is better than old.

(SAM brings over two glasses of Irish whiskey)

KIP
Then your ideal man would be nine feet tall and five years old.

VALERIE
Most men are five years old.

SAM
And think they're nine feet tall.

(VALERIE and SAM high five)

VALERIE
(Takes a sip) Anyhow, he takes me to a nice place for dinner, and we had a nice meal, and a nice chat, and this is totally not a mojito. What is this?

KIP
What is this, Sam?

SAM
Jameson's. Eighteen year-old Irish whiskey.

KIP
That's what it is.

VALERIE
I thought your usual was a mojito.

KIP
No.

VALERIE
But when we met -- ah, screw it. Sláinte!

KIP
What?

VALERIE
You're drinking Irish whiskey and you don't know your Irish toasts?

KIP
Are you Irish?

VALERIE
Not a bit. Sláinte!

KIP
Sláinte!

(They drink)

VALERIE
Where was I?

KIP
Cliff. The word nice kept coming up.

VALERIE
Right. Nice manners, nice walk afterwards, nice kiss good night, nice -- everything. Only --

KIP
Only what?

VALERIE
That was it. Nice. No electricity, no chemistry. You see him now, you see what he's going to be like as an old man.

KIP
You've got a thing about ageing, don't you?

VALERIE
No! Well, no, not like you think. I don't have a problem getting older.

KIP
None of us do.

VALERIE
It's how you age that matters. Okay, like I took this ballroom dancing class once, and they made you go to these places where people still do ballroom dancing, and it was usually an American Legion Hall with a mirror ball and an elderly DJ kind of thing, and sometimes I'd be the only person in the room under sixty.

KIP
You must have been very popular.

VALERIE
Oh, I got danced around, but that's not the point. Most of those people would only dance with each other, and they looked like they'd been danc-

ing together forever. They dressed to kill, they knew all the moves, maybe they couldn't do them the way they used to, but it didn't matter. They were these fantastic, happy, sexy, old people. And I thought, that's the way to age, you know?

KIP
"Grow old along with me. The best is yet to be."

VALERIE
Right. What's that from?

KIP
Uh -- I'm blanking.

SAM
Robert Browning.

KIP
Yes, thank you. So, Cliff doesn't dance?

VALERIE
Cliff doesn't live! It doesn't have to be dancing.

KIP
I think you're being unfair to him. There's something to be said for a solid, comfortable existence.

VALERIE
I agree. And the something to be said is that IT'S REALLY BORING! I want someone who really lives his life, and doesn't settle. There is so much going on in the world right now, and I am not going to settle for anything.

> SONG: I LOVE THESE TIMES

LIFE ONCE WAS ONE HUGE BORE.
THEN THEY PUT IT ONLINE MORE AND MORE.
NOW IT'S ONE BIG CANDY STORE.
I LOVE THESE TIMES.

HERE IT IS IN MY HAND.
ALL THE UNIVERSE AT MY COMMAND.
WATCH ME SURF AROUND IT, AND
I LOVE THESE TIMES.

WHY CHOOSE
WHEN YOU CAN BUY ANYTHING,
TRY ANYTHING?
I CHOOSE
TO MAKE NO CHOICE.
AMUSE
ME AS I HACK EV'RYTHING,
CRACK EV'RYTHING.
GOOD NEWS,
LET'S ALL REJOICE!

WANT A NEW LOVE AFFAIR?
WAIT A NANOSECOND, AND HE'S THERE.
AND YOU'VE ALWAYS GOT A SPARE.
I LOVE THESE TIMES.

ONLINE,
I CAN GO SEE ANYONE,
BE ANYONE.
DEFINE
ME AS I DARE.
I'LL SHINE,
I CAN CREATE ANYONE, DATE ANYONE.
DON'T WHINE,
PERHAPS I'LL SHARE.

TIME IS SHORT, TIME IS FLEET.
HERE'S THE FUTURE, NOW IT'S OBSOLETE.
LIFE'S A BALL, AND AIN'T IT SWEET?

I LOVE THE WAY THERE'S TOO MUCH INFORMATION,
NO DEGREES OF SEPARATION.
LOVE THE CONSTANT REARRANGING, MIND-ENGULFING, ALWAYS-CHANGING PARADIGMS.
OH GOD, I LOVE THESE TIMES.

KIP
So, good-bye to Cliff. Who's the next one?

VALERIE
I don't know yet. I fill out the post-

date form, send it in, and wait for the happy happening.

KIP
Call me when it all goes horribly wrong again.

VALERIE
I'm sure you meant to say good luck with the next one.

KIP
I was thinking it. Well, gotta catch a train. Nice talking to you again. (*He stands to leave*)

VALERIE
Wait. (*She scribbles her number down on a napkin and gives it to him*) I feel bad that I didn't give you this before.

KIP
Thanks. But you keep making the calls, okay? Good night, ladies.

VALERIE
Good night, Kip.

(*He exits*)

SAM
You don't see him as a possibility?

VALERIE
He's a drunk, and this is Switzerland. That's two different rules.

SAM
And you never break your rules.

VALERIE
They're all I've got sometimes. (*Her cell phone rings. She looks at it, but doesn't answer*) Screw you.

SAM
Problem?

VALERIE
The real world calling. I sent it to voice mail. Good night, Sam. (*She exits*)

SCENE THREE

SAM
Men in bars often like to indulge their inner James Bond and order vodka martinis, made from vodka and dry vermouth. Women who date these men describe themselves after the encounters as shaken -- not stirred.

(*KIP and VALERIE enter*)

KIP
Hey, there.

VALERIE
Hi, Kip.

KIP
Special occasion today.

VALERIE
Really?

KIP
It's our tenth dating dissection.

VALERIE
You remembered! That's so sweet. I believe the tenth anniversary involves diamonds.

KIP
Funny you should mention that.

(*He hands her a gift-wrapped box. She looks at him in shock*)

VALERIE
That was just a joke.

KIP
Open it.

VALERIE
(*Unwrapping it*) Kip, there was no need to get me anything. In fact, I am more than a little uncomfortable with --- oh! (*She pulls a box of aluminum foil out of the wrapper*) It's foil. You gave me foil.

KIP
Tenth anniversary is aluminum.

VALERIE
It is?

KIP
Or tin, for some reason. It's hard to find a decent tin gift nowadays. You'll note that I sprang for the brand-name, not the generic. Nothing but the best.

VALERIE
Well. Thank you. You can never have enough foil. And it's shiny, like diamonds. I shall think of you every time I have leftovers.

KIP
Seems appropriate.

VALERIE
Dissection time?

KIP
Absolutely. But first, we must sterilize ourselves with alcohol. Sam, I'll have the usual.

SAM
Coming right up. Valerie?

VALERIE
The same, please. You know, for our tenth anniversary, I think we should try something new.

KIP
Like what?

VALERIE
How about you tell a dating story for me to dissect?

KIP
I don't have any.

VALERIE
You must have done something recently.

KIP
Sam, what's that thing that's the opposite of dating?

SAM
Not dating?

KIP
Right. That's the one I've been doing.

VALERIE
(To SAM) I thought you were going to say marriage.

SAM
I see married people dating all the time in here. Just not each other.

VALERIE
Tell me about it. I saw one last night.

KIP
Ouch.

VALERIE
I mean, he's separated, but still --

SAM
Another rule?

VALERIE
Better believe it. My mom used to say, "Divorced is okay, at least you can get matched, but the separated are forever attached." You're divorced, aren't you?

KIP
Yes. How could you tell?

VALERIE
It shows, somehow. Any good stories there?

KIP
I'm here to do autopsies on the recently deceased. That would be like exhuming the long dead and decayed. I could continue with the metaphor: If you open the coffin lid, the sight and the stench of the...

VALERIE
Got it. Moving on. Apart from her, what's the strangest thing you ever did to get a date?

KIP
You'll laugh.

VALERIE
I certainly hope so.

(SAM brings two chairs forward, sits in one, and turns into KAREN)

KIP
I tried out for a reality show.

(VALERIE starts to laugh)

KIP
See? You're laughing already.

VALERIE
I'm sorry. No, I'm not. Tell me everything.

KIP
This was after we separated. *(He gets up, walks over to the two chairs)* Excuse me, is this where they're holding "The Real World" auditions?

KAREN
Yes. Are you auditioning?

KIP
Sure am.

KAREN
(Rapidly) Me, too, that's so cool, my name's Karen, what's your hook?

KIP
My what?

KAREN
(Rapidly) Your hook, your gimmick, you gotta have a gimmick, my mom used to sing that to me all the time when I was girl which was like completely inappropriate I found out when I got older because it's this stripper song so it probably totally warped my childhood only my therapist thinks that's just an excuse and I think stripping is empowering, don't you?

KIP
Does the lack of oxygen ever get to be a problem?

KAREN
Oh, you're one of those sarcastic guys, that could work for you because they always need to have one of those assholes who puts everyone down, only they usually don't last the whole series, 'cause who wants to live with that, right? Me, I'm manic-depressive so I'm hoping that's my way in, the manic cute girl, you think I'm cute, don't you?

KIP
Uh, sure, but isn't there some kind of medication for this?

KAREN
I stopped taking it a week ago, had to time it for the manic, because they'd totally reject me if I was in the depressive, but my manic totally rules.

KIP
That seems a little extreme.

KAREN
Extreme is what they're looking for. So you're going with the sarcasm thing?

KIP
I thought I'd just be myself.

KAREN
You can't be yourself! This is reality!

(KELLY, played by VALERIE, enters, holding a clipboard and wearing a head-

set)

KELLY
Okay, Karen. They're ready to see you. And you are -- Kip?

KIP
I am.

KELLY
My name's Kelly, I'm a production assistant. You auditioned last season, didn't you?

KIP
And the season before. I must have made a good impression if you remember me.

KELLY
I just remembered the name. I mean, who the hell's named Kip, right?

KIP
I the hell am.

KELLY
I don't know why you bothered coming back. By now, the producers know you. If they didn't like you before, they're not likely to want you now.

KIP
Look, just ask. Please?

KELLY
I'll see what I can do. Come on in, Karen.

KIP
Good luck!

KAREN
Thanks. *(To KELLY)* So is this like an interview or should I just stand there and talk because I'm really good at talking...

(KELLY and KAREN exit)

REALITY

KIP
AT THE END OF EACH DAY
I KNEEL DOWN AND PRAY
TO THE GODS WHO HOLD SWAY
OVER ME.

AND I WANT THEM TO SEE
THAT I'M DESTINED TO BE
PART OF WHAT WE CALL REALITY.

MY BRAIN OVERFLOWS WITH QUESTIONS.
I HOPE THEY PUT ME WISE.
HOW COME IN THE PEOPLE'S COURTROOM
THERE'S NEVER COMPROMISE?
AND WHY IS IT CALLED SURVIVOR WHEN
NOBODY REALLY DIES?
WHO WANTS TO LIVE IN THE REAL WORLD
WHEN IT'S ALL BASED ON LIES?

I WANT TO BE HIRED BY DONALD,
AND SEE THE LOSERS SCOWL.
I WANT TO BE PRAISED BY PAULA,
AND RIPPED BY SIMON COWELL.
I WANT TO MAKE THINGS WITH MARTHA
WITH KRAZY GLUE AND A DOWEL.
I WANT TO LIVE ON "BIG BROTHER,"
WITH A CAM'RA UP MY BOWEL.

I WANT SOMEONE TO RAID MY ROOM.
I WANT SOMEONE TO PIMP MY RIDE.
TAKE ME OVER, MAKE ME OVER,
I WANT TO BE QUEER-EYED.

I WANT REAL HOUSEWIVES ON EACH ARM.
I WANT TO WAGE A STORAGE WAR.
PUMP AND FLEX ME, OVERSEX ME.
TAKE ME TO JERSEY SHORE.

GIVE ME A TASTE OF REALITY.
ONE HEALTHY DOSE OF REALITY.
MAKE ME A PART OF REALITY.
I WANT TO BE REAL.

SOMEDAY, I WILL TELL MY CHILDREN
OF HOW THEIR PARENTS MET.
IT HAPPENED IN FRONT OF MILLIONS,
A DAY I WON'T FORGET.

SHE GAVE ME HER LAST RED ROSE WHEN
SHE STARRED ON THE BACHELORETTE.
AND WE'LL BE MARRIED FOREVER
INSIDE A TV SET.

I WANT SOMEONE TO SWAP MY WIFE.
I WANT SOMEONE TO DATE MY MOM.
WASH AND DRY ME, TEASE AND DYE ME,
THEN TAKE ME TO THE PROM.

I WANT TO DANCE WITH WASHED-UP STARS.
I WANT SOMEONE TO TRICK MY TRUCK.
COME PROCLAIM ME, USE ME AND SHAME ME,
BUT LET ME CHANGE MY LUCK.

GIVE ME A TASTE OF REALITY.
MAKE ME A PART OF REALITY.
BIG HONKING GOBS OF REALITY.
HOT STEAMING PILES OF REALITY.
AND WHEN I'M A PART OF REALITY,
THEN I WILL BE REAL.
PLEASE LET ME BE REAL.
I WANT TO BE REAL.

(KELLY enters)

KELLY
Kip, I'm sorry. They said no.

KIP
Oh. Okay. Well, thanks for asking, anyway.

KELLY
Listen, you didn't hear this from me, but my friend down at the History Channel says they're casting for a show where you live like they did in the Neolithic Age. They're calling it "The Modern Stone Age Family." Here's her number.

KIP
That's great. I can do Neolithic in my sleep. This is so nice of you. Listen, if you're not doing anything, maybe I could buy you a drink or something.

KELLY
(Snorting) Get real!

(KIP walks back to the bar as the others change back)

KIP
And that was that.

VALERIE
Why did you even try? Even if you had met someone there, she would have been a reality contestant. Someone totally superficial.

KIP
Maybe that's what I needed at the time. Someone to pull me out of my funk. So, there. I have provided you entertainment through my humiliation.

VALERIE
They say the best comedy comes from pain.

KIP
That's said by people with no pain of their own.

VALERIE
Relax, Kip. Everyone has pain.

SAM
(Handing them their drinks) Here. For your pain.

KIP
To pain.

VALERIE
To pain.

(They drink)

KIP
Interesting, Sam. What's in it?

SAM
Gin, lemon juice, Cointreau, Lillet blanc and a dash of absinthe.

VALERIE
What's it called?

SAM
A Corpse Reviver.

KIP
Well, Dead Man commuting. See you two for the eleventh autopsy.

VALERIE
Good bye, Kip. *(He leaves. Then she remembers, and yells)* Oh. Thanks for the foil! *(Her cell goes off. She looks at it, then answers)* What. None of your business where I am. Yeah, keep dreaming. The house is mine. You want to talk? We'll talk at the lawyer's office. *(She disconnects)* Good night, Sam. *(VALERIE exits)*

SCENE FOUR

SAM
Cocktails made a comeback in the Eighties when the economy was booming. New combinations were invented with sassy, erotic names, aiming for alcoholic yuppies and ironic hipsters. There was Sex on the Beach, which was vodka, peach schnapps, orange and cranberry juice; the Orgasm -- Cointreau, Bailey's Irish Cream and Grand Marnier; and the Screaming Orgasm -- Vodka, Amaretto, Triple Sec, White Creme de Cacao, and light cream. Personally, I think that equating sex with drinking cheapened the experience. Of drinking.

(VALERIE enters, carrying a shopping bag)

SAM
You're early.

VALERIE
I was in the neighborhood. I was at this crazy thing.

SAM
What?

VALERIE
My girl friend got into this business where she sells stuff at these events like Tupperware parties, only she isn't selling Tupperware.

SAM
What is she selling?

(VALERIE pulls a catalog out of the bag and hands it to her)

SAM
"Pleasures Pour Elle," a catalog for -- sex toys? You went to a sex toy party! Oh, those are so fun!

VALERIE
It was so weird. There we were, sitting and drinking tea in this nice living room, beautifully decorated, and there were these obscene toys laid out on the fancy Belgian lace tablecloth. I was shocked, shocked, I tell you.

SAM
Did you get any?

VALERIE
Come on, I was just there to provide moral support. I don't need --

SAM
How many?

VALERIE
Three. *(She flips the catalog open)* I got this one, it has these two rotating ---

SAM
Oh, yeah. I've got one. You're gonna love it.

VALERIE
And then there's this.

(She opens it to another page. SAM leans in for a closer look, then VALERIE opens out a centerfold)

SAM
(Leaping back) GAH!

VALERIE
I know, right? It's like riding a giraffe.

SAM
I love this ad copy: "Ladies, are your lives in a rut? Has the sparkle vanished from your bedrooms? Are you tired of making love only during halftime?"

VALERIE
Although they had some cheerleader outfits for that. And you will not believe what they use the pom-poms for.

SAM
Rah! "Our products are made in America by Americans for Americans. Never again will you be disappointed by the inadequate size and shoddy workmanship of foreign manufacturers." That's good. It appeals to the horny patriot in all of us. "At Pleasures Pour Elle, we stand behind all of our products. Except for the ones you stand in front of, or the ones where you…"

VALERIE
Stop, okay, completely embarrassed now.

SAM
And the catalog layout's just like the FAO Schwartz one.

VALERIE
I know. I kept expecting to see a section with Barbies gone wild. Toys sure have changed since we were kids.

SONG: TOO OLD FOR TOYS

VALERIE
THEY SAID GIVE UP YOUR TOYS
IF YOU WANT TO GROW UP.

SAM
AND CHILDREN MUST OBEY.

VALERIE
THEY SAID WAIT FOR ROMANCE,
THAT IT'S BOUND TO SHOW UP.

SAM
IT'S JUST A BEAT AWAY.

VALERIE
NOW I'M GROWN, AND THERE'S NO DENYING
THE EXPERIENCE CLOYS.
WHY DID THEY ALWAYS TELL ME I'M TOO OLD FOR TOYS?

SAM
I WOULD PLAY WITH MY DOLL
AND TAKE OFF HER CLOTHES.

VALERIE
IT'S NORMAL CHILD'S PLAY.

SAM
I WOULD STARE AT HER BREASTS, AND WISH MINE WERE LIKE THOSE.

VALERIE
A REASON YOU SHOULD PRAY.

SAM
NOW I SIT BY THE WINDOW SIGHING FOR THE NEIGHBORHOOD BOYS.
WHY DO THEY ALWAYS TELL ME I'M TOO OLD FOR TOYS?

BOTH
TOYS WON'T LEAVE OR TRICK YOU WITH EMPTY FLATTERIES.
ALL THEY NEED IS LOVE AND DOUBLE A BATTERIES.
AND BATTERIES, OH.

NOW, I'M HOME ALL ALONE

WITH SOME TIME ON MY HANDS.
IT'S SUCH AN EMPTY DAY.
I COULD PUT THEM TO USE.
I THINK GOD UNDERSTANDS.
WE'RE SURE SHE'D SAY, "OKAY!"
WITH THESE, THERE WILL BE NO MORE CRYING
FOR MY VANISHING JOYS.
WHO CARES IF PEOPLE TELL ME I'M TOO OLD FOR TOYS?

MEN ARE GREAT IF YOU NEED SOMEONE TO LAY AROUND.
BUT WITH TOYS, YOU'RE ALWAYS READY TO PLAY AROUND.
AND ROUND AND ROUND, OH.

WITH A GADGET LIKE THIS,
GIRLS WON'T BOTHER WITH MEN.
FROM HOME WE'LL NEVER STRAY.
SMURFETTE STANDS ON HER OWN,
BARBIE DOESN'T NEED KEN.
GOOD-BYE TO LIVES OF GRAY.
NO ONE WHINING IT'S TERRIFYING,
'CAUSE WE MAKE TOO MUCH NOISE.

VALERIE
WE'RE LOOKING FOR GOOD VIBRATIONS!

BOTH
WHO CARES IF PEOPLE TELL US WE'RE TOO OLD FOR --
WHO CARES IF PEOPLE TELL US WE'RE TOO OLD FOR --
WHO CARES IF PEOPLE TELL US WE'RE TOO OLD FOR TOYS?

SAM
Could I ask you something?

VALERIE
Okay.

SAM
Does the fact that you're buying sex toys mean that the dates aren't going too well?

VALERIE
You mean, did I sleep with any of them?

SAM
Not that I'm judging.

VALERIE
You're judging but not saying anything. That's not the same as not judging.

SAM
Okay. But did you?

VALERIE
A few. In the beginning. I mean, that's one of the reasons I was doing it, right?

SAM
What's the other one?

VALERIE
Ooh, that slipped out, didn't it? Yeah, I want to be a girl gone wild for a while. I wanted to make up for lost time.

SAM
Where did you lose it?

VALERIE
I was kind of stuck with someone for a medium-sized eternity.

SAM
But you didn't tell Kip that.

VALERIE
He doesn't need to know everything. Anyway, I'm not doing the really crazy stuff on the dates any more.

SAM
Why'd you stop?

VALERIE
Because they didn't call back afterwards, and I didn't want to be just another notch on whatever it is that

men notch when they score.

SAM
Have you had a second date with any of them?

VALERIE
Not yet. I guess the guys who are still looking are alone for a real good reason. Or maybe I'm the kind of woman who drives guys away. Screaming and at high speeds.

SAM
Except for Kip.

VALERIE
Kip's not a guy. I mean, he's not a guy I'm dating.

SAM
But he comes back. Every single time. Why don't you consider him?

VALERIE
Why hasn't he asked me out if he's such a great possibility?

SAM
What would you do if he did?

VALERIE
I don't know. The best part of these lousy dates has been doing the post-mortem with him. If I went out with him, who would I be able to talk about it with afterwards? He's a friend. I don't want to screw that up by dating him.

SAM
That's seriously messed up.

VALERIE
Tell me about it. You know what's even worse?

SAM
What?

VALERIE
I've hit a dry spell on the dating. I've actually made the last three up.

SAM
You're kidding. Why?

VALERIE
I like coming here and talking about it. I like to talk.

SAM
I've noticed.

VALERIE
What can I say? Scheherezade did fiction; why can't I?

(KIP enters)

KIP
Afternoon, ladies.

SAM
(Shoving the catalog under the bar) Hi, Kip. So, can I borrow this?

VALERIE
Sure, just don't forget to give it back when you're done.

KIP
What's that?

VALERIE
A catalog. Girl stuff.

SAM
Socks, mostly.

KIP
They have catalogs for socks?

VALERIE
Sock technology has come a long way. They've made great strides.

SAM
You'd be amazed.

KIP
Not by socks. The usual, Sam. Valerie?

VALERIE
I'll have what he's having.

SAM
Be right back. I'm making something special, and I need something from the storeroom. *(SAM exits)*

KIP
What fresh hell have you brought for me today?

VALERIE
My mom always told me -- *(Her cell goes off. She looks at it, makes a face, then shuts it down)*

KIP
Anything wrong?

VALERIE
Big Brother is watching. Anyhow, as I was saying, my mom always told me to aim for the stars. So last night, I went out with an astronomer. Fortunately, it was cloudy, not bright. I didn't need any competition.

KIP
Did he only have eyes for you?

VALERIE
He asked a lot of questions.

KIP
Showed an interest. That's a positive, right?

VALERIE
They were mostly about my fertility cycle.

KIP
What?

VALERIE
He spends half his year in an observatory on Mauna Kea. At night, so his social life is nonexistent. He's getting pressured by his parents to start producing grandchildren. He figured he could get five or six out of me before my ovaries shut down. I figured he figured wrong.

KIP
Ah. I'm sorry.

VALERIE
And you?

KIP
And me what?

VALERIE
Honestly, getting you to talk about yourself is like pulling teeth.

KIP
I told you about the reality show.

VALERIE
Like weeks ago. And you didn't get a date out of it. I want a new disaster story. Tell you what, let's play a game.

KIP
What kind of game?

VALERIE
I just invented it. It's called Ask Until Yes.

KIP
How do you play?

VALERIE
I will ask you about outlandish dating possibilities, and gradually move towards normal. When we get to a yes, you tell me the story.

KIP
I'm not sure I like the sound of this.

VALERIE
Come on, it's just a game.

KIP
All right. Let's make it interesting. You only get ten questions. And my ex-wife is off-limits.

VALERIE
You're on. Okay, ever dated an astronomer?

KIP
No.

VALERIE
Ever dated an astronaut?

KIP
No.

VALERIE
Ever been in an orgy?

KIP
Define orgy.

VALERIE
Uh, multiple partners, multiple rooms, same time.

KIP
No.

VALERIE
But I was getting warm on that one, wasn't I?

KIP
No. And that's four questions.

VALERIE
That was sneaky.

KIP
Games have rules, right?

VALERIE
Yes, they do. Okay, ever dated a professional wrestler?

KIP
I wish. No.

VALERIE
Hah! A professional athlete of any kind?

KIP
No.

VALERIE
A porn star?

(KIP doesn't answer)

VALERIE
You're kidding! Really? You dated a porn star?

KIP
I'm not sure it qualified as a date.

VALERIE
You were a porn star!

KIP
(Laughing) That's the nicest thing anyone's ever said to me. No, it wasn't like that.

VALERIE
Okay, this is intriguing. Tell me about it.

KIP
It's not a pretty story.

VALERIE
Like mine were? Come on. Spill it! Or is that a bad thing to say to a porn star?

KIP
This was not too long ago. I had moved out of what used to be my house, and I was on my own. I didn't like it much. I spent too many hours alone, depressed and online. I found myself checking out some rather out-there websites. You sure you want to hear about this?

VALERIE
Keep going.

(An armchair slides out. KIP sits in it)

KIP
And then I found her. *(He picks up a laptop and opens it. At the opposite side of the stage, a bed slides on. Atop*

it is NANCY, played by SAM, wearing lingerie and a day-glo wig. She also has a laptop)

NANCY
Hi, this is Nancy. Are you there?

KIP
Yes.

NANCY
Are you -- Kip?

KIP
Yes.

NANCY
Seriously, you want me to call you Kip?

KIP
It's my name.

NANCY
All right, if you say so. Well, "Kip," I have two pieces of very good news. The first is that your payment has been approved.

KIP
And the second?

NANCY
The second is that I am here.

KIP
So I see. What do we do now?

NANCY
What would you like to do?

KIP
I don't know. I've never done this before.

NANCY
You're a webcam virgin!

KIP
I suppose I am. Please don't tell the other webcam girls. They'll laugh at me.

NANCY
That is so adorable! Well, it's easy. You tell me to do something, and I do it.

KIP
That's it?

NANCY
That's it.

KIP
Like what?

SONG: IN OUR PRIVATE ROOM

NANCY
WHO DO YOU WANT ME TO BE?
WHAT DO YOU WANT TO SEE?
I WILL GIVE YOU MY COMPLETE ATTENTION.
DO WHAT YOU WANT WITH ME.

YOU CAN MAKE ME MOVE,
YOU CAN MAKE ME STRIP,
YOU CAN MAKE ME DANCE.
USE THE CAM'RA, KIP.
YOU CAN MAKE IT PAN.
YOU CAN MAKE IT ZOOM.
'CAUSE I'M YOUR WEB-CAM GIRL
ALL ALONE WITH YOU,
IN OUR PRIVATE ROOM.

KIP
Touch your nose.

NANCY
What?

VALERIE
What?

KIP
Touch your nose.

NANCY
(Hesitantly putting her hand up to her face) You said nose?

KIP
Yes.

NANCY
As in the middle of my face?

KIP
Yes.

NANCY
(Shrugs, then touches her nose. She pauses, then moans) Ohhhhhh. (Pause) Just kidding. Why my nose?

KIP
THE FIRST TIME WHEN I KISSED MY WIFE, IT WAS SOMEWHERE DARK.
I THOUGHT I WOULD LAND ON HER MOUTH, BUT I MISSED THE MARK.
MY LIPS CAUGHT HER SQUARE ON THE NOSE, AND I SENSED HER GRIN.
SINCE THEN, EV-RY TIME WE MADE LOVE, THAT'S HOW WE'D BEGIN.

NANCY
That's so sweet. So, our lovemaking has begun.

KIP
It has?

NANCY
You told me to touch my nose. And I did. Tell me what to do next.

KIP
AND SHE WAITS ON MY SCREEN, LOOKING SO EXOTIC.
WHO KNEW "SIMON SAYS" COULD BE THIS EROTIC?

NANCY
TELL ME WHAT FANCY YOU CRAVE.

KIP
WHAT DO I WANT HER TO BE?

NANCY
HOW SHOULD I MISBEHAVE?

KIP
WHAT IS MY FANTASY?

NANCY
I GUARANTEE THERE'LL BE NO DISSENSION,
'CAUSE, BABY, I'M YOUR SLAVE.

YOU CAN MAKE ME TWIST,
YOU CAN MAKE ME POSE,
YOU CAN MAKE ME SCREAM,
EVEN TOUCH MY NOSE.
YOU JUST PLANT THE SEED,
AND I'LL MAKE IT BLOOM,
'CAUSE I'M YOUR WEBCAM GIRL
ALL ALONE WITH YOU,

KIP
YOU'RE MY WEBCAM GIRL ALL ALONE WITH ME,

BOTH
IN OUR PRIVATE ROOM.

VALERIE
WHAT DID YOU WANT THIS GIRL FOR?
WHY DIDN'T YOU WANT MORE?

KIP
SOMETHING LIKE LOVE, WITHOUT APPREHENSION.
LOVE WITH NO PAIN IN STORE.

VALERIE
You can't have that.

NANCY
Yes, Kip. You can. With me, you can.

LOVE'S JUST AN IDIOT'S GAME,
A REFLEX ROUTINELY AROUSED,
AN EMBER THAT THINKS IT'S A FLAME,
BUT EASILY DOWSED.

VALERIE
She's wrong. Kip, it has to be more than that. You can't play it safe.

LOVE ISN'T ALWAYS RETURNED,
BUT NEVER GIVE UP THAT DESIRE.
YES, YOU MAY RISK GETTING BURNED,
BUT YOU'LL HAVE A FIRE.

NANCY
Meter's running, Kip.

WHAT DO YOU WANT ME TO BE?

KIP
(Overlapping) WHAT DO I WANT HER TO BE?

VALERIE
(Overlapping) WHAT DID YOU WANT HER TO BE?

KIP
THE LAST TIME WHEN I KISSED MY WIFE, IT WAS JUST A PECK.
THE LAST TIME I WROTE MY WIFE'S NAME, IT WAS ON A CHECK.
HOW QUICKLY THE FLAMES CAN DIE DOWN.
THAT'S HOW FAST LOVE GOES.
THE THING THAT I MISS MOST OF ALL --
MY LIPS ON HER NOSE.

NANCY
Shall I be her?

KIP
Her?

NANCY
The one whose nose you kissed. The one you lost. Shall I be her for a while?

KIP
Can you? How?

VALERIE
No, Kip!

NANCY
(Overlapping for the rest of the song) I CAN BE YOUR FANTASY.

KIP
(Overlapping for the rest of the song) THE FIRST TIME WHEN I KISSED MY WIFE, IT WAS SOMEWHERE DARK.

NANCY
REVIVE THAT REVERIE.

KIP
I THOUGHT I WOULD LAND ON HER MOUTH, BUT I MISSED THE MARK.

NANCY
TELL ME WHAT SPRINGS

KIP
MY LIPS CAUGHT HER SQUARE ON THE NOSE,

NANCY
FROM YOUR HEART'S INVENTION,

KIP
AND I SENSED HER GRIN.

NANCY
AND I'LL SET THOSE DREAMS

KIP
SINCE THEN, EV-RY TIME WE MADE LOVE

NANCY
FREE.

KIP
THAT'S HOW WE'D BEGIN.

NANCY
I CAN CHANGE MY EYES,

KIP
LET HER GO.

NANCY
I CAN CHANGE MY HAIR.

KIP
THROW AWAY THAT OLD APPARITION.

NANCY
TELL ME WHAT TO SAY,

KIP
TRY LIVING YOUR LIFE

NANCY
TELL ME WHAT TO WEAR.

KIP
WITHOUT HER PERMISSION.

NANCY
I COULD BE YOUR BRIDE,
YOU COULD BE MY GROOM.
'CAUSE I'M YOUR WEB-CAM GIRL
ALL ALONE WITH YOU,
IN OUR PRIVATE ROOM.

VALERIE
I can't believe you did this.

KIP
I was lonely. I was depressed. And I was afraid.

VALERIE
Afraid of what?

KIP
That this was what my life would be like from now on. Afraid that it would take someone like her to keep me connected.

VALERIE
Was she worth it?

KIP
It didn't get that far.

VALERIE
Why? Was something wrong?

NANCY
Is there something wrong?

KIP
I'm not sure.

NANCY
Tell me what you want, Kip.

VALERIE
What do you want, Kip?

KIP
I don't know what I want.

NANCY
It can be anything, Kip. Just tell me.

KIP
CAN YOU MAKE IT REAL?

NANCY
ANYTHING BUT THAT.
SORRY, KIP.
I DON'T DO REAL.

Pick a fantasy. That's what I get paid for.

KIP
Look, don't get me wrong, you're a dream come true. But --

NANCY
But you don't want a dream.

KIP
I -- I'm sorry. I don't think this is going to work. It isn't you --

NANCY
It never is me, Kip. It's okay. You know there's no refund.

KIP
No, of course, I know that. It's just that --

NANCY
No bother, Kip. Call me when your next marriage breaks up.

KIP
THIS MAY SEEM ABSURD, BUT I WANT TO THANK --

(*The lights go out on NANCY, who exits*)

BUT SHE NEVER HEARD,
'CAUSE THE SCREEN WENT BLANK.
AND SHE DISAPPEARED,
VANISHED IN THE GLOOM.
SO MY WEB-CAM GIRL LEFT ME ALL ALONE
IN MY PRIVATE ROOM.

KIP
And that was my date with a porn star.

VALERIE
Every time I get a story from you,

it's about a fake experience. Reality shows, cybersex --

KIP
The point is, I realized that I needed something more. I had to stop postponing real life.

VALERIE
And having had that revelation, you bravely marched all the way to this bar, and you haven't left since.

KIP
Baby steps, okay? Look, this was your stupid idea of a game. I didn't even want to bring this up.

VALERIE
I thought it would lead to a humiliating but funny dating story. But that -- that was cowardice. And so is being here. You're hiding behind a glass instead of a computer, but it's still shields up, Captain.

KIP
And how is your internet dating any better?

VALERIE
It's legal, for one thing.

KIP
But it's still fake. At least the way you're doing it.

VALERIE
It is not fake! I am out there looking. I'm putting myself on the line every time.

KIP
No, you're not. You're using these dates as a way of avoiding the hard work of actually trying to know someone. You find the flaw in each man, write him off immediately, and come here to tell amusing stories

about it, completely secure from exposing yourself to anything resembling an emotion.

VALERIE
(*Shouting*) That isn't --

SAM
(*Entering with a bottle*) Hey, hey, hey! This is Switzerland! Cease with the shouting, you'll cause an avalanche or something. Now, I have something weird and different for you today. Observe how my hands never leave my arms. Watch! (*She simultaneously pours blue liquid from one bottle into one glass and red from a second bottle into the other, then switches and repeats*) Blue curaçao and raspberry liqueur. Drink up.

VALERIE
I'll pass. Good night. (*She exits*)

KIP
(*Picking up the glass and looking at it suspiciously*) What do they call this?

SAM
A Porn Star.

KIP
No thanks, Sam. I'll see you. (*He exits*)

SAM
Did I miss something? (*She drinks one of them, then grimaces*) Yeesh. That is horrible. (*She drinks the other*)

SCENE FIVE

SAM
I've created a cocktail called First Love. You start with a blush wine; add a cordial infused with rose petals and some soda for bubbles. Then shake, strain, pour over ice, and add bitters. Then watch and see if separation occurs. I'm afraid to try it.

KIP
(Sitting at bar) She's late.

SAM
Yup.

KIP
She's never been late before. Eighteen dates, eighteen post-mortems, right on time for all of them.

SAM
A drink, Kip?

KIP
Usually I drink with her.

SAM
Usually. But she's not here.

KIP
We drink. She talks. I listen.

SAM
Usually. But she's not here, you're talking, I'm listening. And working.

KIP
Point taken. I'll have the usual, Sam.

SAM
Gin and tonic, coming right up.

KIP
Maybe I should try one of those James Bond things.

SAM
Not if you want to keep my respect. Gin and tonic.

(KIP gulps it)

SAM
Easy, sailor.

KIP
It's because I told her about that webcam girl, isn't it?

SAM
Could be. Or maybe this date went better than the others.

KIP
You mean --?

SAM
Maybe she got lucky.

KIP
On a first date?

SAM
It happens.

KIP
I wonder if she'll tell me that part when she shows up. *(He finishes his drink)* If she shows up. Give me another, Sam.

SAM
Coming right up.

KIP
She'll come in, tell me about how wonderful he was, how great he was in bed. *(SAM gives him the drink)* And I'll sit here and listen.

SAM
That's what you do.

KIP
I thought that's what women wanted. Men who listen.

SAM
Some do.

KIP
My wife left me, Sam. She left me after seven years of marriage, some of them pretty good, because she said I wasn't listening. *(Pause)* At least, I think that's what she said. *(Pause)* That was supposed to be a joke.

SAM
Jokes are those funny things, right?

KIP
So, I decided that the next time, I would listen. And here comes Valerie, and I have listened the hell out of her. Eighteen sessions, I have memorized every word, every nuance, every undertone. I could play them all back in my head, splice them into one continuous Valerie-thon. So what happened?

SAM
What did you want to happen?

KIP
I wanted her to like me.

SAM
She likes you.

KIP
Maybe more than like me.

SAM
How was she supposed to know that? You're Mister Safe Guy, Mister No Danger of Emotional Entanglement Here, Ma'am. You're cheap therapy, Kip. You're like a gay best friend without the fashion sense.

KIP
I closed her out.

SAM
Yes.

KIP
Jesus. I shut her out by listening to her. Unbelievable. Do you know what I do for a living, Sam?

SAM
What?

KIP
I design software. Security systems. Spam filters, mostly. I am very, very good at my job. In other words, I'm very, very good at keeping things out.

And the things I keep out usually have to do with sex. See any parallels there?

SAM
Only if you think you are what you do.

Song: Keep The World Out

KIP
There's a world out there
Full of tech-savvy thugs
Hiding weird malware
In Canadian drugs.

But the geek lone ranger
Is ready to ride
To combat the danger
That's lurking outside.

I keep the world out,
A world that's filled with infection
Which a connection can bring about.

You let the world in,
Then ev'ry thing that's desirous
Is probably a virus
That seeps through your skin.
So keep the world out.

Fill me up again, bartender.
Geek man's going on a bender!

There's a world out there
That you cannot defeat
'Cause the game's unfair
And the players all cheat.

So you get some skills
And you learn how to hack.
You defend your hills
From each subtle attack.

You keep the world out,
A world that's all out of kilter,
So put on your filter,
Suppress the doubt.

You let the world in,
Then it will find all your weak points,
The desp'rate and bleak points,
Where membranes are thin.
So keep the world out.

Romance sucks and life is chronic.
Give me one more gin and tonic.
There's a world out there
That I've tried to avoid.
What I have to share
Ends up being destroyed.

So I hunkered down
And I laid in supplies.
I moved far from town
Under desolate skies.

I kept the world out.
Now there's not a whole lot left.
And all that I've got left... is me.

She's not coming, is she?

SAM
Maybe she's running late.

KIP
Why do I waste my time on her? I could have been out there, chasing around, having fun, looking for, looking for -- hey.

SAM
What?

KIP
I've never noticed how pretty you are.

SAM
Thank you.

KIP
And you're nice. You've always been nice.

SAM
It's a harsh world, Kip. I try and make it nicer.

KIP
And you do that, one drink at a time. I never thought about this before, Sam, but you know something? I could really go for you.

SAM
(Beckoning to him) Come here, Kip.
(SAM leans across the bar. KIP, thinking she wants him to kiss her, leans towards her. At the last moment, she stops his progress with one finger to his chin)

SAM
Car keys.

KIP
What?

SAM
Your car keys. Give them to me.

KIP
(Considering the implications for a moment) I'm drunk, aren't I?

SAM
Yes.

KIP
I've never been this drunk before.

SAM
It shows.

KIP
How am I doing?

SAM
Not well.

KIP
(Taking out his keys, but holding onto them) You know, I'll be sober by the time I get to the station.

SAM
How long is your commute?

KIP
Forty-five minutes.

SAM
Not long enough. Car keys.

(KIP hands them to her)

SAM
Thank you. Now, go home. The walk should clear your head.
(KIP walks to the door, then turns)

KIP
Do you think if I had asked her --- ?

SAM
We'll never know, will we?

KIP
I won't be coming back, Sam.

SAM
Car keys.

KIP
I'll be coming back for those. But I won't be staying.

SAM
Okay. Good night, Kip.

(KIP exits. SAM starts washing the glasses. VALERIE enters, wearing sunglasses)

VALERIE
Was Kip here?

SAM
He was here. He waited for a while. Then he left.

VALERIE
What was his usual tonight?

SAM
You figured that out.

VALERIE
A long time ago. The usual was different every time. It was a game.

SAM
Something like that. He had a gin and tonic. In fact, he had four.

VALERIE
That sounds good.

SAM
You want one?

VALERIE
Yeah, I'll have one. Then three more.
(She removes the sunglasses, revealing bruises about her eyes)

SAM
Oh, my God! What happened?

VALERIE
Turned out my date also liked to play games.

SAM
You have to call the police.

VALERIE
Did that. That's why I'm late. I was at the precinct. They arrested the creep. I wanted to tell Kip what happened. But the guy smashed my phone. That's why I couldn't call. I couldn't remember Kip's number. I couldn't even remember the name of this bar.
(SAM places the drink in front of her. VALERIE presses it against her face for a moment, then sips it) Thanks, Sam.

SAM
You could still call him. I've got his number.

VALERIE
No. This game is over. I'm retiring from competition. All these dates, and the best guy I met is some recently divorced drunk working his way through the liquor cabinet.

SAM
He isn't a drunk. I mean, tonight he was, but that wasn't --

VALERIE
Usual?

SAM
That first time you came in and met him? That was only the second time he ever came here. And every time he's been here since, he'd have just the one drink. He wanted the experience, not the drunk.

VALERIE
Until today.

SAM
Until today. You know what his real usual is?

VALERIE
What?

SAM
You. Kip's been burned, but he's coming out of it. He's a nice guy, Valerie. I mean it.

VALERIE
Maybe he is. That's another problem. I wouldn't wish me on anyone nice. *(She finishes her drink)* Forget about the rest, Sam. I'm going home.

SAM
See you around.

VALERIE
No. I don't think you will. *(She exits the bar towards the front of the stage as the lights on the bar fade)*

SONG: NICE GUYS

WEAR THE DRESS.
PLAY THE GAME.
HIDE THE MESS.
HIDE THE SHAME.
TRY NOT TO WONDER
WHERE HAVE THE NICE GUYS GONE?
HAVE A DRINK.

NUMB YOUR SOUL.

ONE MORE KINK.
LOSE CONTROL.
JUST DON'T START THINKING
WHERE HAVE THE NICE GUYS GONE?
NICE GUYS SMILE AND HOLD YOUR COAT,
NEVER KEEP THEIR EYES REMOTE,
AND WON'T LEAVE MARKS ON YOUR THROAT...

PLAY TO WIN.
ALWAYS LOSE.
ONE MORE GIN.
ONE MORE BRUISE.
AND I'M STILL WOND'RING
WHERE HAVE THE NICE GUYS GONE?
WHERE HAVE THE NICE GUYS GONE?

HE'S NOT HIM.
I'M NOT ME.
SINK, DON'T SWIM --
THAT'S THE KEY.
JUST KEEP AVOIDING
THE BITTER LIGHT OF DAY.

DON'T EXPLAIN.
NEVER FEEL.
IF THERE'S PAIN,
IT'S TOO REAL.
DREAM OF A NICE GUY.
THEN WATCH HIM FADE AWAY.

NICE GUYS CALL BACK, PAY THE BILLS,
KISS YOU GENTLY, GIVE YOU CHILLS,
NEVER TIE YOU UP FOR THRILLS...

LIVE TOO HARD.
LIVE TOO FAST.
NO HOLDS BARRED,
IT'S A BLAST.
I'LL JUST KEEP RACING,
I'LL JUST KEEP RACING,
I'LL JUST KEEP RACING,
AND NICE GUYS FINISH...
AND NICE GUYS FINISH LAST.

(VALERIE exits)

END OF ACT I

ACT II
SCENE ONE

(VALERIE's house. A small table and chair are upstage. Some cardboard boxes are scattered about. VALERIE enters, holding a handset to a telephone)

VALERIE
No. No. No, you listen to me, big brother. Mom left the house to me. Not to you, not to Annabeth. To me. You got your money, but the house is mine. I earned it, God damn it. I spent my good years taking care of her. Yes, I know, you had your adorable little family to look after. Get Valerie to watch Mom -- she's the youngest and she's got nothing else going on in her life. Believe me, taking care of Mom was like taking care of a child, only this child knew every single thing you ever did wrong in your life, and reminded you about them every single day. What am I going to do next? I don't know. Whatever I want seems like a plan. Maybe I'll sell the house and travel; maybe I'll drop a match in the basement. I don't know. What I do know is that you and Annabeth have until next weekend to take whatever stuff you want to keep from your rooms, and anything you don't take goes into a yard sale. Or a bonfire. And Paul? I'm moving into your room.

(She hangs up the phone and starts looking through boxes)

VALERIE
I'm fine, go away, leave me alone. What's in this one? (She opens a box and looks inside) No way. No freakin way! (She lifts out a KEBPRO II desktop computer and puts it on the table) I didn't know we still had this!

Song: *Kepbro II*

VALERIE
Moping in my adolescence,
I turned to this brand-new machine. It warmed me with its phosphorescence.
It called me from its tiny screen.

My first love was a Kebpro Two.
It changed me, made the world seem new,
Shook me to the core,
Made my spirit soar.

With it, I could never be bored.
I traveled, playing through the night.
My fingers roamed across its keyboard.
My heart sang, as my mind took flight.

It took me to fantastic lands.
Strange kingdoms lost in desert sands.
It held me, made my dreams seem true.
My first love was a Kebpro Two.

VALERIE
Look at you. You probably haven't even been plugged in for fifteen years. I know what that's like. I wonder if you still work. (She plugs it in. The lights go on. She pats it) Good for you. Let's see what we got. (She pulls a stack of floppies from the box and rummages through them) "Map of the White Wizard!" Oh, cool! I loved that game.

(The telephone rings)

MACHINE
You're talking to a machine. Go away.

KIP
Valerie, it's Kip. Sam told me what happened. Are you all right? Give me a call. I'm worr --

VALERIE
(Picking up the phone) Hi. I'm here.

KIP
How're you holding up?

VALERIE
Okay, I guess. In kind of a self-controlled coma.

KIP
Need company?

VALERIE
No thanks. I've got everything I need right here.

KIP
Okay. Are you working? What do you do, anyway?

VALERIE
I've never told you that, have I? Freelance computer consulting. Beta-testing mostly, but I get called in to check on security systems to make sure they do what they say they do.

KIP
Sounds like fun.

VALERIE
You're the first person ever to say that. But, yeah, it is fun. Although, and I'm not proud of this, I did some work for some spamming companies once.

KIP
Doing what?

VALERIE
Finding ways to get around spam blockers.

KIP
You're kidding. Why?

VALERIE
I needed the money, and I liked the challenge. But I felt so dirty afterwards.

KIP
Huh. So, it's just been you and your computer since -- since that night?

VALERIE
Oh, no ordinary computer. I've got a Kebpro II.

KIP
Are you serious? Those have been obsolete for two decades. It's like coal-powered.

VALERIE
I know. Ain't it cool? It was my first computer. My mom kept it for some reason. And I'm impressed that you know about them.

KIP
I had one, too.

VALERIE
So you were cool like me. I'm about to start playing a game I was obsessed with when I was a teenager.

KIP
Which one?

VALERIE
"The Map of the White Wizard." Ever heard of it?

KIP
Yeah. I remember that one. They say that no one ever finished it.

VALERIE
Including me. Well, I'm in the mood to try something pointless, frustrating and impossible.

KIP
Valerie?

VALERIE
Yes?

KIP
I should have waited longer that night. I'm sorry I didn't.

VALERIE
No, it's okay. I mean, how could you

know, right?

KIP
I should have had more -- faith, I suppose.

VALERIE
It's all right. Thanks for checking up on me.

KIP
That's what friends do, right?

VALERIE
We're friends again?

KIP
We are friends. Not Capital F trademarked computer friends, but actual live friends.

VALERIE
Good. I'm glad.

KIP
Any chance of getting you out to Sam's place sometime soon?

VALERIE
I -- I don't think so, Kip. I don't think I'll be going out anymore.

KIP
Okay. Got it. Well, I'd say call me when you finish the game, but then I'll never hear from you again.

VALERIE
I will make you eat those words.

KIP
Sure you will. Don't overdo it. If the characters start talking back, then it's time to get some sleep.

VALERIE
I'll keep that in mind.

KIP
I'll talk to you again.

VALERIE
Okay. *(She disconnects)*

Please tell me this still works. [She inserts the floppy.] "Choose gender." Holy cow! [She types.] Female. "Choose profession." Mage, thief, bard, ranger, valkyrie … Valkyrie! I remember.

Song: Valerie the Valkyrie

VALERIE
Roll the dice.
Pick a name.
Let's generate her ev'ry trait
So she can dominate this game.
Make her smart.
Give her pluck.
A heroine who's gonna win
With just a little bit of luck.

She's Valerie the Valkyrie.
Scourge of the underworld,
A brave and fearless viking.
She's Valerie the Valkyrie.
Death is her daily bread,
And danger's to her liking.
The darkness holds no terror
And monsters cannot scare her,
No matter what battles occur.
She's Valerie the Valkyrie,
An army of her.

(The VALKYRIE, played by SAM, appears in full regalia, complete with horned helmet, breastplate, sword, shield and spear)

VALKYRIE
Give me wit.
Give me strength.
So I can wield a might shield
Or swing a sword of any length.
Give me guile.
Give me stealth,
So I can slide and creep and glide
To score a massive pile of wealth.

I'm Valerie the Valkyrie.
Foe of the devil's spawn,
More deadly than a ninja.
I'm Valerie the Valkyrie,
Queen of the plunderers,
So hot, I'm gonna singe ya.
The sorcerers won't charm me,
And demons cannot harm me,
Let hell send its whole cavalry.
I'm Valerie the Valkyrie,
An army of me.

Escaped from my indentures,
To go off and have adventures
Wherever the reckless and free go.

VALERIE
And if anything should halt her,
Or her skills or strength should falter,
I can always go alter
My alter ego.

VALKYRIE
I'm Valerie the Valkyrie,
Mistress of Larceny,
A girl who thrives on trouble.

VALERIE
She's Valerie the Valkyrie,
Intrepid paragon,
My bold courageous double.
She's brainy like Athena,

VALKYRIE
And victorious like Nike,

VALERIE
With a body built like Xena,

VALKYRIE
Only just a tad less Dykey.

BOTH
And I know that this will mean a major boost to my poor psyche.
At last I'll be all I can be.

VALKYRIE
I'm Valerie the Valkyrie.

VALERIE
I'm Valerine the Valkyrie.

BOTH
We're Valerie the Valkyrie.
Yo ho ho oh!
Yo ho ho oh!
Yo ho ho oh!
An army of me.

VALKYRIE
Well. We haven't done this in a while. What are you hiding from this time?

VALERIE
I'm not hiding! I'm having an adventure.

VALKYRIE
An adventure. In a cave. Deep underground. Surrounded by darkness.

VALERIE
Now, you're turning me on. Come on, it's just a game.

VALKYRIE
You said that to someone else recently. Remember?

VALERIE
Enough! Are you ready?

VALKYRIE
Are you ready? We've never beaten it.

VALERIE
Yeah. Let's do this. Back to the mines we go.

Song: The Wizard's Map

VALERIE
Start the game.

VALKYRIE
There's a cave.

VALERIE
Go on in. Just be brave.

VALKYRIE
It's so dark. Also damp.

VALERIE
Check your gear for a lamp.
Better light one.
Look around.

VALKYRIE
There's a stair
Going down.

VALERIE
Don't go there.

VALKYRIE
I hear screams, distant roars.

VALERIE
Hang a left.

VALKYRIE
There's two doors.

VALERIE
Take the right one.

BOTH
And ev'ry passage conceals some test,
And ev'ry doorway could be a trap.
It doesn't matter -- we're on a quest
To find the wizard's map.

VALKYRIE
Lots of smoke.
Hard to see.

VALERIE
Take the stairs.

VALKYRIE
Level three.
There's a vault, locked and barred,
And in front, there's a guard.
Can I fight him?

VALERIE
Yes!
Draw your sword!
Parry, thrust!

VALKYRIE
This guy's toast.

VALERIE
Dust to dust.
Pick the lock. Go on through.

VALKYRIE
Here comes guard number two,
Watch me smite him!

VALERIE
Cool!

BOTH
With ev'ry battle, our skill's increased.
We'll storm ahead like a thunderclap.
We'll steal the treasure,
And slay the beast,
Then find the wizard's map.

VALKYRIE
There's a cliff
And a bridge.

VALERIE
Wait. What do you see?

VALKYRIE
Someone big, dumb and male.

BOTH
Just the way I like them.

VALERIE
Okay, when you meet him, look for the flaw. They always have a flaw.

VALKYRIE
Come on! Just because he's flawed doesn't mean we should, you know, kill him.

(The TROLL, played by KIP, enters)

TROLL
Hey, little lady. How about a drink?

VALKYRIE
See? He's friendly. Hey back at ya, big guy. What are we drinking?

TROLL
Your blood!

VALKYRIE
Hold that thought. *(To VALERIE).* I've changed my mind. I'm going to interpret that as hostile. What do I do?

VALERIE
The flaw. Find it.

VALKYRIE
I can't. His skin's too thick.

VALERIE
You have to find it.

VALKYRIE
There's no time. He's attacking.

TROLL
(Advancing, raising his club) Hey, I remember you!

VALERIE
What?

VALKYRIE
Remember me from where?

TROLL
The other night. We sure had some fun, didn't we?

VALERIE
This is impossible.

VALKYRIE
What should I do? Should I use my shield?

VALERIE
It can't be him. He's in jail. They told me he's in jail.

VALKYRIE
I'm thinking shield right about now would be a really great idea.

VALERIE
What?

VALKYRIE
May I use my shield please?

VALERIE
Shield, yes! Use your shield! Use everything!

(A battle, and the VALKYRIE kills the TROLL. He falls off-stage)

VALKYRIE
That was intense. I think I just went up two levels.

VALERIE
You went up three.

VALKYRIE
Damn right. SO WHAT THE HELL JUST HAPPENED? Look for the flaw, you said, look for the flaw. HE WAS ALL FLAW!

VALERIE
But you beat him.

VALKYRIE
We beat him. How the hell did we beat him?

VALERIE
I'm not sure. I don't remember the game being this interactive. How is it that you and I are having a conversation?

VALKYRIE
I have the amulet of Argajed from Level 12. It gives me plus three empathy.

VALERIE
Oh. Okay, cross that bridge. I think I know what's coming next.

VALKYRIE
I'm across.

VALERIE
Here she comes. Be strong, Valerie.

(The WITCH, played by KIP, enters)

WITCH
So, dearie, you've dug deep into the earth and uncovered me. I bet you thought I was dead all this time.

VALERIE
(Typing) No. But you're gonna be.

VALKYRIE
No. But you're gonna be.

WITCH
Hmph.

SONG: UNLIKE YOU

WITCH
LOOK AT YOU,
WITH YOUR CUTE METAL OUTFIT ENTOMBING THE HEART IN YOUR BREAST.
LOOK AT ME,
THE OLD CRONE YOU MUST OUTWIT
BEFORE YOU CONTINUE THIS QUEST.

UNLIKE YOU,
I LOOK BACK AND REMEMBER
EACH MOMENT OF JOY THAT I'VE TASTED.
UNLIKE YOU,
WHEN I'VE ADDED IT ALL UP,
I CAN'T SAY THAT MY YOUTH WAS WASTED.

VALERIE
What?

WITCH
I'M NOW GRAY, AND MY ARTERIES THICKEN,
EVEN THOUGH I'M A PRACTICING WICCAN,
BUT THERE'S NOTHING IN LIFE THAT I RUE.
UNLIKE YOU.

LOOK AT YOU,
FIGHTING WARS IN A DUNGEON.
IS THAT HOW A GIRL SHOULD BEHAVE?

VALERIE
Mom?

WITCH
LOOK AT ME.
WHEN I FIND LOVE, I PLUNGE IN.
I DON'T LIVE MY LIFE IN A CAVE.

(At this point, the dialogue below begins)

UNLIKE YOU,
I'VE RUN NAKED THROUGH FORESTS,
AND TASTED THE WINE OF DESIRE.
UNLIKE YOU,
I'VE DANCED UNDER THE MOONLIGHT,
MADE PASSIONATE LOVE BY THE FIRE.

I HAVE FLOWN TO THE STARS WITH THE FAIRIES,
SUCKED THE NECTAR FROM JUICY RED BERRIES,
BIT OFF MORE FROM LIFE THAN I COULD CHEW.

(Song ends with "You're the boss.")

UNLIKE YOU.
UNLIKE YOU.
UNLIKE...

VALERIE
(Overlapping at moment indicated) Will you please kill her already?

VALKYRIE
But she's not finished.

VALERIE
No, she is finished. We are finished! I am sick and tired of you undermining my life! I said kill her!

VALKYRIE
You're the boss. (She battles the WITCH and kills her, not easily) That -- that was really hard. She took a lot out of me.

VALERIE
Tell me about it. She took a lot out of me, too. And I knew her first.

VALKYRIE
Maybe I should have asked her questions first. She might have had some wisdom to share.

VALERIE
Yeah, I've tried talking to her. She destroyed me every time.

VALKYRIE
Are we talking about the same thing?

VALERIE
I'm not sure anymore. Let's move on.

VALKYRIE
Where?

VALERIE
I don't know. I've never gotten past her before.

(The IMP, played by KIP, enters)

IMP
Where the heck have you been? I've been waiting for ages.

VALKYRIE
What are you?

IMP
Oh, you know, just one of those things, spirit guide, confidante, bosom buddy, traveling companion. They tell me I'm imp-petuous, imp-pertinent, downright imp-probable, imp pfact.

VALKYRIE
You're an elf!

IMP
Hate them.

VALERIE
You're a sprite.

IMP
Getting colder. I'll give you a hint. Sounds like blimp.

VALERIE and VALKYRIE
You're an imp!

IMP
You guessed! So, where are we going?

VALKYRIE
To find the Wizard!

IMP
You don't look like you're from Kansas. I don't want to seem imp-polite, but I knew Dorothy, I was a friend of hers, and you're no Dorothy.

VALERIE
To find the Wizard's Map, I mean.

IMP
Oh, that old thing. You shouldn't be imp-precise, it's confusing. Fine, follow me. Remember, we have to stick together. Although you have to do all the fighting.

(The IMP leads the VALKYRIE around. Twice, he screams and hides behind the VALKYRIE, who kills the unseen enemy with her sword. He screams a third time. She gives him a look of disdain, then squashes a tiny bug with her foot. He shrugs in embarrassment)

VALKYRIE
Why have we stopped?

IMP
This is as far as I take you, little sister.

VALERIE
What? What did you just say?

IMP
I said, this is as far as I take you, Valkyrie. What's out there is too imp-posing.

VALERIE
Wait. I'm going to save the game here. I've never done this part.

VALKYRIE
There's a fork in the path. Which do I take?

IMP
(Pointing) That one. Good luck, it's

been fun.

VALERIE
Okay, position saved. Are you ready?

VALKYRIE
Are you ready?

VALERIE
Yeah. Let's do this.

(The VALKYRIE charges off-stage right. Battle sounds, and she falls back, dead)

VALERIE
First try, not so good. Restore saved position.

VALKYRIE
There's a fork in the path. Which do I take?

IMP
(Pointing the other way) That one. But I wouldn't do it. Turn back, I imp-plore you.

VALKYRIE
After getting this far?

IMP
I imp-portune you.

VALKYRIE
Not a chance.

IMP
Good luck, it's been fun.

VALERIE
Go!

(The VALKYRIE charges off-stage left. Battle sounds, dead again)

VALERIE
Restore!

VALKYRIE
There's a fork in the path. Which do I take?

IMP
(Pointing) That one. Good luck, it's been fun.

VALERIE
Let's try doing the opposite of what he said. Take the other fork.

IMP
Fine. Be that way.

VALERIE
Go! *(The VALKYRIE charges the opposite way. Same result)* I don't understand. Restore!

VALKYRIE
There's a fork in the path. Which do I take?

IMP
(Pointing) That one. Good luck, it's been fun.

(Same result)

VALERIE
Restore! Why can't I do this?

IMP
(To VALERIE) You're not good enough. You're not smart enough.

VALERIE
Shut up! Restore!

IMP
You're not strong enough. It's too hard for you.

VALERIE
Restore. Restore! RESTORE!

VALKYRIE
I've tried forty times! I'm sorry, there are too many of them.

IMP
Repeated attempts, identical results, yet you expect it to be different. Insane, much?

VALERIE
AND IF ANYTHING SHOULD HALT HER,
OR HER SKILLS OR STRENGTH SHOULD FALTER,
I CAN ALWAYS GO ALTER
MY ALTER EGO.

(She stands up, moves to the VALKYRIE, who turns over her sword, shield, etc)

VALKYRIE
It's not me. You know that.

VALERIE
I know. Thank you for getting me this far.

(The VALKYRIE exits)

IMP
Back for more of the same? Look at all the demons waiting for you. More than you thought would be there. Looks imp-possible.

VALERIE
I'm not listening to you any more. I have to think.

IMP
But you need me. You can't make a decision without me. You can kill all the rest, but I will always be with you.

VALERIE
When I listened to you, I was killed. When I did the opposite of what you said, I was killed. Maybe that's the problem. When what I do is a reaction to what you say, I get killed. What if... *(She hurries back to the KEBPRO and types)* Kill the imp.

IMP
Excuse me? What did you just say?

VALERIE
(Coming back to him) Nothing personal. I'm just thinking outside the box.

IMP
By putting me in one?

(She stabs him)

VALERIE
You see, by killing you, I'm asserting my independence. It's a metaphor.

IMP
I have to say, as metaphors go -- this one really sucks. *(He falls off-stage. VALERIE partially drags his body [a dummy to allow for KIP's fast-change] back on)*

VALERIE
Sorry. It's hard out there for an imp. Search body. *(She pats him down, and pulls a folded piece of paper from his pocket)* The Wizard's Map! You had it all along, you son of a bitch. *(She unfolds it and reads)* You will not find the Wizard by solving a labyrinth or by slaying a monster, but by conquering the demons...

(The WIZARD, played by KIP, enters)

WIZARD
...within yourself. Hi, there. I'm the White Wizard. I expect you have questions for me.

VALERIE
Do you know Gandalf?

WIZARD
Excellent fellow. Taught him everything he knows.

VALERIE
Oz?

WIZARD
That humbug! He owes me ten bucks.

VALERIE
Dumbledore?

WIZARD
Who?

VALERIE
That's right, this is an old game. Um, meaning of life?

WIZARD
I'm a wizard, not God. What do you really want to know?

VALERIE
Have I really conquered my demons?

WIZARD
Yes. The last was that shell you've been hiding behind.

VALERIE
The Valkyrie.

WIZARD
Always easier to face rejection when it's not you. Am I right? Of course I'm right, I'm the White Wizard.

VALERIE
What happens now?

WIZARD
Excellent question. I have been waiting for an eternity for a champion, a person with the courage, intelligence, strength and empathy to find me. Now, we will undertake the next great adventure together. Will you join me?

VALERIE
You mean the game isn't over?

WIZARD
This adventure is over. The next one begins. You must now play the sequel: The Quest of the White Wizard!

VALERIE
There's a sequel? I never knew about any sequel.

WIZARD
Just hit return, and print out the certificate on the next screen, and you shall receive a 25% discount. You've won! *(He waves a wand. There is a swirl of voices and lines around VALERIE. SAM enters)*

SAM
IN HERE WE PLAY IT SAFE.
DON'T LET EMOTIONS CHAFE.
WELCOME TO SWITZERLAND.

VALERIE
Sam?

SAM
He comes back. Every single time. You know what his real usual is? You.

THE ANSWERING MACHINE
You're talking to a machine. Go away.

SAM
(To WIZARD) Hey, Mister, could you take pity on a fellow human being for a moment?

(The WIZARD removes his hat, beard and robe and becomes KIP. SAM exits, repeating, "He comes back. Every single time, etc.")

KIP
Valerie.

VALERIE
Kip?

KIP
You've won, Valerie.

VALERIE
Kip? What are you doing in my --

KIP
Are you ready for the next adventure?

VALERIE
It's you, isn't it? My next adventure is with you. Yes, Kip! I'm ready! I'm finally --

KIP
Wake up!

VALERIE
What? No, Kip! Not now. Please --

KIP
Wake up, Valerie!

(VALERIE wakes at her computer as KIP exits)

VALERIE
Kip! I did it! I -- Kip? Oh. Right. *(She taps a key and looks at the screen)* There it is! 25% off the sequel! I can't wait to see the look on his face when I show him the ... Oh, shit! The printer! *(She picks up her phone and punches in a number)*

KIP
Hello?

VALERIE
Guess who I just met?

KIP
Who?

VALERIE
The White Wizard!

KIP
No way! And it only took you a week.

VALERIE
A week? *(She looks at her watch)* When did it get to be Thursday?

KIP
Have you eaten anything?

VALERIE
I think so. There seems to be a bunch of empty frozen dinner cartons in the kitchen. Oh, and leftover Chinese takeout.

KIP
Breakfast of champions. What did he look like?

VALERIE
A tiny bearded man with a robe and a hat with a pair of blinking capital W's. A double double-you! A quadruple -- *(Pause)* you! Here's the amazing part -- there was a sequel.

KIP
There was?

VALERIE
Yeah, only I never heard about it coming out. There's supposed to be a certificate to get a discount for it, but the printer I had for the Kebpro burned out when I was fourteen, so I can't print it.

KIP
Well, congratulations on time well-wasted. We should celebrate. How about you come out for that drink now?

VALERIE
I'd like that very much, Kip. You could buy me a usual. At Sam's. And we could talk. There's something I want to tell you, but I don't want to do it on the phone.

KIP
You're on. There's something I want to tell you, too. Usual time, usual place?

VALERIE
I'll be there.

SCENE TWO

(The bar. SAM is in there alone)

SAM
A cocktail by definition requires at least two ingredients. They can be mixed in different ratios, or rest on top of each other. One flavor can

dominate, or they can alternate on the palate, or they can combine to make something completely new. The flavor can be affected by proportion, temperature, humidity, vintage, accident, and most importantly, the subjective taste of the person drinking it. That's why I like making cocktails. The infinite variety of the experience.

(VALERIE enters)

VALERIE
Hey.

SAM
Hey back atcha. You okay?

VALERIE
Getting there. Kip's not here yet?

SAM
He called, said he'd be running late, but don't start talking without him.

VALERIE
I've decided to stop with the stories with Kip and go with the truth from now on.

SAM
I think that's a good idea. You know, I looked up that Scheherezade chick, and I just don't get why anyone would think that story's so romantic. I mean, she settled.

VALERIE
She settled? She tamed a powerful king with her stories and made a happy marriage out of it.

SAM
She married a man who had raped and murdered a thousand women on their wedding nights all because his first wife cheated on him. What a catch.

VALERIE
But she stopped him from doing it to anyone else. And in time he came to love her.

SAM
Okay, so she took one for the team. Great. But she was still the Queen of Settling as far as I'm concerned.

VALERIE
I never thought about it like that. Maybe she wasn't the best role model for me.

(KIP enters, carrying a laptop)

KIP
Valerie.

VALERIE
Kip, hi. I'm really glad to see you.

KIP
Doing better?

VALERIE
Yes. I mean, at the time, I thought the next post-mortem might be real, but I got out alive.

KIP
I'm glad for that. So, we won't talk about it if you don't want to.

VALERIE
Not right now. Look, Kip, I haven't been honest with you. Or myself.

KIP
No?

VALERIE
My mom died six months ago.

KIP
I'm sorry.

VALERIE
It was a relief. I had been taking care of her for years while trying to work out of an office I set up in the basement. She was demanding, needy,

abusive, and in a lot of pain, and it wore me out. So, when she died, and I was finally free, I went crazy with it. You were right about that dating website. I was using it to hide myself. I've been doing a lot of hiding.

KIP
You don't have to --

VALERIE
There were a lot of dates, Kip, and a lot of men, before I fled into this bar. And met you, and made you listen to me.

KIP
I liked listening to you.

VALERIE
Thank you. You're a good listener.

KIP
Thank you, but - You were right, too.

VALERIE
I was?

KIP
I'm the one who's been hiding – and I've decided to take the plunge. I'm signing up for that dating website. Would you help me with that?

VALERIE
You--

(He sets up the laptop)

KIP
I filled out the questionnaire already. Forty-six questions. They've cracked the human genome for love and put it on a computer, and that's the future of dating.

SAM
It's just a Myers-Briggs personality test tarted up with some music and movie preferences.

KIP
No, no, don't take the mystery out of it, Sam. Okay, so I have to post a picture for the profile, and that's where I need your help. I've narrowed it down to five. This is one.

VALERIE
No. The smile looks forced.

KIP
Okay. Two.

VALERIE
No woman dates a man in a sweater.

KIP
Good to know. Three.

SAM
Yuck.

VALERIE
How much product did you put in your hair? It looks flammable.

KIP
I'll put that down as a no. Four.

SAM
Ugh.

VALERIE
Serial killer!

SAM
Definitely.

KIP
And five.

VALERIE
Hmm. I like that one. Go with five.

KIP
Great. Let me just upload it -- there. Now, let the magic happen.

VALERIE
Kip, I think it's great that you -- No, screw that! What the hell are you doing? You are making the same stupid

mistake that I just wasted six months of my life making. You're going to be wasting your money and time on a bunch of desperate, isolated losers when you could be -- okay, so I was one of those desperate, isolated losers, but the point is --

(The computer beeps)

KIP
Hey, that was fast. They've sent me a picture already. Well, will you look at that?

VALERIE
No. No, that's not possible.

KIP
Pretty. Don't you think?

VALERIE
That's me!

KIP
Sure looks like you.

VALERIE
This is some kind of joke. No, you spoofed the site. You copied the format--

KIP
If I had done that, then you wouldn't have anything sent to your end, right?

VALERIE
Right.

(He slides the laptop over to her)

KIP
Log on to your account. See if they sent you me.

(She hesitates, then types rapidly on the laptop)

VALERIE
There. *(Computer beeps)* It's you. My next date is you.

KIP
Well, hard to tell how accurate these things are. I mean, look at all the losers they've fixed you up with. Maybe I'm just another one.

VALERIE
You hacked it, didn't you?

KIP
What do you mean?

VALERIE
You hacked the dating site.

KIP
Yes.

VALERIE
You rigged the game!

KIP
Yes.

VALERIE
But that's supposed to be impossible. They have one of the top security systems around.

KIP
It was a challenge, I must admit. But it was fun. I haven't done that in years.

VALERIE
Jesus Christ, Kip! Do you know what could have happened if you got caught? That's like a felony! You could've been arrested! You still can! Just to get a date with me?

KIP
Yes.

VALERIE
That's the most romantic thing anyone's ever done for me in my entire life!

SAM
(Looking at the screen) Christopher Skellen.

VALERIE
What?

SAM
On his picture. It says Christopher Skellen.

VALERIE
Who's Christopher Skellen?

KIP
I am. They needed a real name for the profile.

VALERIE
Your real name is Christopher Skellen?

KIP
Nice to meet you. But, please, call me Kip. Everyone I care about does.

VALERIE
Christopher Skellen. I know that name. You're Skellen Software!

KIP
I am.

VALERIE
I think I've hacked you.

KIP
Wouldn't surprise me.

VALERIE
Wait -- you wrote "The Map of the White Wizard!"

KIP
I did! A long time ago. So long that I had given up on anyone ever finishing it. I made the game too hard.

VALERIE
I finished it!

KIP
I know. You're amazing, Valerie.

VALERIE
Do you still have the sequel?

KIP
In a shoebox in my closet. I'd like it very much if you played it.

VALERIE
Oh, you are so on. Wait! No, no, this is all wrong!

KIP
Why?

VALERIE
You're breaking the rules. You're hitting on me in Switzerland!

KIP
But --

VALERIE
You can't break the rules of the game, Kip. Any game.

[Note: If the set has no exterior to the bar, use the alternate dialogue in the Appendix.]

SAM
Get out!

KIP
What?

SAM
The two of you. Get out of my bar. Cross the border, go into hostile territory, use whatever stupid metaphor you need to make it work. But get out now.

KIP
The rules permit that?

VALERIE
I don't see why not. Let's go.

KIP
Wait. We've forgotten something.

VALERIE
What?

KIP
Sam?

SAM
Yes?

KIP
I'll have the usual, please.

SAM
(*Pulling out a bottle of champagne*) I've been saving this one. Now, get out.

KIP
What do I owe you?

SAM
I'll put it on your tab.

KIP
That works.

VALERIE
Thanks, Sam. For everything.

(*KIP and VALERIE walk to the front of the stage*)

KIP
So. Here we are. In the cold, cruel world.

VALERIE
Here we are.

KIP
Valerie, would you --

VALERIE
Yes.

KIP
Okay. Back to your place to pick up the Kebpro, then back to mine to play the sequel. Think you can beat it in ten days?

VALERIE
Eight days, max. You're going to be with me?

KIP
A Kebpro II, the Quest of the White Wizard, and a beautiful evil genius hacker in the same room? Better believe I'm gonna be there. It's why I started making games in the first place.

SONG: FINALE
(KEBPRO II AND GEEK MASHUP)

KIP
FREEZING, IN THAT DRAFTY LOFT WHERE
I TYPED CODE, FINGERS TURNING BLUE,
CREATING MY ATTEMPTS AT SOFTWARE.
WHO KNEW THAT THEY WOULD BRING ME YOU?

VALERIE
(*Overlapping KIP's next verse*)
DROWNING, WHEN I SHOULD BE LIVING,
I SURFACED, SUMMONED BY YOUR VOICE.
THE WORLD NOW SEEMS MUCH MORE FORGIVING.
AT LONG LAST, I CAN MAKE A CHOICE.

KIP
THE WORLD NOW HAS
A NEW DIMENSION TO EXPLORE
ALL FOR THE GEEK NEXT DOOR.

VALERIE
SUPRESSING MY EMOTIONS,
I WOULD SABOTAGE EACH ROMANCE.
THERE'S NOTHING MORE PATHETIC THAN
A NERD ALL FULL OF RAGE.

KIP
I LIVED TOO LONG IN HIDING
WATCHING LIFE PASS BY MY DOORWAY,
AFRAID THAT I WOULD END UP LIKE
A BIRD TRAPPED IN A CAGE.

VALERIE
I LIVED TOO LONG IN HIDING.
FEARFUL OF DECIDING.
I COULDN'T TURN THAT PAGE.

BOTH
BUT THEN CAME OUR ENCOUNTER
ON AN ORDINARY TUESDAY.
A TUESDAY FULL OF MIRACLES
WE TOOK TOO LONG TO SEE.

Through all the random hazards,
And the self-imposed obstructions,
It took a tiny valkyrie
To bring you here to me.

It's wondrous how two lives converge.
And from them, romance may emerge.
'Cause sometimes, youthful dreams come true,
When they start with a Kebpro Two.
When they start with a Kebpro Two.

(They kiss)

END OF PLAY

APPENDIX

Alternate dialogue for last scene:

VALERIE
You can't break the rules of the game, Kip. Any game.

SAM
(Frantically erasing the Swiss flag from the chalkboard) No! You are no longer in Switzerland. *(She waves her arms as if doing magic)* You are now back in the real world!

KIP
(To VALERIE) Do the rules permit that?

VALERIE
I don't see why not.

And continue as before.

EBENEZER

A PLAY BY
JOSEPH ZETTELMAIER

CAST OF CHARACTERS

EBENEZER SCROOGE - a businessman (retired), late 70s
TIM CRATCHIT - a soldier, 20s
MISS POOLE - a nurse, 20s

TIME

December 24th, 1863

PLACE

St. Bartholomew's Hospital, London, England

EBENEZER received its world premiere in November 2012 at the Williamston Theatre (Williamston, MI). It was directed by John Lepard. Set Design by Janine Woods-Thoma, Lighting Design by Alex Gay, Sound Design by Tony Caselli, Costume Design by Karen Kangas-Preston, Prop Design by Stefanie Din. Stage Managed by Rochelle Clark.

The cast was as follows:

EBENEZER: Arthur J. Beer
ALICE POOLE/HELEN: Alysia Kolascz
TIM: Joseph Seibert

For information about production rights, visit www.jzettelmaier.com.

Ebenezer

(Lights up. A nice room in St. Bartholomew's hospital. EBENEZER lies on a bed, dressed in nightclothes and under blankets. Next to him, sitting in a chair, is MISS POOLE, a nurse. She's reading to him. There is a coat rack with coats and a pile of presents in the corner. The wind can be heard roaring outside)

MISS POOLE
"It was the day before Christmas; such a cold east wind! such an inky sky! such a blue-black look in people's faces, as they were driven out more than usual, to complete their purchases for the next day's festival. Before leaving home that morning, Jenkins had given some money to his wife to buy the next day's dinner.

'My dear…'"

EBENEZER
No, no. You must do a voice.

MISS POOLE
I don't think that's necessary.

EBENEZER
Oh, please.

MISS POOLE
Mr. Scrooge…

(EBENEZER uses a put-on, gruff voice)

EBENEZER
Make him talk like this.

(Beat. MISS POOLE continues, using such a voice for the character of the Husband)

MISS POOLE
"My dear, I wish for turkey and sausages. It may be a weakness, but I own I am partial to sausages. My deceased mother was. Such tastes are hereditary."

(EBENEZER chuckles at that)

MISS POOLE
"As to the sweets -- whether plum-pudding or mince-pies -- I leave such considerations to you; I only beg you not to mind expense. Christmas comes but once a year." *(She looks up)* Satisfied? *(Notices that he isn't paying attention)* Mr. Scrooge?

EBENEZER
It doesn't, you know.

MISS POOLE
How's that?

EBENEZER
Not once a year. Many times. Many

times a year.

MISS POOLE
My calendar might disagree with you.

EBENEZER
Trust me, dear. I know of what I speak.

(Beat. She goes back to reading, initially forgetting the voice)

MISS POOLE
"And again he had called out from the bottom of the first flight of stairs, just close to the Hodgsons' door ('such ostentatiousness,' as Mrs. Hodgson observed), 'You will not forget the sausages, my dear?'"

(EBENEZER immediately turns to her. She sighs, then reads again, using the voice)

MISS POOLE
"You will not forget the sausages, my dear?"

(EBENEZER smiles, perhaps claps a little)

MISS
I hope you're quite pleased.

EBENEZER
I am.

MISS POOLE
Making a fool of myself like that…

EBENEZER
You read very well.

MISS POOLE
Only for you, Mr. Scrooge. Only for you. *(She kisses his forehead)* Now get some sleep.

(She starts to leave. He becomes agitated)

EBENEZER
Don't go.

MISS POOLE
I have to make my rounds.

EBENEZER
Please.

MISS POOLE
Besides, you could use a bit of peace. Been nothing but well-wisher after well-wisher for a week. Just lie back and…

EBENEZER
Please don't go.

MISS POOLE
Mr. Scrooge…

EBENEZER
What if they appear? I want you to see them.

MISS POOLE
See who? *(Beat)* See who, Mr. Scrooge?

EBENEZER
Just sit down.

MISS POOLE
I asked you a question.

EBENEZER
Did you?

MISS POOLE
I did.

EBENEZER
Can't you just humor a sick old man?

MISS POOLE
You've got more life in you than a buck half your age.

EBENEZER
That's a lie. But it's a sweet lie, so I forgive you.

MISS POOLE
I promise, you'll wake up tomorrow.

EBENEZER
You don't know that.

MISS POOLE
Of course I do. I made a wish. And if Christ can't grant a wish made on Christmas Eve, then what sort of world is this, I ask you?

EBENEZER
It's only Christmas Eve for an hour more.

MISS POOLE
What? *(She looks at the clock)* Ebenezer Scrooge! You've had me talking half through the night!

EBENEZER
So what's one more hour?

MISS POOLE
It's the rest of the nurses working double-hard because I...

EBENEZER
I paid them.

MISS POOLE
You what?

EBENEZER
Well, I paid your supervisor. Who then paid everyone else. You'll get your Christmas bonus in the morning, courtesy of me.

MISS POOLE
Why would you go and do such a thing?

(Beat)

EBENEZER
Charming senility?

MISS POOLE
You're senile like a fox, you are.

EBENEZER
Allow an old eccentric one last...um... eccentricism. Is that a word?

MISS POOLE
Doesn't sound like one, does it?

EBENEZER
It most certainly does not.

(She just stares at him, deciding what to do. He pats the chair next to him)

EBENEZER
Sit. Sit sit sit.

(She doesn't move)

EBENEZER
You're alone tonight, yes?

MISS POOLE
I fail to see how that's your business.

EBENEZER
Well, you volunteered for the night shift. On Christmas Eve. And I heard Dr. Halsey refer to you as "Miss" Poole. Hence...

MISS POOLE
You're not currying my favor, sir.

EBENEZER
I can't help but draw the conclusion. *(Beat)* Although why such a lovely young lady hasn't found herself a husband...

MISS POOLE
If I stay, will you refrain from the... personal inquiry?

EBENEZER
I'll try, but it's doubtful.

(She smiles at him)

MISS POOLE
You're awful.

EBENEZER
I am.

MISS POOLE
Utterly, terribly, irredeemably awful.

EBENEZER
But I'm also so very charming. Wouldn't you agree?

MISS POOLE
Only under duress. *(Sits back down and picks up her book)*

EBENEZER
No more stories.

MISS POOLE
You're certain?

(He nods)

MISS POOLE
Then what shall we do while we wait for your mysterious guest?

EBENEZER
I have no idea what you're referring to. And it's "guests". *(Takes the book from her hands)*

MISS POOLE
Hey!

EBENEZER
"Christmas Storms and Sunshine"? Feeling sentimental?

MISS POOLE
(Holds her hand out) I'll be feeling cross if you don't give me back my book.

EBENEZER
One shouldn't speak of crosses on Christmas Eve! You never know who might be listening. *(He roles his eyes heavenward. She still holds her hand out)* Don't do that.

MISS POOLE
Don't do what?

EBENEZER
Don't hold your laughter back. I did that for many years. Too many.

MISS POOLE
Perhaps I simply didn't find your joke funny.

EBENEZER
Oh. We both know that isn't true.

(She smiles slyly)

EBENEZER
It's a start. *(Hands her the book)*

MISS POOLE
She's my favorite.

EBENEZER
Who is?

MISS POOLE
Elizabeth Gaskell. She wrote this.

EBENEZER
You're a reader then?

MISS POOLE
Oh yes. Very much so.

EBENEZER
Some men might be put off by that. Fortunately, I am not one of those men.

MISS POOLE
Don't you start.

EBENEZER
Start what?

MISS POOLE
You're not the first old gentlemen to flirt with me. You're not even the first one today.

EBENEZER
Oh I say!

MISS POOLE
Old Mr. Danforth down the hall? He was this close to getting down on one knee.

EBENEZER
How close?

MISS POOLE
This close.

EBENEZER
Well! It appears none of us are immune to your charms.

MISS POOLE
Ha! There's a laugh.

EBENEZER
I'm being quite serious.

MISS POOLE
Charm isn't something I'm often accused of.

EBENEZER
Then clearly your other acquaintances aren't as perceptive as I.

MISS POOLE
They call me the Needle. Behind my back, of course, but I hear it nonetheless.

EBENEZER
Because you're so thin?

MISS POOLE
Because I'm cold, I'm hard, and I'm not afraid to draw blood should I need to.

EBENEZER
So others find you…prickly?

MISS POOLE
Just so.

EBENEZER
Well, that seems quite foolish to me. You are, without a doubt, my favorite of the nurses.

MISS POOLE
What did I say about flirting?

EBENEZER
No, no. That's God's honest truth. I was quite happy to hear you'd be present this evening. In fact, I requested that you be in this wing.

MISS POOLE
I know.

EBENEZER
Oh yes?

MISS POOLE
Dr. Halsey told me.

EBENEZER
The man never could keep a secret. *(Tries to sit up, but finds it difficult)*

MISS POOLE
(Helping him) There now. Easy.

EBENEZER
Thank you.

MISS POOLE
How's the pain?

(He shrugs, saying nothing)

MISS POOLE
If you don't tell me when it hurts, then there's not much I can do for you, is there?

EBENEZER
There's not much to be done for me at all, so I'd rather not complain.

(The clock outside chimes quarter-past. EBENEZER lights up)

EBENEZER
Do you hear that?

MISS POOLE
The clock?

EBENEZER
Quarter past.

MISS POOLE
Yes.

EBENEZER
It's almost midnight.

MISS POOLE
Don't remind me.

EBENEZER
They're not here! They have to arrive before...

MISS POOLE
Who?

EBENEZER
Who do you think?

MISS POOLE
Mr. Scrooge, visitation hours were done at eight. Whoever you think is coming...well, they'll have to come back in the morning.

EBENEZER
No! It's imperative! I don't have much time, you see.

MISS POOLE
Enough of that talk.

EBENEZER
I wasted so many years. And now...it's all slipping away from me.

MISS POOLE
This fear you're feeling...it's perfectly natural. You should think of...

EBENEZER
I do not fear death. No. Only that... when I am gone, everything I've tried to do stops. I can't let that happen.

MISS POOLE
There's no point in dwelling on that.

EBENEZER
I need help, I know that. But they haven't arrived and...

MISS POOLE
Who? Who hasn't arrived?!

(Beat)

EBENEZER
I somehow doubt that you'll believe me.

MISS POOLE
I am a font of imagination, sir.

EBENEZER
I simply mean...I didn't believe it when it happened to me. Not at first. I thought it was indigestion. A bad bit of potato or some such.

MISS POOOLE
I had a lovely chicken broth for dinner, and a sweet cake after. Not a potato to be had. So out with it.

(He says nothing, unsure)

MISS POOLE
Fine, fine. Keep your secrets. I'm sure whoever they are...

EBENEZER
They're ghosts.

(Beat)

MISS POOLE
Ghosts?

EBENEZER
Ghosts.

MISS POOLE
Is that a fact?

EBENEZER
Oh, it's the very definition of a fact. *(He waits smiling, excited for her response. Finally--)*

MISS POOLE
Time to go to sleep. *(Starts tucking him in)*

EBENEZER
(Pulls the blankets aside) Don't you believe me?

MISS POOLE
...none of that now...

EBENEZER
They're coming! I know it in my bones!

MISS POOLE
Yes, yes. That's very nice.

EBENEZER
This is my hour of need! They must know that!

MISS POOLE
Mr. Scrooge, you need to calm down.

EBENEZER
They're coming! They have to!

(She stops, surprised by his outburst)

EBENEZER
Miss Poole, they have to come.

MISS POOLE
I don't like it when you thrash around like that. There's no telling...

EBENEZER
I have to see them one more time. Don't you understand?

MISS POOLE
I'm sorry. I don't.

(He stops, becoming confused. She can read it in his expression, so she goes to him)

MISS POOLE
Mr. Scrooge, you're...you're not well. I think that, perhaps, your mind is having a bit of fun with you. I know that, in your head, this all makes sense to you. But there are no ghosts. There's just you and me.

(He struggles to regain lucidity)

EBENEZER
Just you and me?

MISS POOLE
That's right?

(He looks around the room, sitting up more)

EBENEZER
No...I can see it clearly...right there... he was like a little boy, but like an old man, too.

MISS POOLE
Who?

EBENEZER
The ghost! The first ghost! He glowed with a bright light and carried a candle-cap with him...

MISS POOLE
Mr. Scrooge...

(He rises, going to the window)

MISS POOLE
...lord help me...

EBENEZER
He took me out the window...took me back home....

MISS POOLE
Back to bed with you.

EBENEZER
I saw Fan...my sweet Fan...

(She leads him back towards the bed)

MISS POOLE
Come on now.

EBENEZER
She was my sister. She died when I was... *(He pulls away, back to the window)* And Fezziwig's! He took me to Fezziwig's! *(He turns suddenly, with renewed energy, and grabs MISS POOLE in a waltz)*

MISS POOLE
OH!

EBENEZER
There was dancing! Oh and the food and the music! It was wonderful!

MISS POOLE
Put me down this instant!

EBENEZER
I had forgotten, you see? Forgotten what it was to laugh…to feel alive!

MISS POOLE
You're going to hurt yourself.

EBENEZER
(Sniffing the air) I can smell it…the spiced punch, the roast beef…and listen! *(He stops dancing, holding her by the shoulders)* There's music. Carols. They're singing Christmas Carols.

MISS POOLE
The carolers are long in their beds, sir.

EBENEZER
Listen! *(He quietly sings)* …I saw three ships come sailing in, on Christmas Day, on Christmas Day…I saw three ships come sailing in…

MISS POOLE
On Christmas Day in the morning.

(He smiles, turns her to him)

EBENEZER
You hear it too?

MISS POOLE
I'm sorry, I don't.

EBENEZER
But you were…

MISS POOLE
Everyone knows that carol, Mr. Scrooge. I just got caught up in the moment.

(He wanders around the room, singing, searching for the source of the music only he can hear)

EBENEZER
…And all the souls on earth shall sing, on Christmas Day, on Christmas Day…

MISS POOLE
Back to bed. Now!

EBENEZER
…and all the bells on Earth shall ring, on Christmas Day in the… *(He stops at the window. A surprised sadness hits him)* Belle?

(MISS POOLE goes to him, gently touching his shoulder)

MISS POOLE
Be a good fellow then. Come on.

EBENEZER
I loved her. God, how I loved her. And I let her go.

MISS POOLE
All right then.

EBENEZER
My whole life…I never loved another…never…and I let her walk out of the door. *(He goes to the coat rack, looking for his coat)* …told me I loved only gold…that she was setting me free. She gave me back the ring, but I kept it! I… *(He stops, remembering. His sadness grows)* No. No. I didn't keep it, did I?

(MISS POOLE finally manages to lead him back to the bed, sitting him there)

EBENEZER
I thought I did. But I didn't.

MISS POOLE
All right now. Just relax.

EBENEZER
(Starts to cry a little) I sold it. I was angry…hurt…I thought that, if money was all she thought mattered to me, that I… *(He looks up at MISS POOLE)* Why would I do that?

MISS POOLE
I'm sure I don't know.

EBENEZER
Why would I sell Belle's ring?

MISS POOLE
Listen to me. It's the past. That's all it is. We all do things we regret, but you can't let it stay with you. Selling a ring doesn't mean you didn't love her. Or that you don't still. All right?

(He nods. She takes out a handkerchief, cleans his face)

MISS POOLE
There we are. No room for tears on Christmas Eve. Unless you're the Virgin Mary, of course. I imagine she shed a few birthing that baby, savior or no.

(He smiles a little at that)

MISS POOLE
Now, will you be a good fellow and lie down before you give me a conniption fit?

EBENEZER
All right. *(He lies down)*

MISS POOLE
Shouldn't let yourself get all worked up by that.

EBENEZER
Yes. Of course. I…I don't know what came over me.

MISS POOLE
What's done is done.

EBENEZER
I must have given you quite a fright.

MISS POOLE
I've seen stranger. 'Least you kept your clothes on.

(He stares at her)

MISS POOLE
Oh yes. Some things cannot be unseen, if you get my meaning.

EBENEZER
My goodness.

(They sit in silence for a bit, neither sure how to continue)

MISS POOLE
Well, I know it isn't the day proper, but perhaps you'd like to open a present?

EBENEZER
That's quite all right.

MISS POOLE
Just one. I won't tell.

EBENEZER
Miss Poole, it is my belief that I'll be dead in the morning.

MISS POOLE
Don't…

EBENEZER
As such, I'd take it as a great personal kindness if you could have those gifts given to a poorhouse.

MISS POOLE
You can't stop, can you?

EBENEZER
I'm sorry. I know this talk of passing doesn't…

MISS POOLE
No, I mean…the giving. You can't stop, can you?

EBENEZER
Oh. That. *(Smiles)* Considering how long it took me to start, I'd say I'm still making up for lost time.

MISS POOLE
For as long as I can remember, you've been the heart of the city, sir. If you don't mind my saying.

EBENEZER
That's sweet, dear. But for most of my life, I was as cruel, as covetous and as cantankerous a sinner as ever walked the earth.

MISS POOLE
I find that hard to believe.

EBENEZER
Ah, the sweet ignorance of youth.

MISS POOLE
I'd wager there's not a soul in the old town that hasn't been touched by your generosity.

EBENEZER
Even you?

(Beat. She goes to the presents)

MISS POOLE
I'll see to it that your presents find good homes.

EBENEZER
Thank you.

MISS POOLE
Think nothing of it. *(She picks up a wrapped gift that is obviously a walking stick)*

EBENEZER
Whatever could that be?

MISS POOLE
One wonders why they even bothered to wrap it. *(Reads a card on it)* It's from your nephew.

EBENEZER
Ah, Fred. Good lad. Wonderful lad.

MISS POOLE
I could tell. He adores you.

EBENEZER
And I him.

MISS POOLE
Thought we'd have to use a shoe-horn to get him out of this room.

EBENEZER
He's my sole relation.

MISS POOLE
I'd wager half these presents are from him.

EBENEZER
Oh no. Fred...lives within his means. Not to say he's stingy, mind you. But the boy just won't accept my help.

MISS POOLE
Then he's about the only one.

EBENEZER
It doesn't matter, I suppose. If I did give him money, he'd just give it to someone he thought needed it more.

MISS POOLE
Sounds like he takes after you.

EBENEZER
Would you believe that I actually took after him? When I first decided to change my ways, Fred was very much my mentor. Ah, if he were but twenty years younger. And unmarried, of course.

MISS POOLE
Stop.

EBENEZER
I can't. Matchmaking is a favorite hobby of mine.

MISS POOLE
I beg you. Please stop.

EBENEZER
He's a handsome fellow.

MISS POOLE
Lord help me...

EBENEZER
If I had more time, I'd find you a proper husband.

MISS POOLE
Delightful.

EBENEZER
As it is, I suppose it will be your father's job to find you one.

(She stares at him)

EBENEZER
Did I misspeak?

MISS POOLE
I don't have a father. Or a mother. Not anymore.

EBENEZER
Oh. My dear, I'm so sorry.

MISS POOLE
You really don't remember, do you?

EBENEZER
Remember what?

(Beat. She stares at him, uncertain if he's serious or putting her on)

MISS POOLE
My parents were killed in a fire when I was ten. I lived on the streets for eight years. Does any of this sound familiar?

EBENEZER
Too familiar. London's streets are over-full with unfortunates.

MISS POOLE
No…Mr. Scrooge. Look at my face.

(He stares at her)

MISS POOLE
Is there nothing familiar about this face?

EBENEZER
(Staring, trying to remember) I'm sorry, dear. My vision is all but gone.

(She goes to him)

MISS POOLE
I'm Alice. Alice Poole. And seven years ago, you saved my life.

EBENEZER
I did?

MISS POOLE
You did.

(Lights change. The sound of a busy tavern fills the room. TIM enters, dressed warmly. He places a ragged coat on MISS POOLE, who falls into his arms. EBENEZER rises, donning a coat as well. It is seven years ago)

EBENEZER
Tim! Set her down there.

(TIM seats her, trying to get her to wake up. She does so, groggily)

TIM
She's waking up.

EBENEZER
Good.

TIM
Poor thing's near-frozen.

EBENEZER
Then let's see what we can do about that.

(TIM wraps his coat around her)

EBENEZER
See to getting her some soup, bread too. I'll stay with her.

TIM
Yes, sir.

(TIM rushes off. MISS POOLE stirs. EBENEZER sits with her)

EBENEZER
There you are. Come back to us.

MISS POOLE
…where am I…?

EBENEZER
Dorry's Tavern. No more than a block

from where you were...

MISS POOLE
What am I doing here?

EBENEZER
We brought you here.

(Beat. She pulls a small knife from her jacket)

EBENEZER
Oh!

MISS POOLE
You keep your hands off me! Don't you touch me or...

(She breaks into a fit of coughing. TIM rushes over with a glass of water. She drinks deep)

EBENEZER
And the soup?

TIM
I'm just one man, Ebenezer! Give me a moment. *(TIM rushes back off)*

EBENEZER
(Gently taking the glass from her) Easy now. Slowly.

(She backs away from him)

EBENEZER
I'm not going to hurt you.

MISS POOLE
Not like you'd tell me if you would.

EBENEZER
You have my word.

MISS POOLE
Oh! Well thank God for that then. *(She still holds out her knife)* Old codger like you drags me to some dank pub, thinks I'm gonna...

EBENEZER
Ma'am, you fainted.

(Beat)

MISS POOLE
I don't remember that.

EBENEZER
I imagine you wouldn't. But it happened nonetheless.

(She coughs again, drinks more water)

EBENEZER
That's quite a cough.

MISS POOLE
Well, I'm quite the lady.

EBENEZER
I have no doubt about that. *(He points offstage)* That fellow there...he's a friend of mine.

MISS POOLE
So?

EBENEZER
You were picking his pocket.

(Beat)

MISS POOLE
The hell you say.

EBENEZER
You had his pocket watch half-out when you collapsed at our feet.

MISS POOLE
You got no proof.

EBENEZER
I would need proof if I meant to see you in prison. That isn't my intention.

(She stares at him, uncertain)

EBENEZER
What is your name?

MISS POOLE
What's yours?

EBENEZER
Ebenezer Scrooge.

(Beat)

MISS POOLE
You're having me on.

EBENEZER
No.

MISS POOLE
You're Ebenezer Scrooge?

EBENEZER
You've heard of me?

MISS POOLE
Show me a Londoner who hasn't. You're Robin Hood with white hair.

EBENEZER
I...it's more silver than white, I thought.

MISS POOLE
You're the one that's kept half the charities in town alive.

EBENEZER
I suppose I am.

MISS POOLE
What good's that done me?

(Beat)

MISS POOLE
I'm not like the rest, Mr. Scrooge. You done a lot of good, I know that. But did it save my ma and da when our shack burned down? Did it keep me out of the workhouse, or off of the street?

(He has no answer)

MISS POOLE
If you want to peddle your charity, find someone else.

(She rises, but staggers from weakness. He helps her sit)

MISS POOLE
I don't mean to spit in your face, sir. I'm just saying...I never asked no one for help in my life, and I'm not going to now.

(TIM returns with a bowl of soup and some bread)

EBENEZER
I'm sorry for the hand you've been dealt. I truly am. And I apologize if I've made you uncomfortable. I just didn't want to leave you there in the snow. *(He rises, goes to TIM)* Come, my boy. Let's find a table.

TIM
But I just...

MISS POOLE
Wait.

(They stop)

MISS POOLE
Is that soup for me?

TIM
And the bread.

EBENEZER
I wouldn't want to offend your pride with my offering of soup.

(Beat)

MISS POOLE
Sit down already. I'm starving.

(They do so. She dives into the soup, talking as she eats. TIM tips his hat to her)

TIM
Tim Cratchit.

(She offers a soup-soaked hand)

MISS POOLE
Alice.

(He shakes it)

MISS POOLE
Christ…I haven't eaten like this in a year easy.

TIM
I can tell.

EBENEZER
How long have you been on the streets?

MISS POOLE
(Shrugging) Years. Seven or eight. About that.

EBENEZER
Forgive me for saying so, but you'll not last another.

MISS POOLE
Oh? You're not just the Patron Saint of pinch-pockets? You're a doctor, too?

EBENEZER
You're frail, you're cold, and that cough would be dangerous for a healthy man.

MISS POOLE
If you're trying to make a point, you're taking the long road to get there.

(EBENEZER rises and walks away)

TIM
That was rude.

MISS POOLE
My favorite opinions are solicited, Mr. Cratcham.

TIM
Cratchit. You speak well.

MISS POOLE
When the mood strikes me.

TIM
You are educated then?

MISS POOLE
Before my life went to Hell. I liked to read.

TIM
I was like you once.

MISS POOLE
Pffft.

TIM
It's true. And not just poor. I had the Rickets.

MISS POOLE
You?

TIM
Me.

MISS POOLE
You don't look it.

TIM
This was years ago. I got the medicine I needed, thanks to the man you just chased away.

MISS POOLE
I didn't chase him anywhere. He probably just had to piss. Old men piss a lot, don't they?

TIM
That old man saved my life. He'll save yours, if you let him.

MISS POOLE
Who asked him to?

TIM
No one. It's just what he does.

MISS POOLE
It's none of his damn business.

TIM
Mankind is his business. You need help, Alice. And you need it badly. Don't let your pride put you in an early grave.

(MISS POOLE stops eating, the reality of that hitting her)

MISS POOLE
A fire killed my parents. Burned 'em alive. And I'd have been better off if I'd gone with them. A life like I'm living now...there's no good in it. I'm just...I'm just a rat that can talk. Sometimes, I think death would be... kinder.

TIM
Then you don't know what kindness is. *(He reaches into his pocket, producing a watch. He gives it to her)* Here.

(She just stares at him, confused)

TIM
You seemed quite intent on taking it not thirty minutes ago.

MISS POOLE
I don't want it like this.

TIM
Like what?

MISS POOLE
Like...like this.

TIM
It's better to have stolen it?

MISS POOLE
Yes! That way, I wouldn't have to...I...

TIM
Take it. Please. I'd rather it do you some good than just have it sit in my pocket all day.

(She thinks about it, then takes it)

MISS POOLE
You're just like him, aren't you?

TIM
(Smiling at that) That's...I can't think of nicer thing to hear. Thank you.

(Beat. It's the first time someone's said that to her in years. She smiles and takes his hand)

MISS POOLE
You're a good sort.

TIM
I'd like very much to be.

MISS POOLE
You are.

(EBENEZER returns. She immediately pulls her hand away)

EBENEZER
Enjoying your soup?

MISS POOLE
I'd lick the bowl but for fear of splinters.

EBENEZER
Excellent. Because I have a proposition for you.

(Beat)

MISS POOLE
A proposition for soup?

EBENEZER
No. For shelter. Mr. Dorry is that jolly fellow there. He owns this establishment. It just so happens that he has a small room for rent above the kitchen. If you'd like it, it's yours.

MISS POOLE
How am I supposed to pay for it? In fleas?

EBENEZER
Your rent has been paid for. All you have to do is move into the room, and help Dorry with the cleaning.

(Beat)

MISS POOLE
Don't do this.

TIM
What?

EBENEZER
I haven't done…

MISS POOLE
I don't want your kindness. I don't want it, and I don't need it.

EBENEZER
My dear, there is not a soul on this planet that does not need kindness.

(She is quiet, fighting a mix of sorrow and gratitude)

MISS POOLE
I don't want your help.

EBENEZER
Yes, you do. You just don't want to ask for it. Now, you don't have to.

TIM
He's giving you a chance to start over, Miss. That's all this is.

MISS POOLE
You make it sound like such a…small thing.

EBENEZER
It isn't. I know that better than anyone. I also know how terrifying it can be.

(She says nothing)

EBENEZER
I have stared at my own grave. I have felt the urge to step into it, to let the ground bury me. And every day since then, I thank God that I fought that urge.

(Beat)

MISS POOLE
I'll stay here then.

EBENEZER
I'll let Mr. Dorry know. *(He heads off)*

MISS POOLE
Why would he do that?

TIM
A question like that can drive you mad. Just be grateful that he did.

MISS POOLE
I haven't had a home in years. I don't…

TIM
Alice. You'll be fine.

MISS POOLE
But I…

TIM
You'll be fine.

(EBENEZER returns)

EBENEZER
I'm afraid we must be off, my dear. But let me introduce you to your new landlord first.

MISS POOLE
Oh, I…yes, of course. *(She starts to go, then turns to TIM)* Will I see you around?

TIM
I'm afraid not. I've joined the Royal Navy. I ship out in the new year.

MISS POOLE
Oh. Well, then. *(She offers her hand again)* Best of luck to you, Mr. Cratchit.

TIM
And to you, Alice.

(The lights change. TIM exits. MISS POOLE & EBENEZER are back at the hospital)

EBENEZER
My God. That was you?

MISS POOLE
It was. Is. I…yes, I'm her. I'm Alice.

EBENEZER
I had all but forgotten.

(She lowers her head a bit)

EBENEZER
I'm sorry. I didn't...

MISS POOLE
I understand.

EBENEZER
I meant only that my memory is not what it once was. I remember that day. I remember you.

MISS POOLE
Oh.

EBENEZER
I should have checked in with you, I know. But I felt that you'd resent any further intrusion...

MISS POOLE
You did more for me than any other. You never have to apologize to me.

EBENEZER
That's kind of you to say.

(An awkward pause between them)

EBENEZER
So you're a nurse now?

MISS POOLE
For five years. It still seems like a dream, sometimes.

EBENEZER
I'd imagine.

MISS POOLE
That winter...you were right. That cough was more than a cough, and was very nearly the death of me. Dorry sent for a doctor not a week later, and he saved my life as surely as you did.

EBENEZER
Dr. Halsey?

MISS POOLE
Indeed.

EBENEZER
Well...the old rogue can keep a secret after all.

MISS POOLE
I couldn't pay, of course. Nor could Dorry. But he offered me a trade, to help in the laundry here.

EBENEZER
My goodness. You worked your way from a laundry maid to a nurse?

MISS POOLE
I wanted to help people. That need can be contagious too, spreading from one person to the next.

EBENEZER
Are you comparing kindness to illness?

MISS POOLE
Having experienced both, I'd rather have the former.

EBENEZER
If only we had that choice.

(He lies back on the bed. She goes to him, wiping his brow)

MISS POOLE
Mr. Scrooge, it is most unseemly to perspire so on such a chilly night.

EBENEZER
How bad is it?

MISS POOLE
Not so bad as all that.

EBENEZER
Alice, please.

(Beat)

MISS POOLE
It could be better.

EBENEZER
I told you, I believe...

MISS POOLE
Yes, yes! I've heard what you've said already!

EBENEZER
There's no need to shout.

MISS POOLE
I just... For God's sake, Mr. Scrooge. You're not even trying to fight this!

EBENEZER
Of course I am. But it's not as simple as all that.

MISS POOLE
What of your nephew? What of your friends? Are they ready to be parted from you?

EBENEZER
I'm an old man. This is not new information to them. But...no. No one is ever ready to let go of what they love. It happens nonetheless.

MISS POOLE
It's damn selfish is what it is.

EBENEZER
Come now.

MISS POOLE
It is! I don't have a single soul who cares a whit about me, but I'd still fight 'til there's no fight left in me.

EBENEZER
You're still very young. But Alice... fifteen years ago, I was given a second chance. I've lived long enough to make some good of it. I have but one task ahead of me now. *(Pats her hand)* But it's lovely to know that I'll be missed.

MISS POOLE
Half of England will mourn for a week. The other half for a month.

EBENEZER
I've set up funds and charities. I don't know if it will be enough, but...

MISS POOLE
It's not about the charities or the businesses or...it's you, Ebenezer. The multitude of small kindnesses that you did personally, every day. So many that you can't even remember all of them. Who will do that?

EBENEZER
Why not you?

MISS POOLE
I...that's ridiculous.

EBENEZER
No it's not.

MISS POOLE
I'm not you! I'm just...me.

EBENEZER
I wasn't me either. That is...I mean, of course I was me, but...A life changes because you choose to change it.

MISS POOLE
It's not that simple.

EBENEZER
(Chuckles) In fact, it is. You just can't see it until you're on the other side of it.

MISS POOLE
Pfft.

EBENEZER
Look how much your life has changed.

MISS POOLE
Yes, because of you.

EBENEZER
Because of you.

(She doesn't respond)

EBENEZER
All I ever did for you was give you an option. You're the one who took

it. You're the one who rebuilt a life. Never marginalize that.

(Suddenly, the window blows open. A howling wind can be heard)

MISS POOLE
Lord, what now... *(She runs to the window)*

EBENEZER
Wait!

MISS POOLE
You'll catch your death.

EBENEZER
I've already caught it. Just...listen.

MISS POOLE
(Listening to the snowstorm) I don't...

EBENEZER
There's a voice on the wind.

MISS POOLE
Yes. It's telling you to let poor Alice close the window.

EBENEZER
They're speaking to me! Oh my dear Miss Poole...they're...!

(He coughs loudly. She slams the window shut and goes to him)

EBENEZER
No...

MISS POOLE
Whatever else is going on, I am a nurse, Mr. Scrooge. And I'll not let a man freeze to death, even if he's already... *(She immediately changes the subject)* So what did the wind say, hmm?

EBENEZER
Beg pardon?

MISS POOLE
Your howling wind there. You said it spoke to you.

EBENEZER
Oh, the wind didn't speak to me, dear. It simply carried a voice on it.

MISS POOLE
Fine. What did the carried voice say?

EBENEZER
Well, if you're going to be short with me...

(She glares at him, frustrated)

EBENEZER
I'm afraid I couldn't make it out.

MISS POOLE
All right. Play your games.

EBENEZER
I would tell you if I could.

MISS POOLE
Of course.

EBENEZER
But when a ghost speaks....

MISS POOLE
There are no ghosts, Mr. Scrooge! I've walked this hospital for many years, and have seen more than my fair share of passing-ons. But in all that time, never once have I seen a single specter, spook, or spirit.

EBENEZER
Is it so hard for you to believe?

MISS POOLE
In ghostly visitations? Yes, I should say so.

EBENEZER
In anything? Anything at all?

(Beat)

MISS POOLE
I believe in myself.

EBENEZER
An excellent start. What else?

(She thinks on it, but has no answer)

EBENEZER
Is that why you're alone on Christmas Eve?

MISS POOLE
I'm not alone. I'm with you.

EBENEZER
Alice, I have only one regret left me, and it's that I never told Belle how sorry I was that I drove her away. Don't walk through this world alone.

MISS POOLE
And what, get married and play the doting wife? Do you know what I see when I come home at night?

EBENEZER
What?

MISS POOLE
Everything exactly where I left it. All of my food uneaten by anyone but myself. If I decide to go out for a pint, I don't have to discuss it with anyone. What do I need a husband for? To order me around, to get him Christmas sausages?

EBENEZER
You've been reading too much of your Mrs. Gaskell.

MISS POOLE
A good book, a nice fire and a hot toddy. That's all I need.

EBENEZER
If you say so.

MISS POOLE
I do say so.

EBENEZER
All right then.

MISS POOLE
So no more discussion of a romantic nature.

EBENEZER
I'm flattered, dear, but you're much, much too young for me.

(She laughs)

EBENEZER
Ha! That's the spirit!

(The door opens and TIM enters. He's a young man wearing a military uniform and a thick winter coat)

TIM
Uncle Ebenezer, I just....

(MISS POOLE lets out a little yell and jumps. TIM stops)

TIM
Oh. I...goodness. Terribly sorry.

MISS POOLE
Who are you, and what are you...?!

EBENEZER
Tim! My good Tim! *(Waves him over. They embrace)* Oh, my fine lad! How good it is to see you!

MISS POOLE
Excuse me...

TIM
Merry Christmas, Ebenezer.

EBENEZER
I thought you were still overseas. America, yes?

MISS POOLE
Please excuse me...

TIM
I've only just returned. I....

MISS POOLE
Excuse me, gentlemen!

(They turn and stare)

MISS POOLE
I'm not sure what time the sun rises and sets in America, sir, but visiting hours have long since passed.

EBENEZER
Miss Poole, this is Tim, one of my dearest...

TIM
Ebenezer, please. It's Timothy.

EBENEZER
Of course, of course. *(Leans in to MISS POOLE)* He doesn't like to be called "Tim" because it makes him feel young and childish. But I always say...

MISS POOLE
Tim or Timothy or Timon of Athens....Do you have any idea what time it is?

TIM
No, actually. I don't have a watch.

(She pulls out her pocket watch)

MISS POOLE
It's half past Eleven, and I've spent the better part of an hour trying to get Mr. Scrooge to sleep. Your presence isn't conducive to that.

TIM
Of course, I only...

MISS POOLE
So kindly return in the morning, when St. Bartholomew's welcomes visitors at...*(Notices TIM staring at her watch)* Eyes forward, sir.

TIM
I'm sorry. I just...I once had a watch very much like that one.

EBENEZER
Of course you did! Timothy, do you remember...?

(The clock tolls 11:30)

MISS POOLE
And it appears the old clock tower agrees with me. Out you go.

TIM
Please, just a moment.

MISS POOLE
How on earth did you even get in here?

TIM
It wasn't very difficult. The hallways are all but abandoned, and most of the patients are asleep.

MISS POOLE
Then you should have no difficulty retracing your steps out.

EBENEZER
No! Timothy, please sit down.

MISS POOLE
Mr. Scrooge, there are rules to take into consideration.

EBENEZER
Yes, but you never really know if the rules work unless you bend them now and then.

(TIM goes to MISS POOLE)

TIM
Miss...?

MISS POOLE
Poole.

TIM
Miss Poole, I have traveled a very long way to be here, and I would implore upon any sense of Christmas charity you might have to let me visit with my dear friend before sending me back out into the cold.

(She stares at him for a bit, then opens the door. TIM sighs and starts to go. Before he gets there, she stands in the doorway)

MISS POOLE
I was just about to find a warm cup of tea. If you managed to sneak in while I was away...well, these things happen, I suppose.

TIM
Thank you.

MISS POOLE
You're welcome, Mr. Cratchit. *(She exits)*

TIM
Did she just call me "Mr. Cratchit"?

EBENEZER
Indeed.

TIM
How did she know my name?

EBENEZER
I...I'm sure you should ask her when she returns.

TIM
If she doesn't throttle me first.

EBENEZER
Oh, I think she likes you better than that.

TIM
Then you were witnessing a very different conversation than I was.

EBENEZER
Alice puts up a stone wall, surely. But if one gets close, they can see the many cracks.

TIM
"Alice" is it, you old rascal?

EBENEZER
You're never too old, Tim.

(TIM just stares at him)

EBENEZER
Timothy.

(TIM sits next to him)

TIM
You look well.

(EBENEZER laugh/coughs at that)

EBENEZER
Come now. I may not have a mirror, but if my appearance reflects my condition at all...well, it doesn't matter. It was kind of you to say.

TIM
Here.

(TIM gives him some water. EBENEZER drinks)

EBENEZER
What did Bob tell you? About my... situation?

(Beat. TIM isn't sure how honestly to answer)

TIM
Father said you should've gone to the hospital a month ago.

EBENEZER
We both know I couldn't do that.

TIM
We do?

EBENEZER
I would've missed the Season. Unacceptable.

TIM
You should've come here at the first hint of trouble! My father could run Scrooge & Cratchit without you for a little while.

EBENEZER
Come the morrow, he will have to do that anyway.

(Beat)

TIM
What are you saying?

EBENEZER
Tell me of your travels, boy! You've been gone for three years!

TIM
Ebenezer...how bad is it?

EBENEZER
(Taking TIM's hand) You're a sweet lad to ask, but there's nothing can be done.

TIM
I'm sorry.

EBENEZER
Oh, it's quite all right. Every book reaches its final chapter. *(sensing TIM's sadness, he changes the subject)* So how are your dear parents?

TIM
You saw them yesterday.

EBENEZER
So I did, so I did. But you know Bob...trying so damn hard to put on a cheerful face for me, never saying a peep about himself.

TIM
He misses you. We all miss you.

EBENEZER
Besides that, Timothy.

TIM
I think he's finally begun to accept himself as your partner.

EBENEZER
I would hope so! Adding his name to the sign should have given him an inkling.

TIM
You have to understand...he never thought of himself as a man of business. Just a clerk. You were the one who saw what he could become. Sometimes... sometimes it takes a while to see in yourself what others see in you.

EBENEZER
Of course.

TIM
Peter is helping him now. Did you know he'd hired Peter on?

EBENEZER
Oh yes. I suggested it, in fact. I felt that Scrooge & Cratchit might live longer as a family business.

TIM
Peter has father's gift for numbers. He's an asset.

EBENEZER
I'm sure there would be room for you there, should you want it.

TIM
No. I'm not a businessman.

EBENEZER
You're a Navy man.

(TIM says nothing)

EBENEZER
Tell me of America. I've heard so many contrary reports, I don't know what to believe.

TIM
That's understandable. It's a divided country, still very much trying to find itself. Frankly, I don't know that it ever will.

EBENEZER
You paint a bleak picture.

TIM
They're in the midst of a civil war, Ebenezer. The country isn't even 100 years old, and already it's coming

apart at the seams.

EBENEZER
There's always hope, Timothy.

TIM
You always say that! You've been saying it ever since I was ten, but... *(He collects himself)* They're very different from us.

EBENEZER
The Americans?

TIM
Yes. They have...there's a fire to them. A great passion.

EBENEZER
You're not calling we fine Britains passionless, are you?

TIM
It's not the same. With an American... you never have to wonder what they're feeling. It's all right there, on the surface. They laugh easily, and they fight just as easily. They love deeply, with every fiber of their being...but they lack a sense of identity.

EBENEZER
You make them sound like children.

TIM
They very much reminded me of children.

(Suddenly, the window blows open again. A gusting storm is heard)

TIM
Good Christ!

EBENEZER
It's been doing that all night.

(TIM goes to it)

EBENEZER
Wait!

TIM
It's freezing out there! Do you want it to be freezing in here?

EBENEZER
Give it a moment, please!

TIM
The whole damn room will be covered in snow if I don't...

EBENEZER
Tim! Please!

(TIM just stares at him)

EBENEZER
Just leave it for a moment. I beg of you.

TIM
You're mad. You know this.

EBENEZER
I do.

TIM
And I know there's always method to your madness. *(Moves away from the window)*

EBENEZER
Thank you.

TIM
Well, it's as good a time as any for your Christmas present, I suppose. *(Pulls a poorly wrapped present from his coat pocket)*

EBENEZER
I was actually just telling Alice, I'd rather have any gifts donated to charity.

TIM
Of course you would. *(Begins to unwrap it)*

EBENEZER
I appreciate the kindness, of course. But there are so many more in greater

need than I that...

(The gift is a knitted cap. TIM puts it on EBENEZER's head mid-sentence. It looks a bit silly on him)

EBENEZER
Oh. I see.

TIM
It'll keep the nip off your ears, at any rate.

EBENEZER
Thank you, Timothy. It's lovely.

TIM
That would have been more convincing if you said it after the lights had blown out.

EBENEZER
Those are paraffin lamps, my boy. It would take quite a gust to extinguish them.

TIM
The storm outside might be up to the task.

(EBENEZER holds his finger up, silencing TIM)

TIM
Did you hear something?

EBENEZER
Shh!

TIM
I simply...

EBENEZER
Shh! *(Listens intently)* ...I can almost make it out...

TIM
Make...?

(EBENEZER glares at him. TIM holds his hands up in surrender and is silent)

EBENEZER
It's a voice! I know that voice! *(EBENEZER rises and goes to the window)*

TIM
Oh lord...

EBENEZER
(Calling out the window) You have to speak louder! I can't quite hear you!

TIM
No you don't. *(Grabs EBENEZER, who shakes him off)*

EBENEZER
Tell me what to do! Tell me what you want me to do!

TIM
You'll wake the whole damn hospital!

EBENEZER
Tell me! Please!

(TIM slams the window shut, latching it tight)

EBENEZER
No!

TIM
You have to calm yourself.

EBENEZER
What have you done?!

TIM
Kept you from falling to your death!

EBENEZER
I was so close! I could almost hear them! *(He clutches TIM)* Bring them back! Oh God please...I'm ready...I... *(He weeps. TIM holds him)* I want to talk to them. Why did you shut the window?

TIM
There's no one out there.

EBENEZER
Please...I just need to know what to do...

TIM
I know you think you heard something, but...

EBENEZER
I'm not some befuddled dolt! There are things...God, Timothy....there are things that you can't possibly understand. Mysterious and beautiful things...and they came to me once, years ago. They showed me my past and...

TIM
Back to your bed.

EBENEZER
LISTEN! You have to listen. The man I was before...Do you remember the Christmas fifteen years gone, when that great roast turkey arrived at your doorstep?

TIM
Of course. Father told us you sent it.

EBENEZER
I did. But...you see, the night before... ah, where do I start...Timothy, everything you'd heard about me up to that point was true. Every curse your mother uttered at my name was earned. I was as black-hearted and vile a man as ever walked the earth.

TIM
That doesn't matter, sir.

EBENEZER
It matters. Matters more than anything. Because you....(*His mood softens, smiling at* TIM *with great affection*) You never spoke ill of me. Not once.

TIM
How could I? I'm alive now because of you.

EBENEZER
No, before you'd even met me...before I'd changed...Even when others spat at my name, you never did.

TIM
I don't...did Father tell you that?

EBENEZER
He didn't have to. I saw it with my own two eyes.

TIM
What?

EBENEZER
The night before my redemption, a spirit...a ghost...took me to your house. I watched your whole family gather around the fire. You couldn't see me, of course, but...

TIM
That's enough. Get back into bed or I'll call for a nurse.

EBENEZER
Your father tried to toast me, but your mother protested. Said she'd give me a piece of her mind and hoped I'd choke on it. But you...you raised your glass to me. All of ten years old, you raised your little glass and toasted me.

TIM
Why are you telling me this?

EBENEZER
And slowly...one by one...your brothers, sisters...your mother and father... all raised their glasses too. And do you remember what you said then?

TIM
That was a long time ago, Uncle Ebenezer. I don't...

EBENEZER
You do! You have to remember!

TIM
So much has happened since then. You can't expect me to remember one Christmas Eve out of so many.

EBENEZER
(Laughs) Lord love you, but you're a terrible liar, Tim. Always were. You know what you said. "God bless…"

(EBENEZER's weakness catches up to him & he falters. TIM helps him sit on the bed)

TIM
Uncle, you shouldn't agitate yourself like this.

EBENEZER
I always appreciated that affection, Tim. "Uncle." I couldn't love you more if you were my own flesh and blood.

(TIM backs away, wrestling with his emotions)

EBENEZER
Tim?

TIM
Timothy. How many times must I tell you? Timothy.

EBENEZER
I've upset you. I'm sorry. I didn't…

TIM
I'm not a boy! That's all I'm saying, Ebenezer. I just…you look at me, and you see the crippled child I was. The tiny lad you carried on your shoulders and…I'm not him! Why can't you see that?

EBENEZER
You will always be that boy to me.

TIM
Don't! Don't say that.

EBENEZER
Whatever else, to me…you're still Tiny Tim.

TIM
No! Don't bloody say that! Don't…!
(TIM paces, trying to hold back his anger)
I just wanted to see you one more time. That's all. To sit at your bedside and to remember better times. Why do you have to make it so damn difficult?

EBENEZER
My boy, what is it?

TIM
You have no idea. The world you've spent so much time trying to brighten, it didn't even notice. All the good you've done in London…go fifty miles in any direction and it means nothing.

EBENEZER
That's not you talking.

TIM
It's not the Tim you remember, but it's Tim nonetheless.

EBENEZER
Has being an officer changed you so much?

TIM
I'm not an officer!

(Beat. EBENEZER stares at him)

TIM
Not for much longer.

EBENEZER
What happened?

TIM
The world happened. As it always happens.

(TIM sits by the Christmas Tree. He inspects the presents as he speaks)

TIM
Have you ever heard of Thanksgiving? *(EBENEZER shakes his head "no")* An American holiday celebrating... it's hard to say. They celebrate every damn thing. This year, their President proclaimed it a national holiday. A day to be thankful for their country's great bounty.

EBENEZER
There's nothing wrong with celebrating, Timothy. The world would be a merrier place if we had more of it.

TIM
Doesn't it seem odd, though? Setting up a holiday in the middle of this great war?

EBENEZER
Perhaps that's when a sense of hope is most needed.

TIM
Hope? Christ almighty, I don't know that I'd even recognize hope if I saw it.

(TIM looks up at EBENEZER)

TIM
The truth is, we don't all deserve God's blessing.

(The lights change. The setting is the kitchen in a mansion in Mississippi, a month earlier. TIM is walking about with a candle. HELEN, a kitchen maid, is loading food into a basket. She stops)

HELEN
Who's there? Is somebody there?

TIM
I'm sorry. I didn't mean...

HELEN
Oh! Leftenant, I didn't realize...

TIM
Perhaps you could...

HELEN
Just give me a moment to clean up and... *(She puts the basket under the table as he enters)*

TIM
It's Helen, yes?

HELEN
Leftenant.

TIM
Timothy. Please.

HELEN
Sir.

TIM
Could you help me please? I was looking for the kitchen and...

(She just stares at him)

TIM
I was hoping there might be some pie left.

(She continues to just stare at him)

TIM
It's a terrible habit, I know. Ever since I was a child, I've always been ravenous in the evening. And the feast tonight was truly exceptional and I... *(Looking around)* I am in the kitchen, aren't I?

HELEN
You are.

TIM
Well. Apparently my gullet sees better than my eyes.

HELEN
Yes. Well. Let me just clean this up....

TIM
Please, let me help. *(He sits, begins eating)* This is quite a place.

HELEN
One of Virginia's finest.

TIM
Have you been in Mr. Comstock's service long?

HELEN
Since I was a girl.

TIM
Ah. Are all his gatherings so…lavish?

HELEN
No, sir. Mr. Comstock enjoys celebrating holidays, even the ones endorsed by Lincoln.

TIM
I see.

HELEN
And having you and the Ambassador here…He wanted to make a good showing. *(Beat)* Did he make a good showing?

TIM
Hard to say. The Ambassador is a difficult man to read.

HELEN
But you're his…I'm sorry, I forget the word.

TIM
Attaché?

HELEN
Yes.

TIM
I'm not, actually. Captain Halliwell is the Military Attaché. And I'm the Captain's assistant.

HELEN
Of course.

TIM
In fact, you might say we're both servants. Please, join me.

HELEN
I really shouldn't. I…

TIM
Is that stuffing?

(TIM digs in ravenously. HELEN laughs a little. TIM looks up)

HELEN
I'm sorry. I just thought…. I imagined all Englishmen to be very…proper.

TIM
I'm eating like a wolf bringing down a deer, aren't I?

HELEN
It's all right.

TIM
My appetite got the better of my manners. But please don't let it besmirch your opinion of the English.

HELEN
Actually, I think they've improved my opinion.

TIM
Excellent.

(He wipes his mouth on his sleeve. She laughs again)

HELEN
Is it true what they say?

TIM
That depends. What do they say?

HELEN
Is Britain going to recognize the Confederacy as its own country?

(TIM shrugs as he eats)

HELEN
Is that a yes or a no?

TIM
It's not my place to say.

HELEN
Oh.

TIM
I'm only here to assist the Captain. I don't attend the more important meetings.

HELEN
But the Ambassador is here.

TIM
Yes he is.

HELEN
I can't help but draw the conclusion.

TIM
I'd say more if I could.

HELEN
But you can't.

TIM
But I can't.

HELEN
The South could certainly use Britain's support. And supplies.

TIM
And I could use a plate that never runs out of pie. Some prayers go unanswered.

HELEN
So the meetings aren't going well?

TIM
I didn't say that.

HELEN
No. Of course. Pardon me.

(She smiles a bit. TIM catches it)

TIM
That pleases you?

HELEN
Hmm?

TIM
That the talks aren't progressing as Comstock would like them to.

HELEN
I don't have an opinion on it, sir.

TIM
I find that very hard to believe.

HELEN
I'm just a kitchen girl.

TIM
Who asks a lot of questions. And smiles at the news she's glad to hear.

HELEN
I didn't…I was smiling about something else.

TIM
You have no love for the Confederacy.

(She says nothing)

TIM
I'll let you in on a secret. Neither do I.

HELEN
Truly?

TIM
I don't care for slavery.

HELEN
(Looking around nervously) I wouldn't say that too loudly.

TIM
The house is asleep. Besides, I'm a guest.

HELEN
That sort of thinking isn't popular around here.

TIM
And yet, you think it. *(rising, bumping his foot on the basket. He stares at it)* This food isn't for me, is it?

HELEN
Of course it is. I...

TIM
You weren't cleaning the table. You were packing this food up. Which makes me wonder who this feast is for.

(Beat. She says nothing)

TIM
Helen, what's wrong?

HELEN
Did you mean what you said? About your feelings for the Confederacy?

TIM
Yes.

HELEN
Then please, just go back to your room and forget you ever saw me.

TIM
Are you in danger?

HELEN
We're all in danger. Each and every one of us. *(Beat)* There is a group of men about a half mile into the forest, just past the manor house.

TIM
The people you were bringing the food to?

HELEN
Union sympathizers. Mr. Comstock's slaves are with them now.

TIM
Dear God.

HELEN
I had to do something! I have friends among them and I knew Comstock would drink himself into a stupor tonight.

TIM
If he catches you, he'll...

HELEN
I know.

TIM
Then why in God's name...

HELEN
A countryman of yours once said, "All that is required for evil to prevail is for good men to do nothing."

(Beat)

TIM
You have to get out of here.

HELEN
I was trying to do just that. Somehow, my plan was interrupted.

(TIM digs some money out of his pocket)

TIM
Here. I don't have much American currency, but take it.

HELEN
If Comstock discovers you helped me...

TIM
He won't. And even if he did, he'd never lift a finger. He wants my country's help too dearly.

HELEN
You don't even know me.

TIM
I know you had a choice, and you chose something over nothing.

HELEN
Thank you.

TIM
You can thank me by leaving with all haste.

(She starts to go, then runs back and hugs TIM. He is momentarily stunned, and half-hugs her back)

HELEN
Goodbye, Leftenant.

TIM
Goodbye, Helen.

(She runs off. Lights return us to the hospital room)

TIM
Comstock's men found them the next day. He had them all shot.

EBENEZER
Oh God.

TIM
The slaves, the Union men and Helen. All dead.

EBENEZER
My boy, I'm so sorry.

TIM
And when I arrived home…I'm not a soldier anymore, Uncle.

EBENEZER
Tim…

(He tries to rise, but is too weak. TIM helps him lie back down)

TIM
I shouldn't have told you.

EBENEZER
It was good that you did. That's too great a burden to bear alone.

TIM
They were hunted down like animals! This woman…this poor woman saw injustice and acted! She asked for nothing, she just listened to her conscience and she lost everything because of it.
(Fighting his tears) I have wanted to be like you since I was ten years old. My God, I joined the Navy because I wanted to serve England in my own way, just as you did in yours. I was going to see the world, and bring with me the same kindness you've always given others…but that world is a lie, Ebenezer. This world…THIS world…

EBENEZER
Tim…

TIM
Everywhere I went, I saw the same thing. Men in power, using their influence to turn one against another. Men who truly believed themselves good, rising up against their neighbors for the sin of looking differently, thinking differently. There is no peace on earth, just intolerance and fear and…

(EBENEZER rises, shaky. TIM goes to him)

TIM
What are you doing?

EBENEZER
You're wrong, Tim.

TIM
Lord, you're burning up.

EBENEZER
Listen to me, please…

TIM
Miss Poole! My Uncle is…

(EBENEZER claps a hand over TIM's mouth)

EBENEZER
You have to listen to me, Tim. I know with great certainty that I am not long for this world, but so help me, I will not leave it until you have heard me out. So be…quiet. *(He removes his hand)* That world you speak of…I helped

to make it. For much of my life, I spread sorrow and hatred like a sickness. Everything I've done for the last fifteen years, I did to...to...

(His weakness catches up with him, and he falters. TIM lies him in bed)

TIM
I'm getting your nurse.

EBENEZER
(Grabbing TIM's arm) I won't let it take you, Tim. The darkness of the world will not have you.

TIM
You have to let me go.

EBENEZER
(Smiles) Never.

TIM
Uncle Ebenezer, please...

EBENEZER
...my nurse...Alice...

TIM
I'll get her.

EBENEZER
No, dammit! Listen to me...You helped save her life.

TIM
What?

EBENEZER
Years ago, we found a sick girl and...

TIM
You're not thinking clearly.

EBENEZER
Your watch! That's why she has your watch!

TIM
I don't understand.

EBENEZER
Don't you remember? Seven years ago...a street urchin tried to steal your watch. When you turned around, she collapsed in your arms.

(Beat. TIM remembers the moment)

EBENEZER
We took her to a pub and gave her food.

TIM
She'd lost her family to a fire.

EBENEZER
Yes.

TIM
I gave her my watch.

EBENEZER
Yes, you did.

TIM
And her name was Alice.

(EBENEZER smiles)

TIM
You're saying...that Alice...is this Alice?

EBENEZER
Yes.

TIM
My God.

EBENEZER
You want proof that something good still exists in this world? There it is! A poor, lost girl with no hope...and you gave her hope.

TIM
No. It was you who...

EBENEZER
Tim. She spoke with me tonight, told me her story. I may have gotten her off of the streets, but you saved her life.

TIM
How?

EBENEZER
You gave her your watch.

(Beat)

TIM
That doesn't make any sense.

EBENEZER
Of course it does! It was her first gift in…I don't even know how long. Why do you think she's hung on to it all these years?

TIM
I can't imagine.

EBENEZER
Because it meant everything to her. That one thing, a small pocket watch, was what reminded her that no one is so far gone that they cannot be… redeemed.

(Beat. The truth of that hits TIM)

EBENEZER
That's the beauty of this world, my boy. A simple act of kindness, given for no reason other than the giving… that's what changes the world.

TIM
I tried. I tried to help, and I failed.

EBENEZER
Then you try again. And again. And a thousand times more if you must. If you make even one life better, then it was worth the effort.

(MISS POOLE returns)

MISS POOLE
What on earth is happening here?

TIM
Alice, I…

MISS POOLE
(Going to SCROOGE, placing a hand on his head) Mr. Scrooge, how do you feel?

EBENEZER
Tired.

MISS POOLE
Yes, I'd imagine.

EBENEZER
And very warm.

MISS POOLE
That's not so bad a thing on as cold a night as this. Perhaps now's the time to get some rest.

EBENEZER
Not yet.

MISS POOLE
You were waiting for a mysterious guest? Well, here's Mister Cratchit. You two have had your fun, but…

EBENEZER
Timothy, don't give up.

TIM
Uncle, you mustn't…

EBENEZER
Don't close your heart, as I did long ago.

MISS POOLE
Rest your eyes, sir. It's been quite a day.

(The clock outside chimes 11:45)

EBENEZER
The bells….Timothy, the bells….

MISS POOLE
They'll be there tomorrow.

EBENEZER
If they come…you have to wake me if they come…

TIM
Who?

EBENEZER
I'm very tired.

MISS POOLE
Then sleep. And dream of Christmas morning.

(EBENEZER motions TIM over. When he's near enough, EBENEZER moves him next to MISS POOLE. He then falls asleep. She goes to him)

TIM
Is he...?

MISS POOLE
Sleeping. Just sleeping.

TIM
Will it...will it be long?

(Beat)

MISS POOLE
I don't think so.

TIM
(Fighting back his sorrow) Even at the end, he was trying to help me.

MISS POOLE
It's his way.

TIM
I should have just talked with him, remembered better times. Instead I'm nattering on about my own damn concerns and...

MISS POOLE
Mr. Cratchit, your guilt does him no good. Whatever you had to say, I'm sure he wanted to hear it.

(He sits)

TIM
I remember you.

MISS POOLE
You do?

TIM
Now. Uncle reminded me.

MISS POOLE
Oh.

(Beat. She takes out her watch and offers it to him)

MISS POOLE
I suppose you'd like your watch back.

(He smiles a little, shakes his head "no")

MISS POOLE
All right then.

(She pockets it. They share an awkward beat)

MISS POOLE
I know what kindness is now.

(He stares at her)

MISS POOLE
When we met, all those years ago... you said I didn't know what kindness was. I do now. You taught it to me.

TIM
I did?

MISS POOLE
Yes.

TIM
But it was such a little thing, I...

MISS POOLE
Don't say that. Never say that again. I am here now, alive, because of you. And him. Thank you.

(Beat)

MISS POOLE
The proper thing would be to say, "You're welcome."

TIM
Oh. Yes. You're welcome, of course. *(He's still very much lost in his thoughts)*

MISS POOLE
Have you seen the world?

(He stares at her)

MISS POOLE
You were joining the Royal Navy. I imagine you've seen many things by now.

TIM
More than I would have liked. I'm leaving the service.

MISS POOLE
Oh.

TIM
I thought the sea would show me one adventure after another.

MISS POOLE
I think we may have read the same books.

TIM
It didn't turn out like it did in the stories.

MISS POOLE
I suppose it never does.

(Beat)

TIM
I'm glad you're here.

MISS POOLE
I'm sorry?

TIM
With him. I'm glad he's had someone with him who knew him. Someone he helped.

MISS POOLE
Oh. Well. I am a nurse. This is what I do.

TIM
It suits you. Better than pick-pocketing did, at any rate.

MISS POOLE
(Smiles) I was a terrible pick-pocket.

TIM
When you tried to steal that watch…

MISS POOLE
Oh god.

TIM
You might as well have introduced yourself and given me a business card.

MISS POOLE
I was that bad?

TIM
Oh yes.

MISS POOLE
Well, it was your own fault! Walking through that alley with this bit of gold just swinging from your pocket. What did you think would happen?

(He laughs a little. She smiles)

TIM
I apologize if my being here upset you.

ALICE
It didn't.

TIM
You seemed…displeased with it earlier.

ALICE
Surprised is all.

TIM
I believe you said I wasn't conducive to my uncle's rest.

ALICE
I only meant…Mr. Cratchit…

TIM
Timothy. Please.

ALICE
Timothy…when you've had to fight

your whole life, you forget that...I don't mean to push people away. I just don't know how to stop.

TIM
You're not pushing me away.

ALICE
Now. But when you came in, I...

TIM
I'm still here, and you haven't tossed me out the door.

ALICE
No. I suppose I haven't.

(Beat)

ALICE
I'm glad you're here too.

(Suddenly, the window blows open again. The sound of the storm is louder. The lamps blow out, and the stage goes dark. A light slowly rises on EBENEZER. He bolts up from his sleep, as if waking from a dream)

EBENEZER
Hello? Hello, who's there?

(TIM starts to laugh a little)

EBENEZER
Who's there?!

(TIM laughs louder now, a huge laugh filling the room)

EBENEZER
I know that laugh.

(The lights rise. TIM & MISS POOLE are still there, though their demeanors have changed. They both smile at EBENEZER, and TIM continues laughing)

TIM
Well I'd hope so, man! Few know me better than you!

EBENEZER
You're...you're not Tim.

TIM
(Laughing again) Not at all! I've just borrowed him for a moment.

EBENEZER
Then you are...?

TIM
I think you know.

EBENEZER
Can you not say your own name?

TIM
Oh, I've said it so many times. Why don't you?

EBENEZER
You...you are the Ghost of Christmas Present.

TIM
(Laughing) Indeed I am!

(EBENEZER rises, suddenly full of life again. He runs to TIM, shaking his hand vigorously)

EBENEZER
You came! I knew you would, you see! And you...

(He goes to MISS POOLE, taking her by the shoulders. Her demeanor is more gentle and kindly)

MISS POOLE
Christmas Past. It's so very good to see you again.

(He hugs her. She lets out a surprised shout & hugs him back)

EBENEZER
You're here! This is glorious! Beyond glorious! Resplendent! Heavenly! *(He paces the room excitedly)* I'd almost lost hope, you see. I knew in my heart that

you'd come to me again, but when it took you so long, I began to worry. I said to myself, "Ebenezer, you mustn't lose faith in..." Wait. Why are you here like this?

MISS POOLE
Like what?

EBENEZER
Why are you her? And why are you him? When we met all those years ago, you had your own forms, your own shapes.

MISS POOLE
Then, we appeared to you to take you to our respective domains. The past...

TIM
And the present.

MISS POOLE
But to step out of our realms, to appear together on the night before Christmas, we needed to borrow these mortals for the briefest of times.

EBENEZER
I didn't realize you could do that.

TIM
It's perhaps not as impressive as traveling through time, but we do find it useful, on occasion.

EBENEZER
I never realized.

MISS POOLE
Our task is to lead lost souls back to a better life. No easy thing, that.

TIM
Many consider you to be our greatest success. Well, not mine per se, but...

EBENEZER
No need to be modest. You were instrumental in my redemption.

TIM
Not me, Ebenezer. My brother.

EBENEZER
Your...brother?

TIM
Born fifteen years ago.

EBENEZER
Ah, yes! Of course! You told me this before...

TIM
Every year another Christmas Present, as it were. Ha!

EBENEZER
Over 1800 then!

TIM
The family outings can get...complicated.

EBENEZER
It was you, wasn't it? Yours were the voices I've been hearing?

MISS POOLE
Indeed.

TIM
We've been whispering to you on the wind for quite some time now.

MISS POOLE
Gently at first, reassuring you of our presence.

TIM
Speaking so quietly you barely noticed.

MISS POOLE
But as your time drew near...

TIM
So did we.

EBENEZER
But why?

MISS POOLE
We have heard the call of your soul, old friend.

TIM
What is it you want?

MISS POOLE
Your time in this world draws to a close.

EBENEZER
I know.

TIM
You've freed yourself from the chains that could have been your damnation.

EBENEZER
And I'm glad to hear it, but…

MISS POOLE
Isn't that enough?

(Beat)

EBENEZER
No.

MISS POOLE
No?

EBENEZER
No. I want to continue.

TIM
You've lived a long life. We cannot extend it.

EBENEZER
There must be something you can do! Please! The boy whose body you inhabit…I love him as though he were my own son. His heart is broken, his hope…shattered. How could I leave this world knowing he might lose his way?

MISS POOLE
There may be a way, but it isn't a decision to be made lightly.

EBENEZER
Anything. Just tell me.

TIM
When we came to you fifteen years gone, there was another with us.

EBENEZER
Yes. Of course. The Ghost of Christmas Yet to Come.

TIM
Old Doom-&-Gloom.

MISS POOLE
Don't call him that.

EBENEZER
I feared him more than any other. But if he is to join us, I will….

TIM
He's moved on.

EBENEZER
What?

TIM
Moved on. Ascended. Gone to his eternal reward.

EBENEZER
Indeed?

MISS POOLE
Oh yes. It is the fate of all Spirits of Christmas. We serve through the years, bringing hope to those who need it most. And when our time has come, we are welcomed into the Heavenly Host.

TIM
Which is why we are here, Ebenezer.

(Beat)

EBENEZER
What do you mean?

TIM
We who were once three are now only two.

MISS POOLE
And there must always be three.

MISS POOLE
So join us, Ebenezer Scrooge.

(Beat)

EBENEZER
You...you mean, as a ghost?

TIM
Not just any ghost.

EBENEZER
The Ghost of Christmas Yet To Come?

MISS POOLE
Yes. But know this; it is no small thing, being a Ghost of Christmas.

EBENEZER
I know.

MISS POOLE
Do you? With each passing year, the world grows colder, men's hearts grow darker, and kindness drifts further from their minds.

TIM
When we came to you fifteen Christmases ago, you retook your own life, and tried to do some good with it. Many have not.

EBENEZER
How many have you visited? How many like me?

MISS POOLE
More than you can imagine. Many turn us away.

TIM
And with each rejection, our light dims in this world.

MISS POOLE
You have seen the desperation of the past.

TIM
And the desolation of the present.

MISS POOLE
Do you truly wish to join our ranks? To light a single candle against the growing darkness?

EBENEZER
Of course. Of course I do.

MISS POOLE
Why?

EBENEZER
Because one candle can light another, and another, and another.

(Beat. TIM laughs)

TIM
An excellent answer, Mr. Scrooge. A most excellent answer.

EBENEZER
Then you will have me? I can join you?

MISS POOLE
It's why we came here, to make you this very offer.

EBENEZER
(Shaking their hands) Thank you! Oh joyous day!

MISS POOLE
There is much you will have to learn.

EBENEZER
Of course. Absolutely.

TIM
We haven't had a new Christmas Yet To Come in...well, since before I started.

EBENEZER
Then it's true. I am to become...the future?

MISS POOLE
Yes. Your story will live on and on, further than you can imagine.

TIM
Three hundred years from now, they will still know the name Ebenezer Scrooge. Parents will tell their children of the hard-hearted, miserly wretch...

EBENEZER
All right.

TIM
...who found his soul one Christmas Day.

EBENEZER
That...I cannot thank you enough.

(The window opens)

MISS POOLE
Come. Your body will remain here. Your spirit will come with us.

EBENEZER
Just...just one more thing.

TIM
The clock is ticking, Ebenezer.

EBENEZER
I wish to be a... different sort of ghost.

MISS POOLE
Oh?

EBENEZER
My predecessor... Old Doom-&-Gloom.... he relied on fear and shadows.

MISS POOLE
It was most effective, if I recall.

EBENEZER
Of course, but...

MISS POOLE
If a method is proven effective, I see no need to change it.

EBENEZER
My friends...when mankind fears the future, they accomplish...nothing. They turn on each other, and finally themselves, and wonder where it all went wrong. I think perhaps I'd like to try a different approach.

MISS POOLE
Every new partner has their own ideas on how to improve the business, but...

TIM
HA!

MISS POOLE
What?

TIM
Oh come now! You were the worst of all of us!

MISS POOLE
That's ridiculous.

TIM
Do not forget, I share the memory of all my brothers before me. Your first day, you came in with your changing forms and your flying through windows and...

MISS POOLE
You're exaggerating.

TIM
Old Doom-&-Gloom was spitting fire! And what did my brother tell him? Hmm?

(MISS POOLE mumbles something)

TIM
I must have missed that.

MISS POOLE
He said "Each spirit is chosen for a reason, and we should honor that."

TIM
Yes. I believe that's the gist of it.

(TIM goes to EBENEZER)

TIM
So you don't want to bring them fear?

EBENEZER
No. A man shouldn't change for fear of the punishment.

TIM
Then what shall you bring them?

EBENEZER
Hope.

TIM
(Smiling at that) Hope. Now that has some potential. Wouldn't you agree?

MISS POOLE
We can try it. *(She motions to the bed)*

EBENEZER
I don't understand.

MISS POOLE
It's as I said, Ebenezer. Your spirit will join us. But your body...

EBENEZER
Remains here. *(He stares at the bed, afraid)* Will it hurt?

TIM
Not at all. You'll simply fall asleep.

EBENEZER
And never awaken.

MISS POOLE
You will awaken. With us. And you will begin your good work.

EBENEZER
I want that. More than anything. But...

TIM
Fear is a natural thing, especially at a moment like this. But there is something stronger than fear, isn't there?

EBENEZER
(Smiling at him) Yes there is.

(EBENEZER lies on the bed. MISS POOLE goes to him)

MISS POOLE
I have a gift for you, old friend.

EBENEZER
You do?

MISS POOLE
Soon, you shall see the future before you in all its infinite variety. Would you like a glimpse at what is yet to come?

EBENEZER
Oh yes. Yes, very much.

(She puts her hand on his head. The lights go out. In the darkness, the clock tolls midnight. The lamps soon relight themselves, and TIM & MISS POOLE are back to where they were before they were possessed. The window is now shut. EBENEZER's eyes are open. He smiles)

EBENEZER
Oh my. How...wondrous.

(He passes away)

TIM
Uncle Ebenezer?

(MISS POOLE goes to him. She checks his pulse)

TIM
Is he...

(MISS POOLE closes his eyes, then pulls the sheet over him. TIM finally cries. MISS POOLE goes to him. She is tentative at first, but puts her arms around him)

MISS POOLE
There's no shame in your tears. Just means that you loved him.

TIM
Everyone loved him.

MISS POOLE
Would you like a moment? Alone, I mean? I have to...

(TIM takes her hand)

TIM
Please don't go.

MISS POOLE
I won't.

(They are silent for a bit)

MISS POOLE
He was waiting for ghosts.

(TIM stares at her)

MISS POOLE
I'm sorry. I don't mean to sound morbid. Only that...he said that ghosts were coming. At midnight.

TIM
Maybe they're here, and we just can't see them.

MISS POOLE
There's a thought.

(TIM goes to EBENEZER. He places a hand on his shoulder)

TIM
Wherever you are now, Uncle...God bless you.

(The window blows open again. MISS POOLE, startled, goes to TIM & takes his hand. EBENEZER's voice can be heard singing, and from their reactions, it's clear that TIM & MISS POOLE can hear him)

EBENEZER
And all the bells on Earth shall ring on Christmas Day, on Christmas Day

And all the souls on Earth shall sing on Christmas Day in the morning

(Lights fade)

END OF PLAY

10:53

A PLAY BY
ANNIE MARTIN

Cast of Characters

KATHRYN: a late-forty/early-fifty-year-old woman; mother of ZOE
JOHN: an early fifty-year-old man
ZOE: a twenty-two-year-old woman; daughter of KATHRYN
CHRIS: a twenty-something-year-old woman

TIME
Present

PLACE
A Hospice lobby at a hospital in Michigan

10:53 received its world premiere on May 28, 2013 at Williamston Theatre (Williamston, MI). It was directed by Tony Caselli. Set Design by Bartley H. Bauer, Lighting Design by Daniel C. Walker, Sound Design by Michelle Raymond, Costume Design by Holly Iler, Properties by Bruce Bennett. Stage Managed by Stefanie Din & Nan Luchini.

The cast was as follows:

KATHRYN - Sandra Birch
JOHN - John Lepard
ZOE - Zachera Wollenberg
CHRIS - Julia Garlotte

For production rights, contact Annie Martin at annielmartin@gmail.com.

10:53

ACT I
SCENE ONE

(Night time, around 10:30. Lobby on the 8th floor, west wing of a hospital. The lobby is near the elevators and is decorated like you'd expect. Chairs and end tables. Windows on one side, a little area with cabinets, coffee maker, and accessories for drinking coffee. There is also a flat screen television on the wall)

(KATHRYN sits alone, watching a show like Law and Order, and talking on the phone. She has a tote bag and purse, maybe a bottle of water. Her cell phone charger is plugged into an outlet. After watching the show for a few moments, she walks to the TV and changes the channel by pressing the button on the side of the TV. She has to keep stepping back to see what's actually on)

KATHRYN
(Into the phone) Honey, please stop sending me... *(Pause)* But I don't text. *(Pause)* Why don't you just call me...

(JOHN walks down the hallway and, as he waits for the elevator, he hears her conversation and watches)

KATHRYN
It's not quicker for me. *(Pause)* Fine, you text and I'll just call back. *(Pause)* I'm older, not old. *(Sighs, keeps changing the channel)* Oh, Honey. Bridget just got here... gotta... *(Pause)* Yep. I will call you if anything changes. *(Pause)* Love you. Bye. *(KATHRYN hangs up and sits back down. Takes a bite out of a fast food container and sighs. Elevator doors open; JOHN goes in)*

SCENE TWO

(A day later. Same lobby, same time. KATHRYN sits again, watching television. Her still-charging phone is vibrating on the table, but she doesn't get up. JOHN walks by again. KATHRYN and he make quick eye contact)

KATHRYN
Hello.

JOHN
Hi.

(JOHN pushes the elevator button. KATHRYN gets up and changes the channel again. JOHN watches)

SCENE 3

(A day later. Same lobby, same time. KATHRYN is again getting up and down to change the channel. JOHN walks by again and KATHRYN turns at the sound of feet. JOHN nods in acknowledgement and KATHRYN smiles. He heads to the elevator, but then comes back)

JOHN
Excuse me. *(Pause)* Ma'am?

KATHRYN
(Turns around) Me?

JOHN
Yes. They have remotes for those things.

KATHRYN
Remotes?

JOHN
For the TV.

KATHRYN
Oh. Oh.

JOHN
I mean the nurses, at the station

KATHRYN
That makes sense.

JOHN
Yeah.

KATHRYN
Thank you.

JOHN
Sure. That's a tough reach.

KATHRYN
Yeah, but I like the exercise.

JOHN
Exercise?

KATHRYN
Cardio. Gets me up and moving. *(Shows off her walking and button-pushing skills)* See?

JOHN
(His phone vibrates from his pocket) Wow. Hadn't thought about that.

KATHRYN
(Smiles) About two in the morning is when I hit my stride and the sweat really pours.

JOHN
(Smiles; pulls out his cell phone and turns it off. Elevator dings) I'll have to give it a try sometime.

KATHRYN
You should. Have a good night.

JOHN
Thanks. You too.

(KATHRYN finds a program and sits back down)

SCENE 4

(A day later. Same lobby, same time. KATHRYN is sitting, watching the TV again. JOHN walks by and they catch each other's eye)

KATHRYN
Hello.

JOHN
(Pushes the button) Hi. No workout tonight?

KATHRYN
Nope. I think I may have overdone it yesterday.

JOHN
Oh no.

KATHRYN
Happens as we get older.

JOHN
Don't I know it? *(Pause)* Well, have a

good night.

KATHRYN
Thanks. You too.

(KATHRYN goes back to watching TV. Something about the TV catches JOHN's eye. The elevator comes and goes as he's watching the show, confused. A moment passes as they are both engrossed in the TV. JOHN sneezes, KATHRYN jumps)

KATHRYN
Jesus!

JOHN
Sorry.

KATHRYN
I thought you left and...

JOHN
I was leaving and...

JOHN
What are you watching?

KATHRYN
Oh god.

JOHN
Is this supposed to be good?

KATHRYN
This?

JOHN
Yes.

KATHRYN
No.

JOHN
I didn't think so.

KATHRYN
Hey, no judgment. It's not the worst one.

JOHN
No?

KATHRYN
Definitely not.

JOHN
You sure about that?

KATHRYN
Yes. There's good and bad. And then there are the good-bads.

JOHN
Good-bads? Is that an official ranking?

KATHRYN
It's more theory.

JOHN
(Points to the TV) But this is bad.

KATHRYN
It's a good-bad.

JOHN
Right.

KATHRYN
Typically, I would watch this with my blinds drawn, in the privacy of my own home.

JOHN
Because you're ashamed?

KATHRYN
A little.

JOHN
I get the feeling you should be.

KATHRYN
Hey, don't insult The Bachelorette.

JOHN
The Bachelorette?

KATHRYN
Reality show.

JOHN
Never heard of it.

KATHRYN
No?

JOHN
No.

KATHRYN
Really?

JOHN
Honest.

KATHRYN
It's exactly what you'd expect. A woman has something like twenty-five men trying to marry her. She narrows it down every week by giving roses and going on dates and, in the end, she gets engaged.

JOHN
Actually engaged?

KATHRYN
Yep.

JOHN
Do they ever get married?

KATHRYN
Maybe once. Twice.

JOHN
That's love, huh?

KATHRYN
No. Of course not.

JOHN
Because it sounds like prostitution.

KATHRYN
Basically. Although some could argue that marriage is a form of solicitation.

JOHN
What?

KATHRYN
I'm not saying that. I mean, I guess I could probably make an argument that marriage, at its most basic, can sometimes seem like a business arrangement and that sex for money can indeed be part of the contract. Which, in some views, could make it seem like legal prostitution.

JOHN
That's your argument?

KATHRYN
I'm not making an argument, I'm just saying that if I had to make an argument, that might be a path I take.

JOHN
Marriage equals prostitution.

KATHRYN
When did I say that? I didn't say that.

JOHN
You were kind of saying that.

KATHRYN
No. You said this is prostitution. I agreed, but then I...

JOHN
You took it to the next level.

KATHRYN
I did, didn't I? Well, I guess The Bachelorette really makes you think.

JOHN
It does?

KATHRYN
Of course not.

JOHN
It can't.

KATHRYN
Listen, I know this show is bad... it's appalling. I'd never let my daughters go on it, but it's also just stupid and I don't have to think about anything while watching it. And it makes me feel secure in my own life... just comparing it to this.

JOHN
Guilty pleasure. I get it.

KATHRYN
Everyone's got one.

JOHN
Everyone?

KATHRYN
Of course.

JOHN
I hate to ruin your theory, but I don't think I do.

KATHRYN
Trust me, you do.

JOHN
No. Sorry.

KATHRYN
It can be anything.

JOHN
Got nothing.

KATHRYN
I don't believe that.

JOHN
It's true.

KATHRYN
Do you turn on anything to relax, just to veg? Music? TV?

JOHN
NCAA tournaments.

KATHRYN
Well, there you go.

JOHN
Wait a second, basketball isn't a guilty pleasure.

KATHRYN
I think it's stupid.

JOHN
You think basketball is stupid?

KATHRYN
Yeah. You aren't playing. You're doing nothing but watching and yelling at a screen.

JOHN
Millions of people watch it.

KATHRYN
Just like The Bachelorette.

JOHN
No. No. You cannot compare the two.

KATHRYN
You take this very seriously.

JOHN
I just don't think it deserves the same treatment.

KATHRYN
I struck a nerve.

JOHN
No you didn't. I have other things that I'm ashamed of.

KATHRYN
Really?

JOHN
I'm merely pointing out there's no shame in basketball.

KATHRYN
Fair enough. Even if I think there is. So you said you have lots of things to be ashamed.

JOHN
I don't know you.

KATHRYN
I don't know you, but you just encroached on my secret, so let's go. Tit for tat, buddy.

(Pause)

JOHN
I read the Harry Potter books.

KATHRYN
No. Try again.

JOHN
They are kids' books.

KATHRYN
I know but they are amazing.

JOHN
You feel strongly about that.

KATHRYN
I do. Didn't you love them?

JOHN
I did. I read them with my kids.

KATHRYN
Me too. So that doesn't count. Come on. *(JOHN starts to smile)* What is it? You got it don't you?

JOHN
Yep.

KATHRYN
Spit it out.

JOHN
It's more embarrassing than this. *(Pulls out his phone and checks it)*

KATHRYN
Probably not.

JOHN
Oh, it is.

KATHRYN
Come on.

JOHN
Twilight.

KATHRYN
Twilight?

JOHN
Twilight, the teenage vampires...

KATHRYN
Twilight?

JOHN
I read it and actually--

KATHRYN
No.

JOHN
--liked it.

KATHRYN
(Laughing) Ew.

JOHN
I didn't like the movie.

KATHRYN
But you bought the book. And you read it.

JOHN
All four.

KATHRYN
Team Edward or Team Jacob?

JOHN
Edward. *(KATHRYN laughs and he realizes he's said too much)* I burned the books after I read them.

KATHRYN
Thank God.

JOHN
I just wanted to see what the whole thing was about and then... I committed.

KATHRYN
And you liked it?

JOHN
Not like Faulkner or Tolstoy, but... *(Phone vibrates for a second, but he turns it off)* Yep. There you have it. Are we even?

KATHRYN
Yes. I think it was a fair trade off.

JOHN
I think I'm through embarrassing myself tonight.

KATHRYN
No more Bachelorette for you?

JOHN
(Starts to the elevators) No. No offense.

KATHRYN
None could be taken.

JOHN
(Presses the button) All right. Well, thank you for the education.

KATHRYN
You are welcome.

JOHN
Hey, do we have to promise to keep this to ourselves?

KATHRYN
Um, no. We're adults. Unless you feel the need to pinky-swear or something.

JOHN
I'm good.

KATHRYN
Hopefully, I'll see you around again. *(Laughs)*

JOHN
Count on it.

(Elevator arrives)

JOHN
Bye.

KATHRYN
See ya.

(JOHN exits into the elevator. KATHRYN returns her attention to the TV)

SCENE 5

(One night later, lobby again. KATHRYN is drinking a cup of coffee. She looks at the clock, then at the TV. Once more at the clock. JOHN walks by and approaches)

JOHN
Hi.

KATHRYN
Hi. I was wondering if I was going to see you.

JOHN
Always here.

KATHRYN
Me too.

JOHN
How are you?

KATHRYN
Good.

JOHN
Bachelorette?

KATHRYN
Not tonight. *(Pause)* I'm watching your Edward and Jacob

JOHN
What?

KATHRYN
Twilight.

JOHN
You're kidding.

KATHRYN
I would never kid about your secret passion.

JOHN
(Sits down) That's mean.

KATHRYN
You want some coffee?

JOHN
Um...

KATHRYN
Just made it.

JOHN
Eh, hospital coffee?

KATHRYN
No. Good god, that is horrible. I brought in my own.

JOHN
Smart.

KATHRYN
I think so.

JOHN
Then sure, I'll take a cup. *(Sits as KATHRYN pours him a cup)* I was actually coming to find you.

KATHRYN
Really?

JOHN
Yes, I...

KATHRYN
Cream?

JOHN
Black. *(Pause)* I got a gift for you.

KATHRYN
A gift?

JOHN
Just a little something that...

KATHRYN
For me?

JOHN
Don't get excited. It was free.

KATHRYN
Do we know each other well enough to give each other gifts?

(JOHN takes out a television remote)

JOHN
This seems appropriate and not out of line.

KATHRYN
Is that the...

JOHN
Yes, this is called a TV remote.

KATHRYN
Awesome. Let's see if this puppy works. *(Starts to click it)* Ooh.

JOHN
That's luxury.

KATHRYN
VIP treatment. A remote and an uncomfortable sofas.

JOHN
At least the coffee isn't crap, right?

KATHRYN
Amen.

(They sort of toast each other and both drink. The coffee is horrible. JOHN's face expresses this)

KATHRYN
I thought you were going someplace really creepy for a second with that whole "I got you a gift thing", but I'm sorry... obviously not the case. This is... so kind.

JOHN
It was nothing.

KATHRYN
Thank you.

JOHN
They said just throw it on one of the tables out here.

KATHRYN
I'd never throw it anywhere.

JOHN
See? You didn't even know how much you wanted one.

KATHRYN
You may be right. This is great. Although my exercise--

JOHN
Right. Well, this is a workout for your fingers.

KATHRYN
Thank you.

JOHN
Really. It was nothing.

(Pause)

KATHRYN
It's funny...

JOHN
Yes, it is.

KATHRYN
What's funny?

JOHN
I don't know.

KATHRYN
What?

JOHN
I was agreeing.

KATHRYN
With what?

JOHN
That it was funny.

KATHRYN
But I didn't say what it was.

JOHN
I know.

KATHRYN
You were just going to agree with whatever I said?

JOHN
Looks that way.

KATHRYN
So that was...

JOHN
Overeager. Over-active listening. That's embarrassing.

KATHRYN
I was going to say it's funny-- I have no idea what your name is.

JOHN
That's not funny, though. *(She just looks at him)* Neither am I, apparently. I'm John.

KATHRYN
Hi John. Kathryn. *(KATHRYN's cell phone vibrates loudly on the table)* My daughter. Zoe. *(Picks up her phone and reads a text)*

JOHN
Ah.

KATHRYN
Goes to school in Chicago. Coming home tomorrow.

JOHN
(A vibrating from JOHN's cell phone) She driving or training it?

KATHRYN
Train.

JOHN
Good. I always liked the train.

KATHRYN
Yeah?

JOHN
Oh yeah. Took it every summer with my folks-- Detroit to Chicago and back.

KATHRYN
That's nice. I always drive. I guess I prefer it.

JOHN
That's a control thing.

KATHRYN
Maybe. Probably. *(Pause)* It's on.

JOHN
(Looks at the TV) You really are watching it?

KATHRYN
I told you.

JOHN
Oh god.

KATHRYN
You are welcome to watch it with me.

JOHN
No.

KATHRYN
Will you cry? Is that why?

JOHN
You're a mind reader.

KATHRYN
I can spot a crier.

JOHN
I'm not a crier.

KATHRYN
No?

JOHN
No. I mean, I might cry when I'm sad. I'm not sad that often. Sometimes I'm sad.

KATHRYN
He doth protest too much.

JOHN
I could prove you wrong, but I've actually gotta be on my way.

KATHRYN
That's rather convenient.

JOHN
I could come back.

KATHRYN
Don't worry about it. I was just being a pain.

JOHN
(Turns off the cellphone alarm) Oh. OK. Well, it was no pain.

KATHRYN
Thanks for the remote.

JOHN
You're welcome. I'll see you around Kat.

KATHRYN
You know where I live. *(Indicating the lobby)* Oh wait, don't forget your coffee.

(JOHN saunters to the elevator and throws out his cup of coffee. KATHRYN bangs her head with the remote and Twilight music can be heard. Elevator doors open. Elevator door closes)

SCENE 6

(One day later. Night time but an hour earlier, lobby again. JOHN walks by and looks around for KATHRYN, but doesn't see her. He presses the elevator button, but continues to casually look around. When the doors open, two girls are laughing, holding hands, and cuddling. They walk out. JOHN sees them and they see him)

JOHN
Hi.

ZOE
Yeah. Hi.

CHRIS
Hi.

(JOHN gets on the elevator)

ZOE
Perv.

CHRIS
Stop.

ZOE
Seriously. He was, like, ogling us.

CHRIS
Whatever.

ZOE
(Looks around) Where is she?

CHRIS
(Takes her hand and kisses it) How you doing?

ZOE
Fine. It's all fine.

CHRIS
Liar.

ZOE
Yep. (Looks around and sees her mom's bags in the lobby) This is her stuff. Where is she?

CHRIS
Hey. (Gives ZOE a kiss) It's gonna be OK.

(ZOE kisses her back. Then KATHRYN walks in and ZOE jumps)

KATHRYN
Zo?

ZOE
(Goes to hug her) Hey Mom! (They hug)

KATHRYN
You didn't call? I was...

ZOE
I came straight here.

KATHRYN
You look good. Are you sleeping? You look tired. Exhausted really.

ZOE
I'm glad I look good and like shit at the same time. I don't know how that's possible, but...

KATHRYN
That's not what I meant.

ZOE
How's he doing? Is he awake anymore?

KATHRYN
Basically he's... he sleeps a lot. But he'll be happy you're here.

ZOE
He won't even know.

KATHRYN
Of course he will. They say he can still hear you.

ZOE
OK. OK.

KATHRYN
(Hugs her again) Everyone here has been great. The nurses are amazing. Funny and nice. They would do anything for him.

ZOE
That's good.

KATHRYN
Bridget's been here all week.

ZOE
Well, she doesn't work or go to school, so...

KATHRYN
She said she'll see you tomorrow.

ZOE
Ok.

KATHRYN
(Noticing CHRIS) Hello.

CHRIS
Hi.

ZOE
Mom. This is Chris.

KATHRYN
Hi Chris. Kathryn.

CHRIS
Hi.

ZOE
I mentioned she might be coming with me.

KATHRYN
You did? *(Pause)* Oh my god, yes. I remember. I thought Chris was a boy, your boyfriend. I was wondering what the hell you were thinking bringing home a boy to meet us at a time like this. *(To CHRIS)* I'm glad you're here, Chris. Sorry for the confusion. My brain must not be…

ZOE
Mom.

KATHRYN
What?

ZOE
She's my boyfriend.

KATHRYN
What?

ZOE
We're together. Girlfriends.

KATHRYN
It's important to have girlfriends. *(To CHRIS)* So thank you.

CHRIS
(To KATHRYN) You're welcome.

ZOE
Mom, we're in a relationship. *(Pause)* Mom, do you understand? *(Pause)* We love each other. We have sex. *(Pause)* Mom? *(Pause)* Mother? *(Pause)* Hello?

KATHRYN
Yes.

ZOE
Can you say something?

KATHRYN
No.

ZOE
No?

KATHRYN
You don't want me to say anything right at this moment.

CHRIS
I'm gonna go get something to drink.

ZOE
No. Stay.

KATHRYN
(To CHRIS) Follow your instincts.

CHRIS
How about I just go over here, OK?

(CHRIS walks over to the other bench of chairs and picks up a magazine. There's a moment of awkwardness between ZOE and KATHRYN, but that soon passes for anger)

ZOE
How dare you treat her like--

KATHRYN
How dare you treat me or her like that?

ZOE
You tried to kick her out--

KATHRYN
What the hell are you thinking?

ZOE
Are you gonna kick me out now? Disown me and--

KATHRYN
Keep your voice down.

ZOE
No. I won't. I'm not ashamed.

KATHRYN
Shut up.

ZOE
You shut up.

KATHRYN
You're a goddamn lesbian now?

ZOE
I'm bi.

CHRIS
I am too.

(Pause)

KATHRYN
(To CHRIS) Uh-huh. Yeah, OK. *(To ZOE)* I told you it was inappropriate to bring someone home. This is a private time for our family and to bring in a new element... no matter the element. It's unacceptable. That's not what we need. And I can't deal with it...

ZOE
It's what *I* need.

KATHRYN
You don't need her to--

ZOE
I love her.

KATHRYN
Sure.

ZOE
I do.

KATHRYN
We can talk about this later.

ZOE
This?

KATHRYN
Zoe, be here. This is about family.

ZOE
She is my family.

KATHRYN
You can't be family after knowing someone what... two weeks?

ZOE
Don't do that. Don't reduce my feelings to a--

KATHRYN
OK. OK. OK. Let's stop. Breathe. *(Breathes)* I understand you are going through things. We are all going through things. But this is about being supportive of each other.

ZOE
So be supportive.

KATHRYN
I am supportive. I am not supportive of this method right now. But I understand that perhaps this is how you are dealing with it.

ZOE
I suddenly like girls because Dad's dying?

KATHRYN
I understand you're scared. This is all a lot to process. Trust me. I get it. And I want to be here for you. This is a moment. Your moment. Our moment. And this moment with you and Chris can and should happen later.

CHRIS
Sure.

ZOE
Mom, with Chris... I don't have to worry about her loss, about her emotions, I can just be. She reminds me that I've got a lot more life ahead of me. That this is just one horrible moment in my life, just one. With her here, I don't feel like I need to roll up into a ball and die. She gets me. She understands and she...

KATHRYN
Honey...

ZOE
Won't let me fall.

KATHRYN
I won't let you fall.

ZOE
Of course you will. I mean, I'm gonna fall. We are all gonna fall. We already are.

KATHRYN
You're right. But, as a family, we'll be able to share--

ZOE
Mom, I love you, but just because I go through this with you, it doesn't mean you and I will bond over it. Doesn't mean it will be the same for either of us.

KATHRYN
Why are you making this so hard?

ZOE
You're not listening. I can't take on your issues now.

KATHRYN
Excuse me? I didn't ask you to.

ZOE
You never do and yet somehow I always end up with...

KATHRYN
Are you kidding me?

ZOE
No.

KATHRYN
Do you ever think about anyone other than yourself?

ZOE
Nope.

KATHRYN
Good. Great.

ZOE
Did Bridget bring Damon over here?

KATHRYN
Yes.

ZOE
Does Damon get to be here?

KATHRYN
Damon is like family. Chris, you seem nice, but I don't know you. You don't know me.

CHRIS
I look forward to getting to--

ZOE
Then get to know her.

KATHRYN
Every time I try with anyone you bring home, they're gone the next day.

CHRIS
Really?

ZOE
Now you think I'm a slut or something?

KATHRYN
(Pauses) Let me repeat. This is not

about Bridget or you or Chris. This is about the appropriateness of...

ZOE
Fuck appropriate. I'm sorry I'm not a fucking bore like Bridge. I'm sorry I can't be like her--

KATHRYN
(Interrupting) Your sister is practical, yes, but...

ZOE
--and settle with some dude who happened to be the only guy I've ever slept with.

KATHRYN
Don't talk about her like that.

ZOE
I'm in love. Accept it.

KATHRYN
I do. It's just how frequently you happen to fall in love. You don't know what it means to be...

ZOE
You don't know how I feel.

KATHRYN
You just like the excitement of--

ZOE
Yes, I do. I love love. The infatuation, the constant thinking about that person, the sick yummy feeling it gives you to even be near them—

CHRIS
I love it too.

ZOE
But I also love the fighting, the hating—how can I hate the person I want so much, the pushing and shoving for domination, for being right, and I love the devastation I feel when my heart breaks.

CHRIS
I don't. I hate that.

ZOE
I might not love it at the time, but I do love it. The clichés are all true and then I somehow dig my way out and it happens again a little different. It makes me feel so alive.

KATHRYN
Those sounds like the dreams of a little girl who has watched too many movies.

ZOE
It's not.

KATHRYN
It is. Hate to burst your bubble, sweetheart, but nothing that you just said can last. Reality comes in to play. Real life comes knocking and you better hold on because you get stuff like mortgages, bills more than you can imagine, children, aging, joblessness, and yes even illness. So, that really exciting love that you're talking about fades and is replaced with reality. You'll see.

ZOE
I've already seen. I lived with you and Dad. Trust me, it's amazing I even want to fall in love after living with that horror show of a marriage.

CHRIS
Zoe.

ZOE
I'm sorry.

KATHRYN
No you aren't. And I don't accept.

ZOE
Mom.

(KATHRYN leaves. ZOE follows after and then decides against it)

ZOE
That was fun. *(Starts to cry)*

CHRIS
Oh babe. *(Comes to comfort her)* I love you.

SCENE 7

(About an hour later, lobby again. KATHRYN is lying very still on the sofa staring at the TV, which is on QVC. The elevator opens and out comes JOHN, who looks around for a minute. He doesn't see KATHRYN and then presses the down button. KATHRYN hears this and pokes her head up. They see each other immediately)

BOTH
Hey.

KATHRYN
Hi.

JOHN
Hi. *(Pause)* What're you doing?

KATHRYN
Nothing. What are you doing?

JOHN
Just my normal walk around. Figured I'd find you here.

KATHRYN
Where else?

JOHN
I think I might've seen your daughter earlier.

KATHRYN
Here?

JOHN
At least I thought it was. She looked a lot like you.

KATHRYN
She does not look like me.

JOHN
This girl did. She was with her... friend?

KATHRYN
Oh Jesus. *(Lays back down)*

JOHN
(Comes over) So it's been a good night.

KATHRYN
It's been one of those nights that will go down in history.

JOHN
So you didn't know she was a... a... is she a...

KATHRYN
Lesbian? Yes. I mean, no. She's bi. Bisexual. Yep. Bi-sex-ual.

JOHN
Maybe she's just going through...

KATHRYN
Hey listen, I'm an open person. I am. I mean, if that's what she needs to be, to be happy, great. Besides that this literally came out of nowhere, she decides now, right now, is the perfect time to introduce the girlfriend to the family and then to top it all off, she tells me I am a horrible mother. I just wanted to hit her. I mean, HIT HER.

JOHN
My daughter once said I was the reason she was in therapy.

KATHRYN
No.

JOHN
Yeah.

KATHRYN
What did you say?

JOHN
I told her that was the reason I agreed to pay for it.

KATHRYN
John.

JOHN
What am I supposed to say? You can't argue with them. If that's how they feel, OK.

KATHRYN
It's not OK.

JOHN
(Pause) What am I supposed to do, Kat? Punish myself by watching... *(Looks at the TV)* Are you seriously watching this? That's Marie Osmond. *(Indicating to the TV)*

KATHRYN
(Laughs) And her dolls.

JOHN
She makes dolls?

KATHRYN
Apparently.

JOHN
For children?

KATHRYN
Adults.

JOHN
Well, that's scary.

KATHRYN
Yes.

JOHN
You could buy Zoe one.

KATHRYN
What will that do?

JOHN
Confuse her.

KATHRYN
And?

JOHN
That's it.

KATHRYN
I should do that.

JOHN
Make sure it's a scary one.

KATHRYN
I think they all are. I made coffee.

JOHN
(Gets up) You want a cup?

KATHRYN
I can get it.

JOHN
I think I can handle it.

KATHRYN
OK then. Yes. Please. *(Silence, then she laughs)* I did something wrong.

JOHN
And you're laughing about it?

KATHRYN
It's not very nice.

JOHN
(Pours her coffee) Can't be nice all the time.

KATHRYN
I wanted to see how he'd react.

JOHN
Who?

KATHRYN
My husband.

JOHN
And?

KATHRYN
Well, he's officially dying.

JOHN
Ah. I'm sorry. *(Hands her a cup of coffee)*

KATHRYN
Thanks. Didn't even make a peep or moan. Nothing. I leaned over the bed and I said, "Zoe's here. She's here and she brought a friend. Her girlfriend." I waited. Nothing. Then I said "our daughter just came out to me as a lesbian bisexual and brought home a girlfriend named Chris." I just stared, waited and got nothing.

JOHN
Well.

KATHRYN
If he was really there, he'd have shot up or done something. Trust me. I just wanted to tell him because...

JOHN
You wanted to share it with him.

KATHRYN
I kinda just wanted to see what would happen. That's horrible.

JOHN
Nah.

KATHRYN
It is, but he's just not there, you know. *(Pause)* Tell me something. Talk to me.

JOHN
About?

KATHRYN
Anything. Anything good.

JOHN
OK.

KATHRYN
Any time.

JOHN
OK. *(Long pause)* I..I...I got nothing.

KATHRYN
What do you mean you've got nothing?

JOHN
I don't do well under pressure.

KATHRYN
Are you kidding me?

JOHN
Don't judge.

KATHRYN
I'm just shocked.

JOHN
Come on. Just wait a second. *(Pause)* When I got up this morning, I noticed it was a perfect Fall day. It's my favorite time of year.

KATHRYN
Everything is dying.

JOHN
No. It's just transition, change. The leaves and flowers come back in the spring. But the colors--right before they drop for good--they are electric. And the smell of burning leaves and the dampness... the kind of mildew that surround you as you...

KATHRYN
Mildew?

JOHN
Mildew.

KATHRYN
You like mildew?

JOHN
Only in this context. Don't make fun.

KATHRYN
Well, you *are* talking about mildew like it's an aphrodisiac.

JOHN
You're mocking me.

KATHRYN
Don't get defensive.

JOHN
Oh, yes, your highness.

KATHRYN
I apologize for hurting your sensibilities.

JOHN
I will ignore that tone.

KATHRYN
Please do. *(Pause)* Please.

JOHN
So I started to think about all the things I haven't done in a while. Orchards. Cider. Pumpkins. About this time of year, we used to take the kids to the orchard. To pick apples, eat doughnuts and cider.

KATHRYN
We only took the girls once.

JOHN
Once?

KATHRYN
Yeah. It was OK. The girls were little so they liked it.

JOHN
It's not just for little kids. It's fun even when they get older. Something about that place, we all fell into our roles. My daughter picking out the five-ton pumpkin no one could carry, my son chucking apples at his sister, and, inevitably, on the way home... and, I swear to God, this happened every year... one of them would barf in the car.

KATHRYN
That doesn't sound fun.

JOHN
No, that was terrible. It was like clockwork, but never once did we come prepared. It was like we forgot every year until the moment we heard "I don't feel so good."

KATHRYN
(Laughing) I know those words well.

(CHRIS and ZOE walk down the hallway and ZOE stops CHRIS as she sees her mom talking with John. They watch from a distance)

JOHN
We always went. Always just loved it. I don't know why we stopped going.

KATHRYN
Kids grow up.

JOHN
Yes. They do and they become involved with everything else except their family.

KATHRYN
Yep. Although now I can't stop picturing those doughnuts. Hungry and curious, thanks. Maybe I'll have to give the orchard a try again.

JOHN
You should. I can tell you the best ones or I'll even go with you.

KATHRYN
As my guide?

JOHN
Yeah. You're a novice. You could screw up the whole thing. I mean, do you even know how to dunk a doughnut properly?

KATHRYN
There's a specific way?

JOHN
Kat.

KATHRYN
You are making this up. That's like caring about the type of apple you eat. It's an apple.

JOHN
Kat, you are killing me. You are a Michigan girl. You should know about apples.

KATHRYN
There's a difference between knowing and caring.

JOHN
You need more help than I thought. We'll start you with a Golden Delicious.

KATHRYN
Those are red ones?

JOHN
Lady!

(KATHRYN laughs)

JOHN
And here I am trying to be nice and talk about good things.

KATHRYN
It is nice. Go on. I won't say anything else. Promise.

JOHN
Don't make promises you can't keep.

KATHRYN
I don't. So, I'll get a Golden Delicious and what's next?

JOHN
You'll eat it. We'll sit you on a hill. And you'll look at the trees and eat your apple and think about nothing and everything.

KATHRYN
It's that simple?

JOHN
Yeah, it is.

KATHRYN
I'm sold. If not this year…

JOHN
Then maybe next. Maybe you can take your daughter and her girlfriend. (KATHRYN stops smiling) Or not. (Looks at the clock and his pocket buzzes)

KATHRYN
You need to go?

JOHN
I do.

KATHRYN
No worries. Thank you for talking to me.

JOHN
Thank you for talking to me.

KATHRYN
You know what I mean. I'll see you…

JOHN
Tomorrow?

KATHRYN
Perfect.

JOHN
Nite, Kat.

KATHRYN
Have a good night, John.

(JOHN leaves and throws the coffee out again. KATHRYN watches TV smiling. ZOE looks at CHRIS)

ZOE
Who the hell is that?

CHRIS
Remember, you are gonna apologize.

ZOE
Yeah. Yeah. Who the hell was that?

(ZOE marches in. CHRIS just sighs)

SCENE 8

(The next night. Lobby again. KATHRYN is crying in her chair. It's not a loud cry, but it's probably ugly. She's trying to keep it private. The television is, of course, on. After a few moments, JOHN walks in. He sees her and comes in with two coffees)

JOHN
I thought you might like something better than the... *(Sees she's crying)* Kat. What's wrong? *(KATHRYN shakes her head - no words can get out)* I... I... what can I do? *(KATHRYN shakes her head "No")* OK. OK. *(He sits)* I'm here.

KATHRYN
(Sobbing) It's Derrick.

JOHN
(Arm around her) I'm sorry. *(KATHRYN nods)* It's going to be OK.

KATHRYN
This is so silly. I'm sorry. *(Wipes her eyes with her tissue, but needs another one. She rummages through her purse)*

JOHN
It's not silly. It's human. It's completely natural.

KATHRYN
It's stupid. This is stupid. But... I can't help it.

JOHN
You're supposed to cry. *(Gets up and gets a handful of paper towels and brings them to KATHRYN)*

KATHRYN
(Taking the paper towel) Thank you.

JOHN
What can I do to help?

KATHRYN
(Laughing) Nothing. I'll be fine. I feel better already.

JOHN
OK.

KATHRYN
Feels good to get it out. Let's talk about something else. What were you saying?

JOHN
When?

KATHRYN
Before. Something about me liking something.

JOHN
Coffee. I brought you a coffee. *(Hands it to her)* You don't have to...

KATHRYN
(Takes a huge gulp) Mmmhmm. Thank you. I needed this...

JOHN
How are the girls? Are they...

KATHRYN
They're good. How are you doing?

JOHN
I'm fine... Are you OK? I mean, you aren't OK, but I think you might be in shock.

KATHRYN
Why?

JOHN
Because of Derrick.

KATHRYN
No, I've seen it before.

JOHN
Before?

KATHRYN
Last year.

JOHN
He died last year?

KATHRYN
It's a repeat.

JOHN
I'm a little confused.

KATHRYN
He lives. He makes it.

JOHN
Derrick?

KATHRYN
Yes, Christina operates on him. Saves him.

JOHN
Who's Christina?

KATHRYN
Meredith's best friend. And Meredith saves Owen.

JOHN
Meredith? Your other daughter?

KATHRYN
What?

JOHN
Who's Meredith?

KATHRYN
Meredith Grey.

JOHN
Is that a relative?

KATHRYN
On Grey's Anatomy.

JOHN
But your husband...

KATHRYN
Paul?

JOHN
Wait, are you--

KATHRYN
I feel you're confused.

JOHN
Your husband died.

KATHRYN
Paul died?

JOHN
I don't know.

KATHRYN
Did Paul die?

JOHN
Isn't that why you're crying?

KATHRYN
No.

JOHN
No?

KATHRYN
It was a sad episode.

JOHN
So nobody died?

KATHRYN
Here?

JOHN
Yes.

KATHRYN
No. It's Grey's Anatomy. TV.

JOHN
Jesus!

KATHRYN
Did you think I was... *(Laughing)* Sorry.

JOHN
It's not funny.

KATHRYN
It is.

JOHN
It's not. What was I supposed to think with you here and crying and...

KATHRYN
I get it.

JOHN
TV?

KATHRYN
Yep.

JOHN
That's stupid.

KATHRYN
It's not stupid.

JOHN
Isn't that a hospital show?

KATHRYN
And?

JOHN
And you don't think that's a little odd.

KATHRYN
Out of everything going on, do I think it's odd I like to watch a television show?

JOHN
Forget it.

KATHRYN
No. I think it's odd that I got a little shot of excitement and fear when you mentioned that Paul died.

JOHN
But he didn't.

KATHRYN
Yeah, but I can't tell if I'm happy or sad about that.

JOHN
I think that's normal.

KATHRYN
It is? Is it normal to be relieved that your husband's never gonna wake up again? Because it's one less person to pretend for. It's like I'm following a script; I'm in one of these shows. And when those doctors told us news, more horrible news, they waited for me to cry on cue. There was this pause in their speech that indicated that I was supposed to cry. I did. And then Paul would sometimes look at me, and I'd give him some tears. We would pretend that we were that couple that we've always see on these shows, right.

JOHN
Kat, you don't have to tell me this

KATHRYN
I don't love him, John. I mean I do, *(Pause)* but not really. I did. A long time ago. I think I did. And I don't think he loves me. And we are both maybe ok with that. I feel bad for him, sad really. He's too young. And it's horribly unfair to the girls. They love him and it's been so hard. Hard on all of us, but then I think maybe this is just the change I need. Right? Maybe I can start over. Here my chance and then I think of all the things I don't know. That I don't want to know. That I will be forced to know. And if it was my choice. If this was all my choice, then maybe it'd be ok, but I don't know how to run the mower. No idea. And I don't understand IRAs and our 401K. It's not a female thing, it's a me thing. I've tried and I don't get it. That was his job. And

gas grills scare me and I hate spiders. He killed the spiders. And I can hire people to do repairs, but how do I know that I'm not getting ripped off. Who am I supposed to ask? And I always figured if we were robbed, he gets shot first because I would make him go check on the sound. Now I have to go and I have to get shot. This is what I think about and you know what, there's a lot of other stuff I don't even know about yet. And I'm too old to learn and I don't want to make more mistakes. Ok, wait maybe not too old, but too tired, too lazy, too something. We ran a tight home, tight life. And while I've daydreamed of changing it, of wanting something more, maybe there's a reason it never happened. And so you know, I watch tv here. I like it here. Right here. It feels good. I got my coffee. The cafeteria is actually pretty good. The magazines are stellar. And I mean this is a nicer tv than I've got at home. People leave me alone here. When I go home... home sucks. The neighbors come over demanding updates, the family wants to know why I'm not here with him. And right here, I'm close enough to Paul. And so you know, watching grey's anatomy doesn't feel odd to me. It feels normal. So yeah. *(Takes a sip of the coffee)* Thank you for the coffee.

(JOHN just sits as KATHRYN drinks. She changes the channel. Silence still)

KATHRYN
Stop looking at me like that.

JOHN
I'm not.

(Pause)

KATHRYN
I'm replaying what I just said, hearing what I actually said, and your look...

JOHN
There's no look.

KATHRYN
And that sounded really bad. I sound really bad.

JOHN
It didn't. I...

KATHRYN
I don't think I meant that. Who says that?

JOHN
You.

KATHRYN
That's not a good answer

JOHN
I liked it.

KATHRYN
Please. Did you listen to any of that?

JOHN
I did.

KATHRYN
Are you thinking "what a bitch?"

JOHN
No. Not at all.

KATHRYN
Why not?

JOHN
Because it makes sense to me.

KATHRYN
Really.

JOHN
Yes.

KATHRYN
So I should think less of you as well?

JOHN
Looks that way.

(A beat)

KATHRYN
And then there's you.

JOHN
Me?

KATHRYN
You and the TV. I feel kind of normal with you. Not so unsure of everything.

JOHN
You always seem sure.

KATHRYN
I do?

(KATHRYN kisses him and he kisses her back. This kiss isn't a hungry, eat-your-face kiss, but a kiss that is simply that - two lips that are meant to be attached to each other. John pulls away. At the same time, CHRIS walks in with a bag of chips and pop. She sees JOHN and KATHRYN and freezes. They don't see her)

JOHN
Kat.

KATHRYN
I'm sorry?

JOHN
Are you?

KATHRYN
Are you?

JOHN
No.

KATHRYN
Me neither. *(Goes back in for another kiss)*

JOHN
Hold on. Hold on. I have to... tell you. For the past sixteen years, every night, I've been coming to this hospital.

KATHRYN
What?

JOHN
You should know that--

(CHRIS opens her bag of chips and begins to eat them while watching the events unfold)

KATHRYN
Are you sick? *(Touches his face)*

JOHN
No. I'm dying.

KATHRYN
So, you're sick?

JOHN
No. Listen.

KATHRYN
Just tell me.

JOHN
I'm trying.

KATHRYN
OK.

JOHN
I have an ability. Not an ability. Maybe more like a curse. I know the time of my death. I'm dying at 10:53.

KATHRYN
10:53?

JOHN
I've known this since I was younger. And so, because of this, because I know the time of my death, I come to the ER every night just before 10:53 to make sure it doesn't happen. And I know this sounds crazy.

KATHRYN
Yes. It does.

JOHN
I know. I know, but...

KATHRYN
Did you say sixteen years?

JOHN
Yes, but...

KATHRYN
(Smiles) You don't have to explain.

JOHN
There's more.

KATHRYN
I don't really think I wanna hear more. (Laughs) In fact, I know I don't.

JOHN
This isn't a joke.

KATHRYN
Oh, it is. It's a cosmic joke.

JOHN
I'm trying to be honest.

KATHRYN
(Laughs) Ok.

JOHN
Kat.

KATHRYN
(Laughing as she gathers her purse) Wow. Wow. I am... I am... (Laughing harder) I'm a fucking idiot.

JOHN
No.

KATHRYN
This is good. Thank you. Thank you. (Laughing as she heads out)

JOHN
You are not an idiot. I thought I should tell you.

KATHRYN
Yeah, yeah, absolutely. Have a great night. I hope you don't die.

JOHN
Can't you just wait? (Pause) Kat! (Pause) Please.

(KATHRYN is continuing to laugh painfully and walk toward the rooms in the hospital. She passes CHRIS)

JOHN
(Overlapping KATHRYN) Please just give me a second to explain.

KATHRYN
(To CHRIS) Is Zoe in there?

CHRIS
Yes.

JOHN
Kat?

KATHRYN
Great. Thanks. (Walks in the other direction)

JOHN
Don't go. Please. Just give me a... (KATHRYN's gone) Shit.

(CHRIS walks over with her chips and pop and sits a few seats away from JOHN. She then picks up the remote and begins to flip through the stations. Vibrations can be heard in JOHN's pants. JOHN looks at CHRIS and takes out his phone)

CHRIS
(Offering the bag to JOHN) Chip?

(JOHN gets up and leaves)

BLACKOUT

END OF ACT ONE

ACT TWO
SCENE ONE

(The next night. Around the same time, lobby again. KATHRYN, ZOE, and CHRIS are sitting around watching TV. ZOE has the remote and is flipping through channels)

KATHRYN
Will you just pick something?

ZOE
I'm looking.

KATHRYN
You've been looking for a half hour. Just leave it on a station.

ZOE
I wish they had good cable.

CHRIS
HBO or something.

ZOE
Right?

KATHRYN
Then go home and watch something there.

ZOE
We don't have HBO.

CHRIS
(To KATHRYN) Is there anything you want? Did you see something?

KATHRYN
I couldn't even tell what she flew past. I think American Idol is on.

ZOE
Oh god, you watch that? It's so... stupid.

KATHRYN
You used to watch it.

ZOE
I did not.

KATHRYN
You did.

CHRIS
I don't think less of you, babe.

ZOE
Shut up.

CHRIS
Let's watch it.

ZOE
No.

CHRIS
For your mom.

ZOE
(Pause) Fine. *(Turns it to American Idol)* Happy?

CHRIS
(Grabs her hand) Yes. *(They watch)*

ZOE
I'm sorry, I can't. *(Flips the station)*

CHRIS
Zo.

KATHRYN
You really can go home. There's no need to stay.

ZOE
(Flipping) Just hold on.

(CHRIS grabs the remote and gives it to KATHRYN)

ZOE
HEY!

CHRIS
Kathryn. Save us.

ZOE
Thanks a lot. *(Pushes CHRIS)*

CHRIS
You're annoying. *(Pushes her back)*

ZOE
You're more annoying. *(Pushes her and playfully twists her arm)*

CHRIS
Ow.

ZOE
Apologize.

CHRIS
Never.

ZOE
Come on.

CHRIS
(Puts her onto the ground) Please. You can't beat me. *(They both laugh. There is a sexual tension in the air)*

KATHRYN
Girls, get up. *(Flips through channels)*

ZOE
Tell her to get off me.

CHRIS
(Whispering) You sure you want that?

(ZOE smiles)

KATHRYN
I'm right here.

CHRIS
I'm sorry. That was.. sorry. I…

ZOE
We're all adults.

KATHRYN
Are we?

ZOE
Nice, mom. *(Looks at TV)* Friends?

KATHRYN
Yes.

ZOE
OK.

CHRIS
Great.

(They sit and watch. ZOE and CHRIS are trying to be discreetly close without letting on to KATHRYN, which is just stupid. They mouth "I love you" to each other, squeeze each other's legs, and things of that nature. KATHRYN gets up to get coffee and takes the remote with her. JOHN walks in with a bag of donuts and cider and looks around for KATHRYN. CHRIS and ZOE see this. KATHRYN sees this and tries to walk away before she is seen by JOHN)

JOHN
Kathryn.

KATHRYN
(Sees JOHN) Oh, Hi John.

JOHN
Hi.

KATHRYN
I was just going to check on… getting coffee.

JOHN
(Walking toward her) Do you have a minute to talk?

ZOE
(To JOHN) I saw you the other day.

JOHN
(To ZOE) Ok. *(To KATHRYN)* Kat, I was…

ZOE
You work here?

JOHN
At the hospital? No.

ZOE
But you work?

CHRIS
I apologize for her. She's…

JOHN
Yes. I do. *(To KATHRYN)* Just a couple minutes...

ZOE
But not here?

JOHN
No.

KATHRYN
(Comes and sits back down) No time. Not really.

ZOE
(To JOHN) You seem to be here a lot.

JOHN
(To KATHRYN) Listen, if you could give me five minutes...

KATHRYN
We are kind of having a girl's night here, so...

(The dialogue here should slightly overlap with ZOE and CHRIS talking - with ZOE trying to listen in, JOHN trying to talk with KATHRYN, and KATHRYN trying not to talk to anyone)

ZOE
We are?

CHRIS
(To ZOE) Babe, let's go get some food. I'm starving.

(CHRIS pulls ZOE up and tries to walk her away. ZOE is interested in what is going on with her mom and JOHN)

ZOE
We just ate.

JOHN
Kat. I know you must have questions.

KATHRYN
No. Not really.

CHRIS
(To ZOE) Come on.

ZOE
Hold on.

KATHRYN
(Watching TV) Oh, I love this episode.

JOHN
I'm sorry.

KATHRYN
It's the smelly cat one.

(JOHN sits down next to KATHRYN)

JOHN
I ruined the moment and I...

KATHRYN
Please don't do that.

JOHN
I... it's hard for me to talk about...

KATHRYN
I just wanna watch TV. That's it.

CHRIS
(Pushing ZOE) Just give them a....

ZOE
Mom, you OK?

KATHRYN
I'm fine. It's all fine

JOHN
Zoe, can you give us a minute?

ZOE
Zoe? You don't know me.

JOHN
You're Zoe.

CHRIS
Babe, come on.

JOHN
I'm John.

ZOE
So?

CHRIS
Zoe. Now.

JOHN
(To KATHRYN) I wanted to make sure you were OK.

CHRIS
Zo!

KATHRYN
I am. Thank you.

ZOE
What is going on?

KATHRYN
Nothing. Absolutely nothing.

CHRIS
See? Come on. Kathryn, you want anything?

KATHRYN
No. Just gonna watch my show.

CHRIS
(Finally making headway with ZOE) Come on, brute.

(ZOE starts to walk with CHRIS, but slowly)

JOHN
(To KATHRYN) I didn't mean to surprise you, not after... you know, but...

KATHRYN
I'm watching.

JOHN
It meant something.

KATHRYN
OK. But I just wanna watch...

JOHN
I thought I should be honest. It was the wrong moment. It was...

ZOE
Did you guys have sex?

JOHN
No!

KATHRYN
NO!

CHRIS
They just kissed.

ZOE
WHAT?!?

KATHRYN
Chris!

JOHN
Jesus.

ZOE
You what?

KATHRYN
Honey.

CHRIS
They kissed, babe.

ZOE
(To JOHN) You kissed her? You kissed her?

CHRIS
Come on, remember we're all adults.

(ZOE pushes him and is ready to fight)

JOHN
Shit.

KATHRYN
Zoe!

CHRIS
(Tackling ZOE) Stop. Stop.

ZOE
(Yelling) How dare you? Trolling around here--

CHRIS
(To ZOE) Stop.

ZOE
--for women who are lonely and sad and pathetic like her.

KATHRYN
Hey!

ZOE
It's disgusting.

JOHN
There's no trolling, no hitting on.

CHRIS
Maybe a little.

KATHRYN
Zo.

ZOE
I knew it.

KATHRYN
Zoe Elizabeth.

CHRIS
(To ZOE) She kissed him.

KATHRYN
Oh god.

ZOE
She what?

CHRIS
She was having a moment.

ZOE
(To KATHRYN) You?

CHRIS
Hold on.

ZOE
Did you?

KATHRYN
Is there any way we can not talk about this?

JOHN
It was my fault.

ZOE
Like I don't know that.

CHRIS
Hon. Hon.

ZOE
(To CHRIS) How long have you known?

CHRIS
Since last night.

ZOE
Why didn't you tell me?

CHRIS
I didn't want to upset you.

JOHN
Unlike now?

CHRIS
I'm not gonna lie to her.

(KATHRYN goes back to the sofa and sits)

ZOE
Mother.

KATHRYN
I'm not discussing this.

CHRIS
(To ZOE) She didn't know he was... off.

JOHN
"He" meaning me?

ZOE
Off?

JOHN
I'm not off. I mean, everyone is a little off.

ZOE
How? How is he "off"?

CHRIS
It's hard to explain.

JOHN
Exactly. It is hard to--

KATHRYN
John believes he knows the time of his own death and he comes to the hospital, the ER, every night to try to stop it from happening.

ZOE
What?

CHRIS
John, he thinks he's dying at 10 something.

JOHN and KATHRYN
10:53.

CHRIS
Right, 10:53 every night. So that's why he's here. To make sure he doesn't die.

ZOE
What?

JOHN
For Christ's sake, I'm dying at 10:53. I don't know the day.

(Pause)

ZOE
What?

KATHRYN
Just give her a minute to process.

(They all wait and look at her)

ZOE
You know when you are going to die?

JOHN
Yes.

ZOE
You're lying.

JOHN
No.

CHRIS
That'd be a ridiculous lie.

ZOE
Then what? Are you psychic or something?

JOHN
No. It's just something I've seen. Known since I was a boy.

ZOE
Nobody knows when they're gonna die.

CHRIS
My grandma knew.

ZOE
Your grandma?

CHRIS
She knew. Knew before she stepped foot in the doctor's office. Always kept a positive outlook, but she was just going through the motions. Even when they said they got it all, she smiled, but she said she knew. She swore that you just know these things if you really listen. Died the next day.

(ZOE is looking at CHRIS. JOHN smiles)

ZOE
Hey, Hon. Get on my side.

CHRIS
I am. I'm just saying that it's not unbelievable. Weird, yes. But unbelievable, no.

ZOE
Mom! *(Pause)* Mother.

KATHRYN
Stop whining.

ZOE
I'm not whining.

KATHRYN
You are.

ZOE
Aren't you gonna do something? Say something?

KATHRYN
Like what?

ZOE
What were you thinking?

KATHRYN
Don't yell at me.

ZOE
(To JOHN) Have some respect. He's lying in there...

JOHN
I know. Kat and I --

ZOE
Kat?

JOHN
--we just happen to meet and just talk.

KATHRYN
That's right.

ZOE
THEN WHY KISS HIM? *(To JOHN)* You are totally taking advantage of her.

KATHRYN
I'm right here.

JOHN
I wouldn't do that.

ZOE
(To KATHRYN) You aren't saying anything. It's disgusting. *(To JOHN)* You are disgusting.

JOHN
I'm not here to talk with you. Kat, can we--

ZOE
She doesn't want to talk to you.

JOHN
(To KATHRYN) I am sorry for the mess.

ZOE
Mess? This isn't a mess. It's a... it's a... it's something much worse than a mess.

CHRIS
(To ZOE) Disaster. Apocalypse.

KATHRYN
Shut up, Chris.

ZOE
Don't talk to her like that, Mom. You kissed this weirdo.

KATHRYN
Get out.

ZOE
Dad's dying and you are losing it. Let's focus on getting you help--

KATHRYN
All of you.

ZOE
And not on the...

KATHRYN
Get out!

ZOE
Yeah, John.

KATHRYN
(Yells) No! Every one of you. Get out.

ZOE
Mom.

KATHRYN
Go home. I am begging you to go home.

JOHN
I think that's a good…

KATHRYN
And you… no. No one say anything else, OK? This is my place. My space.

ZOE
It's a public lobby.

KATHRYN
No, it's not. It hasn't been for a while. And you are all ruining my one spot. Ruined my sanctuary. Here it doesn't matter that… *(To JOHN)* …that you are gonna die. We all are. Doesn't matter that you… *(To ZOE)* …like girls. Be happy however you can. And Chris, I don't know what the hell your deal is, but good luck with that. And now, you come in and attack. You don't get to tell me how to feel or judge me. No. Nope. Absolutely not. I'm an adult woman damn it. Capable of making my own decisions, thank you all. And now, you all have just fucked up my peace. Hope you are happy. Now I have to go watch TV in your father's room. Thanks a fuck of a lot!

(KATHRYN leaves. JOHN, ZOE, and CHRIS all stand there in silence. JOHN's pants vibrate. The elevator bings open and they all pile in very unhappy. Door shuts)

SCENE TWO

(One night later. Lobby again. KATHRYN is watching TV again but she looks sleepy. ZOE comes out and sits on the other side of the couch. She is stoned. They watch TV in silence)

ZOE
Could you turn it up?

KATHRYN
It's loud enough.

ZOE
I can barely hear it.

KATHRYN
If I can hear it, you can hear it.

ZOE
Fine.

(Silence. ZOE then gets up and manually turns up the TV. KATHRYN used the remote to turn it back down. ZOE turns it up again. KATHRYN turns it off)

ZOE
I couldn't hear it. *(Pause)* I'm the one who should be mad at you.

KATHRYN
Blah, blah, blah…

ZOE
Chris says you're just grieving and acting out, but…

KATHRYN
Is Chris a psychologist, a phrenologist, a phlebotomist?

ZOE
How could you do that to him?

KATHRYN
I don't know.

ZOE
You don't know?

KATHRYN
No. I don't.

ZOE
Are you at least sorry?

KATHRYN
Sorry?

ZOE
For fucking kissing him?

KATHRYN
Don't talk to you... nope, talk to *me* like that.

ZOE
Well are you? Sorry?

KATHRYN
I don't know. Whatdaya think about that? I'm just... not sure of much. I'm sorry that I can't give you more than that, honey, but, honestly, some things—like this—are mine and not yours. You are my daughter. My beautiful, smart, gay-or-bi or something daughter.

ZOE
What is wrong with you?

KATHRYN
What's wrong with *you*?

ZOE
Are you on something?

KATHRYN
Are *you* on something?

ZOE
Stop repeating me.

KATHRYN
Stop repeating me.

ZOE
I'm serious.

KATHRYN
Fine.

ZOE
What are you on?

KATHRYN
The nurses thought I was too wound up.

ZOE
(Laughs) You are stoned.

KATHRYN
This is prescribed.

ZOE
Yeah, you're stoned.

KATHRYN
I know everything I'm saying. It just takes the edge off the cliff.

ZOE
You're funny.

KATHRYN
You're funny too. Mean but funny.

ZOE
We can sit here stoned together.

KATHRYN
We can. *(Pause)* Wait, are you stoned?

ZOE
Yeah.

KATHRYN
WHAT?

ZOE
I just smoked a bowl.

KATHRYN
You're doing drugs?

ZOE
Oh my god, calm down.

KATHRYN
That's illegal.

ZOE
Shhh. It's like barely illegal.

KATHRYN
No such thing.

ZOE
I use it medicinally.

KATHRYN
You do not.

ZOE
I've got depression.

KATHRYN
Oh my god.

ZOE
Calm down, I smoke weed, you kissed a crazy. It's all fair.

KATHRYN
(Laughs) He is crazy and you cannot smoke that stuff anymore.

ZOE
OK.

KATHRYN
Promise me.

ZOE
No.

KATHRYN
Then lie.

ZOE
OK. I won't.

KATHRYN
Thank you. Oh my god, do you do anything else?

ZOE
Nope.

KATHRYN
Would you tell me?

ZOE
Not at this point. But I don't. Really.

KATHRYN
Good.

(Pause)

ZOE
Do you love him?

KATHRYN
John? I just met him.

ZOE
Not him. Dad.

KATHRYN
Do I love your dad? Do I love your dad? Do I? *(Pause)* Yes. I do.

ZOE
Love your enthusiasm.

KATHRYN
What do you want me to say?

ZOE
That you love him. That you adore him. That what I perceived to be a miserable marriage was actually a great one. Am I wrong?

KATHRYN
Here's what you need to know. Your dad and I did at least two things right in our twenty-seven year marriage. Bridget and you. We love... most of the time... we love being your parents. We messed up all the time, but you girls have bonded us always together.

(Pause)

ZOE
How long have you been practicing that answer?

KATHRYN
Since you were about ten.

ZOE
Do you even like him?

KATHRYN
Come on.

ZOE
I'm serious.

KATHRYN
This is silly.

ZOE
He's a good man.

KATHRYN
He's a good father.

ZOE
Why are you even here?

KATHRYN
Because I can't drive home on these...

ZOE
I mean, why wait here like this with him?

KATHRYN
Because it's what I do. It's what I've always done. I'm not gonna leave him alone. He wouldn't do that to me. I won't do that to him. I'm doing what I'm supposed to do, just like you. Just like Bridget.

ZOE
You should have just left. Gotten a divorce.

KATHRYN
Maybe.

ZOE
If you were so miserable being in the...

KATHRYN
I don't know what I was. I had two little girls who needed me—no matter how unhappy or unsatisfying it sometimes was. I wasn't just going to blow that up because your father and I were... whatever we were.

ZOE
So it's our fault you didn't leave?

KATHRYN
Did I say that? (Pause) Seriously, did I? Because I wouldn't. Stop being dramatic. You want to be an adult, so here it is.

ZOE
So you aren't sad? You aren't upset? Just getting ready to move on?

KATHRYN
Yep, this is me happy, Zoe. Get a good look.

ZOE
Well, I saw you with John. You looked happy there.

KATHRYN
I enjoyed myself for a second. One tiny second.

ZOE
Real nice.

KATHRYN
I don't deserve a second of laughter during this? Are those your rules? Let me know what they are so I can be sure to make this all perfect in your mind. You need to see me a mess? You saw that yesterday. Now you're here for the show tonight. You want to see me cry? You should have been here a couple months ago. Give me your checklist so I can make sure I make this as much about you as possible. Because everyone knows I don't really care, right?

(Silence)

ZOE
I'm sorry.

KATHRYN
Me too.

(Silence)

ZOE
I don't want to be here.

KATHRYN
I know.

ZOE
No, I mean I want to leave. I don't want to see him or you and definitely not Bridget.

KATHRYN
I get it.

ZOE
I love him though.

KATHRYN
I know. He loves you too.

ZOE
He'd hold my hand though.

KATHRYN
Huh?

ZOE
If that was me, Dad would hold my hand. He'd tell me he loved me. He wouldn't leave my side.

KATHRYN
You're right.

ZOE
But I don't want to hold his hand.

KATHRYN
You don't have to.

ZOE
But I do. I'm supposed to.

KATHRYN
Says who?

ZOE
Says Bridget...

KATHRYN
(Interrupting) Tell her to shut up.

ZOE
Says anything on TV.

KATHRYN
We're all just making it up.

ZOE
I mean, wasn't this supposed to go quick? It shouldn't take so long for... it always seems so quick, but this isn't quick. And I'm just wishing that it would... it would be...

KATHRYN
I've wished it too.

ZOE
But it's not normal. This isn't how I should feel. I love him.

KATHRYN
Zoe, our lives have ceased at the moment. We're stuck in repeat here, waiting for one action to occur and it's something we don't control. At all. It's frustrating. Nobody wants to be here. Not your dad, me, anyone.

ZOE
He shouldn't have to be here.

KATHRYN
I can't have him at home not with--

ZOE
This is his worst nightmare.

KATHRYN
Yes. Of course it is. But he's got the morphine. He was excited about that.

ZOE
Mom.

KATHRYN
He was. Said it was the only part he was looking forward to.

ZOE
Dad said that?

KATHRYN
Yes.

ZOE
He hates drugs.

KATHRYN
Yes. *(Smiling)* Well, not always.

ZOE
What's that mean?

KATHRYN
He's not as innocent as legend has it. You take after him.

ZOE
What?

KATHRYN
If I tell you this…

ZOE
Tell me.

KATHRYN
You keep it to yourself.

ZOE
OK.

KATHRYN
You know that Dad and I met in college.

ZOE
Yeah. His roommate was dating a friend of yours.

KATHRYN
Yeah, well, we actually met when I went to his dorm room with Lindsay Miller. Lindsay was looking for some… pot.

ZOE
Did his roommate smoke?

KATHRYN
He had a single.

ZOE
What?

KATHRYN
Your dad was the weed dealer for the dorm.

ZOE
DAD!

KATHRYN
Yes.

ZOE
My dad?

KATHRYN
Yes.

ZOE
He sold drugs?

KATHRYN
Just pot. Some mushrooms sometimes.

ZOE
Shut up!

KATHRYN
But he only sold to people he could trust.

ZOE
Then why are you on my ass?

KATHRYN
Because you're smarter than he or I. I'd just like you to stay away from it. You don't know what people put in it. Could be laced. Could be--

ZOE
Wait, did you smoke too?

KATHRYN
I tried it once…

ZOE
OH MY GOD!

KATHRYN
…but I didn't like it. Just made me sleepy. Anyway, we went to his room and that was the first I'd ever seen him. So Lindsay and your dad were taking care of business and I remember your dad wouldn't stop looking

at me. I was so uncomfortable already because I'd never been to an actual dealer's place.

ZOE
It was a dorm room.

KATHRYN
Listen, I was a good kid. To me, it was a crack house. Anyway, Lindsay gets her stuff and we're leaving and your dad asks me if I want anything. I said, no thanks. He asked for my name and wanted us to stay and hang out.

ZOE
Did you want to stay?

KATHRYN
Oh yeah. Your dad was so cute. But I was dating Simon still, so I felt it would be wrong, plus your dad was way too intense. Scared me.

ZOE
I cannot believe you bought drugs from Dad.

KATHRYN
I didn't. Lindsay did.

ZOE
So then...

KATHRYN
He kept showing up at our room. Lindsay and him would smoke and I'd just talk with them while they got high like idiots. But nothing happened because I was still with...

ZOE
Yeah, yeah, so...

KATHRYN
So there was a party at a frat house. It was really stupid and so crowded. Simon was an idiot and drunk and I was miserable and drunk. So I went outside and there was your dad, just waiting.

ZOE
For you?

KATHRYN
For me. So he was a gentleman and walked me back to my room. We just talked and laughed. And when we got to my room, he finally kissed me. God, it was a good kiss, that I remember. Simon had fish lips, so when you kissed, well, you know.

ZOE
Yeah. But Chris is a good...

KATHRYN
So he came in and slept...

ZOE
Oh my god.

KATHRYN
We didn't do that.

ZOE
Right.

KATHRYN
No. We literally just slept next to each other all night. We talked and kissed, but that was it. One of the most exciting nights ever. That next morning, he told me he loved me. When I tried to tell him it was moving too fast, he said--it was so cheesy--he said "I've loved you before I ever met you, so, to me, this timing is just right." Oh my god, he had me. I knew I was gonna marry him after that night. I called grandma to tell her I was pretty sure I met the one.

ZOE
Really?

KATHRYN
Yeah.

ZOE
You did love him.

KATHRYN
Probably a little too much, for a while anyway.

ZOE
See you were happy.

KATHRYN
The beginnings are always the best, right?

(Pause)

ZOE
You sure can ruin a story.

KATHRYN
It's not the epic love story you want, but it's a story. Our story.

ZOE
How'd you guys screw it up?

KATHRYN
(Starts to lay down) You want some kind of concrete thing. There isn't anything, we just changed, we grew and not together.

ZOE
Something must have happened. Did you cheat on him, I mean, before crazy guy?

KATHRYN
Never.

ZOE
Maybe he did.

KATHRYN
I don't know. I don't think so. I mean, maybe he did and he found some happiness. Good for him.

ZOE
You got any more of that stuff the nurse gave you?

KATHRYN
Not that I'm willing to share.

ZOE
This sucks. You and he suck.

KATHRYN
There's my adult girl.

(CHRIS walks into the room with a pizza)

CHRIS
Pizza delivery.

ZOE
I'm so hungry.

CHRIS
I knew you would be.

ZOE
(Kissing CHRIS) You are the best.

CHRIS
Uh-huh.

ZOE
I'm serious. And it's not just because we are at the beginning of our love.

CHRIS
What?

ZOE
YUM! *(Grabs a slice)*

CHRIS
Kathryn, you want-- *(Turns to KATHRYN who has face planted into the sofa, fast asleep)* OK. *(Pause)* Everything OK?

ZOE
Oh my god, this is so good. *(Chewing)* Wait until you hear about my dad. He was like the Pablo Escobar of MSU...

SCENE THREE

(Next night. Lobby again. KATHRYN in her same spot watching TV and

flipping through a magazine. JOHN rounds the corner and they both see each other)

JOHN
Hi.

KATHRYN
Hello.

(Silence)

JOHN
I don't suppose you wanna listen to anything I have to say.

KATHRYN
You don't owe me an explanation.

JOHN
I know.

KATHRYN
(Turns around) Whatdya mean "I know"? Of course you owe me an explanation.

JOHN
You just said I didn't.

KATHRYN
It's an expression.

JOHN
An expression meaning that I don't need to explain myself?

KATHRYN
I didn't mean it that way.

JOHN
You didn't?

KATHRYN
I meant it more off the cuff.

JOHN
How so?

KATHRYN
In an off the cuff way.

JOHN
That is not an off the cuff remark.

KATHRYN
Fine. Not making me really want to hear you out right now, but fine.

(Pause)

JOHN
I botched it, I know I did. And it was never my intention to hurt you or make you feel bad.

KATHRYN
You don't need to worry about me.

JOHN
I know. But I...

KATHRYN
It would have been nice if you mentioned your thing earlier.

JOHN
My thing?

KATHRYN
Yes. Your thing. Your quirk. What do you call it?

JOHN
I don't typically call it anything.

KATHRYN
What do you say when you tell people?

JOHN
I don't go around telling most people.

KATHRYN
I guess you wouldn't.

JOHN
No. Because they think I'm crazy. Or laugh like you.

KATHRYN
I *did* do that.

JOHN
My timing is not usually so bad.

KATHRYN
It was pretty bad.

JOHN
Yeah. Typically I plan out what I'm gonna say.

KATHRYN
You never thought about telling me?

JOHN
No. Not until that moment.

KATHRYN
Thanks.

JOHN
I didn't think it was necessary. But now you know and I want to answer your questions. Tell you what I can. Let you know I'm not crazy.

KATHRYN
You don't think you're crazy?

JOHN
I think I have some issues. I know I do.

KATHRYN
Yes. Some pretty big ones.

JOHN
I know. *(Pause)* So ask me.

KATHRYN
What will it change?

JOHN
Change?

KATHRYN
The damage is done.

JOHN
We can't be friends?

KATHRYN
Is that what we were? What were we?

JOHN
I guess we weren't friends.

KATHRYN
No. We were more like...

JOHN
Companions.

KATHRYN
Army buddies.

JOHN
Really? OK. And there's no going back?

KATHRYN
We can't. I can't. There's no ignoring it.

JOHN
Ignoring what?

KATHRYN
The warning signs.

JOHN
What signs?

KATHRYN
Oh, that my husband is dying. I live in this lobby basically. You come to the hospital every night with the plan of dying.

JOHN
The plan is *not* to die.

KATHRYN
But those are the signs. And I'm not ignoring them this time.

JOHN
So you believe in signs?

KATHRYN
Yeah. I do.

JOHN
Me too. That's why I come here every night and stop my life for a few minutes. The sign started when I was a boy.

KATHRYN
And this is what makes you so sure you are going to die at 10--

JOHN
(Finishing) --53? Yes. I know I am. I saw it.

KATHRYN
As a boy?

JOHN
And now I don't know if it's me having the dream anymore or if it's me remembering it.

KATHRYN
I've had those dreams.

JOHN
But this isn't a dream, although I suppose that's the best thing to call it. It's real. It's hard to explain to someone that's never experienced it.

KATHRYN
I wasn't trying to downplay the intensity of--

JOHN
It seems far-fetched. Even silly. But this is what haunts me, demanding my attention. At first, I just see me standing in the middle of nowhere and there's this look of utter panic on my face. I'm watching me. And I am gasping. Gasping for air. I feel it. Can't get enough into my lungs. Trying hard to breathe in something and nothing. My eyes are burning into me. Pleading. I'm pleading with myself for help. As if I could do something, anything. And, in my brain, on a loop, is the number 10:53, over and over. Flashing in my brain. I feel this man's fear, my fear. There is pain. There is regret. There is panic like you wouldn't believe. And then I see I am dead and, for a moment, in my mind watching this, I feel relief. Like it's over. But it's not. I watch myself disappear. Disappear into nothing.

Like watching existence end and there is nothing. I'm left with nothing. Nothing. No corpse, no bones, no soul. Just a nothingness. Even these words that I'm trying to say to you, feelings I'm trying to convey to you, doesn't measure up to this thing that terrorizes me. And so, when I keep seeing this, how do I not listen?

KATHRYN
You don't have a choice. You have to.

JOHN
So I listen. And, when I come here, it seems to keep it at bay. I'm not asking you to understand everything I'm saying...

KATHRYN
But I do.

JOHN
You do?

KATHRYN
Yes.

JOHN
Oh. *(Pause)* OK.

KATHRYN
That doesn't mean I think you are going to die at 10:53. You do, but I don't.

JOHN
Yes.

KATHRYN
I'm sorry for you. It must be horrible.

JOHN
I'm used to it.

KATHRYN
Do you get used to it?

JOHN
Sure.

KATHRYN
Really?

JOHN
Sometimes. Occasionally.

KATHRYN
And are your kids used to it?

JOHN
They accept their father, although their mother... that's a different story.

KATHRYN
I bet.

JOHN
We didn't like each other to begin with, so this was just icing on the cake.

KATHRYN
Because I think, if I were you, I'd be mad.

JOHN
At who?

KATHRYN
Myself mostly.

JOHN
I'm not mad at myself.

KATHRYN
No?

JOHN
No.

KATHRYN
Because, in the amount of time I've been here, all I feel is this growing anger.

JOHN
You're mad at me?

KATHRYN
No. At me.

JOHN
About what?

(CHRIS *enters with a drink and bag of chips, once again overseeing the situation and unsure what to do. So she just plays possum and freezes*)

KATHRYN
About everything. That I'm not who I thought I was. That I'm not where I thought I'd be. That I sit here and watch TV because out of everything I could be doing, this feels best to me. How are you not angry?

JOHN
I... I'm trying to live the best I can.

KATHRYN
And you're supposed to be the crazy one. I did nothing. I didn't leave him. I didn't even try to change. I just accepted my lot because what if I was more miserable without him? And now I'm getting some freedom and all I can do is freeze. I'm frozen. But you, you keep living in spite of...

JOHN
I am a slave to a clock. To a persistent ticking that demands all my attention.

KATHRYN
I'm not saying your way is perfect.

JOHN
No. It's not. It's nice to hear someone thinks I have it together. Because I hear that clock every day. And I think about the things I still want to do before my time is up. I think about my children and wanting to travel and wanting to find that woman and I just think about all the possibilities. So I get in the car and come here, just in case I can be saved. As I drive, I realize that even if I don't die tonight, I'm still going to think I will the next day. So all those things

I dream about doing—falling asleep at 10 o'clock, traveling, staying in, making love to a woman at 10:53... I can't because I'm like Sisyphus. I keep pushing the boulder up the hill and I make it to the top and then the day starts again and the rolling starts again and... and... Maybe I'm already dead. I don't know. But I can't stop coming here. This is what makes me feel safe, if only for five minutes a day. And then you. You with your issues and coffee and horrible TV shows. I know when you and I... I know that talking with you... I love talking with you. Because I don't hear the clock. I never hear the clock when I'm with you. And I just want to keep you near so I... I can have another second to feel normal again.

KATHRYN
Oh.

JOHN
I get you, Kat. I do. And I... I...

(JOHN kisses her and, for a second, they are connected again. She pulls away and stands up)

KATHRYN
Goddamn it!

JOHN
That was on me.

KATHRYN
What the hell?

JOHN
Sorry. Sorry.

KATHRYN
I'd be going from one dying man to another.

JOHN
OK.

KATHRYN
This... this cannot happen.

JOHN
I don't know what *this* is.

KATHRYN
This is nothing. Cannot be anything. It is just desperation.

JOHN
I'm not desperate.

KATHRYN
Look at us. We are both desperate.

JOHN
No. I'm sorry. I didn't just kiss you out of desperation. I find you...

KATHRYN
Don't. Don't say anything else. It's not fair.

JOHN
Fair?

KATHRYN
You're taking advantage of me.

JOHN
Bullshit.

KATHRYN
I'm not in my right frame of mind.

JOHN
Yes, you actually are.

KATHRYN
This is just loneliness.

JOHN
Yes.

KATHRYN
And... and I... I don't want crazy.

JOHN
You don't think I'm crazy.

KATHRYN
I do.

JOHN
(*Pants are vibrating*) No, you don't.

KATHRYN
I feel sorry for you.

JOHN
And I feel sorry for you.

KATHRYN
Well, my husband is dying.

JOHN
No, I feel sorry for you because you are so sad. You are so sad you don't even know you're broken.

KATHRYN
I am not broken.

JOHN
Broken and scared for so long that you don't recognize a kindred spirit right in front of you.

KATHRYN
That's convenient for you.

JOHN
Nothing about this is convenient. (*Pulls out his phone*) I have to go.

KATHRYN
Exactly.

JOHN
I'll come back and we can finish this--

KATHRYN
It's finished.

JOHN
It's not.

KATHRYN
For me, please. It's finished. It has to be. Because I can't handle this, whatever it is. I don't want it and it isn't healthy for me. Please just respect that.

JOHN
But...

KATHRYN
I'm done.

JOHN
You're scared.

KATHRYN
I am just tired. I can't help you and my girls and myself. I don't have enough to go around.

JOHN
I don't want your help.

KATHRYN
Of course you do, you said it yourself. I don't make the clock tick.

JOHN
That's not called help, Kat.

KATHRYN
I don't care what it's called.

JOHN
Fine.

KATHRYN
Fine.

JOHN
Glad we could talk. Good luck to you.

KATHRYN
No. Good luck to you.

(*JOHN gets on the elevator. The next lines they are trying to one up each other*)

JOHN
Good Luck to you!

KATHRYN
Good Luck to you!

JOHN
(*Gets the last line in before the elevator doors shut*) Good Luck to you!

(*Elevator doors close. KATHRYN sits back down. A moment passes until CHRIS*) *drops her drink)*

CHRIS
Shit.

KATHRYN
(Turns around) Chris? Hi.

CHRIS
Hi.

KATHRYN
What are you...

CHRIS
I spilled.

KATHRYN
(Getting some paper towels) I see.

CHRIS
Sorry.

KATHRYN
It's not a big deal.

(They are both wiping it up together)

CHRIS
I won't say anything. Just so you know.

(KATHRYN stops cleaning and looks at her)

KATHRYN
About what? *(Silence)* Why are you always lurking?

CHRIS
I don't mean too. *(Pause)* So he kissed you, huh?

KATHRYN
How long were you standing there?

CHRIS
I just freeze like a deer when I--

KATHRYN
Here's some helpful advice when you find yourself in a situation that is none of your business: turn and walk away.

CHRIS
OK.

(They finish mopping up the floor)

CHRIS
It's just hard to do that.

KATHRYN
I don't care. It's polite.

CHRIS
Yeah, but I didn't know how long it was going to take or what was happening so... I guess I'm just kind of rooting for you.

KATHRYN
Rooting for me?

CHRIS
Yeah.

KATHRYN
I don't need you to.

CHRIS
You do though. Maybe. I don't know. You just seem... stuck.

KATHRYN
I'm not.

CHRIS
OK.

KATHRYN
What I'm dealing with is normal.

CHRIS
It's not.

KATHRYN
It--

CHRIS
It seems to me that this whole thing, the whole act of death is the exact opposite of what feels normal.

KATHRYN
It is, right?

CHRIS
And Zoe is so freaked out right now.

KATHRYN
I know. She and her dad--

CHRIS
No, about you and him. *(Indicating JOHN)*

KATHRYN
She doesn't need to be.

CHRIS
But she's seeing you as something you've never been.

KATHRYN
I'm the same...

CHRIS
Yeah, but no. It's all gonna be different. And it's weird. She saw you with John and you looked... different.

KATHRYN
I really didn't do anything.

CHRIS
But she's just used to seeing you... as what she thought was her mom. I mean, that girl of yours fights any change. She likes people to fit in the right boxes.

KATHRYN
I always thought she leads the charge of change.

CHRIS
No. Sometimes, but it takes her a while. We were friends all freshman year and when she and I first realized there was something going on between us, she bolted. Summer came and she just cut me out. We'd been friends all this time and suddenly nothing. And then this fall, she started to date all these guys. They were nasty. She'd bring them to any event that I'd be at and parade them around. I mean, it totally annoyed me, but I figured she'd talk to me at some point again. There was no denying there had been something between us. So, after a month, I finally cornered her. I was like, "What is going on with you? If you don't like me like that, fine, but we're friends." And then she just started to cry. She was so scared of everything she was feeling for me and I just held her and said "Let's be scared together." And then, well, you know, I'm here.

KATHRYN
Yes. You are.

CHRIS
It's hard to be honest and then to act on that. That's what people never tell you. They act like it's so easy, but really, it's not and sometimes it just sucks, you know.

KATHRYN
I do.

CHRIS
Zo's gonna be wondering where I am.

KATHRYN
Yeah.

CHRIS
Just so you know, in case you didn't, I do love her.

KATHRYN
Good.

CHRIS
OK. *(Pause)* Thanks for helping me clean up.

KATHRYN
You're welcome.

(CHRIS pauses and heads back in the opposite direction. KATHRYN watches her walk. She turns around, sits, and watches TV. A beat. Elevator doors open and JOHN huffs out)

JOHN
I think we should go for a walk.

KATHRYN
John?

JOHN
Let's go for a walk.

KATHRYN
Now? It's almost 10...

JOHN
Do you wanna take a walk?

KATHRYN
To the ER?

JOHN
No. Outside.

KATHRYN
Outside?

JOHN
Walk the grounds.

KATHRYN
John, I... I...

JOHN
Come on, Kat.

KATHRYN
No. I can't I'm sorry. And you, you're supposed to be in the...

JOHN
But I don't want to go.

KATHRYN
(Pressing the elevator button) I'll still be here when you're done.

JOHN
But I don't want you here.

KATHRYN
Stop being an idiot.

JOHN
Then I'll take a walk by myself.

KATHRYN
Ok. Good for you.

JOHN
What are you doing?

(JOHN is in the elevator and the doors begin to close)

KATHRYN
I'm scared all the time.

(JOHN's arm comes out and he steps out again)

JOHN
I'm scared too. We could just be scared together. Not together-together. But just together. What's the worst that could happen?

KATHRYN
You could die.

JOHN
But you said I wouldn't.

KATHRYN
You won't. But what if you do?

JOHN
Ok. That's horrible, but what about you? What's the worst that could happen?

KATHRYN
I don't know.

JOHN
That you'll be just as sad as you are in here? That life will be just as hard? That you'll have to kill that spider yourself?

KATHRYN
Don't make fun of me.

JOHN
I'm not. I wouldn't. But if you stay here, if I stay here, we... we are just stuck. We stop growing. We stop dreaming of all the things we want. No possibilities. Don't you want some possibilities again? Just the notion of them? I think you want to come with me. If just for tonight, right? Because tomorrow will come regardless, the future will come no matter what we do. *(Pause)* I think we should take a walk.

KATHRYN
Ok.

JOHN
OK?

KATHRYN
(Turns off the TV and drops the remote) Ok.

(The clock turns 10:53. They're in the elevator and the doors close. Lights fade)

END OF PLAY

The Gravedigger
A Frankenstein Story

A PLAY BY
Joseph Zettelmaier

Cast of Characters

VICTOR – the Doctor
KURT – the Gravedigger
ANTON – the Monster
NADYA – a Gypsy

TIME
The Late 1700s

PLACE
A cemetery outside of Ingolstadt, Bavaria

The Gravedigger: A Frankenstein Story was originally produced as a joint premiere between First Folio Theatre (Oak Brook, IL) and Williamston Theatre (Williamston, MI) in October of 2014.

First Folio Theatre's production was directed by Alison C. Vesely. Stage Managed by Sara Gammage. Sound Composed and Designed by Christopher Kriz. Costume Design by Rachel Lambert. Lighting Design by Michael McNamara. Scenic Design by Angela Weber Miller. Prop Design by Cassy Shillo. Fight Choreography by Joe Foust. Melanie Keller was the Assistant Director. The cast was as follows:

KURT: Craig Spidle
VICTOR: Doug MacKechnie
ANTON: Joshua Carroll
NADYA: Simina Contras

The understudies were David Rice (KURT), T. Isaac Sherman (VICTOR), Ben Muller (ANTON) and Yesmeen Mikhail (NADYA).

Williamston Theatre's production was directed by John Lepard. Stage Managed by Stefanie Din. Scenic Design by Kirk A. Domer. Lighting Design by Daniel C. Walker. Costume Design by Karen Kangas-Preston. Prop Design by Bruce Bennett. Sound Design by Michelle Raymond. Fight Choreography by Zev Steinberg. The cast was as follows:

KURT: Mark Colson
VICTOR: Joe Seibert
ANTON: Alex Leydenfrost
NADYA: Alysia Kolascz

For information about production rights, visit www.jzettelmaier.com.

THE GRAVEDIGGER

ACT I
SCENE ONE

(Lights up. KURT's small shack. VICTOR sits at the table, waiting for KURT to return. Thunder is heard peeling in the distance. The door flies open. KURT enters. He is a large, strong man in his late 40s. He walks with a pronounced limp, leaning on his cane. He has a burlap sack slung over his shoulder. KURT starts at the sight of VICTOR)

KURT
Dammit all to hell! What are you doing here?

VICTOR
It's raining.

KURT
Of course it's raining! Been raining every day for a week.

VICTOR
You have them then?

KURT
I do.

VICTOR
Good.

(KURT drops the sack onto the table. It is large, and whatever's inside is heavy)

KURT
Pay me.

VICTOR
In good time.

KURT
Not "in good time." Now!

(KURT advances on VICTOR. VICTOR produces a knife. KURT stops)

KURT
So that's how it is, then? I dirty my hands for you, and you cut my throat?

(VICTOR stares at him, then cuts the tie-string on the sack. He looks inside)

KURT
Don't open it here. The stink...

VICTOR
...is something men like you and I should be used to.

(VICTOR looks inside, examining his merchandise. KURT mutters to himself)

KURT
Christ help me.

(VICTOR examines the merchandise, then ties the bag back up)

VICTOR
Well done.

KURT
Hmmm.

(VICTOR speaks as he examines)

VICTOR
What happened to your leg?

KURT
God.

VICTOR
What?

KURT
God happened.

VICTOR
Indeed?

KURT
Sometimes, we pay for our sins even before we die. You might want to think on that.

VICTOR
I might. But I don't.

(VICTOR takes out a sack of coins, & sets them on KURT's table)

KURT
I'm done.

VICTOR
Yes?

KURT
Yes. Find what you need from some other poor bastard. I can't do this anymore.

VICTOR
A little late for a weak stomach, don't you think?

KURT
This job's all I have. I can't risk it, no matter how much you pay me.

VICTOR
So that's it? A fear of unemployment? I'd have thought it might be something more…substantial.

(KURT hobbles to the door, opening it)

KURT
Get out.

VICTOR
(Pointing to KURT's leg) I could have a look at that sometime. If you'd like.

KURT
No, I wouldn't like. Get out.

VICTOR
I am a doctor, whatever else you might think of me.

KURT
I'd rather not think of you at all.

VICTOR
You may be causing undue stress on your good leg, trying to overcompensate for your limp. If the brace isn't properly aligned…

KURT
I don't want your help.

VICTOR
Please. I don't like to see a man suffer.

(KURT can tell he genuinely means it. He softens his attitude & takes an old rosary from his pocket. He absently holds it as he speaks)

KURT
The damage is already done.

VICTOR
I'm sorry.

(KURT shrugs)

VICTOR
If it's any solace, the work I'm doing may one day make you whole again.

KURT
I'll pray for the day, sir, but not expect it.

VICTOR
Just know that…the work you've done for me…great good shall come of it.

(Beat)

KURT
You know what they call men like me? Resurrection men. Families come into a graveyard, see the dug-up plots…like their loved one's been resurrected. Except that's not it, is it? They've just been defiled. By men like me.

VICTOR
I won't bother you again. You have my word.

KURT
Thank you.

VICTOR
Well, then…

(VICTOR offers his hand to KURT. After a moment, KURT shakes it. VICTOR starts to leave)

KURT
God watch over you, Doctor.

VICTOR
Hmm. What an archaic notion.

(VICTOR exits. KURT takes out a flask and takes a long drink. Lights change)

SCENE TWO

*(A year later. Lights up. The graveyard. A pile of dirt lies outside. KURT enters, limping worse. He's a bit drunk, and singing **Gaudeamus Igitur**)*

KURT
Gaudeamus igitur
Juvenes dum sumus.
Post iucundam iuventutem
Post molestam senectutem
Nos habebit humus.

(He stops at the dirt pile, preparing to urinate into the grave. He looks down)

KURT
Hey! What's this then?

(He sees a man lying in the open grave)

KURT
You! Get out of there.

(No response)

KURT
I know you can hear me! I said out!

(No response)

KURT
You asleep? Huh?!

(KURT pours his flask in the hole. ANTON speaks from within the hole)

KURT
Rise and shine, little dumpling.

ANTON
Leave me alone.

KURT
Ah! There! Now get out.

ANTON
No.

KURT
This hole's got a coffin going in it

tomorrow. Sleep it off somewhere else.

ANTON
I'm not drunk.

KURT
More's the pity.

(KURT circles the hole, trying to figure out how to get down inside it)

ANTON
What are you doing?

KURT
I can't get down there on my own. So do an old sot a favor and…

ANTON
LEAVE ME BE!!!

KURT
Don't you shout at me! This is my damned boneyard!

ANTON
Let me die in peace!

KURT
Oh no. No, no, no.

ANTON
Please!

KURT
This place isn't for the dying; it's for the dead.

ANTON
I'm begging you.

KURT
I'm sorry, but…

(ANTON begins to cry)

KURT
Oh. Oh. None of that.

(ANTON lets out a roar of anguish and rage. KURT staggers back. As ANTON rants, he crawls out of the hole)

ANTON
All I want is to die! My whole wretched life, it is the only thing anyone wished on me! And now.. NOW…I am stopped!?

(ANTON is fully out of the hole. He is a large man, his face mostly wrapped in bandages. Only his mouth and eyes are fully visible)

KURT
Oh my God…

ANTON
Why?! Why can't you just leave me be, and let me die?!

(KURT has fallen to his knees)

KURT
Please…please no…

ANTON
What are you…?

KURT
I'll go. I swear. Just don't hurt me. I'm begging you.

(ANTON's rage diminishes)

ANTON
I won't hurt you.

KURT
I'm sorry I shouted at you. I…

ANTON
Listen to me. I said I won't hurt you.

(He walks towards KURT. KURT tries to back away. ANTON reaches down and helps KURT stand)

KURT
What…?

(ANTON starts to leave. For reasons even he's unsure of, KURT speaks)

KURT
What happened to you?

(ANTON stops)

ANTON
I am…damaged.

KURT
Do you need help?

ANTON
No one can help me.

KURT
That's why you want to die.

(ANTON says nothing)

KURT
Perhaps I can help you.

ANTON
Why?

KURT
Because…I used to help people.

ANTON
Why?

KURT
It's what people do.

ANTON
No. It isn't.

KURT
Well…it's what we're supposed to do.

(They stare at each other for a bit)

KURT
Come with me.

ANTON
Where?

KURT
I have a shack, just past that mausoleum.

(ANTON doesn't move)

KURT
Come on. It's going to rain.

ANTON
Rain doesn't bother me.

KURT
Well, it bothers me. And I don't intend to leave you out here.

(Beat)

ANTON
You…don't want to leave me?

KURT
No. I suppose not.

(ANTON is silent for a while, taking that in)

ANTON
I'll go with you.

KURT
All right then.

(KURT leads the two of them off. Lights change)

SCENE THREE

(KURT's shack. KURT enters, followed by ANTON)

KURT
And…here we are.

(ANTON looks around)

ANTON
It is small.

KURT
Well, I was going to take you to my mansion, but I prefer my dingy shack and its rustic charm. *(Beat)* That was a joke.

ANTON
I…I don't understand jokes.

KURT
I see.

(KURT hobbles to his chair and sits. He pulls out his flask, and offers it to ANTON)

ANTON
No.

(KURT drinks)

KURT
You don't have to just stand there.

(ANTON sits. He stares at a painting on the wall)

ANTON
Who is that? Your father?

KURT
Father of all of us, I guess. Saint Anthony.

ANTON
Your father was a saint?

KURT
No, but...old Anthony up there. He's the Patron Saint of many things. Including gravediggers.

(ANTON says nothing, continuing to stare at the painting)

KURT
Not one for conversation, are you?

ANTON
No.

(They sit in silence for a bit)

KURT
So what's your name?

ANTON
I have none.

KURT
You don't remember your name?

ANTON
I was never given one to remember.

KURT
You're putting me on.

ANTON
No.

KURT
Well, what do people call you?

(ANTON shrugs. KURT rubs his eyes in frustration)

KURT
What the hell am I supposed to call you then? Hmm!?

(Again, ANTON shrugs)

KURT
Just pick something, will you? A name you like. Anything.

ANTON
I don't know many names. And the ones I know, I do not want.

KURT
All right then...

(KURT thinks for a moment)

KURT
Helga.

ANTON
What?

KURT
That's your name now. Helga.

ANTON
No.

KURT
What's wrong with Helga? It's a good Bavarian name.

ANTON
It's a woman's name.

KURT
I thought you didn't know many names.

ANTON
Don't mock me.

KURT
Well then what about Ingrid? Or Eva? Or...

ANTON
Do not mock me!

KURT
Then pick a name, dammit!

(Beat)

ANTON
You raised your voice to me.

KURT
You raised yours first.

ANTON
Aren't you afraid of me?

KURT
I am. But I'm also in my cups. Means I can do stupid things even when I'm scared.

(For the first time, ANTON smiles, almost chuckling)

ANTON
You are a strange man.

KURT
Oh? What does that make you then?

ANTON
Just...strange.

(Beat)

ANTON
Anton.

KURT
What's that?

ANTON
You can call me Anton. Like your saint.

KURT
Anton it is, then. I'm Kurt Volker.

(KURT offers his hand. ANTON shakes it. KURT winces at his grip)

KURT
Good Christ!

ANTON
Did I hurt you?

KURT
Yes! That's my drinking hand, too!

ANTON
I am sorry. I did not mean to...

KURT
It's all right. Give me a moment.

(KURT wrings his hand out)

KURT
You're quite the ox, huh?

ANTON
I'm strong, if that's what you mean.

KURT
Good for you. The world always needs strong men.

(He pours some booze in a glass and offers it to ANTON)

KURT
It'll keep you warm.

(ANTON drinks, KURT sits)

KURT
So what brings you to my boneyard, Anton the ox?

(ANTON doesn't respond)

KURT
Most folks don't find themselves here accidentally. They're either mourners

or...well, the ones being mourned.

ANTON
I was drawn here.

KURT
Really?

ANTON
This place is familiar to me.

KURT
So you've been here before.

ANTON
Perhaps.

KURT
Did I put one of yours in the ground here? Your mother? Your father?

ANTON
Why do you limp?

(Beat)

KURT
Beg pardon?

ANTON
You walk with a limp. I want to know why.

KURT
Don't see how that's any...

ANTON
Are you damaged?

KURT
I don't want to talk about it!

ANTON
I'm only asking...

KURT
And I'm telling you, leave it alone. Just because I took pity on you doesn't mean I want to tell you my Goddamn life story. *(Beat)* Do you have any family hereabouts? Someone to take you in?

ANTON
I have a father. But he won't claim me.

KURT
So you're a bastard then?

ANTON
I've been called that.

KURT
You and me both. *(Drinks)* Well, it's not a palace, but you can sleep here tonight if you want. At least you'll be dry. Then you can...go wherever you're going.

ANTON
I'm not going anywhere. I was trying to die.

KURT
Well, you can't do it here. I won't let you.

ANTON
If I decided to, you couldn't stop me.

KURT
Oh! You're a tough one, then.

ANTON
You know I am.

(KURT puts his arm on the table, ready to arm wrestle)

ANTON
What?

KURT
Put your arm up here and show me.

ANTON
I don't understand.

KURT
You've never done this before?

ANTON
I don't know.

KURT
All right, all right. Put your arm up here, like mine.

(ANTON *does so. KURT grabs his hand*)

KURT
Now, you try to push my arm down, and I'll try to push yours down. Whoever does it, wins.

ANTON
This is childish.

KURT
Let's see how strong you are when I know what's coming.

ANTON
I don't see...

KURT
Don't let my limp fool you. I've got muscles that...

(ANTON *slams KURT's arm down with ease. He's so forceful that KURT falls out of his chair*)

KURT
Jesus Christ!

ANTON
I win.

KURT
I wasn't ready yet, dammit!

ANTON
Yes. But I won.

KURT
Again! We're going again.

(*He puts his arm up.* ANTON *grabs it*)

KURT
Now this time, don't move til I say so. On the count of three. One...

(KURT *immediately starts to push, hoping to trick* ANTON. ANTON's *arm doesn't move*)

KURT
...move, dammit...

ANTON
Are we going again?

KURT
...come on....come on...

(ANTON *slams* KURT's *arm down again, knocking him out of his chair.* KURT *lies there, stunned*)

ANTON
I win again.

KURT
Sweet merciful Jesus. I've never seen anything like that.

ANTON
Shall we go again?

KURT
No, no. If there's one thing life's taught me over and over again, it's to know when I'm beat. (*He rises, dusts himself off*) You're with the circus, aren't you?

ANTON
What?

KURT
A strongman or something? Pulling nails out of boards with your bare teeth? Bending iron bars in two?

ANTON
I've never even seen a circus.

KURT
You should seek one out. They'd welcome you, no doubt.

ANTON
I do not do well in the company of others.

KURT
We're getting along fine.

ANTON
Hmm.

KURT
Is it your face? Trust me, a circus wouldn't care about that. They might love it, in fact.

ANTON
I don't like being stared at.

KURT
You might want to unwrap yourself then. Draws a lot of attention.

ANTON
I would draw even more attention without the bandages.

KURT
Can't be that bad.

ANTON
It's that bad and worse.

KURT
Do you mind if I ask?

ANTON
Ask what?

KURT
About your face. Was it an accident? I know a man, worked at the University. Knocked over a beaker of acid. Damn near melted his left side.

ANTON
It wasn't acid.

KURT
Poor fellow looked like an old candle.

ANTON
I do not wish to discuss it.

KURT
I'm just asking.

(Beat)

ANTON
I will tell you about my face when you tell me about your limp.

(Beat)

KURT
Fair enough.

(He rises)

KURT
Well, Anton the Ox, I'm off to bed. It's the only one I got, but... *(He looks into another room offstage)* I've got the side room there, where I keep my tools. There's some haybales that'll serve for a bed. It's yours if you want it.

ANTON
I should leave.

KURT
And go where?

ANTON
You should not take me in.

KURT
Well, I already have, so...

ANTON
Wherever I go, tragedy follows.

KURT
Tragedy and I know each other very well. I don't fear it, and neither should you.

(ANTON stands there, unmoving. The room fills with the sound of thunder and a flash of lightning)

KURT
Besides, the downpour's still going strong.

(ANTON says nothing)

KURT
Ah, do what you will. I'd tell you not to steal anything, but I've got nothing worth taking.

(KURT heads off, stopping at the doorway. He stares at ANTON for a bit, clearly waiting for him to say something. Finally--)

KURT
You're welcome.

(ANTON doesn't respond. KURT sighs and goes to bed. ANTON stays at the window, watching the lightning. Finally, he goes to to the door and leaves the shack. Lights change)

SCENE FOUR

(The graveyard, the same night. A fog hangs in the air. NADYA is at a grave, throwing things into a sack. She carries a small, dim lantern. ANTON approaches silently)

ANTON
What are you doing?

(Startled, she spins around, drawing a knife)

NADYA
Stay back.

ANTON
What are you doing here?

NADYA
Another step, and I'll slit your throat for you.

(He steps close enough that she can see him better. She's taken aback at his size)

NADYA
Good God.

ANTON
Put your knife down.

NADYA
I think I'll keep it where it is.

ANTON
Put it down or I'll break your arm, woman.

(Beat. She sheathes the blade)

NADYA
Don't touch me.

ANTON
I won't.

NADYA
Good. (She grabs her bag, backing away) I didn't hear you come up on me.

ANTON
I didn't wish to be heard, so I wasn't.

NADYA
Simple as that?

ANTON
That was all the thought I put into it.

NADYA
Neamt Jegos.

ANTON
What?

NADYA
What?

ANTON
I don't know what you said.

(Beat)

NADYA
It loses something in translation.

ANTON
What are you doing here?

NADYA
I could ask you the same question.

ANTON
I could break your neck and take that sack from you.

NADYA
Doamne! Not one for social graces, are you?

ANTON
No.

NADYA
How does this sound? Why don't I just leave the graveyard, and you go back to wherever you came from?

ANTON
No.

NADYA
You're the gravedigger. Is that it? A loyal dog guarding his hole?

ANTON
I am...Anton. Yes.

NADYA
Are you certain?

ANTON
I am only recently named. It does not sound like my own yet.

(Beat)

NADYA
I don't know what that means.

ANTON
I don't know how else to explain it.

(She smiles. He stares at her for a bit)

ANTON
I like the way you smile.

NADYA
Yes?

ANTON
Your face is lovely.

NADYA
So I've been told.

ANTON
What is your name?

NADYA
Nadya.

ANTON
Nad-ya...

NADYA
That's it.

ANTON
What is in your bag, Nadya?

(Beat)

NADYA
Bones.

ANTON
Why do you have a bag of bones?

NADYA
Why do you think?

ANTON
I have no idea. That's why I asked.

NADYA
I'm Romani.

(ANTON pauses, trying to place the word)

ANTON
A gypsy.

NADYA
That's right. And I use these...*(Shakes the bag)*...to see the future.

ANTON
You're lying.

NADYA
Don't call me a liar.

ANTON
No one can see the future.

NADYA
I have a long list of clienti who'd say otherwise.

ANTON
I do not believe in superstition.

NADYA
Then what?

ANTON
Science. I believe in science.

NADYA
Are they so different?

(She sits down. He stares at her)

NADYA
Well, if we're going to have a chat, sit down already.

ANTON
The ground is wet from the rain.

(She immediately stands up, examining her dress)

NADYA
Dammit! Soaked right through.

(ANTON smiles, laughs a little)

NADYA
That's funny to you?

ANTON
Yes. Your bottom is wet.

NADYA
Thank you, I'm well aware.

(He starts to laugh more)

NADYA
Yes, yes. Please, remain amused.

ANTON
You knew that it had rained, and you sat down anyway. That was foolish.

NADYA
I wasn't thinking.

ANTON
You behaved foolishly.

NADYA
Are you quite finished?

ANTON
And now your bottom is wet.

(His laughter peters out naturally. He just smiles)

NADYA
You're a strange giant.

ANTON
I haven't laughed before. At least...not that I remember.

NADYA
Nonsense.

ANTON
It's true. I am younger than I look.

NADYA
I cannot tell how you look at all, wrapped as you are.

(She reaches for his bandages. He backs away)

ANTON
No.

NADYA
Am I so terrifying?

ANTON
Do not touch me.

NADYA
Hmm. Not something I am often told.

ANTON
Why would you want to...?

NADYA
See your face? I am always curious. The more something is hidden, the more I want to take it out of the

shadows.

ANTON
I belong where no one can see me.

NADYA
That only makes me…oh!

(She pretends to trip. ANTON instinctually catches her. She holds onto him)

NADYA
And look. We're touching. Not so bad, is it?

(ANTON feels conflicting emotions, but does not release her)

ANTON
Don't.

NADYA
Don't what?

ANTON
My face…do not touch it.

NADYA
I haven't, and I won't.

ANTON
But before…you tried to see it and…

NADYA
I will see it when you let me, not before.

ANTON
I will never want that.

NADYA
Oh, I can be very persuasive. *(She jumps out of his arms)* Well, since I've provided the evening's entertainment, perhaps you'll let me leave with this bag and with my limbs intact.

ANTON
I will not hurt you.

NADYA
I wouldn't have let you if you tried.

ANTON
I don't want you to leave.

NADYA
That's sweet, but I'm not staying in a graveyard all night. Lots of strigoi about.

(Beat)

NADYA
Evil spirits.

ANTON
You like to use words that I don't know. It makes you feel smart.

NADYA
You're a clever maimuță. *(Starts to leave)* I'll see you next time, Anton.

ANTON
You will return?

NADYA
Yes. I think I will.

ANTON
Then…are we friends?

(She smiles)

NADYA
Stranger things have happened.

(She exits. Lights change)

SCENE FIVE

(KURT's shack, the next morning. KURT staggers about the room, hung over. He splashes some cold water on his face)

KURT
Ah! Dammit!

(He shakes it off, and goes to ANTON's room. No one is there)

KURT
Back to the circus with you then.

(*He grabs a shovel for the day's work. He goes to the door and opens it. ANTON is standing there. KURT jumps back, startled*)

KURT
This is not the ideal face to wake to.

ANTON
I want to stay.

KURT
What?

(*ANTON mistakes the question for not hearing him. He speaks unnecessarily loud*)

ANTON
I WANT TO STAY!

KURT
I heard you, you damn lummox! I just...get inside already!

(*ANTON enters*)

ANTON
If your offer still stands, I would like to stay here with you.

KURT
My...what the hell?

ANTON
You offered me the tool room.

KURT
For one damn night!

ANTON
I wish to stay longer.

KURT
Well, I wish for a buxom lady with a stein between her breasts. Mine is a life of disappointment.

(*ANTON just stares at him*)

KURT
And now I remember that you don't understand jokes.

ANTON
A gypsy sat on wet dirt and got her bottom wet.

(*Beat*)

KURT
I don't get it.

ANTON
It was a joke.

KURT
I still don't get it.

ANTON
It made me laugh.

(*KURT rubs his eyes in frustration*)

KURT
So you want to stay.

ANTON
Yes.

KURT
Why?

(*Beat*)

ANTON
I have nowhere else to go. I came here to die, but I no longer wish that. And I like it here.

KURT
You like the graveyard?

ANTON
It's peaceful. I've known very little peace in my life.

KURT
I like the quiet myself.

ANTON
So I can stay?

KURT
Give me a damn minute, will you? I'm barely awake and....

(KURT sits down. ANTON joins him)

KURT
You have no money, no prospects, and I should just...what? Give up my peace and quiet for a boarder? I don't even know you.

ANTON
I don't know you either.

KURT
That's hardly the point, is it?

ANTON
Is it?

KURT
Jesus, every time you open your mouth, I don't know whether to laugh or punch you!

ANTON
You helped me before. Why won't you help me now?

KURT
Not that simple.

ANTON
Explain it to me.

KURT
I can't.

ANTON
I want to understand.

KURT
Stop talking! Just...can you shut your flapping jaws for a trice?

(Beat. KURT composes himself)

KURT
I've been alone here for a while now. That's the way I prefer it. When other people are around...they complicate things. I don't like complication.

ANTON
I am a complication?

KURT
Yes. I'm sorry, but yes.

ANTON
And so you do not like me?

KURT
I didn't say that. You're all right, I guess. You either talk too much or too little, but...yes, I've known worse than you.

ANTON
Thank you.

KURT
I just... I'm a drunken, crippled ass. I'm not a good companion.

ANTON
I like you.

KURT
Why?

ANTON
Because you have been kinder to me than anyone has been in my entire life.

KURT
I'm sorry to hear that. *(Thinks for a bit)* I'll tell you a secret.

ANTON
All right.

KURT
I'm a hair's breadth from losing this job.

ANTON
Really?

KURT
I can't dig for shit anymore. I have

a hard enough time getting around with this... *(He taps his brace)* And the church...they keep me on as a kindness, but there's no way I can keep up. People drop like flies in this town. They can't afford to hire another man to help, so...there it is.

ANTON
I could dig for you.

KURT
Yes. You could.

ANTON
I'm stronger than anyone. I can dig many graves.

KURT
At night. You dig at night, stay in this shack during the day. That way no one will know.

ANTON
That works well for me. I have no desire to draw attention to myself.

KURT
I won't be able to pay you, but you can stay here and share your meals with me.

ANTON
That is all I ask.

KURT
All right then.

ANTON
You are helping me again.

KURT
No. I'm helping myself. You just happen to be here.

ANTON
I think it's more than that.

KURT
It's not.

ANTON
I think it is.

KURT
Shut your gob before I change my mind, lummox.

ANTON
Thank you.

KURT
And don't thank me! This is entirely self-serving.

ANTON
You are a good man.

KURT
And you're one sentence away from fouling the deal.

(ANTON offers his hand)

KURT
Gentle this time. I like my knuckles lined up the way they are.

ANTON
All right.

(They shake. ANTON doesn't hurt him)

KURT
All right.

(Lights fade)

SCENE SIX

(That night, the cemetery. ANTON is rising out of the hole, shovel in hand. KURT is watching him)

KURT
That was a hell of a thing.

ANTON
This is large enough for a casket, yes?

KURT
That's large enough for a fat burgo-

meister and half his fat family.

ANTON
Then you are satisfied?

KURT
Stunned is more like it. But...yes, well done.

ANTON
Good.

KURT
That took you...*(Checks his pocket watch)*...not even an hour. And I don't see a drop of sweat.

ANTON
It was not difficult work.

KURT
How can you say that? In my prime, that hole would've taken me half the night.

ANTON
Your prime and mine are two different things.

KURT
And that's God's truth. *(offers ANTON his bottle)* You may not need it, but you earned it.

(ANTON takes the bottle and drains it)

KURT
Hey! Not the whole thing!

ANTON
Oh. I'm sorry.

(KURT takes out another and drinks)

KURT
Ah, no harm done.

ANTON
It's good. This...what is it?

KURT
Schnapps.

ANTON
I like it.

KURT
If there's one thing we Bavarians know, it's schnapps.

(They sit by the hole, drinking)

KURT
Where are you from, Anton?

ANTON
Many places, I suppose. I think I was born in Ingolstadt, but...most of my life was spent in Switzerland.

KURT
An orphan?

ANTON
Abandoned. My father saw my face and left me.

KURT
Christ, I'm sorry to hear that.

ANTON
I hate him. Or...I hated him. I can no longer tell the difference.

KURT
You must've done well enough. Got an education.

ANTON
Only experience. Little of it good.

KURT
You speak proper.

ANTON
I enjoy language. For a time, I could barely communicate. It was maddening...to have these thoughts and these feelings...to have the urge to express them, but no ability to do so.

KURT
For some people, that would be an improvement.

ANTON
It is a hard thing. I imagine all who live wish to be understood.

KURT
Anton, my friend, I will drink to that. *(Drinks)*

ANTON
I've never had a friend.

KURT
Come now.

ANTON
Truly. Those who did not wish me dead simply ran from me.

KURT
You're a hunted man, then?

ANTON
Once. But I've fled beyond their reach.

KURT
A criminal?

ANTON
I've done…terrible things. I was very young and had no control over what I felt. I raged against those who hurt me most, and some died because of it.

(KURT makes the sign of the cross over ANTON and splashes his face with alcohol)

KURT
Ego te absolvo.

ANTON
I am wet. And confused.

KURT
I just absolved you of your sins. And I did it in Latin.

ANTON
You did?

KURT
Oh yes. It's the language God likes his prayers in.

ANTON
Are you a priest?

(KURT drinks, then rises)

KURT
Well, Brother Anton. I'm off to perform a miracle: Turning schnapps into piss. If that's not a sign of the Lord's existence, I don't know what is.

ANTON
What should I do?

KURT
Whatever you'd like. This is your home now.

ANTON
I need…guidance.

(KURT puts a hand on ANTON's shoulder)

KURT
You know what I do when I'm in need of thinking?

ANTON
No. How could I know that?

KURT
I walk amongst the graves. I read what little I can on the stones, learn of the people this earth holds. I suggest you take your past, and bury it in one of these plots. And then, start thinking about your future.

ANTON
I've never thought of the future. Only where I was, and what I felt at the moment.

KURT
Pfft. A fine way to achieve nothing.

You want to find happiness, lummox? Decide what you want your life to be, then make it that.

ANTON
Is that how you ended up a gravedigger?

(Beat. KURT chuckles)

KURT
That's a story for another time.

(He exits. Lights fade)

SCENE SEVEN

(A month later. ANTON has found better clothes, though his face is still bandaged. NADYA pokes her head up out of the burial hole. ANTON stands above her, offering her his hand. She lets out a startled cry, then laughs)

NADYA
Hello, giant.

ANTON
Hello, Nadya.

(She takes his hand. He lifts her out of the hole with great ease, almost hurling her. She staggers but catches herself)

ANTON
Oh! I'm sorry.

NADYA
Christos! If I was meant to fly, I'd have a beak and feathers.

ANTON
Chickens have beaks and feathers, but they do not fly.

NADYA
Yes they do.

ANTON
I do not think so.

NADYA
Chickens fly, Anton.

ANTON
I've never seen them do so.

(She laughs)

NADYA
I have seen many strange men in my day, but you may well be the strangest.

ANTON
You do not need to insult me.

NADYA
Not an insult. Strange means interesting. Very, very, VERY few men are interesting anymore.

ANTON
Oh. Thank you.

NADYA
Bentru Putin.

ANTON
Did you come for more bones?

NADYA
Not this time.

(She tosses him a bag. He looks into it)

ANTON
You have a bag of dirt.

NADYA
Grave dirt. Very potent.

ANTON
How can dirt be potent?

NADYA
Good for seeing the past or the future.

(He just stares at her)

NADYA
I have a new client. Wants to see his future. I asked him some questions, and he mentioned this graveyard several times. So I'll take the dirt, mix it with some wax and make a candle.

ANTON
To see his future?

NADYA
Yes.

ANTON
With a candle?

NADYA
Yes.

(Beat)

ANTON
You are just as strange as I am.

NADYA
What I am is penniless. I'll take whatever clientii I can get. So, this last month has been good to you, yes?

ANTON
What?

NADYA
You're looking less...ragged.

ANTON
I do not understand.

NADYA
Those clothes. Better than the scraps you were wearing before.

ANTON
I took them off a dead man.

NADYA
Ha! Well, he did not need them anymore.

ANTON
My thought as well.

NADYA
We have something in common. We are both of us corbi, picking off the dead.

ANTON
You mean crows.

NADYA
Very good, giant! You've learned some of my language.

ANTON
I was hoping to see you again.

NADYA
And you were hoping to impress me, yes?

(Beat)

ANTON
I would ask a favor of you.

NADYA
Oh yes? What might that be?

ANTON
I want to know my future.

NADYA
Ah. Is that all?

ANTON
Should I ask for more?

NADYA
You should always ask for what you want. And be prepared not to get it.

ANTON
My life has taught me to expect nothing from anyone.

NADYA
And yet here you stand, with a set of new clothes.

(Beat)

ANTON
You make a good point.

NADYA
So what of your future do you wish to know?

ANTON
Anything. Everything.

NADYA
Those are two very different answers.

ANTON
I have never thought of my future. In fact, I doubted I would ever live this long. But now…

NADYA
Your life has changed.

ANTON
Yes.

NADYA
For the better?

ANTON
I think so. I hope so.

NADYA
And you wish to know if this better life will last.

ANTON
Very much.

NADYA
Sit with me. *(She takes him by the hand and they sit)* Why do you hide your face?

ANTON
I have no face.

NADYA
You have eyes. Two different colors.

ANTON
It is how I was made.

NADYA
And a mouth. And I'm guessing a nose.

ANTON
Yes. But together they are… monstrous.

NADYA
I'm sorry.

ANTON
I have always looked this way. This graveyard is the first place where people have not fled from me.

NADYA
It's why I like places like this. A sanctuary for outcasts. *(Notices him staring at her)* I am so lovely you cannot help but stare? Is that it?

ANTON
You do not seem like an outcast.

NADYA
I am a gypsy. We belong nowhere.

ANTON
You have tribes. Your friends and family who…

NADYA
I am the last of my people here. The others have moved on.

ANTON
And you did not go with them?

NADYA
I couldn't. They cast me out.

ANTON
Why?

NADYA
It hurts to tell it.

ANTON
I understand.

NADYA
You couldn't. It didn't happen to you.

ANTON
My own life...what little I had, I have lost. I carry that loss with me everywhere I go.

(She stares at him)

NADYA
Is that where your kindness comes from?

ANTON
Am I kind?

NADYA
Very. You have a child's heart. It gives itself completely, and shatters at the smallest hurt.

ANTON
I wish I was stronger. Inside.

NADYA
You will be strong, or you will be dead. The world welcomes no others.

ANTON
It is that cruel?

NADYA
That cruel and worse.

(Beat)

NADYA
I had a child.

ANTON
You seem too young.

NADYA
Not so young as all that. My child... my girl...she was încrucișat... *(She struggles to translate the word)* Mixed. Her father was not of my tribe. Not of any tribe.

ANTON
That is why they sent you away?

NADYA
Yes. With my people, that is a great shame. It does not wash off. They cast me to the winds.

ANTON
I'm sorry.

NADYA
I was young. A fool. I went to the father...a man of numbers. A...what is a man who counts money?

ANTON
A banker?

NADYA
Banker, yes. He had come to my camp, and I had loved him. But I loved him with a child's love...foolish. I came to his house, and his wife answered.

ANTON
He was married to another?

NADYA
As I said...I was a fool. He came to the door, dragged me to the field and threw us to the ground. Me and my Dorina.

ANTON
I don't know that word.

NADYA
Not a word; a name. It means "gift." My gift. Her father wanted nothing to do with us, swore to kill us if he saw us again. So I ran. Tried to live in the wood, but... *(Beat)* Dorina did not survive a year.

(ANTON struggles to reign in his emotions)

NADYA
I see your rage, Anton. But this is the past, and cannot be changed.

ANTON
I want to hurt this man.

NADYA
As did I. But it would help nothing. Murder does not bring peace. *(She looks in his eyes)* You know this better than most.

ANTON
I do.

NADYA
And so I came here. Ingolstadt is a good enough place. Lots of places to hide. Lots of drunks who don't guard their pockets.

ANTON
You are a thief?

NADYA
I am whatever I need to be to survive.

ANTON
I understand that. *(He realizes they're still holding hands)* You have my hand.

NADYA
I've been reading it.

ANTON
What?

NADYA
Your hands hold many things, including the future. I've been following their lines, trying to learn where they lead.

ANTON
Oh. I...should I pay you?

NADYA
You have let me steal bones and dirt. And eased my burden a little. No charge, this time.

ANTON
What do you see?

NADYA
It is...confusing. Yours is a strange hand.

ANTON
It is?

NADYA
You are...were a man of the fields. A farmer.

ANTON
No.

NADYA
You were. I can see it.

ANTON
I have never spent a day in the fields.

NADYA
You are certain?

ANTON
I am.

(She stares at him, confused, then tries to read on. She smiles)

NADYA
You have known great love.

ANTON
I have?

NADYA
I see it here. A wife that you loved above all others.

ANTON
No.

(She stares at him, frustrated)

NADYA
I know what is on your palm, Anton.

ANTON
Whatever you are reading there...

that life didn't belong to me.

NADYA
I think you are being stubborn.

ANTON
I think you are perhaps not as good at this as you think.

(She gasps in mock outrage, smacks his arm)

NADYA
You would say such things to one you fancy?

ANTON
You think I fancy you because of what you see in my palm?

NADYA
Because of what I see in your eyes. And I do not "think". I know.

(He is embarrassed by this)

NADYA
There is no shame in this, my giant. Few can resist my charms.

ANTON
You are very confident.

NADYA
(shrugging) I am many things, all of which are Nadya. (She can see he is embarrassed) Do not look away. What you feel is a good thing. The rush of blood, the blush of the cheek... nothing is better.

ANTON
I do not want to discuss it.

NADYA
So bashful, you are.

ANTON
It makes me feel strange. Weak. Confused.

NADYA
It is the way of affection. But it should be embraced, not feared.

ANTON
But what if the...what if it is not returned?

(Beat. NADYA smiles, understanding)

NADYA
My sweet, kind-hearted friend...why do you think so little of yourself?

(He pulls his hand away)

ANTON
I am a monster.

NADYA
Not in my eyes.

ANTON
You would not say that if you knew the things I've done. The people I've hurt...killed...

NADYA
A monster would not hurt inside as you do now.

ANTON
I do not know how to atone for them.

NADYA
You can't. You can only do what you have already done.

ANTON
Start over.

NADYA
Yes. Give me your other hand.

ANTON
What?

NADYA
This hand tells me your past. It is your future you wish to see, yes?

ANTON
I do.

NADYA
Then my friend, give me your other hand.

(He gives it to her. She stares at it for a moment, then leaps up & backs away)

NADYA
Cacat!

ANTON
What is it?

NADYA
What are you?!

ANTON
I do not understand.

NADYA
Why do you have two hands?

ANTON
Is that…most people have two of them.

NADYA
Not… (She grabs his hands, holding them up to inspect them) These are not the same hands! Nothing about them is the same!

ANTON
Each has four fingers and a thumb.

NADYA
They do not even feel the same! The palm, the knuckles…even the skin… you have the hands of two different people.

(ANTON pulls his hands away, his anger rising)

NADYA
Is your face like this? A collection of other men's faces?

ANTON
Do not ask me that.

NADYA
Good God, what are you?

ANTON
I told you before. I am a monster.

NADYA
I didn't believe you.

ANTON
Do you now?

(She backs away, her hand on her knife)

NADYA
Don't hurt me.

ANTON
Why do you…?

NADYA
(Draws her knife) Don't!

ANTON
I am not your enemy!

NADYA
I'm going to leave now, Anton.

ANTON
No!

NADYA
I am going to leave, and you are going to stay. Do you understand me?

ANTON
Please. You are my friend.

(She is about to respond, but thinks better of it. She sheathes her knife)

NADYA
Just let me go.

ANTON
Do not hate me, Nadya. I could not bear it.

(He goes to her. She backs away)

ANTON
You were going to tell me my future. Please, just sit. We can talk and...

NADYA
You have no future, giant. None at all.

ANTON
Nadya...!

(She runs off. ANTON stands there, a storm of anger and sorrow. In his rage, he rips a headstone from the ground. Lights fade)

SCENE EIGHT

(That same night, but several hours later. It is almost dawn. A table is set in the corner of the stage, with a cloth cover and a small bowl of water. NADYA enters with a hand-made candle. She lights it, lets the flame grow)

NADYA
You can come in.

(VICTOR enters. He is a changed man, much more haggard than in Scene 1)

NADYA
Sit.

(He sits at the table)

VICTOR
I appreciate your expediency.

NADYA
I appreciate your gold. Good motivation to get this done tonight.

VICTOR
Did it take you long? To make the candle?

(She fans the flame)

NADYA
You don't believe in this, do you?

VICTOR
It's up to you to make a believer out of me.

NADYA
Give the fire a moment to do its job. *(She sits down)* Dawn is a good time to tell the future, just as a new day is born.

VICTOR
What is this ceromancy supposed to tell me?

NADYA
That is a doctor's word for seeing in wax, yes?

VICTOR
Yes.

NADYA
I like you, domnule. We both use strange words to confuse those around us.

VICTOR
I did not pay for banter.

NADYA
I am to see in the wax, yes? Hard to do until the candle melts some. *(She leans over the table, showing her cleavage)* There are other things we can do to pass the time.

VICTOR
No.

NADYA
I promise you, I am worth the price.

(She reaches to touch his face. He grabs her wrist tightly)

VICTOR
The only woman I ever loved had her neck snapped like dry wood. Don't

touch me again.

NADYA
I do not like threats so much.

(VICTOR rises, crosses to her)

VICTOR
Do not mistake me for some common alley-rat you can gut and leave in the snow. I am a baron, a doctor and in no way a man to be trifled with.

(She rises, meeting his gaze)

NADYA
Then why come to me?

VICTOR
Because all sane means of finding my quarry have failed, so I must resort to...this.

(They stare at each other for a bit. She then laughs)

NADYA
Desperation can be a good thing, boierule. It can be the best thing.

(NADYA motions for VICTOR to sit. He does so. She takes the candle and holds it above the bowl, carefully letting a small amount of wax drip into it)

VICTOR
What do you see?

NADYA
Give me a moment. This is an art, not a science.

VICTOR
Do not bait me, woman. I...

NADYA
Who do you seek? Tell me of him.

VICTOR
What?

NADYA
Speak while the wax forms! The more I know, the clearer I will see.

VICTOR
He is large...very tall and broad.

NADYA
Good.

VICTOR
He burned through my life like a wildfire. Murdered my brother, my friends, my father...my wife.

NADYA
Yes. I can see it. He is close.

VICTOR
How close?!

NADYA
Very. You have tracked him to Ingolstadt, yes?

VICTOR
Yes. I was a student here. It was where we were first...acquainted. I thought perhaps he would return and...

NADYA
He has but...wait....

(She drips more wax into the bowl. She starts at what she sees within)

NADYA
You must stop this hunt.

VICTOR
What did you see?

NADYA
There is a chain wrapped tight around the two of you. If you continue to hunt him, it will be death for you both.

VICTOR
I don't care! If my death brings his

about, then it will be worth it.

NADYA
You speak madness. Stop, and rebuild a life. If you leave this place, you and your prey will never see each other again.

VICTOR
I can't. He's more than my prey. Any lives he takes will fall squarely on my head.

NADYA
I don't understand.

VICTOR
I made him.

NADYA
This man is your son?

VICTOR
He is no man. He's a monster. Scarred and malformed…he…

(She backs away. VICTOR sees the recognition in her eyes)

VICTOR
You've seen him.

NADYA
No.

(He grabs her roughly. She doesn't fight back)

VICTOR
Where is he?!

NADYA
Let me go!

VICTOR
You have no gypsy camp to come to your rescue, woman. Tell me where he is!

NADYA
I saw death in the water! If you chase him any longer, you will meet your end in a land of snow and frozen seas!

VICTOR
I don't give a damn for your prophecies. Just tell me where he is!

(He takes a knife and holds it to her)

NADYA
Kill me and you'll never find him.

VICTOR
There are other gypsies besides you. I imagine my coin will make them forthcoming.

(She is about to speak, but stops)

VICTOR
Ah. Is that it?

(He opens a belt-pouch, and produces several gold coins. She reaches for them, and he drops them on the floor. She scrambles to pick them up. A moment of shame takes VICTOR)

VICTOR
I should be a better man than this.

NADYA
So say all dogs.

VICTOR
But for one mistake, my life would have been full of light. A family, a noble title, and scientific advancement. Now…

NADYA
Yes. All eyes weep for you, rich man.

VICTOR
I would gladly part with every franc if it would put an end to this nightmare.

(She rises, clutching the coins. He reads her expression)

VICTOR
Yours has been a hard life, I take it.

(*She spits on the ground*)

NADYA
That is what I think of your pity.

VICTOR
Then what do you think of this? (*Removes his coin pouch, holds it*) There is enough here for you to start over. The dream of every pauper. And all you have to do is tell me where to find the monster.

NADYA
So that you can kill him?

VICTOR
I'm not killing him. I'm taking back a life I should never have given.

(*Beat*)

VICTOR
This is not your story. Take these coins, and remove yourself from it.

(*A long beat. She reaches out. He puts the coin pouch in her hand*)

NADYA
Sit. We have much to discuss.

(*They sit. She blows out the candle. Blackout*)

END OF ACT I

ACT II
SCENE ONE

(*Lights up. KURT's shack. It is a mess. ANTON is huddled in a corner. KURT enters, carrying a small barrel*)

KURT
Stop your worrying, lummox. I have returned with beer and... (*Sees the wreck of his room*) Christ almighty... (*Sees ANTON*) Anton! Are you hurt? Anton!

(*ANTON rises. His chest is bleeding, & he holds a bloody knife*)

ANTON
...Kurt...

KURT
Oh God, boy. You hold still. I have bandages and...

ANTON
...why won't I die?

KURT
Don't you worry. You're not dying, not so long as I'm here.

ANTON
This knife...I buried it deep...no man could have survived...

KURT
What?

ANTON
A man can die. A man should die. But I am not a man.

(*KURT has found a cloth, tries to press it to ANTON's chest. ANTON holds his knife up and KURT stops*)

ANTON
I thrust it all the way into my heart. Through the muscle, between the ribs...I felt the blade touch my back-

bone...I saw my blood pour out of the hole.

KURT
That's impossible.

ANTON
But my heart did not stop beating. The pain didn't leave me. I live and...

(In a sudden rage, ANTON thrusts knife into the table)

ANTON
I should not live! I never should have lived, but here I am, a mockery of nature and... *(Grabs KURT by the shoulders)* The night we met...I had come to this cemetery to die. Can you help me? Will you help me?

KURT
Help you what?

ANTON
Die! I want to die, I...

(He starts pounding on his bloody chest)

ANTON
I cannot take the pain! Everything I feel turns on me, and then...Kurt, you are my only friend. If you do not kill me...

KURT
I won't!

ANTON
...then I will kill you.

(Beat)

ANTON
I do not wish to. But already, I can feel murder rising up inside me. Soon, I will go mad and when that happens... *(He grabs some rope)* This. Take this. Strangle me. If my breath stops, my heart might follow.

KURT
No.

ANTON
Please! I'm begging you!

KURT
Listen to me. I have broken damn near every vow I've ever taken, but I will never kill a man. Certainly not you.

(ANTON falls to his knees, weeping)

ANTON
...please...I want the pain to stop...

(KURT kneels next to him)

KURT
It doesn't. I know that better than anyone. But life isn't about the absence of pain. It's about enduring it.

ANTON
I cannot. I love, I find peace, and every time it is taken from me. And when it is...I've felt a neck break in my hands. I don't want it to be your neck.

KURT
Nor do I.

ANTON
You should fear me. You should fear what I can do.

KURT
Don't tell me what to do, lummox.

(KURT smiles. ANTON's mood softens. KURT puts his arm around him)

KURT
Whatever happened to you while I was in town...for God's sake, you don't have to kill yourself over it.

ANTON
She was my friend. She was kind to me. Then she saw what I am, what I truly am, and she fled.

(There is a long silence between them)

KURT
A woman. I should have known.

(ANTON just stares at him)

KURT
You're not the first to go mad over a broken heart, Anton. Nor will you be the last.

ANTON
All my life, I have been betrayed. Always.

KURT
"Always?" No such thing. A child is always a child until it becomes a boy, then a man, then a corpse. Trust an old gravedigger on that.

ANTON
She said I had no future.

KURT
Pfft! Will you wake up tomorrow? Will you do something then? That's the future. Happens whether we think it will or not.

(KURT pats ANTON on the chest, then winces)

KURT
Oh God, I'm sorry.

ANTON
Why?

KURT
Didn't that hurt? Where you cut yourself?

ANTON
No. And I didn't cut myself. I stabbed myself.

KURT
I'd think you were drunk if I hadn't drained the last drop yesterday.

ANTON
You don't believe me?

KURT
Well...when you love a woman and then...I think you're not thinking straight is all.

ANTON
Do you know much about women?

KURT
Yes! Or...perhaps not as much as some, but...what kind of question is that?

ANTON
I don't know. How many kinds of questions are there?

(Beat. KURT starts to laugh. ANTON smiles. As the laughter peters out--)

KURT
You were right about me.

(ANTON stares at him)

KURT
I was a priest. Long ago. A lifetime ago. I was happier then...until I met a woman.

ANTON
Had you not met women before?

KURT
No, I...this woman in particular.

ANTON
Oh.

KURT
A married woman at that. The Father had hired her to clean the church and...she wasn't a great beauty, Anton. But her heart...kind, and pure, and nothing but love for this whole rotten world. We would talk, and she would laugh and...God,

that laugh. Hers was a marriage of convenience, though not damn convenient for me. I loved her. I didn't want to, I tried not to, but it happened all the same.

ANTON
Did she love you in return?

KURT
She did. And so I abandoned everything I believed in, the life I thought would be my fate forever, all for her.

ANTON
What of her husband?

KURT
We kept it a secret at first. Her from him, me from the church. But secrets never keep, so I left the clergy. She left her husband too, but...

(Beat. He takes a drink)

KURT
He killed her, Anton. Took a knife and just...and then he came for me. I was in the church, saying my goodbyes and this madman bursts in. Grabs me, throws me into the altar and...he set the church on fire. Said he was gonna send us all to Hell. Damned fool didn't count on him dying first. The old timbers went up like matchsticks, and the burning curtains fell on him.

ANTON
That seems just.

KURT
There was justice to be had that night, but that wasn't it. So there I am, watching everything I'd ever known burn around me...except it wasn't just me. Five other priests, men who'd been my friends all my life, and they were going to die because of what I'd done.

ANTON
You did not set the fire.

KURT
Oh, I didn't strike the tinder, but I lit it all the same. But I knew I had to get these men out. The church was falling in on itself, and I just started grabbing these men and dragging them out. The last of them, my friend Gregor...I had him over my shoulder and suddenly...

(KURT claps loudly)

KURT
A support beam comes crashing down. I managed to toss him out the door, and then everything went black. When I woke up, the church was gone and my leg...crushed. Broken beyond repair. And that was justice, Anton.

ANTON
I do not understand.

KURT
God was punishing me for what I'd done. He could've killed me that night, but he's kinder than that, I suppose. Or crueler. Hard to tell sometimes. And so the church set me up here, tending to the dead. I've spent every day since that day cleaning the paths, reading the gravestones and trying to drink away a life that I remember the way one remembers a story he was told long ago.

ANTON
Why did you tell me this?

(KURT is silent, thinking)

KURT
The day will come, Anton, where I will look God in the eye and have to answer for what I've done. I think it will be easier if I could...do something good again.

(ANTON rises)

KURT
You don't have to leave. I don't want you to.

ANTON
I'm not.

(ANTON begins to remove his bandages)

KURT
What are you doing?

ANTON
I said I would tell you about my face when you told me about your leg.

KURT
You don't have to.

ANTON
Yes. I do.

(He has unwrapped his face. It is a scarred & mangled mess. KURT just stares at him)

KURT
Oh my God.

ANTON
God had nothing to do with this.

(KURT can only gape at ANTON. After a bit, ANTON starts to leave)

KURT
Don't go.

(ANTON stops, turns)

KURT
Whatever you've done...whatever's been done to you...This is your home now, if you want it.

ANTON
I've never had a home.

KURT
"Never" is a lot like "always." It only exists until it doesn't.

(Beat. ANTON shuts the door)

KURT
Good. I'm going to cook us up some supper. Sit down already.

(ANTON sits. KURT begins to re-assemble his shack)

KURT
Where the hell did you throw my beans?

(ANTON begins to wrap his face again. KURT speaks without looking at him)

KURT
Put those down. You don't need them here.

(ANTON leaves his face unwrapped. Lights fade)

SCENE TWO

(The cemetery at night. KURT walks in holding a lantern. He makes sure no one is present, then motions ANTON to enter. ANTON, no longer bandaged, enters)

KURT
How does it feel?

ANTON
Strange.

KURT
To be out in the open, as you are?

ANTON
Yes. I feel...taller? I am unsure...

KURT
Christ, don't get any taller on me. I already need a damn ladder to look you in the eye.

ANTON
I am so used to hiding myself. When I went unmasked before, the result was...violent.

KURT
You never need to worry about that here. Here, it's just me and buried bones.

ANTON
I like your company...and theirs... more than any other.

KURT
You can still do your work at night, but without them rags on your face. This is your graveyard now as much as it's mine.

ANTON
Perhaps more so. I do more work than you.

(KURT stares at him)

KURT
You just made a joke, didn't you?

ANTON
I did.

(KURT laughs, claps him on the back)

KURT
Ha! Not bad, lummox! Not bad.

ANTON
Thank you. Runt.

KURT
What?

ANTON
If you can call me "lummox," I can call you "runt."

KURT
I'm not a runt! You're just enormous! Everything looks smaller to you.

(ANTON wanders around)

ANTON
It is so beautiful here.

KURT
You think so?

ANTON
I do. There is such order to these grave markers. Like a garden of stone. And the trees that guard over them. And the moonlight shining between the branches, making paths of light in the mist. It is so quiet... and so alive.

KURT
Not many'd say that about this place.

ANTON
They do not see it as I do. You cannot see the dead here, just the growing, living things. The trees, and the vines, and the birds that sing at night. It is perfect.

KURT
I never saw it that way.

ANTON
Do you now?

(A breeze blows in, moving the mist. ANTON feels it against his face. The emotion is almost too much)

KURT
Cold wind. Might be another storm coming. Come on.

(He tries to move ANTON, who stands still, savoring the wind)

KURT
We should get inside.

ANTON
No.

KURT
You want to get thunderstruck? Tall as you are, you…

ANTON
I do not fear lightning or thunder. I…I can feel the wind on my face.

KURT
So can I, so let's just…

ANTON
Is this God?

(KURT stops, sees ANTON enjoying the moment, and closes his eyes, trying to do the same)

ANTON
What do you feel?

KURT
Nothing.

ANTON
Here. What do you feel here? *(Taps KURT's chest)*

KURT
I don't…

ANTON
The breath of God. Life. It is all around us.

KURT
How do you know?

ANTON
I just know.

(Beat. ANTON can tell something is upsetting KURT)

ANTON
Kurt? What is it?

KURT
Nothing. Let's go inside.

ANTON
I am your friend, yes?

KURT
Yes.

ANTON
If I have upset you…

KURT
You didn't upset me, I just…

(Beat)

KURT
When the wind blows, all I feel is the wind. But you stand here and talk of God and…you have no idea. Do you know what I would give to feel God's presence again?

ANTON
You were a priest.

KURT
And a poor one at that. Since the day God took my leg and my church… he wants nothing to do with me. He turned his back, I turned mine, and that was that.

ANTON
A man burned your church. You tried to stop him.

KURT
And I'm sure the ashes thank me for my efforts. *(He pulls the old rosary out of his pocket)* You see this? This is all I have left of that place. Back then, when my thoughts turned dark, all I had to do was hold this, look at this…and it was as though God was taking my hand, consoling me.

Now...now it's just cold, dead wood.

ANTON
Then why do you still have it?

(They are quiet for a moment)

KURT
Enough of this standing around. My leg's locking up. *(He turns to go)*

ANTON
May I stay here, just a while longer?

KURT
We have no graves to dig tonight.

ANTON
I know. I just...I am happy here. I want to stay.

KURT
I said this was your home, didn't I? Don't have to ask my permission. You want to stay, stay, you lummox.

ANTON
Thank you. Runt.

(They smile at each other, and laugh a little. KURT heads off. ANTON sits, listening to the night birds sing. He whistles, trying to mimic their calls. NADYA approaches from the darkness)

NADYA
Trying to speak to birds? I wonder what they think you said.

(ANTON rises, stares at her)

ANTON
Nadya.

NADYA
Salutari, Anton.

ANTON
What are you doing here?

NADYA
I came to warn you.

(He stares at her, confused)

NADYA
There are worse things in this cemetery than you and I this night.

(Lights fade)

SCENE THREE

(The shack. VICTOR stands warming his hands at the stove. His back is to the door. He wears a high-collared coat & a hat, so his face is obscured. KURT enters & sees him)

KURT
Hey! Hey! Who the hell are you?! Get out of my...

(VICTOR turns to him)

KURT
Wait...I know you, don't I?

VICTOR
We worked together, after a fashion, a year ago.

KURT
You...you're that doctor, yes?

KURT
Victor.

KURT
Christ, you're the one I dug up the corpses for.

VICTOR
Yes. That's why I'm here, in fact.

KURT
No. No no no. I told you then what I'm telling you now.

VICTOR
Listen to me.

KURT
I'm not pulling another pour soul

out of the earth for you. Never again.

(VICTOR smiles)

VICTOR
That's just it, though. They don't have souls. That was the mistake I made. There's no equation for it, no chemical formula...that part of them is gone forever.

KURT
What are you talking about?

VICTOR
Our child has come home, Mr. Volker.

(KURT stares at him)

VICTOR
I made life, with your help.

KURT
Didn't your pa ever talk to you? I'm certain there has to be a lady involved somewhere.

VICTOR
What I did goes far beyond impregnating some girl. I made life...I...

(KURT grabs VICTOR's arm)

KURT
I don't know what you're talking about. I don't want to know. Just get out before I toss you out.

VICTOR
Why do you think I asked for parts instead of entire bodies? I wanted the strongest arms, the sharpest eyes, the fiercest heart...each individual piece had to be perfect. But their sum total was...abominable.

KURT
Get yourself to an inn and sleep it off.

VICTOR
And now that abomination is here.

(VICTOR pulls a gun from his belt, checking it. KURT freezes)

VICTOR
Calm yourself. I won't hurt you.

KURT
You've got a gun.

VICTOR
The bullet isn't for you. Sit.

(KURT sits)

VICTOR
You were a priest, yes? Or something of the sort. I think I remember you saying that once.

KURT
Yes.

VICTOR
Can you still absolve a man of his sins?

(Beat. KURT's demeanor softens)

KURT
No. That part of my life died a long time ago.

VICTOR
What if...could you try?

KURT
I'm sorry. That's not how it works.

(VICTOR sits, his emotions rising)

VICTOR
I never wanted to hurt anyone. You have to believe me.

KURT
All right.

VICTOR
The work I was doing...it was to

preserve life. Perhaps indefinitely. And it...I don't know how it became what it became.

KURT
Doctor, I...

VICTOR
Victor. Please.

KURT
Victor. You're seeking absolution from a man...and not much of a man at that. My days in the confessional are long behind me.

VICTOR
Just hear me out. I beg of you. *(Collects himself)* Mr. Volker, when a child is born...naturally, as God intended, they have time to grow, to learn and adapt. I think...I think this is how a soul is formed. But my creature lacked all of that. It began its existence fully formed, in a body stronger than any ten men, but with an emotional capacity no greater than an infant's. Do you understand what I'm saying?

KURT
I'm sorry, I don't.

VICTOR
A baby is upset, it lashes out. But it is small, fragile...it can harm no one. Now, imagine that blind emotion, pure and unfettered by thought, but with the strength of a giant behind it.

(KURT begins to understand)

KURT
What?

VICTOR
I fled from it. I saw it rise up, saw its scarred and mangled face...its dead, soulless eyes...and I ran. I left it to the world in hopes that it would sputter out and die. But it didn't die. It endured, in a world that offered it nothing but hate. And so it became as monstrous within as it was without. It tracked me down and...

(Beat)

VICTOR
It killed my brother first. William. No more than 10 years old, and it snapped his neck, for no other reason beyond bringing me anguish. My servant Justine was next. Then ...my friend Henry, a man who'd never hurt any living being... dead. My servants, dead. My father and...and my wife...my beautiful Elizabeth...I saw him. Standing over her broken body, pointing at it as he glared at me. But he left me alive... always alive to suffer his wrath. I have hunted him these long months, and my hunt has led me here. I have come to warn you. The creature...

KURT
Anton.

VICTOR
What?

KURT
His name is Anton. And he is that man no longer.

VICTOR
You know him?

KURT
He is my friend.

(VICTOR grabs him, lifting him up)

VICTOR
What? What did you say?

KURT
Please...he's not the way he was. He's

found peace here.

VICTOR
He has deceived you! He is as clever as he is savage.

KURT
He came here to die! He wanted to die. That's what he said. But... no, what he really wanted was hope. Friendship.

(VICTOR releases him)

KURT
I'm sorry for what he's done to you. I am. No man should ever suffer like that. But I'm telling you, if you leave...if you let him go...he'll never hurt another soul again.

(Beat. VICTOR considers this, then points his gun at KURT)

VICTOR
I'm afraid I can't take that chance.

(Lights fade)

SCENE FOUR

(The cemetery, with ANTON & NADYA, shortly after we saw them last)

NADYA
So this is your face.

ANTON
Yes.

NADYA
Would you...can I touch it?

ANTON
Why would you do that?

NADYA
I am curious.

ANTON
The last time you laid your hands on me, you ran in fear.

NADYA
I know.

ANTON
I am not inclined to trust you now.

NADYA
How could I hurt you?

ANTON
You have already hurt me. Deeply. I have no desire to experience it again.

(She lowers her head, ashamed)

ANTON
You came to warn me? Then do so and be gone.

NADYA
There is a man in Ingolstadt. He is hunting you.

ANTON
I am no stranger to that.

NADYA
He's your father.

(Beat)

ANTON
What did you say?

NADYA
About this tall. Dark hair, wild eyes. He came to me last night, paid me to read his future. To help him find you.

ANTON
And you did this?

(She says nothing. He grabs her arm)

ANTON
Did you tell my father I was here!?

(She pushes him away)

NADYA
I live in filth! I have no family anymore, no friends! Only men who would see their future or see up my skirts! And this man...he offered me more gold than I could earn in a year!

ANTON
You have betrayed me.

NADYA
Yes, dammit. And I am trying to make it right.

ANTON
Why?! What do you care if he finds me, if he ends my life? I am only a monster to you!

NADYA
Stop attacking me! I...

(ANTON closes on her quickly. She falls backward, terrified)

ANTON
I have not attacked you yet, little gypsy. You should know this because you are still breathing.

NADYA
I'm sorry for what I said to you... what I did to you. I am!

ANTON
Your word means less than nothing.

NADYA
He told me what you did. The people you killed. His brother. His wife.

(ANTON backs off)

NADYA
You may look down your crooked nose at me, but you are no innocent. You've bloodied your hands more in a year than I could in a lifetime.

ANTON
I am trying to be something better than I was! I have left behind man's world and entombed myself here!

NADYA
I have travelled further than you can imagine, and this much I know; unless you flee to the frozen North itself, you will never be free of men. *(Beat)* The doctor said he had business to attend to, someone he had to warn about you. Do you know what that means?

ANTON
No.

NADYA
It means you can leave here, tonight, and be gone before he finds you. That is what I came here to say.

ANTON
First you sell me to my enemy, now you would aid in my escape?

NADYA
Do not presume to know my mind.

ANTON
This is my home.

NADYA
Then it is good there are many graves here, for the doctor will likely put you in one. *(She crosses away)* I have done what I came to do. Flee or die; the choice is yours.

ANTON
I should break your neck. I have done worse for less.

(She pulls her knife)

NADYA
Try it and I'll cut your throat.

ANTON
You can try.

NADYA
Stay back.

(She starts to flee, but ANTON grabs her. She tries to stab him, but he catches the knife and lifts her high. She cries out in pain)

ANTON
You were the only woman who ever looked at me with kindness. I should have known better than to trust you.

NADYA
Let me go!

ANTON
Why? So you can cut my throat?

NADYA
I won't hurt you! Please!

ANTON
We are far past begging, Nadya.

(He squeezes her wrist until she drops the knife. She cries out again)

ANTON
A part of me loved you the minute I saw you. You are very beautiful, and I wanted to be close to that beauty.

NADYA
You still can be.

ANTON
You say that only to save your life. I can hear the lie in your voice.

NADYA
I'm not lying.

(He grabs her hair, pulling her face to his)

ANTON
Look at me! Would you have these dead lips kiss you? These patchwork hands caress you? Or does your bile rise to be this close to my face?

(She leans forward and kisses him. He releases her, and backs away, confused & perhaps afraid)

NADYA
I could run from you now, but I am still here. There is no gain in this for me.

ANTON
Why...?

NADYA
Because I have hurt you. Because I will not do it again.

(She walks to him. He backs away)

NADYA
Stop.

ANTON
What do you...?

NADYA
Anton. Stop.

(He does. She reaches up slowly and puts her hands on his face)

NADYA
This face is not so bad a face.

(He takes her hands and begins to weep. She squeezes his hands)

ANTON
I was going to kill you.

NADYA
No.

ANTON
I had my hands around your throat.

NADYA
You lashed against one who had hurt you. But no, you would not have killed me. You are that man no longer.

ANTON
How do you know?

NADYA
That man hid his face from the world. You have nothing to hide now.

(He looks around)

ANTON
I will be sad to leave this place.

NADYA
I am sorry that you must. But you found a piece of your soul here. Perhaps other pieces are out there, waiting.

(He rises)

ANTON
You kissed me.

NADYA
Yes. I...I think it was goodbye.

(He lowers his head)

ANTON
As do I.

(Lights fade)

SCENE FIVE

(KURT's shack. It is dark. ANTON enters)

ANTON
Kurt?

(No answer)

ANTON
If you are asleep, I am sorry to wake you but...

(A match is struck, and a candle lit. VICTOR is illuminated by its light. ANTON stands very still. VICTOR points the pistol at him)

ANTON
Father.

VICTOR
Do not move. Do not think of moving. Am I understood?

ANTON
I do not fear you.

VICTOR
I don't need your fear. I need your acquiescence.

ANTON
Where is Kurt?

VICTOR
He is safe. If you wish him to remain thus, you will do as I say. Sit.

ANTON
If you have harmed him...

VICTOR
I said sit.

(ANTON just glares at him, then sits)

VICTOR
Can you sense it, in the dark? The hatred between us clings to the air like a cold mist.

ANTON
What do you want, father?

VICTOR
Don't call me that! I am not your father!

ANTON
If not you, then who?

VICTOR
You are the Devil's orphan, if you are anything at all.

ANTON
God and the Devil...I thought you put no stake in such things.

VICTOR
My perspective has grown since you destroyed my life.

(He pushes a glass towards ANTON)

ANTON
What is this?

VICTOR
If you wish to see the gravedigger again, you will drink.

(ANTON suddenly rises, grabbing VICTOR by the throat)

VICTOR
Kill me and you'll never know where I hid Mr. Volker. He'll die of his wounds unless I tend to them.

(ANTON lets him go)

VICTOR
I have every advantage now. Even if you kill me, you're only bringing me peace. But for your friend's sake, quench your thirst.

(ANTON takes the cup)

ANTON
You mean to poison me.

VICTOR
I mean to drug you, actually. Poison would end this too quickly.

(ANTON stares at the cup)

VICTOR
I had to guess at the dosage, considering your distinct metabolism. But I am confident that the contents of that cup will weaken your body without dulling your mind too much. I want you awake for what comes next.

ANTON
What does come next?

VICTOR
Put cup to lip and find out.

(ANTON stares at the cup for a bit, then drinks)

VICTOR
You willingly cripple yourself, for the sake of a drunken wretch you barely know?

ANTON
He is my friend.

VICTOR
You are a collection of corpses, somewhere between a charnel pit and a butcher's floor. You have no friends.

(ANTON staggers a bit)

VICTOR
And so the chemicals do their work. Don't bother fighting them.

ANTON
I have..fought...all my life.

VICTOR
No one knows that better than I.

(VICTOR checks the gun)

VICTOR
I thought I wouldn't be able to control myself when I saw you again. I have a great desire to revenge myself upon you but...you have no idea. No idea of the time, the resources, my very lifeblood....all these things I poured

into your creation. You were meant to be the greatest scientific achievement mankind ever witnessed. I want very much to know what went wrong.

ANTON
You will never know.

VICTOR
Don't be petulant, beast. Let your death mean something.

ANTON
I have...no answers...for you.

VICTOR
You are in many ways a perfect being. Stronger than any man before you; Senses sharper than any animal's. And your mind...I put within your misshapen skull the mind of a genius. And yet here you are, a rag-covered madman. What a waste. *(Grabs ANTON's face roughly)* Why did you become this demon?! What turned you into this?

ANTON
You.

(VICTOR backs away)

ANTON
For most of my short life...I wanted only one thing. Your love. Even... when you abandoned me...I wanted to know you. A father's love...all any child wants.

VICTOR
Quiet.

ANTON
You gave me...only hate. I took that hate, and put it in the place...where my soul should have been.

(VICTOR sets the gun down)

VICTOR
I am sorry. Sorry that I ever made you. Sorry that you lived long enough to become this...thing. Sorry that yours has been a life of unending horror. But I have paid for my mistakes. You have to pay for yours. Do you understand that?

ANTON
I do not know. After all...I have done...it seems that you should kill me. But for the first time...I do not wish to die.

(Beat)

VICTOR
The answers I seek...I'll never find them, will I?

ANTON
I do not know.

VICTOR
I just...if I could make some sense of this, everything that has happened, perhaps then I would...I suppose it doesn't matter, in the end.

ANTON
Is this the end?

VICTOR
Yes. I believe it is. *(Rises, crosses to ANTON & puts the gun to his head)*

ANTON
Wait.

VICTOR
No.

ANTON
My friend...please let me see my friend.

VICTOR
I owe you nothing.

ANTON
You owe me everything! I exist only because of you!

VICTOR
You won't trick me again.

ANTON
Please! I beg of you! Just let me tell him goodbye!

(Beat. VICTOR lowers the gun)

VICTOR
It seems there's still something human left inside me.

(VICTOR leaves. ANTON tries to stand, succeeds in doing so, but is still very weak. He flops back into the chair. VICTOR soon returns with KURT, bound and gagged and injured)

ANTON
Kurt...

VICTOR
Here. Say your goodbyes. (Throws KURT into the chair)

ANTON
I thought...you left him near death.

VICTOR
A small lie will be the least of my sins.

(VICTOR ungags KURT)

KURT
Untie me, you whore-son!

ANTON
Kurt...

KURT
I'll rip your throat out with my teeth!

ANTON
Kurt, listen to me.

KURT
Has that bastard hurt you?

ANTON
A sedative only.

KURT
Christ, I'm glad to hear that.

ANTON
You have to listen...

KURT
I'll get us out of this, boy. Trust me. I...

ANTON
Thank you, Kurt.

KURT
Don't thank me yet.

ANTON
Thank you...for teaching me...everything that was worth knowing.

KURT
What?

ANTON
These past weeks...I have become something...better than I was. Because of you.

KURT
What are you saying?

(ANTON smiles)

ANTON
Goodbye.

(VICTOR closes on him, gun to his head)

KURT
No!

VICTOR
Close your eyes, Mr. Volker.

ANTON
Kurt, it's all right.

KURT
I'll give you anything!

(VICTOR just stares at him)

KURT
What do you want?! If I don't have it, I'll get it! Just don't hurt him!

VICTOR
It's true then. You care for each other.

KURT
I don't want to see him die and I don't want to see you damned.

VICTOR
My damnation is foregone at this point. But... (Circling behind ANTON) I have an idea, beast. You were right about me, partially at any rate. I never taught you anything. Every lesson you learned, you learned at the boot heel of the world. But now I can show you something important, before you cease to be.

(VICTOR pulls a long knife from his belt)

ANTON
What...?

VICTOR
This? This is to slit your throat in a moment.

ANTON
But...the pistol...

VICTOR
The pistol isn't for you anymore. (He points it at KURT)

KURT
Christ!

ANTON
NO!

VICTOR
You have murdered every single person I ever cared about. I will show you what that feels like.

(ANTON lurches up but stumbles. VICTOR kicks him hard)

VICTOR
The pain you've lived with all your life? It is nothing compared to this lesson I give to you.

(He fires. ANTON lurches up, clenching his fist in front of KURT. VICTOR just stares, shocked. When ANTON opens his fist, a metal ball drops from his hand)

ANTON
The dosage was not correct, father.

(VICTOR lunges at ANTON with the knife. ANTON grabs him, slamming him into the wall. He cries out)

KURT
Anton! Don't!

ANTON
You would have killed the only person who ever showed me kindness, and called it justice?

VICTOR
...burn in hell...

(ANTON slams him again)

ANTON
You said if I killed you, you would be at peace? Let us see.

(ANTON puts a hand on VICTOR's head begins to squeeze)

KURT
Stop it!

ANTON
Soon your fragile skull will break, father, and I will be free of you at last.

KURT
Stop!

ANTON
You should not have hurt my friend.

KURT
STOP!

(ANTON turns, stares at KURT)

KURT
God almighty...you say you regret the things you've done? Then please... please, don't do them again.

ANTON
He has to die!

(ANTON turns back to VICTOR, begins to squeeze again. VICTOR cries out)

KURT
You're a better man than this, Anton.

ANTON
I am not a man!

KURT
You are. You are a man, a good man... and my friend.

(ANTON is about to kill VICTOR, but stops. He drops him. They are all still in tense exhaustion, then VICTOR raises his knife. ANTON hits him and he flies into the wall, then lies unconscious. ANTON takes his knife and cuts KURT's bonds)

KURT
Anton, you didn't...?

ANTON
He still lives.

(KURT checks on VICTOR)

ANTON
You did not believe me?

KURT
Had to be sure. Give me the rope.

(ANTON tosses it to him, and KURT begins to tie up VICTOR. ANTON collapses into a chair)

KURT
You all right?

ANTON
No. But I will live.

(KURT goes to him)

KURT
What do we do now?

(ANTON looks up at him. Lights fade)

SCENE SIX

(The graveyard. No one is there. KURT walks in, making sure the place is empty. Once he's satisfied it is, he heads over to the grave ANTON emerged from in Act I. He hollers loudly at the dirt)

KURT
All's clear!

(The earth shifts, and ANTON rises from the ground. He shakes off the dirt)

KURT
You're quite a sight.

ANTON
So I've been told. The policemen?

KURT
Gone. Took the doctor with them.

ANTON
What did you tell them?

KURT
The truth, more or less. The doctor came in, raving. Attacked me. I managed to fight him off.

ANTON
That's not the truth. I am the one who fought him.

KURT
I could've taken him out if you hadn't gotten there first.

ANTON
I think you are wrong.

KURT
Pfft. What do you know?

ANTON
I know what "embellishment" means.

(KURT chuckles)

KURT
You're getting a feeling for jokes.

ANTON
I am learning.

KURT
That was a fancy trick, by the way. Catching that bullet.

ANTON
I am faster than most.

KURT
Thank you.

ANTON
For being fast?

KURT
For saving my life, you lummox.

ANTON
Had I not come here, your life would never have been in danger.

KURT
I don't care about the whys and wherefores. I'm just…thank you.

ANTON
You are welcome.

(Beat)

KURT
The doctor kept mum about you.

ANTON
I thought as much. He wants to kill me himself.

KURT
Maybe he'll stop now.

ANTON
No. He will never stop. All I have done is gained a little time.

KURT
All right then. What will you do with that time?

(Beat)

ANTON
I have to leave, Kurt.

KURT
No you don't.

ANTON
I do. You know I do.

KURT
Because of that doctor? Who knows how long they'll put him behind bars? He attacked a priest!

ANTON
A former priest.

KURT
Still pretty bad.

ANTON
He will escape. He will hunt me until he is dead. And…I no longer

have it in me to kill him.

KURT
I think maybe you never did.

ANTON
I did. Before I came here, before I met you...murder came as easily to me as breathing.

KURT
I want you to stay.

ANTON
As do I. But where I am, no one is safe. Tonight taught me that.

KURT
Where would you go then? There are people...well, everywhere.

ANTON
North.

KURT
There are people North.

ANTON
Not to the farthest North.

(KURT just stares at him)

ANTON
I have a friend...a gypsy. She told me that it would be the only place free of mankind. I will go there.

KURT
What if the doctor follows?

ANTON
He will. But this time, there will be no one he can use against me.

KURT
This is your home.

ANTON
And no matter how far I go, I will always think of it that way.

(Beat)

KURT
The doctor told me something. I think you need to know.

ANTON
What?

KURT
Do you know why you came here?

ANTON
To this graveyard?

KURT
Yes.

ANTON
I was lost, wandering. I found myself here.

KURT
I think it's more than that.

(Beat)

KURT
I know what you are. A man made from the parts of others.

ANTON
Yes.

KURT
This is where those parts came from.

(ANTON stares at him)

KURT
A year ago, this young doctor came to me, offered me a bag of gold for dead bodies. Or parts of 'em, anyways.

ANTON
You are the one who found me?

KURT
Yes. I didn't know what the doctor was doing. It's not so strange a thing, medical students paying for fresh corpses. Had I known...

ANTON
I am alive because of you.

KURT
I suppose so.

ANTON
I have always thought of the doctor as my father.

KURT
All right.

ANTON
Does this make you my mother?

(Beat. KURT glares at ANTON, who starts to laugh. KURT does as well)

KURT
Christ, I'm glad I didn't have to nurse you!

(They both laugh more, letting it die out naturally. They enjoy the quiet night)

ANTON
I will miss you, gravedigger.

KURT
Wouldn't have to miss me if you just stayed, dammit.

ANTON
You understand that...

KURT
Yes, yes. I understand. I hate it, but I understand. Just doesn't seem fair.

ANTON
I know.

KURT
You've done bad things, but you were just a child then.

ANTON
It was not even a year ago.

KURT
You know what I mean.

ANTON
I know that...Kurt, I have a soul now. I did not then, but I do now. Because of you.

KURT
I don't give souls, Anton. I just... helped you recognize it for what it was.

ANTON
No one has ever given me so much. *(Offers KURT his hand)* Thank you.

(KURT takes it, then pulls him into a hug. After a bit, they let go)

KURT
Goodbye, lummox.

ANTON
Goodbye, my friend.

(ANTON exits. KURT watches him go, then takes his rosary out of his pocket. He looks at it, speaks to it)

KURT
Just...watch over him, all right?

(Nothing happens. He shakes his head, laughs at his foolishness. Then wind blows through the graveyard)

END OF PLAY

The Decade Dance

A PLAY BY
JOSEPH ZETTELMAIER

Cast of Characters

ROGER WEEMS
NINA REYNOLDS

THE DECADE DANCE premiered at Williamston Theatre, in Williamston, Michigan on April 8, 2016. It was directed by Joseph Albright. Set design by Bart Bauer. Lighting design by Daniel C. Walker. Costume design by Karen Kangas-Preston. Sound Design by Julia Garlotte. Prop Design by Michelle Raymond. Stage managed by Stefanie Din.

The cast was as follows:

NINA REYNOLDS - Tiffany Mitchenor
ROGER WEEMS - Mitchell Koory

For information about production rights, visit www.jzettelmaier.com.

The Decade Dance

ACT ONE
SCENE 1
May 6, 1970
Roger's House, Lansing MI

(ROGER's house. It is a bit of a mess, with pizza boxes, beer cans, etc. Some various music & comic book posters are on the wall. The door flies open. ROGER & NINA enter in the throws of passion. As they fool around, NINA's foot goes into a pizza box. They stop)

NINA
Baby?

ROGER
Yeah?

NINA
I think I'm stepping in pizza.

(Beat. ROGER looks on the ground)

ROGER
Ah, shit. *(He grabs the pizza box, sets it on the stove. He makes a barely successful attempt to clean up a bit)*

ROGER
Sorry. Lemme just…sorry.

NINA
So this is your place?

ROGER
Ta-da!

NINA
It's…something.

ROGER
Yeah. I just…so, I wasn't expecting company.

NINA
You woulda cleaned up otherwise?

ROGER
Honestly, I'd need like a week's notice. Maybe two.

(NINA giggles. She walks around as he cleans. She finds a washcloth on the couch)

NINA
Can I use this?

ROGER
Uh…

NINA
For my foot.

ROGER
I…probably fine, yeah.

(She cleans her foot, looks around. ROGER talks as he cleans)

ROGER
Hey, you want anything to eat? Or drink?

NINA
I'm good.

ROGER
I've got some pretty good weed. You smoke, yeah?

NINA
Yeah.

ROGER
Cool. If you want, we...

NINA
This place is kinda funky.

ROGER
In a good way?

NINA
Um...

ROGER
I like it. It's me, you know?

NINA
I guess? I don't really know you. At all.

ROGER
Fair enough.

(He's at least cleaned the couch off. He sits next to her)

ROGER
What's your name?

(She laughs. He smiles)

ROGER
What?

NINA
Now you wanna know my name? You had your hand up my shirt without it.

ROGER
I'm Roger. Or Rog. Lots of people just call me "Rog."

NINA
Saves a lot of time?

ROGER
One syllable's worth, at least.

NINA
I'm Nina.

ROGER
Yeah, you are.

NINA
I am?

ROGER
You give off a very "Nina" vibe. It's like, I look at you, and you're totally just...Nina.

NINA
Cool. *(Beat)* Introductions over?

ROGER
Yep.

(They go at it again)

NINA
I didn't go to this thing to mess around.

ROGER
Cool.

NINA
We were protesting, Rog.

ROGER
Right.

NINA
Nine students were shot. Four died. We have to say something.

ROGER
Yep.

NINA
It was amazing. The energy, baby. The

fuckin' energy.

ROGER
Yuh-huh.

NINA
We're right on the edge. This country, I mean. We're right on the edge and we're about to go over unless somebody does something.

ROGER
Totally agree.

NINA
It's crazy, man. But you get it. That's why you were there. We had to stand up and say "No fucking way!" And then those guards showed up and... Jesus, look who I'm talking to. Mr. Big Hero Man. You know what happened when those dicks showed up.

(ROGER smiles & shrugs)

NINA
Why'd you do it?

ROGER
Punch that guy?

NINA
Yeah. He was a security guard.

ROGER
He was an asshole is what he was. People have a right to protest.

NINA
Yeah we do.

ROGER
I saw him goin' for that hose and...I don't know. I got all Hulk.

NINA
Got all what?

ROGER
Hulk. You know...raaaaaargh! Hulk Smash!

(She stares at him, unsure. He points to a poster of the Hulk on the wall)

NINA
Oh! The INCREDIBLE Hulk.

ROGER
You have no idea who that is.

NINA
I do not.

ROGER
You just said that 'cause the title is on the poster.

NINA
I sure did.

ROGER
He's the guy who got blasted with radiation and...know what? Doesn't matter.

(They kiss)

NINA
It was so brave.

ROGER
C'mon.

NINA
The way you were out there, defending everyone. It's like the whole college was there, watching you.

ROGER
Yeah.

(Beat)

ROGER
Which college?

NINA
MSU.

ROGER
Oh. Totally.

NINA
Wait. Are you...you're a student,

right?

ROGER
Nope.

NINA
Really?

ROGER
Yep.

NINA
Then what were you doing there?

ROGER
I don't know. I saw the crowds, I wanted to see what was up.

NINA
Did you even know about the protests?

ROGER
That one specifically? No. But, I mean, I don't live in a cave. I know about Kent State. I was able to add it up, you know?

NINA
Then why'd you help us out?

ROGER
Well...you know that security guard was pointing the hose at you, right?

NINA
Yeah. Racist asshole.

ROGER
So here's the thing. You're really gorgeous.

(Beat)

NINA
OK.

ROGER
And...I don't know...I'd been trying to get your attention for like twenty minutes, but you were all focused on the, you know...

NINA
The protest!

ROGER
Right. So when that guy grabbed the hose...I was like "Rog, this is your chance."

NINA
Oh my god.

ROGER
Hey! It totally worked, right?

NINA
I gotta go.

ROGER
Why?

NINA
Why?! Why do you think!?

ROGER
I don't know. That's why I asked.

NINA
You lied to me!

ROGER
Nuh-uh.

NINA
I thought you were this, like, activist student! I thought we were on the same side!

ROGER
Baby, I'm on your side. What happened at Kent State is the worst thing that...

NINA
But you just wanted to get some of this! No, sir. I have too much pride and self-respect to...

ROGER
Whoa, whoa, whoa. Maintain. I never once lied to you.

NINA
You did! You totally did!

ROGER
All those things you thought…that's on you. You never asked me anything. We just sorta…collided.

NINA
You're a fraud, man. You don't get it.

ROGER
Nina, a guy can be socially conscious AND want to get laid. They don't cancel each other out.

NINA
I just thought we saw the world the same, you know?

ROGER
You liked me better when you thought that.

NINA
Yeah. I guess I did.

ROGER
Listen. I'm gonna toke up real quick. Will you just stay put and hear me out?

NINA
You gonna share?

ROGER
What am I? An asshole?

(He lights up a joint. As they talk, they pass it back and forth)

ROGER
Do I have a problem with college kids getting gunned down by American troops? Fuckin' right I do. It's everything we're not supposed to be, babe. 'Cause it's a slippery slope, right? You set this, like, precedent where "well, if it's cool to send the National Guard after citizens who do this, then we can send 'em after citizens who do that, and that." And it spirals outta control. And what's it do for the national psyche, you know? How do you recover from looking at the people who your whole life you're raised to believe are on your side, are here to protect you…and now they're shooting kids on their way to class? I'll tell you; you don't. You don't recover from that. It forms these, like, tiny fractures that just spread across a whole generation. And then I hear these people on TV saying that they should've shot ALL the students and I'm like "There! Right there! That's the problem! We're not united!" So long as there are people out there who think shooting unarmed kids is ok 'cause they don't believe what you believe, we're gonna keep disintegrating, as a people.

NINA
Totally.

ROGER
That's the shit that worries me, right? Because I don't know where it leads. We're being raised to…I don't know… deny empathy. Deny that a person can look totally different from you, can see the world totally different from you, and still be a good person. My theory, and again-totally cool if you don't agree-, but my theory is that the government's invested in the chaos. They don't want unity. Unity means you gotta change the way we're doing things. And politicians are like cats, babe. They cannot handle change. But the last two days, I've been watching the news, watching the shit go down in Ohio, and I think if we don't change now…and I mean right fucking now…then we're going right over

that edge you were talking about. Over, and we're never coming back.

(Beat)

ROGER
Jesus. I think that's the most I've said in like a year.

(NINA grabs him and kisses him)

ROGER
I didn't say that to get your pants off, ok?

NINA
I wouldn't kiss you if I thought you did.

ROGER
You got my brain racing and all of a sudden all these words came out.

NINA
You sure you're not a student?

ROGER
Barely made it out of high school. Is that a problem?

NINA
Hey, we're not getting married, right? No problems.

ROGER
So you wouldn't marry a dude who didn't go to college?

NINA
Just…look. Let's have tonight, ok. Let's just have tonight. Tomorrow, the sun will come up and I'll go my way and you'll go yours. Cool?

ROGER
Cool.

(They begin fooling around, undressing)

ROGER
But for the record, I wouldn't hate it if our ways were like the same ways.

NINA
I don't want something serious.

ROGER
OK.

NINA
And you don't know me. At all.

ROGER
It's gotta start somewhere.

NINA
Does pot make you think too much?

ROGER
I'm surprisingly deep.

NINA
Baby, I like you. A lot. But let's not over-think this, ok?

(Beat. He considers it, then smiles)

ROGER
Hulk smash.

(They fall to the couch. Lights fade)

SCENE 2
August 1, 1971 - Behind the Madison Square Garden, NYC, NY

(The sound of The Concert For Bangladesh is heard throughout the scene, as well as the sound of a large crowd. The setting is a parking lot area or something similar. NINA is huddled in a corner, her back to the audience. She is fighting nausea. ROGER enters)

ROGER
(Calling off to someone unseen) I've got it! Baby! You gotta save our seats! Get back in there! *(Muttering to himself)* … not losing my seat to some dumbass hippie…

(NINA vomits. ROGER notices her)

ROGER
Oh jeez! Lady, you ok?

(She waves him off, not turning back)

ROGER
Was it beer? Too much beer? That happens. No shame in it.

(She waves him off again. He remains oblivious)

ROGER
My lady's the same way. More than two and she's inside out.

(No response from NINA)

ROGER
...It's like a volcanic explosion, except with puke...well, I think you're pickin' up what I'm putting down.

(NINA waves him off more emphatically, to no effect)

ROGER
Tell you what. Why don't I keep guard while you finish up here? You don't wanna bork with no one around. That's how Hendrix died, you know? Man, so sad. Did you know he was only 27 and...

(NINA manages to stand up)

NINA
I know!

(They stare at each other for a bit, familiarity dawning on them both)

ROGER
Hey, I know you!

NINA
Un-fucking-believable.

ROGER
You're Nina, right?! From MSU!

NINA
Hey, Roger.

ROGER
It's me! Roger! *(Beat)* You said that. You remember!

NINA
I sure...

ROGER
Holy shit! I mean...what are the odds, right?!

NINA
So tiny.

ROGER
That we'd both be here, I mean! Madison Square Garden! This is nuts!

(He goes to hug her, but is unsure, both at her unreceptiveness and the fact that she just threw up. He instead pats her on the back)

ROGER
So how've you been?

NINA
Sick. Really sick.

ROGER
I noticed.

NINA
My roommate Crystal...she's friends with Ali Akbar Khan's tour manager... we went to this sketchy Indian place right before the show. It was a mistake.

ROGER
Ali Akbar...he's the dude with the big crazy guitar, right?

NINA
Sarod. It's called a Sarod.

ROGER
Uuuuuuugh. Sounded like banjo music put in a grinder.

NINA
It's traditional Hindustani music.

ROGER
Man, I am never goin' to Hindustan.

(Beat)

NINA
It was so nice catching up with you. I…

ROGER
Me, I'm here for Big George! Would you believe I've never seen any of the Beatles perform? And tonight… him AND Ringo! Does it get better than that?!

NINA
I'm just gonna…

ROGER
I mean, yes. Obviously. If Paul and John were there, it would be better. But can I tell you a secret?

NINA
You don't have to.

ROGER
I think John Lennon is WAY over-rated. His stuff is so…like, you can't hum it, you know? And it's like weird for the sake of being weird. People are all "No, man, he's just really deep." Well, I'll tell ya, septic tanks are deep too, and equally full of shit. Am I right?

(Beat)

NINA
Crystal's probably wondering where I got off to.

ROGER
Ah, sorry. I don't mean to keep you. My wife left the brownies in the car, so I was just running back to…

NINA
You're married?

ROGER
Oh! Right! Yeah…married man.

NINA
You weren't…I mean, the night you and I…?

ROGER
Oh! No no no no no. Free and flyin' solo back then.

NINA
Good. I mean, I wouldn't. Not with a married man.

ROGER
Oh, me neither. With a married woman, I mean. Hell, not with a married man either!

(She stares at him, smiles a little)

NINA
You're a weird one. Anyone ever tell you that?

ROGER
All the time. My folks, my sergeant, Betsy…Betsy's my wife.

NINA
OK.

ROGER
Didn't think I was the marrying type?

NINA
What do you want me to say? It was a one-night thing. We had fun.

ROGER
Crazy fun. And you left while I was asleep.

NINA
I…yeah.

ROGER
Was it 'cause I'm white?

(Beat)

NINA
Excuse me?

ROGER
Look, sometimes...colored people... of color...have trouble with...you know...implications.

NINA
And just what implications are those?

ROGER
I just thought maybe you didn't want your friends to know you made it with a white guy.

NINA
Are you serious?! You cannot be serious.

ROGER
Look, some people don't wanna see their kid bring a black guy home. I imagine it goes both ways.

NINA
Oh. Wow. I just...OK, know what? I'm gonna go now, Roger.

ROGER
What?

NINA
For like a minute, it was nice running into you.

ROGER
What'd I do?

(She starts to walk off. He grabs her arm and she turns on him harshly)

NINA
Don't! Do not just grab me like that!

ROGER
I'm sorry! I don't get what's going on here!

NINA
Did you actually not hear the words coming out of your mouth?

ROGER
I mean, I did but I don't always pay attention.

NINA
I don't have an issue with white people!

ROGER
Well how the hell was I supposed to know that?! We had this awesome night, I wake up in the morning and you'd vanished! It was like Cinderella with pot and doin' it!

NINA
Oh lord...

ROGER
I just...I liked you, ok? I really liked you.

NINA
I know. That's why I left.

(Beat. ROGER takes that hard)

NINA
I told you, I didn't want anything serious.

ROGER
I know. I was there.

NINA
But I could tell you did. It was in your face. It was in the way you made love. There was a need there, a powerful need. Like you were holding onto me for dear life.

ROGER
I just...I had so many questions. I thought for sure it was because I was white. Don't yell at me; I know you

can get why I wondered that.

(Beat)

NINA
Sure.

ROGER
I felt like if you'd just stuck around, we could've talked and...

NINA
It's done. Gone. Besides, if I'd stuck around, you wouldn't have found Betsy.

(He smiles)

ROGER
She's pretty great.

NINA
Yeah?

ROGER
Way out of my league.

NINA
Come on.

ROGER
It's true. She's a vice-principal. Smart as hell. And cute? Oh mama...

(NINA laughs)

ROGER
She's got an ass like a perfect peach. Just...

NINA
Roger!

ROGER
Too far? I go too far sometimes.

(She takes his hand)

NINA
I'm happy for you. Really.

ROGER
I'm lucky as hell. I know it.

NINA
That's great.

ROGER
Yeah. We started dating right after... well, you know. She was at the protest too. We ran into each other at the supermarket and she was like "Hey! You're the guy who punched that guy!" Next thing I know, we're... yeah, it was fast. But fast isn't a bad thing. It's better than waiting years and wondering, you know?

NINA
Sure.

ROGER
Ah, enough of my stuff. How're you?

NINA
You know. Good.

ROGER
Come on! We shared something last year! Let me know what's up!

NINA
I don't know, I...

ROGER
Still big into fighting the good fight?

NINA
Is that..? Yes. I'm still fighting the good fight. Why else would I be here?

(Beat)

ROGER
...at a rock concert?

NINA
George Harrison is trying to raise awareness about the Bangladesh genocide!

(Beat)

NINA
Their government is killing their own

people! Right now! This is a big deal!

ROGER
Right, right, right. Betsy was telling me about this.

NINA
You didn't know?!

ROGER
There's a lot of stuff going on all over the world, Nina! I can't keep track of everything.

NINA
This! This is why the concert had to happen. Bunch of ignorant…

ROGER
I knew it was for something big.

NINA
It's for Bangladesh! The title of this concert is The Concert FOR BANGLADESH.

ROGER
That makes sense now.

(She just stares at him, then laughs. He smiles)

ROGER
What?

NINA
I cannot believe we ever slept together.

ROGER
It's pretty wild.

NINA
You're so…I don't know what you are.

ROGER
I'm Rog. I'm pure, 100%, American Rog.

NINA
I just…how do you not care about things?

ROGER
I care about things. Well, not things. People. I care about people.

NINA
I care about people too, but Roger… the world is falling apart.

ROGER
OK.

NINA
You don't think so?

ROGER
I guess I try not to think about it. Nothing I can do, really.

NINA
There is! Of course there is!

ROGER
You say that, but man… Best thing you can do is try to live right and just hope that helps.

NINA
So you're cool with just sitting back and letting America tear itself apart?

ROGER
I wouldn't say I'm cool with it. But I think that change is a messy thing, babe. I've seen enough messy in my life.

NINA
So you're a coward.

(ROGER is suddenly very serious)

ROGER
I am not a coward.

NINA
OK. Sorry.

ROGER
Don't ever call me that. You get me?

NINA
Yes. Roger. I'm sorry.

(Beat)

ROGER
Betsy probably thinks I got lost going to the car. Or that I ate all the brownies myself.

NINA
Roger, what I said, I...

ROGER
Know what? Don't worry about it.

NINA
I am sorry. Really.

ROGER
It's ok. Honest. Look, the truth is we're pretty much strangers who weren't strangers for one night. You don't owe me anything, especially not an apology.

(The Jumping Jack Flash/Youngblood medley by Leon Russell plays)

ROGER
Oh shit! That's Leon Russell!

NINA
Who?

ROGER
Leon Russell! From Delaney & Bobby and Friends! He wrote Delta Lady!

(She stares, unsure who he's talking about)

ROGER
Nina, this is me doing you a huge favor. You get your ass back in there and get blown away by one of the single best organ and guitar players in America.

NINA
I...ok.

ROGER
I'm gonna go get those damn brownies. I'll see you around! *(He starts to run off)*

NINA
Roger! I mean, we're not gonna see each other again, right?

ROGER
Hell if I know. I didn't think I'd see you tonight, but here you are.

NINA
I just... I want to say goodbye this time. Not while you're asleep.

(He comes back, hugs her)

ROGER
I just decided that this isn't goodbye. I'll see you around.

NINA
Yeah, but probably not.

ROGER
Nina, I don't want to alarm you, but I just checked and the glass is half full.

(She laughs. He kisses her forehead)

ROGER
I...*(He points at himself)*...will see you...*(He points at her)*...around. *(He makes a circle with his fingers. She smiles)*

NINA
See you around, Roger.

(He runs off singing Jumpin' Jack Flash)

ROGER
...but it's aaaaaaaaaaaaaall right now...in fact it's a gas...but it's aaaaaaaaaaaaaall right...

(NINA heads back to the concert. Lights change)

SCENE 3
November 16, 1972
A bar in Lansing, MI

(Lights up. A bar. The sound of much activity: music is playing, people are talking loudly, etc. ROGER is at the bar, his back to the audience. NINA enters. She's been drinking and is in high spirits. She holds an empty pitcher of beer. She calls off to her offstage friends)

NINA
Yeah, no, you're right! Morris, I'm agreeing with you! It shouldn't have happened, yes! But what matters... what really matters is we stopped it... we fuckin' stopped it! Justice prevails! *(She turns to the crowd at the bar)* Y'all know what I'm talking about, right?!

UNSEEN SPEAKER
Shut up already!

NINA
Yeah, you feel me!

(ROGER has been watching her the whole time. NINA goes to the bartender)

NINA
Hey! White boy! See this pitcher? Let's say that this pitcher represents the country, and the beer represents justice. Let's fill this country up with some cold, delicious justice! *(She laughs and hands it off. She turns to see ROGER staring at her)*

NINA
What?

ROGER
Unbelievable. Un-fucking-believable.

NINA
I know you?

(He steps closer. She gets a better look at him)

NINA
Oh my god. Roger?

ROGER
Nina...something. Sorry, I don't think you ever told me your last name.

NINA
Reynolds.

ROGER
Nina Reynolds. *(He puts his hand on his chest)* Roger Weems.

(They just stare at each other, stunned)

ROGER
Or Rog. Or "Hey, white boy." That's why I turned around. I heard "Hey, white boy" and I thought you were talking to me. Because I'm white. And I'm a boy.

(She hugs him. He's surprised, but hugs her back)

NINA
Roger! My hero! *(She calls off to her friends, pointing at ROGER)* Hey! Remember when I told you 'bout that guy who socked a security guard to get in my pants?! This is that guy!

ROGER
...oh...I didn't...wait...

NINA
I cannot believe you are here! Tonight!

ROGER
Wow. That dude does not look like he likes me.

NINA
Roger! Rogerrogerroger! *(Hugs him again)*

ROGER
You guys celebrating or something?

NINA
You know what happened, right?

ROGER
Probably not. I've been kinda holed up lately.

(She pulls a folded newspaper out of her pocket, slams it in front of him. He reads it)

ROGER
I don't...Oh! The Tuskegee thing.

NINA
It's over! The Tuskegee Experiment is over!

(Beat. He reads the paper)

NINA
You really don't know?

ROGER
I mean, I heard about it. I just...

NINA
They were experimenting on blacks in Alabama! 40 years, Rog! Been going for 40 years!

ROGER
Jesus Christ.

NINA
Me and my friends... (She points offstage) We just got back from Detroit. We were all ready to protest when the word came down. The Supreme Court shut this shit down! Yeah! And we... (She stares at him) You really didn't hear about this?

ROGER
I did. I heard some. I just...um.... (Beat) I don't wanna keep you. If you gotta go...

NINA
Are you ok?

ROGER
Hmm?

NINA
You just seem...different.

(He smiles a little)

ROGER
From the two times we've seen each other?

NINA
Yeah. You seem kinda...down.

ROGER
It's kinda been one kick in the nuts after another, honestly. Last month, Creedence broke up. Then Nixon got re-elected. Oh, and I got divorced.

NINA
Oh Roger. I'm so sorry.

ROGER
It's ok. You don't...this is your night. I'm shit for company right now. (He starts to rise) Seriously, though. This? (He gives her back her paper) This is incredible. Congratu...

(She takes his hand)

NINA
What're you drinkin'?

ROGER
Oh. I was just gonna go home and...

NINA
You had a beer before, right? I think we can do better.

ROGER
You don't have to do this.

NINA
Of course I don't. But I want to. (She pulls him to the bar. They sit. She calls

off to an unseen bartender) Hey, can we get two whiskeys over here?

ROGER
Whiskey, huh?

NINA
We've earned it. We goddamn earned it.

ROGER
Thanks.

NINA
Hey! You should come hang out. I can introduce you to my friends!

ROGER
Oh. That's ok.

NINA
Don't hate on black, baby!

ROGER
I'm not that way. You know that.

NINA
Shit, I know.

ROGER
I'm just…I'm having trouble. With people. And your friends…I'm sure they're really nice. They're just really…look, you guys are celebrating. You have every reason to celebrate. But I kinda can't handle that just this second.

(Beat. She kisses him on the cheek)

NINA
We don't get a lot of victories in this life, Roger. When they come, you gotta live it up. *(She puts her arm around him. Their drinks arrive)*

NINA
To victory!

ROGER
To…something.

(She clinks his glass. She points at the crowd in the bar)

NINA
You see those good ol' boys? The ones staring at my friends like they should be on the back of the bus? They got a real investment in the status quo. You know why they're here, drinkin' themselves blind? 'Cause the status quo is about to go up in smoke. And to that, I say "Victory!"

(ROGER takes some prescription drugs out of his jacket)

NINA
What are those?

ROGER
This here is Benzodiazepine. *(He takes one, chases it with whiskey)*

NINA
You sure you should take that after whiskey?

ROGER
Probably not. But tonight's the night that was the night.

(She reads the bottle)

ROGER
You gonna give me a talking to?

NINA
I'm not your momma.

ROGER
Thank god. 'Cause we slept together and all.

(She laughs)

ROGER
Who was that Greek guy who did that? Octopus?

NINA
Oedipus.

ROGER
Man, those Greeks had a dim view on marriage. I get that now.

NINA
I'm sorry, Rog. Really.

ROGER
We were stupid. We rushed into the marriage like our lives depended on it. Before we actually knew each other. Unless you were talking about CCR breaking up. 'Cause that was pretty damn terrible too. *(He takes a drink)* Ever since I got back, I've been kind of…I wanted so badly for something to hold on to…something that would make me feel like I was part of the world.

NINA
Wait. Were you in Vietnam?

ROGER
Yes, ma'am. I thought you knew that.

NINA
You never told me.

ROGER
Oh. Yeah. Guess other stuff always came up. *(He salutes her)* Private First Class Roger Allen Weems of the 9th Infantry. Discharged in '69.

NINA
Holy shit.

ROGER
I don't talk about it a lot, to be honest.

NINA
Because of what happened while…

ROGER
Because they spit on me when I came back. I kept thinking "if we can just get Nixon out of office, this whole thing will stop." And…

(Beat. He tries to change the subject)

ROGER
I told you I'd see you around.

NINA
You did. You truly did. *(Beat)* I've thought about you. This last year. You pop into my brain a lot.

ROGER
I do?

NINA
Yeah. It's like…I know Lansing is a big city, but I kept expecting to run into you somewhere. I was beginning to think I never would.

ROGER
You know where I live.

NINA
I totally forgot where. I was only there once, and you drove.

ROGER
Oh yeah. Good point.

(They drink)

NINA
What if it means something?

ROGER
What?

NINA
This. Right here. And the fact that I can sit here, with you, and skin color doesn't mean shit anymore and…Oh! And New York!

ROGER
I don't…?

NINA
That we ran into each other, both times. Hell, all the way back to that rally.

(Beat. He takes another drink)

ROGER
I wonder about that, sometimes.

NINA
Me too.

ROGER
I mean, the New York one in particular. Thousands and thousands of people there...

NINA
...and you happen to step outside at the exact same time I was outside.

ROGER
We coulda been there, opposite sides of the stadium, the whole night and never have known.

(Beat)

NINA
What're you doing tomorrow?

(Beat)

ROGER
I'm not...what?

NINA
Let's have dinner.

ROGER
Why?

NINA
Because of this. Because this keeps happening.

ROGER
I don't get it.

NINA
I just...Rog, this last year...I've come so close to giving up so many times. Every day, I'd pick up the newspaper and want to vomit. But today? Today we won. The same damn day that Pvt. Roger Allen Weems came back into my life. *(She leans over and kisses him)* I think this means something. You and I...this isn't coincidence. Not tonight, and not before tonight.

ROGER
Yeah?

NINA
Yeah. And I don't want to fight it.

(They kiss again. Lights change)

SCENE 4
Jan. 27, 1973
Roger's House, Lansing MI

(Roger's house. It's much cleaner, & there are many Christmas decorations up. There is now a TV in the room, which ROGER is watching, transfixed. NINA enters. She is wearing a nice suit. She is furious)

NINA
GODDAMMIT!

(She hurls her bag on the chair. ROGER tries to focus on her as she rants, but he can't help but get drawn back to the TV)

NINA
You know what that son of a bitch did?!

ROGER
I...hold on...

NINA
He hired this bimbo...this WHITE bimbo...Kelli. With an "I" at the end. K-E-L-L-I.

ROGER
...ok...

NINA
She's got the line right next to mine. She's got this customer making a cash deposit and I'm listening to her,

I'm actually listening to her try to count the money out. "One…two…three…" This is like a five-hundred dollar deposit! I finally step over and help her out and I…Rog, are you listening?

ROGER
Uh-huh.

NINA
So we're on lunch-break and…I knew I shouldn't ask, ok. I knew. But she's sitting there, dumb as a stump, and I just…so I asked her how much she makes. Guess how much.

ROGER
Baby, I…

NINA
Go on. Guess.

ROGER
More than you?

NINA
$5.10 an hour! 5-fucking-10 an hour! I've been there six months, and I make $4.03! I'll give you two guesses why!

ROGER
Baby, you gotta see this.

NINA
So I quit. I had to. I had to, ok?! I just… we marched for this! We fought for this, and…I have a goddamn degree from a great goddamn college and I am smart and I am capable and….

(She collapses on the couch next to ROGER)

NINA
I have to try to get a teaching gig. I have to.

ROGER
OK.

NINA
I can join the union. Yeah. That'll…I mean, right? I gotta get fair treatment, right?

ROGER
Totally.

NINA
Rog, you're not listening.

ROGER
I'm trying, but…

NINA
Rog.

(She grabs his face, turns him to face her)

NINA
Your girlfriend…me…is trying to talk to you about something really serious.

ROGER
Okay.

NINA
She just found out that she's getting screwed at work, and it's almost definitely because she's black.

ROGER
I know. I'm sorry.

NINA
And she…I…I just quit. I lost my shit at work and I quit. Are you hearing me?

ROGER
Yeah. But babe…

(She points at the TV)

NINA
I did not buy you that so you could date it instead of me.

ROGER
It's over.

NINA
Excuse me?!

ROGER
That's what's I...

NINA
You cannot be serious! I came here, poured my heart out to you and...

ROGER
Wait! Babe, wait! Not...slow down!

NINA
I mean...Jesus, Rog!

ROGER
I don't mean us! We're not over!

NINA
What?

ROGER
Huh?

NINA
I don't...

ROGER
Just...I'm sorry. I'm trying to just...absorb it all.

NINA
How many pills did you take?

ROGER
OK, I...That's not what this is about!

NINA
Then what...?

(He takes her, turns her towards the TV. He takes her hand)

NINA
What is?

ROGER
The war. It's over.

NINA
What?

ROGER
Just...

(He turns up the volume. Richard Nixon's voice is heard)

NIXON
The following statement is being issued in Washington and Hanoi. At 12:30 Paris time today, January 23, 1973, the agreement on ending the war and restoring peace in Vietnam was initialed by Dr. Henry Kissinger on behalf of the United States, and Special Advisor Lê Đức Thọ on behalf of the Democratic Republic of Vietnam. The agreement will be formally signed by the parties participating in the Paris Conference on Vietnam on January 27, 1973 at the National Conference Center in Paris. Throughout the years of negotiation, we have insisted on peace with honor.

(He turns down the sound. She stares at him. He's in a sort of shock, having difficulty processing all of it)

NINA
Roger? Honey?

(He turns to her)

NINA
Are you...where are you right now?

(He looks like he's about to speak, but he ends up crying. She holds him)

NINA
Oh god...I know, baby. I know.

(After a few beats, he stops. She kisses him)

ROGER
It's over.

NINA
I know.

ROGER
It's over. It's over.

(He gets up, moving frantically, trying to process everything)

ROGER
Oh my god...I mean...it's over! IT'S OVER! I just...oh, Christ...*(He grabs her up in a bear hug, spins her around)* I thought it wasn't ever gonna happen! And now...they're gonna let it be done! My friend Jimmy... he's still over there, and now he can come home and...oh! He could stay here! Like, if he needs a place to stay or...I don't know, I just...and you'll love him, Nina! I... *(He sets her down, runs to the door. He shouts outside)* It's over! YEAH! *(Beat)* Wait, you quit your job?

(NINA laughs)

NINA
You were listening.

ROGER
I can listen to two things at once.

NINA
Babe, that doesn't matter now. This... *(She points at the TV)* ...what happened today, that's what matters.

ROGER
Oh man. Know what you should do?

NINA
What?

ROGER
Move in.

NINA
What?

ROGER
Seriously! You don't have a job, for like the best reasons, but you don't have one. And if you stay in your apartment, you'll feel all this pressure to take whatever job you can, just to pay rent. Or OR you could move in here, and like...look, I know this place isn't much, but I own it. No rent means you could really take your time, find the perfect job...

NINA
Wait...

ROGER
And you won't have to waste any gas driving here then back to your place. Show those OPEC bastards who's boss!

NINA
Roger, honey, I don't...

ROGER
I know. We've only been together for three months, but...wait. Is this because of what your parents said?

NINA
Rog...

ROGER
Know what? Screw them!

NINA
Hey!

ROGER
I make you happy! That's all that should matter!

NINA
I'm not having this fight again.

ROGER
I'm sorry I'm not black!

NINA
Rog, they marched with Reverend King. they were at the Bus Boycott. They never expected their daughter to end up dating a white man. You gotta give it time.

ROGER
You know, you grew up in a better neighborhood than me. They could afford to send you to college. I had to...

NINA
Hey. *(She takes his hand)* Your brain's goin' too fast. Relax.

ROGER
I know. I'm sorry. I...

NINA
No one's fighting you. So just breathe.

ROGER
Yeah. Yeah, ok.

(Beat. NINA goes to the kitchen, returns with two beers. She tosses one to ROGER. As they talk, he takes a couple pills)

NINA
You gotta slow down.

ROGER
I'm trying, but it's like...

NINA
Everything's different now.

ROGER
I know.

NINA
And I just...you want me to live with you? For real?

ROGER
I do.

NINA
I love you. You know that.

ROGER
I love you too.

NINA
But I don't really know you either. *(Beat)* Three months, and there's still this big question mark hanging over you.

ROGER
Like The Riddler?

NINA
Not like the...no. I mean there's a lot you're not telling me. About your past. About what happened in...

ROGER
I don't wanna talk about that.

NINA
I know. And I understand, as much as I can. But can you see why that doesn't make me feel like we should just jump right into this?

ROGER
I don't feel like we're jumping in. I feel like we've been dancing this dance for years.

(She laughs, both frustrated & amused)

ROGER
Nina, if I could write up a bunch of guarantees about this, I would. Right here, right now. But...and I know of what I speak...there are no guarantees. You can't really test the parachute before you jump. But there's no one in this whole crazy world I'd rather take that jump with.

NINA
Dammit, Roger.

ROGER
Charming, right?

NINA
I hate you. *(She kisses him)* I just don't know.

ROGER
Yeah, but I do.

NINA
How?

ROGER
I don't hurt when I'm with you.

NINA
(Very moved, touches his face) I know what that feels like.

(They embrace, just holding each other for a bit. Finally--)

NINA
You really think this is a good idea?

ROGER
What am I? An asshole?

NINA
Fuck it. Activate the parachute.

ROGER
You don't really "activate" a para...

NINA
Shut up.

(They kiss. Lights fade)

SCENE 5
August 11, 1974
Roger's House, Lansing MI

(Evening, the end of what looks to be a small party. NINA is at the door, saying goodbye to unseen guests. Cars can be heard driving away)

NINA
Hey, so call me tomorrow, ok? Cool? And I'm sorry about Rog! He... OK, but for real, call me tomorrow.

(She shuts the door. She collapses on the couch, clearly upset. After a second, ROGER walks in. He's holding an icepack or wet washcloth to his eye. NINA glares at him. After a beat--)

ROGER
Hey. He hit me.

NINA
Because you're too stoned to...what the hell were you thinking?!

ROGER
Back off.

NINA
This was supposed to be a party, Rog! You come in here...

(He laughs a little)

NINA
That's funny?

ROGER
Just...most people have dinner parties, or birthday parties? You guys have a "Nixon's Out of Office Party." Real fuckin' cheery.

NINA
This was worth celebrating! He... don't. Don't change the subject. These were my friends. We were celebrating something worth celebrating. What I wanna know is why?

ROGER
Why what?

NINA
Why did you go after them?! Why did you try to beat the shit out of Morris?!

ROGER
To hell with this... *(He tries to head off, but staggers)*

NINA
You're a mess.

(He sits, clearly hurting)

ROGER
I think he broke my eyebrow...

NINA
It could've been a lot worse.

Especially after what you said to him.

ROGER
What...what did I say?

NINA
Do you seriously not remember?!

ROGER
...stop yelling...please...

NINA
You called him a short-sighted limp dick!

ROGER
(Chuckling) Yeah, that sounds like me.

NINA
What are you on? *(She takes a pill bottle out of his jacket)*

ROGER
Hey!

NINA
Darvon? For real?

ROGER
My doctor gave those to me.

NINA
How many did you take?

(He doesn't answer)

NINA
Before or after the booze?

ROGER
Get off my back. This whole thing is...Jesus Christ, why did you even have this party?!

NINA
I thought you'd like this! You hated Tricky Dick more than anyone!

ROGER
You know I can't stand groups of people all over...

NINA
It was five people, and us!

ROGER
...acting like you brought down Nixon yourselves...complete bullshit...

NINA
And that's reason to throw a chair at my oldest friend?!

(ROGER stands, finally getting truly angry)

ROGER
You heard him! You heard what he said!

NINA
Yes. I know, but...

ROGER
He said "Anyone who didn't dodge the draft was complicit." HE SAID THAT! HE...! *(He rises, pacing. This is the first we've seen of his true rage)* I could've killed him. I could've just...

NINA
He shouldn't have said that. I understand, but...

ROGER
BUT?! There's no "but!" That privileged shit was safe and secure in his fucking dorm while I was in Khe Sahn...

NINA
He didn't know.

ROGER
What?

NINA
I...never told him you were over there.

(Long beat)

ROGER
Why?

NINA
I never knew how.

ROGER
You never knew..?! You open your mouth and say "My boyfriend was in Vietnam!"

NINA
You never talk about it! You REFUSE to talk about it! How the hell am I supposed to share anything with my friends when you won't share it with me?! And... *(Beat)* The last few months, you been high more often than not.

ROGER
Yeah, like you're squeaky-clean.

NINA
I'm talking about these. *(She shakes his pill bottle)* And like the 10 other different meds in the cabinet. I want to know what's going on that you need painkillers and antidepressants and mood stabilizers and...

ROGER
I don't know, OK?! I don't...look, I'm feeling a lot of stress right now and...I shouldn't have to explain this! *(He starts to leave)*

NINA
ROGER!

(He stops)

NINA
You walk around like there's something inside you, ready to blow.

ROGER
I'm fine.

NINA
You punched a hole through the drywall! And then tonight...!

ROGER
I'm done talking about this. You hear me? DONE!

NINA
Then tell me what's wrong with you!

ROGER
Nothing!

NINA
Rog!

(He starts to go)

NINA
Hey! Don't you just...!

(She spins him around. He immediately reels around, fist raised. He is seconds away from throwing a punch. NINA backs away, stunned. He, too, is shocked by what he was about to do. To release his anger, he flips over a table. Long beat)

ROGER
Baby, you can't come at me like that. I'm not...I'm not ok. In here. *(He taps his head)*

NINA
You can't keep hiding this from me, Rog. It's killing us.

ROGER
We're fine.

NINA
I have a bag of clothes in my car.

(Beat)

ROGER
What?

NINA
Been there for three weeks. Ever since the night you crashed into our mailbox.

ROGER
That wasn't what it looked like.

NINA
We're not fine. You've been pushing me away, pushing everything away. And it feels like it's gonna get worse, not better.

ROGER
I'm trying, babe.

NINA
You want to escape. I can see that. I just don't know what you're trying to escape from.

(Beat)

ROGER
Everything.

NINA
What does that mean?

ROGER
It means...everything.

(Beat)

NINA
I'm part of everything.

ROGER
I know. I don't mean you, specifically, just...

NINA
You mean me non-specifically?

(Beat)

ROGER
You fight. Every job you had, every person of authority...everything is a fight for you.

NINA
You met me at a goddamn rally! You know who I am!

ROGER
I do, but...

NINA
I fight because it's a fight that has to happen! We're at this point...people think that equality is happening...It isn't happening! We are not equal! I am not equal, and I fucking should be!

ROGER
I get that. I agree with all of that.

NINA
You agree with it, but it's a problem, yeah?

(Beat)

ROGER
You come home and you tell me all this stuff, and I want to be there for you, 'cause I love you. And yeah, 'cause I agree with you. On all of it. But I'm not...

(Beat. ROG can barely say what he says next)

ROGER
I...I'm trying to be like I was before I went over there. And it's like...I can remember that person, but...

NINA
And the pills are helping you get back to that?

(Beat. He doesn't respond)

NINA
I'm trying to understand this, Rog. If that's what you want, if that's why you're taking Darvon and whatever else, then are they actually helping you? 'Cause if they are, I'll sign off on them right now.

(He doesn't respond)

NINA
You go to a job where you work in

a freezer, where you don't talk to anyone. I come home and you're in this fog and...am I making you like this? Do you need pills to deal with me?

(Beat)

ROGER
I need them to deal with everything.

(She sits with him)

NINA
But you're not though. You're not dealing with anything. You get that, right?

ROGER
It's not that simple.

NINA
I know that. But do you get that I'm not going to change who I am? I like who I am.

ROGER
I like you too.

NINA
But I feel like I don't know you! There's this huge part of who you are, and you won't talk to me about it!

ROGER
I can't! If I tell you this stuff, you'll leave me.

NINA
I'll leave you if you don't. *(Beat)* It won't be because I want to. But we've got to decide if we're in this together or not. You cry in your sleep sometimes, and I want to know why. You get so scared, and I want to know what you're scared of. But watching you go after my friends, friends who were just here to celebrate the system working for once...This thing inside you is coming out whether you want it to or not. I can only deal with it if you tell me the truth. I have to know who you are, Rog. Or I have to go. That's where we're at. *(She takes his hand)* So what's it gonna be?

(He stares at her. Lights fade)

END OF ACT I

ACT II

SCENE 6
October 1, 1975
A hospital room, Lansing MI

(ROGER lies on a hospital bed. He's fully conscious and functional, but looks unwell. He's listening to the Thrilla in Manila on the radio. It plays in the darkness as the lights rise. He's clearly very into the fight. The fight is near the end. The crowd is chanting "Ali! Ali!")

ANNOUNCER
Ali's slipped.

(Crowd cheers)

ANNOUNCER
Ali holding. Frazier looks awful tired; he's puffed around both eyes now.

(The bell rings)

ANNOUNCER
Ken Norton, down for the first time.

ANNOUNCER 2
Frazier has sustained a small cut under his right eye.

ANNOUNCER
And he's very puffy around those eyes.

ANNOUNCER 2
Very puffy.

ANNOUNCER
Lost his mouthpiece again. I didn't see it come out.

ANNOUNCER 2
As long as the cut is under the eye, it shouldn't be too bad for him. So the blood cannot run into the eye.

ANNOUNCER
Getting a little smelling salts, Ken. We're waiting for Round 14. I would say that Ali has regained control of the fight.

(NINA enters. She's dressed well, business-respectable. The radio's on as they talk)

NINA
Roger?

ROGER
Holy shit. You're here!

NINA
The hospital called me and...

ROGER
I mean...wait. They called you?

NINA
Yes.

ROGER
Why?

NINA
I'm still your emergency contact, apparently.

(Beat)

ROGER
I didn't...I forgot to change the papers, I guess.

NINA
What happened?

ROGER
I don't know. Nobody remembers to do that shit, do they?

NINA
Roger. What happened to you? Why are you here?

ROGER
You look great. Real business.

NINA
Roger...

ROGER
Are you still working for that guy... he's a senator, right?

NINA
Talk to me. Don't just brush this off.

ROGER
It was nothing. Totally ridiculous.

NINA
You look like shit.

(Beat)

ROGER
Real nice.

NINA
Was it the...*(Annoyed with the radio, she turns it off)*

ROGER
Hey! I was listening to that!

NINA
Was it the pills? Huh?

ROGER
It wasn't...turn the radio back on! This is important.

NINA
(Closing in on him) Your life is important, you dumb ass. More important than whatever that was.

ROGER
That's the Thrilla in Manila! I've got fifty bucks on Ali and...

NINA
I don't care. I do not care. I drove thirty minutes to get here, and I...

Fuck, Rog! They said you weren't breathing!

ROGER
I was breathing!

NINA
You want me to grab the nurse? Her name's Maria and she's sweet as pie. She told me how they had to give you mouth-to-mouth. Know who gets mouth-to-mouth, Rog?

ROGER
I don't wanna...

NINA
People who are NOT FUCKING BREATHING. That's who.

(Beat)

ROGER
They're making it sound worse than it was.

NINA
Tell me.

ROGER
I'm trying, ok?! Just... *(Beat. He sits up)* I lost track.

NINA
Of what?

ROGER
Of how many I'd taken. That's all it was. I just...I take them for the pain.

NINA
Jesus, Roger. How much pain are you in?

(He doesn't answer)

NINA
You never told me.

ROGER
I know.

NINA
I mean, I've seen all the scars. I just didn't...

ROGER
And lately, it's been worse. The doctor's say it's in my head, but...I don't know. I just had a bad day, ok?

NINA
How many bad days have you had?

ROGER
I was on the loading dock...I'm still at the Spartan Store...did I tell you that? Doesn't matter. And I'd...so I'd taken a few in the morning 'cause my head was just...and it wasn't getting better, so I took a couple more and...I don't know. I woke up here.

(A long moment. NINA doesn't want to ask this)

NINA
Was it because of today?

ROGER
What do you mean?

NINA
You know what I mean.

ROGER
Nina, pain doesn't give a shit about calendars.

NINA
But you're in good shape! I was with you at your physical last year. If they're telling you the pain isn't real...

ROGER
I don't need you to tell me what's real and what's not, ok!? I can feel it! I can feel the fucking metal moving through my body and I can hear the ringing and...dammit, I just...

(Beat)

ROGER
The pills screw me up, but not most of the time. Most of the time, they help me stay...

NINA
They're not.

ROGER
They are though. When I get it right, I'm me again. It's only when I...

NINA
You gotta look at me when I say this, Rog. These pills are not helping you.

ROGER
Christ, it's not like I'm on horse or anything. This is what the doctors give me!

NINA
The same doctors who told you this is all in your head?

(Beat)

NINA
'Cause seems to me like they wouldn't give them to you, if that's what they thought. Which then makes me ask where are you getting them from?

(ROGER doesn't answer)

NINA
I didn't hold back when we were sleeping together. I'm not gonna go easy on you now.

ROGER
Nina, I...

NINA
You're hooked. You know you are. And you know you gotta stop. That's all there is to it.

ROGER
It's not that easy.

NINA
Shit, you think I don't know that? You think I haven't seen people try to get off the junk before? It's gonna be a damn nightmare for you. But you gotta do it, 'cause if someone hadn't called the hospital when they did, you and me? We would not be talking right now.

(Beat)

ROGER
You're not gonna turn the radio back on, are you?

NINA
What do you think?

ROGER
I just...I really need a win right now.

NINA
You wanna see how many rounds you can go with me, white boy?

(Beat. ROG laughs. NINA does too)

ROGER
You'd kick my ass.

NINA
I would absolutely kick your ass.

ROGER
It's what you do. I pity those senators.

NINA
I'm not working with all of them directly. I'm a Staff Assistant.

ROGER
Forever fighting the good fight.

NINA
...such a stupid saying...

ROGER
But it is good, right? You're doing

something you believe in?

NINA
Hell yeah. We just got the DDA passed. It's all about preserving historical sites and...

ROGER
And keeping business districts alive. I know. I've been following it.

NINA
For real?

ROGER
Sure. Why not?

(Beat. She stares at him)

ROGER
What? I miss you. Can you blame me?

NINA
Oh.

ROGER
I just...not having you in my life... it's killing me.

NINA
Rog...

ROGER
Not seeing you, not hearing you laugh...it's not something I can deal with.

NINA
You have to.

(Beat)

NINA
I'm goin' with Morris now.

ROGER
Ah, Christ...

NINA
It's not...just a couple months now.

ROGER
Goddammit. I'm an idiot.

NINA
You're not. Rog, you're not.

ROGER
I didn't even think...god!

NINA
I just need you to understand. I'll help you however I can, but not like that.

(Beat. She is unsure what to do or say. Then, she goes to her purse, and hands ROG a package)

ROGER
What's this?

NINA
Well, they wouldn't let me see you. Not at first. And I...

(He immediately starts to tear open the wrapping. She laughs a little)

NINA
...every time. Like a damn child...

(It's a small bundle of comic books)

NINA
There's a little news stand in the lobby. Thought maybe you'd...

ROGER
Incredible Hulk.

NINA
Yeah.

ROGER
You got me the Incredible Hulk.

NINA
I didn't know if you already had it but...

ROGER
I didn't. I actually stopped reading them.

NINA
Really?

ROGER
Yeah.

NINA
No. No, I don't like that. That's not Rog. Rog reads comics.

ROGER
Rog has had a very rough year.

(She flips through them with him)

NINA
OK, you got a Hulk, Giant-Sized X-Men, Power Man...by the way, why did I go through an entire rack of comics and not see any black superheroes but Power Man?

ROGER
Power Man's awesome. He's this former criminal who...

NINA
Excuse me?

ROGER
What?

NINA
How come a black superhero has to be a convict?

ROGER
Well, 'cause in prison, they did experiments on him and...

NINA
They did experiments on him?!

ROGER
He ended up with super strength.

NINA
I don't care if it made him bullet-proof!

ROGER
Actually...

NINA
You do NOT experiment on black men, no matter what they've done!

ROGER
I...um...you know that I don't write these, right?

NINA
Ridiculous is what that is.

(He smiles at her. She notices)

ROGER
I can't believe you bought me comics. Today of all days, you bought me something.

NINA
Hey, you said you needed a win. (Kisses his forehead) You got a long road to walk, sugar. And it's gonna be hard as hell. But you gotta walk it all the same. You get me?

(He doesn't answer. She takes his face & turns it to her)

NINA
Hey. You get me?

(He nods. She kisses his forehead & starts to leave)

ROGER
You goin'?

NINA
I've got to. Big plans tonight.

ROGER
Oh. Right. Obviously.

(There is a sad moment between them)

NINA
It was good to see you, Rog. Really.

ROGER
You too.

(She smiles sadly and leaves. ROG is silent, then says to no one in particular--)

ROGER
Happy birthday, Nina.

(He turns the radio on. It announces Ali's victory. He smiles. Lights fade)

SCENE 7
July 4, 1976
Parade route, Lansing MI

(The sounds of many people celebrating. It is dusk, and the fireworks will soon be starting. NINA, dressed casually, has just set up a chair. She has a beer and is in high spirits. She smiles, waves at unseen friends and passersby. She suddenly sees someone she recognizes)

NINA
I'll be damned...

(She puts her hands to her mouth, calling out to him)

NINA
Rog! ROG!

(She waves her hands so he can see her. ROG runs onstage. He's wearing a Captain America t-shirt, & appears much healthier than in the previous scene. He has a stack of fliers in his hand. He almost hugs her, but stops)

ROGER
Oh my god, I...! Wait, is it cool if we...?

NINA
Shut up, white boy.

(She hugs him tightly. He reciprocates)

ROGER
Nina freaking Reynolds.

NINA
Roger freaking Weems.

ROGER/NINA
You look...

(They stop)

ROGER
You go first.

NINA
No no no. I wanna hear what you were gonna say.

ROGER
Awful. I was gonna say "You look awful."

(She laughs)

NINA
Ass.

ROGER
Like, for a second, I thought you actually fell under one of the parade floats.

(She punches his arm)

ROGER
You look amazing.

NINA
So do you. Really.

ROGER
Wait. Was the last time you saw me...?

NINA
In the hospital, yeah.

ROGER
Oh shit. Yeah, I...wow. Yeah, a lot has happened since then.

NINA
I'd hope so. Been almost a year.

ROGER
How are you? How've you been?

NINA
Good. Real good. I...is this weird?

ROGER
The catch-up chit-chat thing?

NINA
Yeah. I feel like...all the shit we've been through, we're kinda past it.

ROGER
I hear ya.

(Beat)

NINA
So how've you been?

(He laughs)

ROGER
I'm clean.

NINA
Oh. I didn't...

ROGER
You did. It's cool. I'm just saving you the embarrassing, meander-around-the-big-issue thing. I'm clean and sober 9 months now.

NINA
I'll be damned.

ROGER
Didn't think I could do it?

NINA
I knew you could do it. I wasn't sure you would do it.

ROGER
It was...yeah, it was pretty fucking awful.

NINA
I'm sure. You've been on one thing or another as long as I've known you. That must've been hard.

ROGER
You cannot image. Well, you probably could, but...yeah, I...yeah.

NINA
We don't have to talk about it.

ROGER
Actually, I'm supposed to talk about it. With people I trust.

NINA
You still trust me?

ROGER
What the hell kind of question is that? Of course I trust you. Always have.

NINA
Thank you. *(She kisses his cheek)*

ROGER
Wow. How many beers have you had?

NINA
Just two. That was a friendly, non-drunken smooch on the cheek.

ROGER
I just...is Morris around?

NINA
He headed home early. Uncle Sam stepped on him.

ROGER
Oh. Is that like metaphor for...?

NINA
No, he actually...you seen those dudes on stilts, dressed like Uncle Sam?

ROGER
Oh shit.

NINA
Yeah, wasn't lookin' where he was going and... *(She claps her hands)* Bam! Right on Morris' foot.

ROGER
That's bogue.

NINA
Doctor said he didn't break it, but he was done for the day.

ROGER
Shouldn't you be tending the fallen hero?

NINA
And miss this? No way. I am really, really confident I won't live to see the Tricentennial. I wanna be here. Morris is cool with that.

ROGER
Tricentennial? Is that a word?

NINA
Yeah. 300 year anniversary.

ROGER
Sounds made up.

NINA
It's not made up! It's a real word.

ROGER
I don't know.

NINA
Pfft. I don't have to prove it to you.

(She pushes him jokingly. He drops his fliers)

NINA
Oh! I'm so sorry!

ROGER
No, it's cool. I got it.

NINA
Lemme help.

(They collect fliers. She reads one)

NINA
What are all these?

ROGER
My new job.

NINA
You make fliers?

ROGER
No, I...Read it.

(He laughs. She reads it)

NINA
"The Gods of Comics?"

ROGER
That's my store! Well, me and a couple buddies.

NINA
You sell comics?

ROGER
I totally sell comics! It's fantastic!

NINA
You know, I've been in the Spartan Store a couple times. Wondered if I'd see you there, but...

ROGER
Oh, no way. They canned me right after I...yeah, turns out managers don't love it when employees stop breathing on the job.

NINA
So unfair.

ROGER
And you wanna know what I have in my office? Three comics. Three comics you gave me.

NINA
Really?

ROGER
Yep. Hulk, Power Man, Giant Sized X-Men. They greet me every morning.

NINA
Come on.

ROGER
It's true. Hand to Gods of Comics.

NINA
Look at you. Roger the big business man.

ROGER
Maybe not what I'd call it but hey, why not do what you love?

NINA
You got that...

(The fireworks start)

NINA
Oh! Look!

ROGER
There they go!

(People cheer. Music plays underneath. Fireworks continue)

ROGER
So you still workin' in the big ol' Capitol Building?

NINA
Yuh-huh.

ROGER
Nina Reynolds...forever fighting the good fight.

NINA
I never got that saying. Like, should I be fighting the bad fight instead?

ROGER
So what's on your agenda?

NINA
It's all Elliott-Larsen right now.

ROGER
I don't know who Elliott Larsen is.

(She laughs)

ROGER
What?

NINA
It's not a person; it's legislation. Gonna make it so you can't pass someone over for a job or for housing just because of age, sex or color.

ROGER
Whoa. That's...that's amazing.

NINA
It'll be amazing if we can get it together. It's gonna be a fight.

ROGER
Come on.

NINA
It's true.

ROGER
Who would fight that?!

NINA
People who look at us like a throwback from the 60s. Bunch of privileged, spoiled hippies trying to...

ROGER
Stop. Stop stop stop. That's...forget that shit. It's gonna pass.

NINA
You're not in these meetings, Rog. You're not seeing the way these bastards dissect every little thing just to stop this from moving forward.

ROGER
"The world must never again mistake compassion for weakness." You know who said that?

(She thinks about it)

NINA
Is it Eisenhower?

(ROGER points to his t-shirt)

ROGER
Cap. The great Boy Scout. Ol' Winghead himself.

NINA
Hey, if you can get Captain America to sign off on this, I'll buy you a steak dinner.

ROGER
I'm just sayin'…look around. *(He motions at the crowd)* Look at all the people out there. Every race, every age, every gender…two hundred years ago, this would've been totally different. This…everything I'm seeing… this is a crazy amount of progress. You kissed a white guy in public, and I don't see anyone runnin' for the hills. You're working for the state government; you're in position to actually make things better. You think that would've been the case fifty years ago?

NINA
No.

ROGER
Exactly. I just…Nina, I lost almost everything I had fighting for this country… But when I look at this… when I think what we might actually be capable of…I don't know.

NINA
It makes you think it might have been worth it.

ROGER
(Nodding) I know that things might be different tomorrow. I get that. But right here, right now…I feel it. People see the good, and they want to keep seeing it. That's how change happens.

NINA
I hope like hell you're right.

ROGER
Remember when you wanted to change the world?

NINA
I want to. I do. I wish the people I work for did too.

ROGER
It's that bad?

NINA
Bunch of petty tyrants and fat cats. It can break you down.

ROGER
Some people maybe. Not you. You're unbreakable.

NINA
Come on.

ROGER
It's true. You're like the whole package. A package full of unbreakable stuff.

NINA
You hittin' on me, white boy?

ROGER
What? No. I just…

(A huge firework goes off. Cheers)

ROGER
I'm sick of us not being friends.

NINA
We're friends. We'll always be friends.

ROGER
Yeah, but not like…we used to hang out. I miss that.

NINA
Yeah. So do I.

ROGER
Really?

NINA
Morris is always swamped with students; I'm always swamped with work. I don't know. It's very…

ROGER
So let's hang out. Just like we're doing now, except not today. Later.

NINA
But not like a date or anything.

ROGER
Oh my god, I get it. You're an old lady now. I don't care. You're my friend. You've helped me more than anyone ever has, and I miss you. That's it.

(She smiles)

NINA
OK.

ROGER
OK?

NINA
Let's catch a movie or something.

ROGER
Yes! Oh god yes! That's what I'm talking about! You have to pay though.

NINA
Oh really?

ROGER
Sister, I am beyond broke. You work for the government. Besides, we're living in the age of equality now. Show your pride by paying for my movie ticket.

(She laughs)

ROGER
Laugh all you want. Selling comic books does not a millionaire make.

NINA
So why do it?

ROGER
I'd rather be happy than financially secure, I guess.

(The band starts to play)

NINA
You are though. You're happy.

ROGER
Yeah. It's weird, but yeah.

NINA
Nothin' weird about it.

ROGER
Hard to be down on a day like today. The Bicentennial. It's cool to live through something like this.

NINA
You're sorta your own kind of patriot, aren't you?

ROGER
I think everyone is. I just kinda came to it in the backwards way.

(As the music plays, NINA sees that ROGER is lost in his own thoughts)

ROGER
They spit on me when I came back. They called me a baby killer.

NINA
I know.

ROGER
I didn't want to go there. I didn't have a choice. And when I got home... sometimes, it feels like 100 years ago. Sometimes it feels like yesterday. *(Beat)* What're you doing?

NINA
Right now? Watching fireworks.

ROGER
Wanna go for a walk? There's stuff I wanna talk with you about. Stuff I should've told you a long time ago.

(She thinks about it, then offers her arm)

NINA
The park's right there. Let's beat feet.

(He takes her arm)

NINA
But no funny stuff, mister.

ROGER
I'll be a perfect gentleman. Scouts honor.

(They start to walk off)

ROGER
You seen Silent Movie yet?

NINA
No. That's the one with the dudes from Young Frankenstein, right?

ROGER
Yeah.

NINA
Well then we gotta see that one.

ROGER
Obviously.

(Lights fade)

SCENE 8
May 25, 1977
Roger's House, Lansing MI

(Cleaner than before, but still maintains its posters. Some may have changed to reflect the year. ROGER & NINA return. It is nighttime, and they're coming back from the movies. ROGER is still in a state of shock)

ROGER
I mean…Jesus! It was like…! Did you see…?!

NINA
I was there.

ROGER
And it was just down to him! He had to blow it up or they were all totally screwed!

NINA
He sure did.

ROGER
And then…oh my god. When he heard that voice, and it was all "Turn off your target and trust your feelings", I was like "No, Luke. No way. You gotta bullseye that thing thing!" But he didn't! He just… he like trusted himself and BAM! I mean…oh man… *(He rests on the couch, emotionally spent)*

NINA
You ok?

ROGER
Yeah. I mean…my life has changed forever, but yeah. I'm good. What're you doing tomorrow?

NINA
Working?

ROGER
I mean, after work. You wanna see it again?

NINA
Star Wars?

ROGER
No, the concessions stand. Of course Star Wars!

NINA
We just saw it!

ROGER
I know, but it's like…I feel like I missed a lot of it. I couldn't take it all in at once. Let's see it again.

(She thinks about it)

NINA
Ok.

ROGER
Really?!

NINA
Yeah. Let's…yeah.

ROGER
Oh man! You are the freaking best! What was your favorite part?

NINA
I...

ROGER
Mine was that crazy bar. Totally. Those freaking aliens were just like...and when that green dude pulled the gun on Han Solo?!

NINA
Harrison Ford.

ROGER
Right, but he played Han Solo.

NINA
No, Harrison Ford was my favorite part.

ROGER
Oh. Which part? Where he shot down the enemy ships?

NINA
Hard to pick. Maybe his pants. His pants might have been my favorite part.

(He laughs, and heads offstage. When he's gone, NINA tries to rein in her emotions. She's clearly upset about something but trying to keep it from ROGER)

ROGER
Like we weren't even watching the same movie. You want something to drink? I got Shasta and...I got water and Shasta.

NINA
What kind of Shasta?

ROGER
Umm...Grapefruit Zazz.

NINA
Water.

ROGER
Cool.

(He returns with a water for her and a Shasta for himself)

ROGER
You rock.

NINA
What?

ROGER
You're the only one who wanted to see Star Wars with me. Freaking Jimmy and Carl...I thought for sure they'd show. They run a comic store, for god's sake!

NINA
They got wives. Carl's got a little girl.

ROGER
Ugh. One more reason not to spawn.

NINA
You still on that, huh?

ROGER
I'd be a terrible father. You know that.

NINA
Why are there no black people in space?

(Beat)

ROGER
What?

NINA
Luke Skywalker: White. Han Solo: White. Princess Leia: Super white.

ROGER
Oh. I guess I didn't really think about it. Maybe the guy who played

Chewie is black?

NINA
Oh no. No. They best not have hired a black man to play Han Solo's dog.

ROGER
I don't think he's a dog. He could fly a spaceship.

NINA
I saw green dudes, I saw blue dudes, but I guess there's one color that even aliens don't like.

ROGER
You ok?

NINA
No, I'm pissed.

ROGER
Yeah, that's clear. What I'm asking is "why are you pissed?"

NINA
Is it not obvious?

ROGER
It's obvious that you're trying to draw me into a fight about Star Wars because you're mad about something and just want to fight.

(Beat. She stares at him)

ROGER
What? I've known you for eight years. I pick shit up.

(She glares at him, furious. Suddenly, she grabs him and kisses him. He initially lets it happen, then pulls away)

ROGER
Whoa. Whoa whoa whoa.

NINA
Sorry, I...

ROGER
I don't...you don't have to apologize. I just...

NINA
That was a bad idea.

ROGER
Not...wait, hold on...

NINA
I'm gonna go. *(She starts to leave)*

ROGER
Wait!

(She stops)

ROGER
For Christ's sake...you can't just kiss me and...what the hell is going on?

NINA
Nothing. Forget it.

ROGER
You tellin' me it's easier to french me than to actually talk?

(Beat)

NINA
What do you want me to say?

ROGER
You think I got a plan for this? Just tell me what the hell's going on.

NINA
Morris is leaving me.

ROGER
Oh. Oh shit. I'm so sorry.

NINA
You are?

ROGER
Yeah. Jesus, of course I am. I don't want you to hurt. *(Beat)* Can I ask why?

NINA
Why do you think?

ROGER
I honestly have no idea.

NINA
Yeah, you do.

ROGER
I think you think I'm smarter than I am.

(Beat)

NINA
The last few months...Christ, almost a year...how much time have we spent together?

ROGER
I don't know. A lot.

NINA
He can't handle that.

ROGER
Come on! There's nothing going on here! I mean, not til like two minutes ago.

NINA
We've been fighting for a while now. This was the final straw, I guess.

ROGER
Me? I'm the final straw?

NINA
You are. Of course you are.

ROGER
(Sitting) You gotta gimme a second. This is...I thought we were just seeing a movie. Honest to god. I mean, it was a freaking incredible movie, but this is...oh man. *(He rubs his face)* I gotta ask it.

NINA
OK.

ROGER
Is this like...are you still in love with me?

NINA
Yeah.

ROGER
Huh.

NINA
I didn't think I was. Last year, at the parade...I was just happy to see you. All the shit we've been through and... the more time we spent together, the more I saw it.

ROGER
Saw what?

NINA
You. Who you've become.

ROGER
What? A broke nerd?

NINA
A good man. Everything you've been able to overcome...you were always a good man, but now...you're who I always hoped you could be.

ROGER
I'm not. Believe me, I'm not.

NINA
I think you can't see it from the inside...

ROGER
I'm still hooked, Nina.

(Beat)

ROGER
I feel like you think that part of me is gone, but it's not. It's no accident I'm drinking Shasta. I had to turn this place into a damn monastery. And I still feel it, every day. The minute something stresses me out, even a

little…my first thought is to reach for my pills, which I don't have. But my hand still reaches for them all the same.

(She sits with him)

NINA
How about now?

ROGER
You kiddin' me? I'm…yeah, I'm stressed as hell.

NINA
But you're not high.

ROGER
'Cause I got nothing to get high on.

NINA
Rog, it's more than that.

(He rises, moves away)

ROGER
What the hell is happening, Nina?! I just…fuck! When you left, it ruined me, ok? Just…total meltdown. And I thought we were getting to this point where we were friends again. I mean, yeah, obviously I still think about you. Everything we've been through, how could I not? But…we're friends. That's all. Your boyfriend shouldn't leave you because…

NINA
He should. He's right. And I hate myself for it. You and me…we'll never be just friends. We were idiots to think anything else. Know why? 'Cause we've never been friends. We had this thing the minute we met, and we've danced around it for years, but we're like an eclipse. Sooner or later, we always line back up.

(Beat)

ROGER
So what do you want? Do we just get back together again? Shit, I don't think I even know how to begin.

NINA
Me neither.

ROGER
Then why did you kiss me?

NINA
I'm sick of pretending I don't love you.

ROGER
When I said we should see Star Wars tomorrow, that's all I meant, that I like hanging out with you.

NINA
Oh.

ROGER
Did you think I meant something more?

NINA
I don't know. I think maybe I hoped so.

(He's silent, conflicted. She rises)

NINA
I'm sorry. I shouldn't have done that.

ROGER
Nina…

NINA
I'm throwing all this stuff at you, and I'm not letting you deal.

ROGER
Hold on.

(She heads for the door)

NINA
You can call me tomorrow, if you want. We can just be friends. Honestly.

I shouldn't...

(He puts his hand on the door)

ROGER
Stop. Just stop.

(She does. Beat)

ROGER
Do not think for a second that I haven't wanted you back.

NINA
Really?

ROGER
I've wanted to be your guy since the day we met.

NINA
I know. *(She comes to him)* Thing is, do you still want that?

(Beat)

ROGER
What am I? An asshole?

(They kiss)

ROGER
We're still gonna see Star Wars tomorrow, right?

(She laughs, hits him. They kiss again. Lights fade)

SCENE 9
January 26, 1978
A Roller Disco, Lansing MI

(The lights and sound of a roller disco. NINA sits on a bench, undoing her roller skates. ROGER soon skates on)

NINA
How's it lookin' out there?

ROGER
There's like a foot of snow on the ground, and it's still goin'.

NINA
Jesus Christ. Are we trapped in a roller disco?

ROGER
I don't..."trapped" is maybe a strong word.

NINA
We're not driving out of here, are we?

ROGER
The plows will come soon. They'll save us.

(He sits down with her, puts his arm around her. She starts to laugh at the ridiculousness of their situation. He laughs too)

NINA
This is just nuts.

ROGER
You're not wrong.

NINA
Why did we even come here?

ROGER
After all the shit this week, you needed to shake your groove thing.

NINA
Yeah, yeah, yeah.

ROGER
You wanna talk about it yet? Or...

(A voice comes over the loudspeaker)

VOICE
Hey, cool cats and kitties! Well the weather outside is frightful, so we're gonna ask you to stay put for just a minute. The plows have been called, and to keep you warm til they get here, we're gonna heat things up with a little...inferno!

("Disco Inferno" plays)

ROGER
One more spin?

NINA
Baby, my feet are killing me.

ROGER
Come on! You look so hot out there.

NINA
You just wanna get me out there so you can stare at my ass.

ROGER
Not to alarm you, but I can do that anytime. And I do. A lot.

(She smiles, puts her feet on his lap)

NINA
Get these things off me already.

ROGER
Fine.

NINA
Thank you. *(She kisses him)*

ROGER
Nina! Not in front of the disco queens!

NINA
They got a problem with it, they can shove it up their YMCA.

(He laughs, removes her skates)

ROGER
Stupid Cleveland Superbomb. I haven't seen snow like that in…

NINA
Wait…Cleveland what-what?

ROGER
Cleveland Superbomb. That's what they're calling it.

NINA
Who? Who's calling it that?

ROGER
I don't know. Clevelanders? Clevelings?

NINA
You don't have to do that.

ROGER
Do what? What am I doing?

NINA
Trying to distract me.

ROGER
If you think I'm good enough to call in a monster snowstorm…darlin', you seriously overestimate my abilities.

NINA
All of it. Taking me dancing, bitching about the weather. I know when you're trying to keep my mind off things.

ROGER
Is that the worst thing in the world?

NINA
No, it's sweet. But you don't have to. We can talk about it.

ROGER
Babe, I'm all ears. *(Beat. She says nothing)* "I'm all ears" means you have to do the talking now.

NINA
I know, I know. I just don't know where to start.

(Beat)

ROGER
You gonna stay there?

NINA
I don't see how I can.

ROGER
Yeah. Me neither.

NINA
I just...you should've seen it. Son of a bitch calls me into his office, and...he literally said to me "this is how you advance in politics."

ROGER
I'll fucking murder him.

NINA
No.

ROGER
I just...god, there's gotta be something we can do!

NINA
There isn't. It's my word against his, and he's been there for twenty years. I'm just an assistant.

ROGER
Dammit!

NINA
I'm positive he's done this before. And he's got enough people to cover for him that...yeah. I'm done.

ROGER
You shouldn't have to give up on your dream because some scumbag wants to fool around in his office! *(Beat)* Okay. Know what's freaking me out?

NINA
What?

ROGER
Why am I way angrier about this than you are?

NINA
I'm angry. I am. But I'm done too. *(She takes ROGER's hand)* I was so excited when I got the job at first. I thought "This is your chance, Nina. Go into the belly of the beast and start fixing things." But the last few years...politics kills the part of you that's human. It's messed up. *(Beat)* I can see everything that's wrong. And now, I'm just trying to think of the right way to fix it.

(ROGER thinks about it for a bit)

ROGER
You can't stop fighting.

NINA
Never thought I'd hear that from you.

ROGER
Look, I used to think that you fought because you couldn't stop. But the thing is, you fight because you can't stand to see a single person treated unfairly, ever. So...I don't know. I wanna beat that fucking senator til he goes cross-eyed. Because I love you, and...yeah, you taught me that people have to be better than that.

NINA
I did?

ROGER
Yeah, you did.

(Beat)

NINA
Then maybe that's what I should be doing.

ROGER
What?

NINA
Rog, I got my teaching degree eight years ago, and I've never used it.

ROGER
You wanna teach?

NINA
It's literally the reason I went to college. Working for the State...that was something Morris got me into,

but...you can't fix government from the inside. Just can't be done. 'Cause they'll talk a big talk, but they don't want it to change. Public servants don't serve, Rog. Even the ones who start out right, they end up either breaking down or...

ROGER
Turning to the dark side?

NINA
You're never gonna stop saying that, are you?

ROGER
Probably not.

NINA
So if fixing the system from the inside is a bust...maybe what I gotta do is stop the problem before it starts.

(Beat)

ROGER
Do it.

NINA
You think I should?

ROGER
Doesn't matter what I think. But yes, I do.

NINA
Yeah.

ROGER
I could see the way this job's been eating you alive. Hell, even back at the Bicentennial. I wanted you there because it was what you believed in. If you think there's a better way, then do that.

NINA
We gotta think it through though.

ROGER
I kinda feel like we just did.

NINA
Rog, I'm the breadwinner. You get that, right?

ROGER
Oh. Yeah.

(Beat)

ROGER
Fuck it. I don't care. We can figure it out. Gods of Comics is doing ok.

NINA
It's not enough. You know that.

ROGER
Then I'll do something else. Anything else. Hell, I can sell the house!

NINA
No. Your parents left it to you. You can't.

ROGER
Babe, you've supported me a while now. And as a progressive, modern man, I felt like it was my duty to let you.

(She laughs)

ROGER
And who knows? You might land a teaching gig super fast!

NINA
Rog...

ROGER
And our overhead is crazy low! It's just you and me! And do you know how much money I saved just by not drinking? We can do this!

NINA
I want to. I do. But not if it screws everything up.

(ROGER laughs)

ROGER
Oh man...how can you be so smart and still just totally look at this thing ass-backwards?

NINA
Hey!

ROGER
If being a teacher will make you happy, then we make that happen. Because if you're happy, then things work. It's that simple.

("Car Wash" is now playing)

ROGER
Man, it is hard to have a serious conversation at a roller disco.

NINA
Screw you, Cleveland Superbomb!

ROGER
Yeah! Screw you, Cleveland Superbomb!

(Some of the skaters cheer)

NINA
So that's it? I tell the Capitol to kiss my grits and...actually, that part sounds pretty great.

ROGER
There's my radical, groovy chick.

NINA
It's gonna take a while, Rog. For me to find a teaching gig. And even if I do, we might have to move, or...

ROGER
You're crossing bridges that are way over there. Let's get past you kicking that dude in the nards and walking out of that dump first.

NINA
I don't know.

(Beat. ROGER looks at her)

ROGER
Holy shit. You're scared.

NINA
What?

ROGER
You. Nina Reynolds, slayer of dragons and bane of junkies everywhere... you're scared.

NINA
I absolutely am not.

ROGER
Are too.

NINA
I'm trying to be practical.

ROGER
"Practical" was invented by cowards.

NINA
Excuse me?

ROGER
Chicken.

NINA
Stop it.

ROGER
Might as well cover yourself in the Colonel's secret recipe.

NINA
(More amused than angry) I know what you're doing, Rog.

ROGER
Why did the Nina cross the road?

NINA
Thin ice, white boy. Thin ice over Lake No-Sex-For-A-Month.

ROGER
You'd never make it.

NINA
You wanna roll those dice?

(Beat)

ROGER
I'll stop now.

NINA
Good boy. *(She kisses him)* Let's do this.

ROGER
Here? There are people watching.

NINA
Finding me a new job, dummy.

ROGER
Yep. Right. Let's do that.

(They kiss)

ROGER
Doesn't mean we can't do the other thing too.

NINA
What?

ROGER
Come on, disco mama.

NINA
We're snowed in! Who knows when the plows will get here?

ROGER
OK, here's what I'm thinking...and just go with me on this...there's only... *(Does a quick count)* Four other couples here, and maybe 3 employees.

NINA
So?

ROGER
So who's gonna notice if we slip off to the restroom for...

(She laughs)

ROGER
What?

NINA
You cannot be serious.

ROGER
Yuh-huh I can.

NINA
We haven't had bathroom sex since... Jesus, when was the last...?

ROGER
July 22nd, 1973.

(She stares at him)

ROGER
Three Dog Night at Cobo Hall.

NINA
Wow.

ROGER
We were pretty baked. I'm not surprised you forgot. *(He puts his arms around her)* I for one think history needs to repeat itself. *(He sees she's thinking about it)* Yes?

(She rolls her eyes)

ROGER
Yes?!

(She starts to lead him off)

NINA
You gotta be quiet.

ROGER
Yes, ma'am!

(They check to make sure no one is watching, then start to sneak off. ROG sings "Shambala")

ROGER
... How does your light shine, in the halls of Shambala?
How does your light shine, in the halls of Shambala?

(She laughs, embarrassed. They run offstage. Lights fade)

SCENE 10
December 31, 1979
Roger's house, Lansing MI

(Lights up. The house is much cleaner/nicer than before, though it still has touches of the old, perhaps a Star Wars poster now, etc. NINA is watching Dick Clark's "New Year's Rocking Eve" on the TV. ROGER soon enters, moving quietly)

NINA
She asleep?

ROGER
Jesus Christ, I hope so. I cannot sing Joy to the World one more time.

NINA
You know Christmas was last week, right?

ROGER
Three Dog Night's Joy to the World. She loves it.

NINA
Really?

ROGER
Oh yeah. Giggles like a loon when I start dancing. *(He joins her on the couch)*

NINA
You wanna grab me a glass of whatever's in that bottle?

(Beat)

ROGER
What bottle?

NINA
The one you think you hid behind the lettuce.

ROGER
Dammit! That was a surprise!

NINA
Then don't hide it behind the lettuce! I reached in for a snack and there it was.

ROGER
You snack on lettuce?

NINA
Lettuce is delicious.

(He laughs)

NINA
We've been together how long, and you don't know this?

ROGER
Who just eats lettuce!? Are you a rabbit?

NINA
I'm gonna be eating it at your funeral when you die of heart disease.

ROGER
(Returning with two glasses) Sparkling apple juice. Ever had it?

NINA
No.

ROGER
Me neither. It's an experiment. *(He clinks her glass, is about to drink)*

NINA
What are you doing?

ROGER
What?

NINA
You see that clock? 11:50. You drink that too early, and you'll ruin the 80s for everyone.

ROGER
Is that how it works?

NINA
Yep.

ROGER
You're the boss.

NINA
'Bout time you figured that out.

ROGER
Are you kidding me? I've known that since our first date.

(She leans back into his arms. They hold each other & watch the TV)

NINA
Our first date was not a date. It was a one-night stand.

ROGER
Fair. But I'm gonna still think of it as our first date.

NINA
This is nice.

ROGER
Yeah. I'm kinda done with New Year's Eve parties. Just some fake champagne with...

NINA
All of it. All of it is nice.

ROGER
Yeah.

(They hold each other. Soon, a baby cries in another room. They groan & laugh)

NINA
Oh my god! Alicia!

ROGER
I got it.

(ROGER goes into the other room. NINA turns down the TV so she can hear him singing "Joy to the World")

ROGER
If I were the king of the world, I tell you what I'd do
I'd throw away the cars and the bars and the wars and...something something something...
Joy to the world, all the boys and girls
Joy to the fishes in the deep blue sea, joy to you and me.

(She smiles. He soon returns)

NINA
That was fast.

ROGER
I'm just that good.

NINA
Yes, you are.

(They go back to holding each other)

NINA
We can never, EVER tell her where she was conceived.

ROGER
Oh, no way. That would screw her up for life.

NINA
Also, we can never take her to that roller rink.

ROGER
Deal. *(Beat)* Flying cars.

NINA
Nope.

ROGER
It could happen.

NINA
It absolutely could not. You know how big a car would have to be to get airborne? It would have to be a plane. Which we already have.

ROGER
You have no idea what the 80s hold. The sky's the limit.

NINA
Okay, but you won't be in those skies in a car.

(Beat)

ROGER
Laser guns.

NINA
Nope.

ROGER
Come on!

NINA
Lasers don't work like that. They're not solid. They're focused light.

(ROGER makes laser gun noises)

ROGER
....bew bew, bew bew bew...

NINA
Nope.

ROGER
I don't want you subbing for science class anymore. It's turning you into a know-it-all.

NINA
Shit, I knew it all before I started teaching. And you better be damn grateful for those checks, mister.

ROGER
Remember how I was able to pay the gas bill this month, which is currently keeping us from freezing to death? I'm grateful.

NINA
Good boy.

(Beat)

ROGER
Robots.

NINA
Oh my god. You're watching way too much Battlestar Galactica.

ROGER
It's the greatest show on TV.

NINA
I don't know. I'll give robots a "maybe".

ROGER
Really?

NINA
It's at least something people are already working on. Robots – maybe.

ROGER
Oh man. Next year, I'm totally buying a robot for Christmas.

NINA
That might be too soon.

ROGER
I'll tell you once more, before I get off the floor, don't bring me down.

NINA
OK.

(They hold each other, watching the countdown)

ROGER
We could put the house on the market in March maybe.

NINA
Let's not talk about that.

ROGER
I could have it ready by then, no problem.

NINA
We're not there yet.

ROGER
We're damn close.

NINA
It's gonna be ok.

ROGER
We've got to think about it. I could still leave the shop.

NINA
No.

ROGER
I just...I want this, all of this...we've gotta be able to make it.

NINA
You built Gods of Comics. You love it, and you're not leaving it.

ROGER
It's not even a choice, if it comes to it.

(She takes his hand)

NINA
It hasn't come to it, babe.

ROGER
I know, but...

NINA
Know what happens tomorrow? A new decade. A whole new start. And...Rog, our whole life together is all about knowing you can't predict the future.

(Beat)

ROGER
So you're saying that laser guns ARE possible?

(She laughs)

NINA
Jackass.

ROGER
Say that to me next year and I'll be a jackass with a laser gun. *(Beat)* I don't wanna be scared.

NINA
Of what?

ROGER
Of the future. Of whatever's coming next.

NINA
Don't call the realtor. Don't sell the shop. Just...just be here, in this moment, right now. There's nothing else but this.

(He holds her closer)

ROGER
Dick Clark is old.

NINA
Yeah.

ROGER
Like, really old. He looks like he's made out of leather.

NINA
People get older. It happens.

ROGER
No. Because in the 80s, they'll have figured out immortality.

NINA
OK, that's just nuts.

ROGER
More nuts than flying cars?

NINA
You know how complicated the human body is? It's a damn miracle we can even walk and talk at the same time. Immortality is off the table.

ROGER
Too bad. I could live forever with you.

(She smiles)

NINA
Not sick of me after ten years?

ROGER
Not even close. You?

NINA
Not even close. You never doubted?

ROGER
Nope.

NINA
Like hell.

ROGER
Hand to God. I can still remember, clear as day, the first time I saw you. You were in a flowered skirt, screaming at that security guard, and all I could think is "There. Right there. That's the girl for me."

NINA
For that night, anyway.

ROGER
For the rest of my life.

(They lie down on the couch)

ROGER
I'm just glad you don't like Pringles.

NINA
So gross. How can you…wait, what?

ROGER
Well, otherwise you might've found this.

(He holds out an engagement ring. She smiles, looks at it)

ROGER
What do you say? Wanna get hitched?

NINA
Rog?

ROGER
Yeah?

NINA
About damn time.

(She kisses ROG, then puts the ring on her finger. They hold each other, looking at it as the lights fade)

DICK CLARK'S VOICE
10, 9, 8, 7, 6, 5, 4, 3, 2…1!

(Blackout)

END OF PLAY

WILLIAMSTON THEATRE

Summer Retreat

A PLAY BY
ANNIE MARTIN

Cast of Characters

AMY: A woman in her early fifties
SIAN: A woman in her early fifties
CAROLINE: A woman in her early fifties
SHEP: A woman in her late twenties/early thirties; Nancy's half-sister
MAN: Somewhere between late 20s and death

TIME
The Present

PLACE
A Summer Cottage in a Rural Area

SUMMER RETREAT received its world premiere on July 22, 2016 at Williamston Theatre (Williamston, MI). It was directed by Suzi Regan. Set design by Kirk Domer, Lighting Design by Alex Gay, Costume Design by Holly Iler, Sound Design by Will Myers, Properties Design by Michelle Raymond. Stage Managed by Nan Luchini.

The cast was as follows:

>AMY - Julia Glander
>SIAN - Sandra Birch
>CAROLINE - Emily Sutton-Smith
>SHEP - Dani Cochrane
>MAN - Patrick Loos

For production rights, contact Annie Martin at annielmartin@gmail.com.

Summer Retreat

ACT ONE

(*Afternoon. The inside of a cottage that is not currently in use. Curtains are drawn shut. There is a rustling sound outside the window*)

AMY (O.S.)
Can something go right? Come on. Open. Open.

(*More pounding and rustling and then the sound of a falling screen and a yelp*)

AMY (O.S.)
Yes.

(*Suddenly, a leg comes through the window, kicking the curtains. There are sounds of heavy breathing and heaving and then Amy falls through the window, taking the curtains with her. Imagine anything but gracefulness as she moves. She gets up quickly and straightens herself out as she takes stock of the cottage. She is wearing a nice black dress but is barefoot. We can now see the window is without a screen. She tries to put the screen back in... no luck. Then she tries to rehang the curtains, which also doesn't work, so she pushes them under the couch. She turns and looks around the cottage again. It is a cabin with male décor... guns hanging, a big buck head, a big fish hung over the fire place. She shakes her head*)

AMY
Ugh.

(*AMY opens the sliding glass doors that face out at a lake and stands there*)

AMY
Stop it. Move. Right? Right.

(*She snaps out of it. She heads down a hallway unseen, but we hear a door open and a screen door hit. AMY then walks back onstage. She is looking for something. While looking in the fridge, she grabs a beer. And continues to search. She is moving onstage and off looking for the unexplained.*

In a hidden spot in a cabinet, she pulls out a tin that she starts to laugh about. She opens it up and inside is an emergency cigarette. She puts it in her mouth as she continues her look around.

We hear a car pull up somewhere, fast and loud as if speeding. AMY is off stage. Car doors slam)

CAROLINE (O.S.)
Amy!

SIAN (O.S.)
Wait a sec.

CAROLINE (O.S.)
Come on.

SIAN (O.S.)
I'll look over here.

CAROLINE (O.S.)
(Louder) AMY!

(The screen door slams)

SIAN (O.S.)
AMY!

(SIAN walks down the hallway. AMY comes into sight)

SIAN
Care, she's here!

CAROLINE (O.S.)
(Yells back) Is she dead?

SIAN
(To AMY) Amy!

AMY
SIAN! (Hugs her)

SIAN
Amy!

AMY
What are you... Do you know?

CAROLINE
(Off-stage, but moving around) Is she still breathing?

SIAN
(To AMY) I don't know why you are... What are you doing here?

AMY
Here? Now? Um.

SIAN
Are you smoking?

AMY
I found it in the... (Holds up the tin)

SIAN
Our emergency smoke. Give that here.

AMY
(Hands it to her) I've been...

(SIAN smells the cigarette and puts it in her mouth)

SIAN
Lighter?

AMY
No. Hey. You got a shovel in your car?

SIAN
No.

AMY
Crap.

(SIAN starts to look)

CAROLINE
(Having walked around and now coming up to the deck) Jesus Christ.

AMY
How mad are you?

CAROLINE
Pretty mad.

AMY
What do you think we should do?

CAROLINE
Well I think I shouldn't've missed my plane?

AMY
Oh the plane. Right.

SIAN
Enough.

CAROLINE
I'm supposed to be in L.A.

AMY
Oh. Yeah. Sorry about that.

SIAN
(To the cigarette) I love you

CAROLINE
What are we doing here?

(AMY shrugs and is looking out the windows)

CAROLINE
We were concerned.

SIAN
You scared us.

AMY
I can explain.

CAROLINE
Threatening to kill yourself--

AMY
(Interrupting) Kill myself?

CAROLINE
--isn't funny. Especially after what we've been through.

AMY
What the hell are you talking about?

CAROLINE
Sian?

SIAN
(Is trying to light the cigarette off the stove) What?

CAROLINE
What are you doing? *(Grabs the cigarette from her mouth and crushes it to nothing)*

SIAN
Hey!

CAROLINE
You need to die of cancer too?

SIAN
Don't say that.

(AMY has started to look around again)

CAROLINE
Then don't be stupid.

SIAN
It's only 1 after 20 years, I don't think one is gonna ...

AMY
(Interrupting) Three.

SIAN
Three?

AMY
Kristi's graduation.

SIAN
That doesn't count. My baby was going off to college and.... this is another big moment.

CAROLINE
Whatever you need to tell yourself. Listen, did she or did she not say she was going to kill herself?

SIAN
She did.

AMY
No.

SIAN
(To AMY) You did.

AMY
I never said anything close to... what makes you think I would ever

CAROLINE
Your text.

AMY
My text? I didn't text you anything

like that.

CAROLINE
(Pulls out her phone and reads) "So good to see you both and so sad that ur leaving. I'm feeling so lost and outside of it all. Going to the old cottage and hang myself."

AMY
Hang myself?

CAROLINE
(Turns the phone to AMY) Hang myself.

AMY
(Seeing it) That's a typo.

CAROLINE
A typo?

AMY
I meant to say, I'm going to come out here to hang with myself.

SIAN
We assumed it was a mistake, but--

CAROLINE
(To SIAN) No, I didn't.

SIAN
We were worried. (To AMY) You didn't say goodbye or anything. You get up, leave, and we get your message.

CAROLINE
(To AMY) And your phone? Why didn't you pick you your phone?

AMY
There's no signal here.

CAROLINE
We tried calling for the two hours it took us to get here.

AMY
Back roads get nothing. You wanna check my phone?

CAROLINE
Yes.

(AMY throws her phone at CAROLINE)

AMY
See?

SIAN
We were gonna call the police.

AMY
You didn't, did you?

CAROLINE
No.

AMY
Thank god.

SIAN
Yes.

AMY
Wait a second, you thought I was killing myself and you didn't call the police?

CAROLINE
I wanted to but---

SIAN
(Looks at CAROLINE) Yeah, I said no.

CAROLINE
We wanted to make sure first.

AMY
Make sure I was dead?

CAROLINE
Yes.

AMY
So you were willing to risk that I might already be dead?

SIAN
Don't get mad.

CAROLINE
Yes.

AMY
What if I was hanging myself, you'd be--

CAROLINE
But you weren't.

AMY
But I might have.

CAROLINE
You'd have been dead long before the police arrived. *(To AMY)* You have no reason to be upset. We just drove--

SIAN
(Interrupting) Sped.

CAROLINE
--all the way here. For nothing.

AMY
I'm sorry I'm not hanging from the rafters.

CAROLINE
I accept your apology.

SIAN
Don't say that.

AMY
I'm kinda happy that you both came because...

CAROLINE
As long as you're happy.

SIAN
Care, let it go.

CAROLINE
What? I'm glad someone is happy because I'm supposed to be in LA tomorrow morning.

AMY
I'm sorry. Christ. I got my own thing too.

CAROLINE
I only mentioned it about ten times today.

SIAN
You can still make it.

AMY
Of course you can. It's not that big of a deal.

CAROLINE
Yes it is. I was supposed to be back to New York tonight to get my things and then...

SIAN
You still need to pack?

CAROLINE
Yes. I was... it was a bit of mad rush for me. I needed to get here, I did, and I didn't really plan ahead.

AMY
None of us planned for this. That's really important for all of us to remember.

SIAN
Maybe you could reschedule. I'm sure they'd understand if you explained...

CAROLINE
Those people don't give a shit. There's no rescheduling a conference I'm speaking at. This has been in the works for a year.

AMY
Well I'm sure Nancy is sorry for her bad timing.

CAROLINE
Fuck you.

SIAN
Hey. Hey.

CAROLINE
I was in London when you called. I flew straight here. Had I actually been told anything, I'd have been here, but none of you fucking told me.

AMY
We didn't know. Nobody knew what the hell was happening.

CAROLINE
Bull.

AMY
I told you as soon as I knew.

CAROLINE
16 days!

SIAN
Care, they originally said 6 months. Then 3. Honest. Nobody knew.

AMY
(To CAROLINE) Plus you've been unavailable.

CAROLINE
I'm here.

AMY
Not before. You've been on your phone all day.

CAROLINE
I had to tie up loose ends. It's called work.

AMY
Who cares?

CAROLINE
Me. My job's a little more important that teaching art to high schoolers.

AMY
Says who?

CAROLINE
Most of the country.

AMY
No. The country hates your money-grubbing profession.

SIAN
You're idiots.

CAROLINE
People like me pay your salary.

AMY
Taxpayers, like me, pay my... I don't have time for your bullshit.

CAROLINE
MY bullshit?

AMY
You can go.

CAROLINE
Great. Let's go.

SIAN
Shut up.

CAROLINE
Sian!

SIAN
You guys are idiots. Let's agree. We all do important work?

CAROLINE
You don't even work.

AMY
There you go. (Searching the cabin)

SIAN
I do work, Caroline. I'm just as busy as any of you. Finances, schedules, juggling family and community obligations. I also teach Sunday school as well as do the banking for the church. You couldn't handle being an SAHM.

CAROLINE
Huh?

SIAN
Stay-at-home Mom.

CAROLINE
Oh. It has its own acronym?

AMY
Don't condescend her!

CAROLINE
I wasn't. *(To SIAN)* I shouldn't have said anything. I know you work hard.

SIAN
It's fine. Amy, what are you doing? Stop messing around.

AMY
I just need a shovel or something.

CAROLINE
You don't need a goddamn shovel. Come on. Stop being so weird.

AMY
You don't know what I need.

CAROLINE
Professional help?

AMY
Shut up.

CAROLINE
No. You shut up. Drag us up here on a damn scavenger hunt while I'm screwed.

AMY
Because everything is always about you. I forgot.

SIAN
Stop being so selfish. You both only think about yourselves and forget about anyone else. I am always the rational one. I always--

(Both have stopped to look at SIAN)

AMY
Excuse me?

CAROLINE
(To SIAN) Did you say rational?

SIAN
Yes.

AMY
No you aren't.

SIAN
Yes I am.

CAROLINE
No.

SIAN
Everyone who knows me, knows I'm exactly that person. Rational.

AMY
No.

SIAN
Yes. I'm the peacemaker.

AMY
People pleaser.

CAROLINE
Perfect. Yes.

SIAN
I do not please people. I mean yes, sometimes I want people to be happy but it's not a necessity or anything.

CAROLINE
Come on.

AMY
Um, remember first week, freshman year, when we couldn't find anyone to buy us beer and we were all pissed off... you made out with um... that guy... we called halitosis.

CAROLINE
Oh my god, yes, she did. Granola

Gary. Down the hall.

SIAN
I got us beer. Problem solver!

CAROLINE
Yeah you absolutely have solved my problems. Dated that statistics TA so I could get a passing grade. Couldn't love you more for that.

AMY
I would never have done it. Especially with him.

CAROLINE
Me neither.

SIAN
Seriously?

AMY and **CAROLINE**
Yeah.

SIAN
Fine. I like to help make people happy, so I guess if that's a people pleaser than...

CAROLINE
Why are you admitting it?

AMY
This is exactly what we're talking about.

CAROLINE
You caved.

AMY
Like a people pleaser would.

SIAN
But you said I was one.

CAROLINE
And you proved us right.

SIAN
My other, better friends, they don't make fun or laugh at me.

CAROLINE
That's because we actually know you.

AMY
We are you.

(SIAN looks through the tin and finds an old picture)

SIAN
Well, this isn't 1984.

CAROLINE
No need to tell me.

AMY
I wish we could go back. Right now I really would give anything. Because right now this sucks.

CAROLINE
You'd want to go back to your mullet phase.

AMY
That was the style.

SIAN
That was never the style.

AMY
(Points to CAROLINE) Yeah, you wore big fake glasses like Sally Jesse Raphael and your flashdance workout clothes and your mom jeans.

CAROLINE
Those pants are back in by the way.

AMY
(Points to SIAN) And you. You wore hideous leggings that gave you cameltoe and shoulder pads that made your neck disappear... so neither of you should judge.

SIAN
I had such a cute little body. And now...I've made peace with this... *(Indicating her body)* ...if only because it's too late.

CAROLINE
What'd you expect after four kids?

SIAN
What's that mean?

CAROLINE
It means you look like you're supposed to now.

SIAN
Which is what?

AMY
You look good.

CAROLINE
Which is fifty-two.

SIAN
I'm fat now?

CAROLINE
It's having babies and Midwest living and… you look like you are enjoying life. Like your happy.

AMY
(To CAROLINE) Come on. Midwest living?

CAROLINE
Don't make it sound like that.

SIAN
Happy, fat and a people pleaser. Golly gee, Caroline, thank you.

CAROLINE
Hey! *(Puts her arm around SIAN)* I… I'm a mean, New York bitch.

SIAN
You really are.

AMY
This. Right now, this feels right, good. not to be so… cautious. We're kind of free… honest… connected and…

SIAN
And mean to Sian.

AMY
You made fun of my hair, which you have to admit was amazing, even in a mullet. So thick and…

CAROLINE
It was not amazing.

AMY
People complimented it. Feel it now. Thinning.

(CAROLINE feels it)

CAROLINE
Well…

AMY
Right?

(SIAN feels it too)

SIAN
Oh. Yeah. *(To CAROLINE)* Is thinning a Midwest thing too?

CAROLINE
I'm dealing with the fact that under this mop, I'm completely white. No gray… just white.

SIAN
I've gotten lucky. Just a few silver strands.

AMY
But you've got the most wrinkles, so…

(AMY and CAROLINE laugh)

SIAN
That's because I don't shoot my face up with Botox like some people. *(Stares at them both)*

AMY
I've never!

CAROLINE
It's not expensive. Lasers, Botox… a fountain of youth for your skin is

out there if you want it ladies. And it looks totally natural.

SIAN
If that's true, then how'd I know?

CAROLINE
I don't have that frozen face thing if that is what you're getting at.

SIAN
Uh-huh.

CAROLINE
I don't.

SIAN
Whatever you say.

CAROLINE
My face moves.

AMY
Does it?

SIAN
Then be surprised.

CAROLINE
What?

SIAN
Show me a surprised face.

(CAROLINE gives SIAN the finger and SIAN gives it back. Everyone laughs)

SIAN
That's it? That's all you got?

AMY
Cheers to that tightly wound face. (Drinks)

CAROLINE
(Points to the beer) Where'd you get that?

AMY
Fridge is full of them.

SIAN
Any Pinot?

AMY
I don't know. (CAROLINE walks into the cottage and to the fridge. Amy and Sian follow) At the funeral, well actually after it...

CAROLINE
I don't want to talk about the funeral. I don't. It was... wasn't about her, not really.

SIAN
Well, this place has... changed.

CAROLINE
Not for the better

SIAN
But it still smells the same.

(They all smell and smile)

CAROLINE
It does. Nancy's dad still owns it?

AMY
You know, here's the thing...

SIAN
I'm sure. Although there isn't a feminine touch in here.

CAROLINE
Key in the shed like always.

AMY
(Nodding and drinking from her beer) Nancy has been talking about it. I mean she did. Remembering us up here. Thought it was magic.

SIAN
It is.

CAROLINE
It was.

AMY
This was her happy place when she was in pain. (Silence for a moment) She wanted to get back here. Thought she'd have time to drive up if only

for a day, but you know didn't. Couldn't.

SIAN
I told her I'd drive her.

AMY
Ok. Well, sure, but...

SIAN
I'm just saying we talked about it too.

CAROLINE
Sian, what do you want? There's no wine.

SIAN
I'll get some water.

AMY
It's brown.

SIAN
(Grabbing a glass) You just need to let it run. *(Turns on the water and begins filling and then dumping her glass over and over again, waiting for the water to run clear)*

CAROLINE
When were we all last here? It had to be before I moved to New York.

SIAN
1991. For a week that summer. She had just gotten married.

AMY
1991? No. That long ago?

SIAN
Yes.

AMY
I must have been engaged to dickhead.

CAROLINE
And I was getting rid of my first one.

SIAN
And I was pregnant

AMY
You didn't even know yet.

CAROLINE
We all thought that kid was going to be born with some serious issues.

SIAN
He, thank the Lord in Heaven, turned out ok. Healthy and happy. So much guilt over....

CAROLINE
Time to let that go. Alcohol did him good.

AMY
So you can see why this place is where Nancy wants to be.

SIAN
Wish we had got up here again.

CAROLINE
You didn't ever without me?

SIAN
It never worked with our schedules.

CAROLINE
I would've been jealous if you did.

AMY
Really?

CAROLINE
I loved it here too.

SIAN
(To CAROLINE) I figured you wanted to avoid it because of the spiders and mice.

CAROLINE
Mice? There was only that one mouse. Remember that thing would scurry across the floor or be up on a ceiling beam.

SIAN
You understand that there was more

than one, right?

CAROLINE
No. Nancy said it was the one mouse, she... *(Realizing it)* That twat. *(AMY and SIAN laugh)* How'd I not figure that out?

AMY
No idea.

CAROLINE
She also called this place a compound and I believed that too.

SIAN
That's right!

AMY
18 and gullible.

SIAN
I pictured the Kennedys compound in Hyannis Port.

CAROLINE
Oh, she oversold it by a lot.

AMY
Every summer it was perfect.

SIAN
So much beautiful wasted potential as my mom kept telling me.

AMY
She was right. We did literally nothing.

SIAN
We swam, drank—

CAROLINE
Fondled a local.

AMY
Chris! He was hottie. Looked like Tubbs from Miami Vice.

SIAN
—ate, drank, slept, drank.

AMY
We shared our dreams.

CAROLINE
We talked a lot of shit.

AMY
Dreams, shit, whatever you wanna call it.

SIAN
I wanted to work, but no one would hire us.

CAROLINE
I wouldn't have either.

AMY
I didn't want to work anyways.

CAROLINE
Shocker.

SIAN
Booze and smokes was all I needed then.

CAROLINE
Hear, hear. *(Drinks)*

AMY
To our college summer days. We didn't know how good we had it.

SIAN
Never do.

AMY
We should have kept up some kind of tradition.

SIAN
Might not have been the same.

CAROLINE
Plus, you can't match that last lost week up here. That was pretty great.

SIAN
Had I known I was with child...

CAROLINE
See? Babies are what really changed it all.

AMY
Says the woman with no kids.

CAROLINE
That's how I know.

SIAN
You've had just as many husbands as I've had kids.

CAROLINE
Yeah, but they don't crap themselves until they are old. And by then, I ditch'em. I have no time for the boredom and static nature of men.

SIAN
Seems a little empty.

CAROLINE
Maybe. But it's amazing. You should try it.

SIAN
I'm quite happy and satisfied where I am.

CAROLINE
It's because it's all you know. But as long as you are getting some still, I'm happy for you. *(Noticing SIAN is still trying to get the water to turn clear)* Sian, get a beer already.

AMY
Told you. It's brown.

SIAN
I don't like beer.

CAROLINE
Drink a beer.

SIAN
Is there a sweet one?

CAROLINE
I'll pick one out for you.

(CAROLINE is looking through the fridge. Amy and Sian are walking around the place)

CAROLINE
(Swigs from her beer) And after this one, I need to head back.

SIAN
Me too.

AMY
(Heads up the stairs to the loft out of sight) Yeah, well, I can't. Not yet. I gotta do a couple things I really really have to do.

(CAROLINE gives SIAN a beer)

SIAN
(Yells up to her) Like what?

AMY
Stuff.

SIAN
Stuff? *(To CAROLINE)* She's got stuff to do.

CAROLINE
Because she's very important, Sian. Boy, she has turned a little nutty, huh? *(SIAN heads into the kitchen)*

SIAN
(In a low voice) She's not normally so…She's off.

CAROLINE
Yeah. She's Amy.

SIAN
Are you?

CAROLINE
Am I?

SIAN
Off?

CAROLINE
Sure. I'm rushing around trying to…

SIAN
I meant... I don't know. Feels strange being here... and I'm thinking about Nancy and us and...

CAROLINE
Don't. Stop thinking. Drink that. It'll help.

(SIAN drinks)

SIAN
Not horrible.

CAROLINE
Best thing we can do—all of us—is get back to the real world. Keep moving ahead. It's not healthy to be here.

SIAN
It's... I feel like there is ... something unfinished or that something missing and I don't--

(Crash offstage is heard)

SIAN
(To AMY) AMY? You ok? (Runs up the stairs)

AMY (O.S.)
I'm okay.

SIAN
She's okay. Everything's fine.

(CAROLINE guzzles her beer and takes stock of the food)

CAROLINE
(Up to them both) Anyone hungry? There's microwave mac and cheese, pretzels, soup, and popcorn. And peanut butter. Crunchy though. Oh... marshmallows too. And that's about it. Wait... Cheez-Its, but they look really old. (Tastes a Cheez-It, spitting it out) No Cheez-Its.

(SIAN comes down the stairs, wearing a strange hunting hat. AMY behind her)

SIAN
New York is all a-twitter about this being the style. I got my Midwest fat ass and this trendy hat... I'm ready for summer now.

CAROLINE
(Seeing SIAN) Now that's a statement. Is that a lumberjack shirt?

AMY
(Follows, wearing a flannel shirt over her dress) Yep.

CAROLINE
Looks filthy.

AMY
I don't want to get my clothes dirty.

CAROLINE
How? Why would you get them dirty?

AMY
You're right. It's not going to work, is it? I can't do anything right.

CAROLINE
It's a flannel. Not an indictment about your entire being.

SIAN
(Stares at the buck head) Hey. I can't stop looking at that dead thing. Can we do something about it? I just...it's so ugly and you know I can't stand to think about death.

CAROLINE
Okay, okay. I'll do it. (CAROLINE drops a comforter over the Buck's head)

SIAN
That's better. Much better. (A car is heard pulling up in the driveway and it gets louder) Did you... did someone just pull in?

AMY
What?

CAROLINE
I think so.

AMY
Is that the police?

SIAN
Police?

CAROLINE
(To SIAN) Did you call'em?

SIAN
No.

AMY
(Running back upstairs) I'm not here.

SIAN
Amy.

AMY
Forgive me.

CAROLINE
(To AMY) Where are you going... *(To SIAN)* Where is she...

SIAN
Should we hide?

CAROLINE
No.

SIAN
OK. What should we do?

CAROLINE
See who it is.

SIAN
Right. Right.

CAROLINE
We aren't doing anything wrong.

SIAN
Right. But Amy...

CAROLINE
Is ridiculous.

(The screen door slams shut. Tension fills the room and the sound of Shep's voice can be heard)

SHEP (O.S.)
LADIES! Oh, Ladies!

SIAN
That's not--

SHEP
(Coming into view) Hello!

CAROLINE
Shep!

AMY
(Upstairs) Did you say Shep?

SHEP
This is where the party is.

CAROLINE
Jesus.

SHEP
Car-o-line!

AMY
(Comes back into view) Shep?

SHEP
Enough with the Shep. Nicole, please.

CAROLIINE
It's Shep.

AMY
What do you know? What. Do. You. Know?

SHEP
Like academically?

SIAN
No. Why are you here?

SHEP
What do you mean?

CAROLINE
She means, why are you here?

SHEP
I was invited.

CAROLINE
By whom?

SHEP
Amy.

AMY
No, you weren't.

SHEP
I got your text. Glad you aren't dead, BTW. No need to steal Nancy's thunder.

AMY
(To SHEP) I didn't text you. *(To Caroline and SIAN)* I did not text her.

SHEP
(To AMY) You actually did.

AMY
No.

SHEP
Um, yeah. *(Pulls out her phone and reads)* Blah, blah, blah, "Worried about" whatever "going to the old cottage and hang myself."

AMY
I don't have your number!

SHEP
(To the group) So I'm here. Plus I saw you two fly off so I figured this was where you were heading.

CAROLINE
We aren't staying.

SHEP
No?

CAROLINE
No.

SIAN
Just a drink and then we are leaving.

AMY
(To SHEP) You need to go. There's already too many of us here. You've got to go.

SHEP
Please. What're we all drinking? *(Silence by the women who are each staring at each other and annoyed by the intrusion. SHEP then heads to the fridge and looks in)* Nice. *(SHEP grabs a beer)*

(AMY has picked up SHEP's phone from the table)

SIAN
Should you be drinking at all because I know...

SHEP
Oh, I'm not an alcoholic, if that's what she told you. Just a binger. Very different. *(Pause)* So, what are we talking about? *(Silence)* The old days? *(Silence)* OK, let's talk about that service. Did you see Kristin? She was tripping and falling all over the place. Had a few too many in the parking lot. Can't say I blame her... did the same thing, but she was a wobbling.

SIAN
She has MS.

SHEP
So.

SIAN
Multiple Sclerosis.

SHEP
You sure?

SIAN
She was using a cane.

SHEP
She was? I don't remember that. Are we talking about the same Kristin?

SIAN
Yes.

SHEP
Ew. Well, I feel bad. I told her to pull it together. But she must get that a lot.

AMY
This is Nancy's phone.

SIAN
You texted Nancy?

SHEP
Dave gave it to me.

AMY
It's not his to give away.

SHEP
(Grabs it back) I needed a phone, so he gave me hers. Nancy wouldn't care.

AMY
(Grabbing it back) This still has personal stuff on it.

SIAN
Come on. Really?

CAROLINE
That's wrong, Shep.

SHEP
Stop calling me that. I won't answer to anything but Nicole now.

CAROLINE
Bummer, Shep.

SHEP
I'm in pain too, Care. *(AMY is going through Nancy's phone)* She was my sister, you know.

CAROLINE
Half-sister.

AMY
(To SHEP) This is private. A violation really.

SHEP
It's only her pics and old emails and text messages. That's all.

CAROLINE
Right. It's private.

SIAN
(To SHEP) Do you think Nancy would like you going through her things, even if she isn't here?

SHEP
Oh, I was looking through this way before she died. I'm not that insensitive.

AMY
That's... You are horrible.

SIAN
Amy.

CAROLINE
It's true.

SIAN
I know, but don't say that to her face.

SHEP
I'm really trying to center myself and not get angry, but you saying that to me now when I'm in mourning. When I've lost my family. Not you. Not any of you. Me. ... I'm trying to adjust to this "new" normal. And you all judging instead of helping me. Selfish! The things I could tell you about my sister. About what she thought about you. You think you know so much, but I know things too. I know all of your secrets, so don't think you're all so high and mighty. I got shit that will take you all down.

(Pause. AMY, SIAN, and CAROLINE all laugh)

CAROLINE
You have stuff on us?

SHEP
You cheated on your first husband.

CAROLINE
That's not a secret. Everyone including him knew. Let's not start talking about skeletons in closets. You've got a house full.

SHEP
I don't have secrets. No skeletons.

AMY
You stole my VISA from of my purse—

SHEP
You dropped it.

AMY
--at Michael's graduation party and how much did you rack up on it?

SHEP
I apologized for that. I was in a tight spot.

SIAN
You bought shoes.

SHEP
I know what I bought.

CAROLINE
My third wedding. Nancy and Dave had you babysit your nieces overnight. You threw a party in their home with the kids.

SHEP
I had a few people over and the kids had a blast. They were up past their bed time.

CAROLINE
They were... how old?

SIAN
3 and 6

CAROLINE
Uh huh. You were arrested when the cops busted it up and found drugs.

SHEP
Lame narc neighbors.

CAROLINE
Emmy and Lucy were taken into child protective services.

SHEP
They thought it was a vacation. Plus, who would leave their kids with me? Think about that.

CAROLINE
How many lawyers have I had to get for you?

SHEP
This is bullying. Nancy forgave me for all of this. It was all so long ago.

AMY
Not her car. You totaled it two weeks ago.

SHEP
Now everything's my fault? I was the victim. I was the one that got hit. Nance got it.

SIAN
Because she was dying, Shep. Dying.

SHEP
Exactly. It was a small thing. And you know, none of this happened to you guys, except for the mix up with Amy's card. Nancy loved me no matter what. Stood by me. Helped pick up my pieces. And never called me Shep. Never. Ever. So why don't you all just respect that. Mic drop, bitches. *(Pretends to drop the mic)*

AMY
(Attacks) Nance only called you Shep.

CAROLINE
I don't think I even knew your name was Nicole.

SIAN
In fact, she actually gave you the name.

SHEP
Nuh-uh.

CAROLINE
Un-huh.

SHEP
Stop messin' with me.

SIAN
This is the God's honest truth.

(CAROLINE goes to the fridge and gets two more beers)

AMY
Way before you came into existence, Nancy wanted a dog.

CAROLINE
When your dad left her mom, Nancy was what? How old?

SIAN
Eight.

CAROLINE
Right. Eight. She was eight and your dad promised her a dog.

AMY
For seven years he kept saying he'd get her one.

CAROLINE
Married your mother and still promised her that dog.

SHEP
I didn't get one either.

CAROLINE
Instead of that dog she'd been promised over and over again, he called her up junior year of high school.

SIAN
Sophomore.

AMY
The summer inbetween.

CAROLINE
Whatever. He calls her and says, "Honey, you are getting something better than a dog--

AMY
--a baby sister."

SHEP
That's exciting news.

SIAN
No.

AMY
Promises had been made and were now broken.

CAROLINE
Nancy is a very type A person--

SHEP
(Interrupting) Anal, yes.

CAROLINE
--especially when she gets her head set on something.

SIAN
Remember her binders. Final exam binders. Wedding binder. Birthing binders.

AMY
Her wedding one was 3 volumes.

SHEP
So she's a binder person.

CAROLINE
You don't get it. She had researched dogs. Every single kind to find the right one.

SIAN
No doubt there was a dog binder.

AMY
No doubt.

CAROLINE
In the end, her heart was set on a shepherd dog... not a German, but a what?

AMY
Australian shepherd dog.

CAROLINE.
Yep. That's it.

AMY
So right after you were born, she baptized you Shep. She refused to call you different and neither will we. So, to us, you will always be Shep.

CAROLINE
Shep the dog who never came to be.

SHEP
Oh.

(CAROLINE, SIAN, and AMY clink drinks and makes dog noises)

SHEP
That is the sweetest story I've ever heard.

AMY
You were named for a dog.

SHEP
But that's what she wanted. I was what she wanted.

CAROLINE
(To AMY and SIAN) How is she missing this?

SHEP
My heart is just so big right now. Sometimes I thought she didn't really like me.

CAROLINE
She didn't.

SIAN
Care.

CAROLINE
What?

SHEP
Tell me more stories. Come on.

CAROLINE
Party's over. I've got a plane to catch.

AMY
(To CAROLINE) Don't leave me. Not yet.

SIAN
(To AMY) One last ciggie for the road. My last one forever.

CAROLINE
Really?

AMY
(To SIAN) That was it. Emergency one.

SIAN
What?

CAROLINE
Darn it.

SHEP
You smoke?

CAROLINE
I thought you knew everything.

SIAN
I quit long ago. I've been jonsing from being here. It's probably best I don't.

CAROLINE
Exactly.

SHEP
I've got an e-cig if you want it.

SIAN
An e-cig? Is that the electronic type of--

SHEP
Yep. But it's kind of through water and is so much better for you. Healthier in fact.

SIAN
Seems a lot less fun.

SHEP
I thought the same, but it's pretty great.

AMY
Care, I think I screwed up.

CAROLINE
Don't worry about it. I'm not mad anymore. *(To SIAN)* Do it and get it over with.

SIAN
Ok. I'm game. It can't hurt and it's not like I'll smell, right?

SHEP
Nope. No smell. I'll go get it. *(SHEP leaves, goes out to her car)*

CAROLINE
Pathetic.

SIAN
(To CAROLINE) You can wait 5 minutes more.

CAROLINE
(Looking at her phone) I don't want to be near her *(Indicating SHEP)* one minute more. *(Walking around trying to get something)*

AMY
Me neither.

CAROLINE
Then let's high tail it outta here.

AMY
I can't yet. I'd rather you guys not either. I think we should...

SIAN
(To CAROLINE) Try the end of the dock.

CAROLINE
What?

SIAN
When we've vacationed up north, I usually get a signal when I'm away from the trees and in the open.

CAROLINE
Ok. Good. *(Heads out)* I want to call and get booked on the next flight available.

(CAROLINE walks out the sliding doors and goes down to the dock with her beer and phone)

AMY
Did you notice she wasn't crying?

SIAN
Who? Care?

AMY
During the service.

SIAN
Everyone shows emotion differently.

AMY
She was checking her phone.

SIAN
It was a long service.

AMY
Come on!

SIAN
It's hard to tell what she's thinking

with the frozen face thing. Do you know if Nancy called her? At all? Or if they talked

AMY
She hasn't said anything to me.

SIAN
I would assume she did. She was calling everyone. I think she was looking for a normal conversation. She called me too and all I could say was "I love you." I couldn't pull myself together—cried like I was dying. Promised her I'd get over to see her the next day. And then, it was too quick.

AMY
I'm sure it made her happy just to hear your voice.

(Pause)

SIAN
Emmie and Lucy held up well today, I thought.

AMY
They did. Although, Lucy wearing that mini skirt, good god.

SIAN
At least she had on underwear.

AMY
True.

SIAN
I thought they were lovely.

AMY
They've got my deepest sympathies. You and I both know it should've been Dave not her.

SIAN
STOP!

AMY
What?

SIAN
You can think that but don't say it.

AMY
Why not?

SIAN
It's just tempting the... well...

AMY
The gods? Fate? What are they gonna do ? Curse me?

SIAN
I will say that it was tacky to bring his girlfriend.

AMY
He's an asshole.

SIAN
He is. That's why she left him.

AMY
Finally.

SIAN
But he's responsible for the girls now.

AMY
They're almost adults, thank god.

SIAN
We need to keep tabs on them. Make sure they know they can count on us.

AMY
Yes of course.

SIAN
(Pause) You gonna tell me what's going on?

AMY
With what?

SIAN
Why are we here?

AMY
You followed me.

(SIAN stares at her)

SIAN
You have no poker face.

(Screen door slams)

SHEP
I've got it.

SIAN
Amy?

AMY
(To SIAN) Don't worry about it. Smoke and then we'll finish.

SHEP
Here you go. *(SHEP holds out her vape pen/e-cigarette)* It's all ready for you.

SIAN
And what do I do?

SHEP
Inhale. Like a cigarette.

SIAN
It won't hurt my lungs?

SHEP
Nope. It's clean and pure.

AMY
You miss it this much, Sianny?

SIAN
(Inhaling) Yes, but I've replaced it.

SHEP
With what? Sex?

SIAN
(Exhales) No!

SHEP
Uh huh.

SIAN
This tastes strange. Jazzercise.

AMY and SHEP
Jazzercise?

SIAN
It's a great workout.

AMY
It was in 1982.

SIAN
There's been a resurgence.

SHEP
Can you do jazz hands?

AMY
That's nice, Sianny

SIAN
You'd both be surprised.

AMY
I am.

SHEP
I think that's awesome.

SIAN
Thank you. *(Keeps smoking away)*

SHEP
So whatcha think?

SIAN
It's pretty smooth. Just the taste.

SHEP
That's quality oil.

SIAN
They use an oil?

SHEP
Yep.

SIAN
Nicotine oil.

SHEP
No.

AMY
Really? I'd think it's all about the nicotine buzz. What's the point of--

SHEP
I don't use the nicotine stuff.

SIAN
So what is it?

SHEP
Hash oil.

SIAN
Huh.

SHEP
Yep. Huh.

AMY
Hash oil? *(SHEP looks at her and smiles)* As in hash hash?

SHEP
Could you be more specific?

AMY
(To SIAN) Stop. Stop smoking it.

SIAN
Why?

AMY
It's laced.

SIAN
What?

SHEP
It's not laced. It just is.

SIAN
Is what?

AMY
Hash.

SIAN
Hash?

AMY
Cannabis.

SIAN
Cannabis?

SHEP
You basically smoked pot.

SIAN
Oh my. Oh my Lord.

AMY
It's fine, Sianny.

SIAN
(To SHEP) How could you do this? Oh lordy. *(Takes another inhale of it without thinking)* Shit!

AMY
(To SIAN) You took one hit. It's not gonna...

SHEP
No way. She took like 5 or 7.

SIAN
Get this away from me! Get it away! *(Handing over to SHEP)*

AMY
How could you do that? What the hell were you thinking?

SHEP
Maybe you should have some too. Make you guys quit being witches.

SIAN
You did this on purpose?

SHEP
Yes.

AMY
Bitch.

SIAN
I've never been high.

SHEP
I'm so happy I'm here for your first.

SIAN
How could you?

SHEP
Everyone is way too uptight.

SIAN
Am I high?

AMY
It's okay.

SIAN
Am I high now?

AMY
You're fine

SIAN
Oh my goodness!

AMY
You are OK.

SHEP
This is good stuff. Just sit back and enjoy it. *(Takes a toke)* So much healthier for you too.

SIAN
I feel sick.

AMY
Sian, look at me…you are fine.

SIAN
Don't tell Tom.

AMY
No. I won't.

SHEP
I've got some premium stuff out there too. I've started a little grow in my basement. I've got a green thumb.

SIAN
No. I'm sick. I feel really…

AMY
(To SIAN) It wasn't much. It'll be out of your system in like an hour.

SHEP
It's a pretty sweet set up. You should see it.

SIAN
My body's on fire.

AMY
It's not.

SIAN
My hands are tingling.

SHEP
Let it do God's work.

SIAN
This is the devil.

AMY
You are panicking.

SIAN
Oh my gosh. Oh my gosh.

(CAROLINE comes back up, angry with a wet phone)

CAROLINE
My fucking phone fell into the lake.

SHEP
Did it fall or did you drop it?

CAROLINE
Sian, I need your phone and… *(Looks around)* What the hell is going on?

(SHEP points to SIAN)

SIAN
I didn't mean to.

CAROLINE
Didn't mean to? Sianny?

AMY
(To CAROLINE) She's freaking out.

SIAN
It's true. I'm freaking out.

CAROLINE
About what?

SIAN
Shep's poisoned me.

CAROLINE
What?

SHEP
She's paranoid.

AMY
The e-cig was full of hash oil and not...

CAROLINE
Are you kidding me?

SHEP
It's legal. I used Nancy's medical card.

(CAROLINE *takes the vape pen from* SHEP'*s hand and smashes it on the counter, breaking it. She throws it to the floor*)

SHEP
Hey! What the hell...

CAROLINE
You don't do that to people, Shep. Are you that fucking stupid? You wonder why we hate you.

SIAN
No littering. Why did you litter?

(AMY *laughs and so does* SIAN)

CAROLINE
I leave for two seconds and hell freezes?

SIAN
Seriously, nobody tell Tom.

AMY
We know.

SHEP
What's it worth to you?

SIAN
I'm so dizzy.

CAROLINE
Sian. Ride it out. Can any of you be useful to me?

SIAN
Put your rice in a bag of phones for a few days and it might work.

CAROLINE
How is that helpful now?

SIAN
Can someone help me?

AMY
I am. Just breathe.

CAROLINE
(*To* SHEP) There's no land line right?

SHEP
Huh.

CAROLINE
Phone?

AMY
Sianny. Deep breathes.

SHEP
My phone?

CAROLINE
No. Is there a phone in the cottage? A land line. One with wires attached.

SHEP
Oh yeah.

SIAN
(*Overlapping*) I'm gonna cry... wait, laugh... wait, no I'm gonna die.

CAROLINE
Where?

SHEP
There was one, but I don't think it's here anymore.

(CAROLINE *starts to search the cottage*)

AMY
I think we should get some food in you.

SIAN
I am hungry. I've been hungry.

AMY
Okay. *(Looks in the kitchen)*

SIAN
Is my tongue supposed to feel thick?

SHEP
You're just thirsty.

SIAN
Right. Thirst. And I'm not on fire?

AMY
No. Hon.

(SIAN sees the mac and cheese)

SIAN
Oh that. Make that.

AMY
No water. Remember?

SIAN
Use beer.

AMY
No.

SIAN
It's like water.

AMY
How about peanut butter and crackers?

SHEP
Beer mac, yummy.

SIAN
(Chants) Mac and cheese. Mac and Cheese.

(SHEP joins in)

SIAN and SHEP
Mac and cheese. Mac and cheese.

AMY
(Yells) CAROLINE! *(To SIAN)* There's no way you are this messed up already.

SHEP
No telling how fast it works. She's a virgin.

SIAN
No. No I'm not. I've got kids and I lost it at 15 to Billy Shelly.

AMY
Sian.

SIAN
I did. It's true. And Tom thinks I saved myself for him. Isn't that hilarious? MAC AND CHEESE!

AMY
Shut up. I'm making it. I'm making it. OK?

SIAN
Yes!

(AMY goes about making beer mac and cheese)

SHEP
The place looks good, though. Quite different, but I like what they're doing to it.

(During the rest of SHEP's time onstage, she picks up and pockets small items)

CAROLINE
(Walking back onstage) No phone and now no working toilet.

AMY
You break that too?

CAROLINE
Smartass, it was already broken.

SIAN
Bushes are outside. Nature is a toilet bowl waiting for you.

(They laugh)

CAROLINE
I already went, so it's your problem now. I need to go, Sianny.

SIAN
I told you go outside.

CAROLINE
I mean I need to leave.

SIAN
OK. *(Gives CAROLINE a hug)* It was so good to see you. I love you.

CAROLINE
Sian. We drove your car.

SIAN
Oh. Right. Do you mind if I eat my mac and cheese first?

SHEP
Made with beer.

AMY
You don't have to go right this second.

SHEP
We're having fun.

CAROLINE
This isn't fun.

AMY
Let me feed these animals and—

CAROLINE
(Interrupting) Amy, I wanna get together and reminisce, but not now. I don't feel like it. You guys come to New York. My treat. Let's plan that, ok?

SHEP
Never been.

CAROLINE
Sian and Amy, you come to New York.

AMY
Sure. That's what you always say.

CAROLINE
And I always mean it.

AMY
There isn't always another time.

SIAN
We'll try and make it—

AMY
(Interrupting) Try.

SIAN
—happen though.

SHEP
I can take your place if you can't make it.

CAROLINE
Exactly. We'll figure it out in the next few weeks.

AMY
This is the same conversation we had six years ago and it never happened.

CAROLINE
And that's all my fault?

SIAN
(Interrupting) Let's make it a priority now.

AMY
You stopped responding to us. We were trying to plan.

CAROLINE
Amy, what do you want? You want to schedule it right now?

AMY
I want you to stop lying about wanting to—

CAROLINE
Lying?

AMY
--yes lying about wanting to see us and that we are so important and that we are like family.

CAROLINE
For Christ's sake.

AMY
I'm sorry if that offends you, but that's the truth.

(Pause)

CAROLINE
That's your truth. You pretend the only friends that truly get us are right here and that isn't true.

SIAN
We need to slrow... I mean slow... *(Laughing)* Slow it down and let's process this.

CAROLINE
I've got a full life. I'm sorry if you feel I haven't made you important enough, but we are adult women now.

SIAN
Yes we are!

CAROLINE
Your pipe dream of us of being Golden Girls together is not a reality. We had our time—

SIAN
Some really good times.

CAROLINE
--and now this is what is left. So either accept it or don't. I can't –

SIAN
We are drifters in each other's lives.

AMY
We don't drift.

SIAN
We have our own lives.

CAROLINE
Exactly.

AMY
So we aren't friends?

SIAN
This transcends friendship.

CAROLINE
But isn't it possible that whatever we have--our friendship--is slightly glorified?

AMY
That is bullshit. Think what you will, Care. But, for me, it's not some made-up story. You are my reflection, my truth tellers. And we should still make time for the important things.

CAROLINE
I do make time.

AMY
You've got a funny way of showing that.

SIAN
Can I just ask about the macaroni?

SHEP
(To SIAN) They're too busy.

CAROLINE
Showing it? Really? I'm fifty. And I have to—

SIAN
(Interrupting) 53.

CAROLINE
--prove my friendship still? I'm here.

SIAN
(Interrupting) Why would you lie about your age? To us?

AMY
Here finally. Your timing is off. Not everyone can be here now. I needed your help and you...

CAROLINE
Nancy needed help not you.

AMY
You ditched her like you ditched all of us.

CAROLINE
(Pushing away) Don't you dare imply that I –

AMY
(Pushing back) I wasn't implying.

(CAROLINE puts AMY in a headlock)

SHEP
Aw, it's a fight!

(SHEP begins a soft chant of "fight, fight, fight" in the background and records the fight on her phone)

AMY
Ow!

CAROLINE
Take it back!

AMY
Let go!

SHEP
Fight, fight!

SIAN
Are you hugging or fighting?

CAROLINE
Take it back! Chicken shit!

(AMY is struggling and grunting)

SIAN
Hugging or fighting?

CAROLINE
You aren't getting out until you say... *(AMY grabs and twists hard CAROLINE's boob)* BITCH!

SIAN
Amy!

AMY
Fake! Those are fake.

CAROLINE
Let it go!

SIAN
I knew it!

AMY
You let go first.

(CAROLINE pulls hard on AMY's hair. AMY screams)

CAROLINE
Let go of the boob first.

AMY
No.

SIAN
Care, let go. Amy, you too.

CAROLINE
(To AMY) I'll pull it all out.

(SIAN starts to hit them both with a flyswatter that was hanging on the wall)

SHEP
Sian, Stop! Get out of the way.

AMY
(Howls) My back. Oh my god. Stop! My back.

CAROLINE
(Lets go) That's what I thought.

(AMY takes a breath and holds her back bent over)

SIAN
Everyone breathe. Just breathe. We've got mac and cheese and beer and let's just all breathe. It's so silly.

You both are ridiculous. Remember you can't be a grouch at the cottage. Fighting like children. Like--

AMY
You abandoned her. Doesn't matter about me or Sian. But you abandoned Nancy and now she's dead. Dead. And now you show up. You weren't her friend. That's not friendship. That's shit. I always sort of held you up to a certain standard. So did Nancy, but we were wrong.

(CAROLINE slaps AMY. AMY slaps CAROLINE, then grabs CAROLINE's purse and runs to the lake. SIAN runs after them. They are off-stage and SHEP is recording all with commentary)

SIAN
Amy!

CAROLINE
Don't you dare!

SIAN
Care.

AMY
Oh, you want this?

SIAN
Stop it! Stop it!

CAROLINE
I swear to god!

AMY
Bye Bye!

SHEP
In the lake it goes.

CAROLINE:
Bitch!

AMY
You're the bitch.

SHEP
OH! NO! Down she goes.

SIAN
I'm done. Kill each other. I don't care. I'm leaving.

SHEP
Watch the...oh! *(SIAN runs into a tree offstage)*

SIAN
Ow!

AMY
Sian.

CAROLINE
Sianny.

AMY
You okay?

CAROLINE
Are you hurt?

SHEP
That was flippin' amazing! *(Laughs a little more while watching it)* You guys are OK, right? Looks like that might have hurt. *(Watching and chuckling)* I gotta watch it again. Anyone need a beer? *(Walks to the fridge and watches the video)* Seriously, this is one of the best things I've ever filmed.

(We see a bleeding SIAN followed by a battered CAROLINE and AMY. They are all breathing hard and heavy. Ripped and dirtied clothes)

SIAN
Assholes. You are both just the biggest assholes.

SHEP
Do you guys wanna see this? Of course you...

SIAN
Shut up, Shep.

CAROLINE
You OK, Sianny?

SIAN
Am I OK? Am I OK? Am I OK? You hit my nose!

AMY
You ran into a tree.

SIAN
Because of you.

CAROLINE
Is it broken?

AMY
Let me see.

SHEP
I'm gonna be honest, I was not expecting that. Maybe some slapping, but you guys went all in, All in. I'm giving you props for it. You committed to it. And seriously, hilarious and vicious. That's the best kind of fight you can have.

SIAN
So let's just end this. Nance is dead and our friendship died with her. I wanna go home. Fuck you both.

AMY
Sian!

CAROLINE
Whoa. Listen. This is just a little…

AMY
It was a little squabble. A little disagreement.

CAROLINE
A little fight.

SIAN
Look around!

AMY
A biggish small fight.

SIAN
You don't own her. Neither of you did. She lent us pieces of herself and, in turn, we gave her pieces of us, but there's no ownership. There's no scale. There's no measurement for that kind of love and friendship. We are all different. All of us! *(Pause)* I was speaking that out loud right?

CAROLINE
I never abandoned her. You told me she had months.

AMY
We didn't know.

CAROLINE
Neither did I. It was two weeks. Two weeks.

SIAN
It was so fast.

CAROLINE
I would have come. But for you to say I abandoned her, I can't even…

AMY
You've been so detached and…

SIAN
You don't get to judge grief. Not mine, or hers, or even hers.

SHEP
Thank you.

CAROLINE
I'm fucking processing! I didn't get to see her. I didn't get to fully understand. She was alive when I was last home and now she isn't.

AMY
Ok.

SIAN
(To AMY) You feel so entitled for some reason. Is it because you saw

her more? You lived 10 minutes away by the way. Doesn't mean you grieve more than us. *(Does something strange with her tongue)*

SHEP
Thank you. She's right, Amy.

AMY
I wasn't. I saw her crumble so fast. It was...

SIAN
I saw it too. Not every day, but it scared the pants off of me too.

AMY
I was being her friend, her family.

CAROLINE
So was I.

SIAN
Me too. You aren't me and I'm not you or you or you. I'm not even sure I'm me. Because I'm currently kind of floating above myself watching this happen and it's surreal. Could I have a concussion?

CAROLINE
You're fine.

AMY
I wanted you both there. For us all to be with her. To say goodbye and be part of her end.

CAROLINE
And I never wanted it to end like it did.

SIAN
Why are we competing with each other?

AMY
We aren't.

CAROLINE
You sure?

SIAN
There's nothing to win anymore. We all fucking lost.

CAROLINE
Sianny, please don't say that.

SIAN
We did, we lost.

CAROLINE
I mean please do not say "fuck" again.

AMY
You say it wrong.

SHEP
Say it again.

SIAN
No. We are all messed up. I mean MESSED UP. You know. Look at us and look at where we are and what we are...

AMY
I did. I MESSED UP! I'm sorry! I'm so sorry.

SHEP
You guys are hilarious. Come on. You're just working it out and beating each other in emotions. Kind of like a gang or like some frat dudes. Taking your whacks. Or maybe you guys are all like jealous and there's this attraction you all have for each other. I don't know, but seriously I cannot think of a more amazing way to end this day then getting back to our primal instincts. Man, I love it here with y'all.

AMY
(To SHEP) You... You, you don't factor into this, any of this, at all.

SHEP
I'm here. That means I'm a part.

AMY
No. Never.

CAROLINE
She doesn't get it. *(To SHEP)* You don't get it.

SHEP
I do completely. I'm the closest thing you have to Nancy.

SIAN
Shep, stop talking.

SHEP
I am in this. I'm like her replacement.

CAROLINE
You could never replace her.

AMY
We aren't accepting your application. Denied. Denied. Denied.

CAROLINE
Sian, let's go.

SIAN
I can't drive.

CAROLINE
I will.

SHEP
You. You are all bitches and liars and... bitches. You can't talk to me like that. You can't treat me like I'm nothing. I am something. I am somebody. I am a person. You owe me. You owe me for being the butt of all your jokes. For laughing it up at my expense. For being horrible people in general with harden hearts and stuff. Oh, and you owe me for that vape pen... that's $100. Pay up. Now! Now! Seriously.

SIAN
(To CAROLINE and AMY) Is she throwing a tantrum?

CAROLINE
I don't have children, but I think so yes.

SHEP
I hate you guys. Elitists. Entitled. Bitches. *(Walks down the hall)*

SIAN
Where are you going? *(SHEP goes into the bathroom, closing the door)* Shep, what are you doing?

SHEP
I need to poop. Can I poop? Is that OK? Are you denying me my right to poop as well?

CAROLINE
Toilet doesn't work.

SHEP
Doesn't work?

CAROLINE
Nope.

SHEP
So, what am I supposed to do?

CAROLINE
Go outside.

SHEP
Outside?

SIAN
Yes.

SHEP
(Mutters) Man, you're all stupid. I'm not stupid. I deny you. You're all denied. Denied. Denied.

(SHEP goes out the sliding door and into the woods)

SIAN
Were we too mean to her?

CAROLINE
Mean but accurate.

AMY
Maybe, but she's... she's so . . Shep.

CAROLINE
I'm ready Sianny. Let's go.

SIAN
Can we wait a second? We can't leave it like this. Such a bad energy. No. We need to be ok and make peace.

CAROLINE
We're good.

SIAN
(All hugging) Because I love you both. And I thank god you are both in my life. Watch the nose. I do. However, it is, I need you both in my life. I'll take however much you can give to me. Ok?

CAROLINE
I love you too.

AMY
Me too. I love you.

SIAN
Ok. *(To AMY)* We will leave you to your whatever you are doing!

AMY
Ladies.

SIAN
Huh.

AMY
Before you go, I need to say... to tell you something. Or rather.

CAROLINE
Now? As we are leaving?

AMY
I need your help.

SIAN
We're in.

CAROLINE
With what?

AMY
Before I say... I want you both not to get too freaked out or...

CAROLINE
Out with it.

SIAN
Is this what you tried to tell me before?

AMY
Yeah.

(Silence)

CAROLINE
Amy, talk!

AMY
Ok. Right. So, she told me... when we were talking, she told me—

SIAN
She who?

AMY
Sorry. Nancy. Nancy told me that. She wanted to be here. This is where she wanted to be forever. So I went to talk to Dave about it. He was handling it all, but he didn't care. He refused to listen to what I was saying. This is where she wanted to be.

CAROLINE
Ok.

AMY
It's not right. To ignore her wishes.

CAROLINE
I agree. But it doesn't matter what you think or I think.

SIAN
Why don't we both talk to Dave? He can be reasoned with. I'm sure if we

explain.

AMY
I tried. I swear I tried. He said "Amy, she's dead. Doesn't really matter where she goes, ok? Plots already been bought."

CAROLINE
He's a prick.

SIAN
Yes.

CAROLINE
All three of us can try. But it's his say not ours. I know it isn't fair, but...

SIAN
But if this was what she wanted, we can at least make sure it's truly considered.

AMY
You don't understand. I tried to no avail. Even today. Before the service and after.

SIAN
Is that when I saw you yelling at him?

AMY
I wasn't yelling. It was a heated discussion.

CAROLINE
That won't help you.

AMY
He's the ex. How does he have the right to decide...

CAROLINE
I don't know. That's not my field, but I'm sure there was something that gave him power.

SIAN
We'll figure it out. There's power in numbers. So the three of us may make a difference and ...

(Screams are heard and SHEP comes running with her pants around her ankles and yelling)

SHEP
Jesus!

AMY
Shep?

SHEP
Help! Oh My GOD!

SIAN
What are you... ?

CAROLINE
Jeez.

(They all run out the sliding door)

SHEP
Something bit me! Something bit me!

AMY
OK.

CAROLINE
Stop running around.

SHEP
It hurts! It hurts!

SIAN
Where did it bite you?

SHEP
On my ass.

(CAROLINE, Amy, and Sian stifle laughter)

SHEP
(To SIAN) Look. Will you look? (SHEP backs her butt up to SIAN)

SIAN
Stop. Stop there.

SHEP
Can you see anything?

SIAN
It looks red.

SHEP
Care? *(Butts up to CAROLINE)*

CAROLINE
Get away. What were you doing?

AMY
I'll grab something cold. *(AMY goes through the freezer, but can't find anything. She grabs a beer for herself)*

SHEP
Can you get me a beer while you're in there!

SIAN
What happened?

SHEP
I was sitting on a log.

AMY
(From inside) Did she say log?

SIAN
On a log?

SHEP
Yes.

CAROLINE
With your pants down?

SHEP
I had to poop.

SIAN
On a log?

SHEP
I have horrible balance and… will you all just look at my ass. It's on fire. I think it was a snake or a black widow or maybe a porcupine.

CAROLINE
A porcupine? *(AMY comes out to the deck, drinking a beer and hands the other one to Shep. Shep takes a sip and put it on her naked butt. To AMY)* And me?

AMY
You wanted one? *(CAROLINE nods)* I thought you were leaving?

CAROLINE
I may never leave at this rate. A beer might give me patience.

SIAN
It never has before.

(CAROLINE goes in to get herself one)

SHEP
I've definitely been bitten. Can one of you look?

SIAN
I told you it's red.

SHEP
(Coming at her with her butt) Look closer.

SIAN
No. I'm sorry.

SHEP
Caroline, please. I may be having a reaction.

CAROLINE
(From inside) I vote Amy. She dragged us here.

SHEP
This is serious! My whole right cheek is numb.

SIAN
You have a cold beer on it.

SHEP
Besides that. Oh my god, it hurts.

SIAN
Amy, you lost the vote.

(CAROLINE comes out with two more beers)

SHEP
LOOK! JUST LOOK!

AMY
Babies. *(To SHEP)* Move the beer. *(Inspecting)*

SHEP
Whaddya see? Whaddya see?

AMY
Looks like a bee sting.

SHEP
Oh my god.

AMY
It's not that bad. A couple mosquito bites too.

SHEP
I'm allergic.

SIAN
To bees?

SHEP
Probably.

SIAN
Probably?

AMY
You are not allergic.

SHEP
You don't know.

AMY
It's a bump. Are you having problems breathing?

SHEP
(Takes deep breaths) I can't tell.

AMY
The stinger's still in there.

SIAN
I've got tweezers in my purse.

SHEP
(Overlapping) I think my throat—it's tightening

CAROLINE
(To SIAN) Get them.

SIAN
Yeah. Yeah.

(SIAN goes inside and grabs her purse)

AMY
(To SHEP, staring at her butt) Is this a tattoo?

(CAROLINE looks with her)

CAROLINE
What is that?

SHEP
It itches and hurts.

AMY
Stay still.

CAROLINE
I can't tell what it is.

SIAN
(With tweezers) Let me see.

(They are all looking at her ass)

SHEP
It's a bear claw. Native American symbol for strength.

SIAN
But you're not Native American

CAROLINE
And that's not a bear claw.

SHEP
It's my spirit animal.

AMY
Have you ever actually seen it? What it looks like? *(To SIAN)* Gimme those. *(Grabs the tweezers and goes for the*

stinger)

CAROLINE
Looks like a turd pile.

SIAN
It does.

(They laugh)

SHEP
Fuck you! Please. Stop. Get the stinger out. I'm dying.

AMY
Hold still.

CAROLINE
Baby.

SHEP
Hold my hands.

SIAN
Did you wash them?

SHEP
No, but I didn't wipe so there's nothing on them.

AMY
(AMY drops the tweezers) Nope! I'm out.

CAROLINE
I'm gonna throw up.

(A scruffy-looking man comes into view behind them, holding a rifle)

SHEP
There wasn't any paper out there and I was attacked goddamnit, ATTACKED.

AMY
I'm not. No. Sorry. No.

SIAN
Go wash your hands and wipe and then we can talk.

SHEP
This is an emergency.

(SHEP is picking at her butt to get the stinger out)

CAROLINE
You couldn't be farther from the truth there.

AMY
Just go wash your hands.

SHEP
It's throbbing. Throbbing. Look. Look. Seriously guys. It's like you don't care! Wait, Wait. I think I got it out. By my own damn hands. Did I get it? At least look at it, please.

(A click is heard in the silence. CAROLINE screams, then AMY and SIAN)

SHEP
Is it that bad?

MAN
How about all of you shut the hell up? *(SHEP turns. More screams)* I said shut up. *(More screams. Man waves the gun and yells)* SHUT UP! And don't move! *(They freeze)* What the hell do you think you're doing?

SHEP
I got stung by something.

SIAN
A bee.

SHEP
And then I--

MAN
I don't know what kind of sick twisted thing you've got going on--

SHEP
I was sitting on a log pooping--

MAN
What?

CAROLINE
(To SHEP) Shut up.

SHEP
I'm unarmed. *(Pulls up her pants)* We don't have any money--

MAN
Be quiet.

SHEP
--well, I don't have any.

SIAN
Shep!

MAN
What you doing here?

SHEP
She's gonna have the most money. *(Looks to SIAN and AMY)* Right?

MAN
Shut up.

AMY
Yes.

SIAN
Amy!

AMY
Sorry.

MAN
Shut up. I don't want your money.

AMY
Are you here for me? Were you sent for me?

SIAN
(To AMY) He's gonna rape us.

MAN
No. No.

CAROLINE
We are post-menopausal. –

MAN
(Overlap) I'm not going to rape you.

CAROLINE
- You don't want us. It's all dried up down there.

SHEP
(To CAROLINE) Is that what happens?

MAN
Jesus, I just wanna know what the fuck you are doing here?

AMY
What the fuck are you doing here?

MAN
This is my house.

CAROLINE
Your house?

MAN
You broke in.

SIAN
This isn't your place.

MAN
The hell it isn't.

SIAN
Are you a Jones family member?

MAN
Who? Jones? No.

SHEP
(To the Man) Yeah. You don't look familiar.

MAN
Neither do you. Now—

SIAN
We used to spend summers here. The Jones owned it.

MAN
I own it. Just me, myself, and I.

CAROLINE
There's been some kind of mistake.

MAN
Not mine.

SIAN
There's been a big misunderstanding, I think. If we can just put that thing... *(Indicating the rifle)* ...down and talk.

MAN
This is my place. You have entered illegally into my home and I could shoot you and be OK with it. And I could do that.

SIAN
(To SHEP) Did your dad sell this off to some relatives, Shep?

SHEP
I don't know. They don't tell me anything. You know that.

CAROLINE
Amy? *(AMY shrugs)* Can you put that goddamn thing down? *(Indicating the gun)*

MAN
No.

CAROLINE
I'd feel more comfortable if you at least--

MAN
Oh yeah. You think making demands to the guy holding the gun is the best idea?

CAROLINE
Strictly speaking, if you were going to have shot us, it would have happened as a reaction to coming in and finding this particular scene--

MAN
(Interjecting) You broke in.

CAROLINE
--but you didn't and therefore won't. Now if you did decide to kill us,

MAN
What?

CAROLINE
--that is premeditation and would be pretty easy to prove in a court of law based on the evidence that would easily be collected here.

MAN
What the fuck are you talking about?

SHEP
The law.

MAN
(Looks around) Is that my beer?

(SHEP throws her bottle far away)

SHEP
What?

SIAN
We will happily replace anything.

MAN
(To AMY) Is that my shirt? *(Looks at the window)* My door is broken. And what the hell happened to the curtains? Shit. What'dya all do to my curtains?

SHEP
It was a bear.

SIAN
Shep. It wasn't a bear.

SHEP
(To the ladies) Wait. Wait. You guys, they totally did sell this place like five years ago. I forgot. Nancy was so pissed. Stopped talking to Dad. *(To the MAN)* You wouldn't know us then. Hi.

SIAN
(To AMY) Did you know that?

AMY
No. Honestly.

MAN
I don't care.

CAROLINE
How'd you get in?

(AMY shrugs)

SIAN
You broke in? *(AMY shrugs and smiles)*

MAN
Yes.

CAROLINE
(To AMY) You broke in here? That's called breaking and entering--

MAN
Exactly.

CAROLINE
--you know that right? That's what people go to prison for.

MAN
You got that right.

SIAN
Oh my gosh. Oh my lord.

AMY
Nancy hadn't mentioned any of this to me. I really thought it was still in the family.

CAROLINE
(To the man) We are extremely sorry for this. We were under the impression that the Jones still owned the cottage.

MAN
Wrong.

SIAN
Absolutely wrong. And boy are we so, so sorry. We've been under a bit of stress and this place holds wonderful--

(MAN looks at the buck covered with a sheet)

MAN
What'd you do to my art?

SIAN
Art?

MAN
Frank.

SIAN
Frank?

MAN
My art.

AMY
Oh, well...

SIAN
It was really creepy.

CAROLINE
In a wonderful way.

MAN
Get it off. Now.

SIAN
Of course. *(None of them move)*

MAN
Now. *(They begin to remove the blanket)* Be careful.

SIAN
Can you put down the gun? We obviously don't mean you any harm

MAN
I don't know that.

(SIAN jumps up in an attempt to get the blanket off the buck's head. She fails)

MAN
You've been drinking my beer, eating

my food--

SHEP
The water is brown and disgusting. Never was like that before when we owned it.

MAN
I don't come here to drink the water.

SHEP
Your toilet too. Plumbing issues.

MAN
You broke my toilet?

SHEP
(Pointing to CAROLINE) She did that.

(MAN lowers the rifle. And SIAN finally gets the blanket off the buck)

MAN
I should call the police.

AMY
No.

CAROLINE
(To AMY) Stop speaking.

MAN
You want me to call the police?

AMY
No. No.

SIAN
Wait a minute.

SHEP
(To the MAN) We can pay you for the damages.

MAN
I thought you didn't have any money.

SHEP
I mean "we" as a group.

SIAN
(To the MAN) I think the best thing for us to do is to leave you to your place. We are happy to reimburse you for any damages this very unfortunate situation has caused.

CAROLINE
Amy caused it, but yes, we can and should fairly compensate you for any damages both structurally and emotionally.

SIAN
We can clean this up too. Put everything back the way it was.

CAROLINE
(To the MAN) What do you think? Can we make this all go away?

MAN
I suppose.

CAROLINE
Will you take a personal check?

MAN
I guess I'll have to.

SIAN
Do you think two hundred sounds fair?

CAROLINE
I do, yes.

SHEP
For the broken door and toilet? Really?

MAN
Curtains too.

SHEP
Right. Curtains too. That's low.

MAN
Agree. I think I need more than that.

CAROLINE
Five hundred?

MAN
And you'll clean this crap up?

CAROLINE
Yes.

MAN
Then I guess.

CAROLINE
A deal. Great.

SIAN
And we are so sorry, again. We'll clean it up and get it back the way it was.

MAN
So if I go down and put my boat it, I expect you guys will be done and out by then, right?

CAROLINE
I hope to god, yes. Who do I make this out to?

MAN
Cash.

CAROLINE
Alright. *(Writes out the check and hands it to him)*

MAN
Settle up and be on your way then.

SIAN
Do you have any cleaning supplies?

MAN
20 minutes until the boat is in.

SIAN
No problem.

SHEP
(To the MAN) You want some help with the boat. I love boats. I used to...

MAN
No.

SHEP
You sure?

(MAN leaves very tentatively. SIAN and CAROLINE turn on AMY)

CAROLINE
What the hell is wrong with you?

SIAN
Amy! Good god.

CAROLINE
B and E. We could have been arrested.

SHEP
We could have died.

(CAROLINE and SIAN begin to clean)

SIAN
Shep's right.

SHEP
I am?

CAROLINE
What is going on with you that you think this is a good idea? That this is a--

SHEP
I mean, it is kind of bad ass of you. It's something I'd do. I'm impressed.

AMY
I'm sorry. I really am. I didn't know.

SIAN
You're lying.

AMY
No. Truly. Honestly I really didn't know.

CAROLINE
You didn't know, but came in through the fucking window.

AMY
Well, I realized later that maybe it had changed hands.

SIAN
Let's clean up and get out of here. I

don't want to be here a second longer.

AMY
Sianny.

CAROLINE
(To SIAN) She has lost it. She can't drive herself; she'll need to come back with us. She can come back and get the car later.

SIAN
Agreed.

AMY
This is what I was trying to get at. To tell you guys.

CAROLINE
But you didn't.

SIAN
You should have told us immediately.

AMY
I know. I'm sorry. I know. That's what I'm trying to tell you now. What I was saying before about Nancy wanting to be—

CAROLINE
If you think I'd help you talk to Dave or whomever about bringing her ashes here now, you're crazy.

SIAN
You're right. We would have, could have helped but this... I get you're sad, but... I'm speechless.

AMY
Right, but—

CAROLINE
No. There's no buts. No excuses.

AMY
I took her.

CAROLINE
Shut up.

SIAN
Who? Took who?

AMY
Nancy.

CAROLINE
Nancy?

SHEP
Nancy?

SIAN
You took Nancy?

AMY
Yes.

CAROLINE
You took her? Explain. Explain... what... explain.

AMY
I thought we could give her the send-off she deserves at the cottage.

(Pause)

CAROLINE
Oh my god.

SIAN
No. No, you didn't.

CAROLINE
You're kidding.

SIAN
She's not. (To AMY) You're not.

SHEP
Did you steal Nancy?

CAROLINE
Jesus. You stole Nancy?

SIAN
Stole?

AMY
I didn't steal her. I can't steal Nancy.

SHEP
But you did.

CAROLINE
WHERE IS YOUR CAR?

AMY
I was doing what she wanted.

CAROLINE
WHERE IS YOUR CAR? TELL ME? WHERE IS IT?

AMY
Behind the trees next door.

(CAROLINE *runs out of the cabin*)

SIAN
Listen. Just listen. We can compromise here. WE can solve this. Spread a few ashes here—

AMY
About that.

SIAN
--and then take the rest back. We'll explain the situation. We won't tell them what we did here and we will chalk this up to an accident.

SHEP
You can say Amy lost her fucking mind.

AMY
Sian, I'm so sorry. I really am. I ... I thought this would have gone better. That I would have... I'm stupid, I know but...

SIAN
You weren't thinking it all out. We will fix this. You're just... you need to just sit back and stay quiet. (*Hugging her*)

AMY
I know it's not the same anymore. We're different. I know, but I still love you and Caroline and Nancy.

SIAN
Of course.

AMY
I just want you to know—to really understand and know--that I always try to have your best interest at heart.

SIAN
I know. You just made some real, real poor choices.

AMY
Understatement.

SIAN
We've got this though. It is actually going to be easier than you or I imagined. Plus, we can honor her request. A hard won win-win... sort of.

AMY
It's not.

SIAN
It isn't?

AMY
Nuh-uh.

SIAN
Is there something else you need to tell me-- (*AMY nods*) --because you're making me paranoid? Please say it. I'm about to have a panic attack if you don't.

AMY
I took Nancy and something else.

(CAROLINE, *out of breath and with crazed eyes, runs in with an orange funeral flag grasped in a hand*)

CAROLINE
(*To AMY*) YOU!

SHEP
The hearse.

CAROLINE
(*To AMY*) YOU!

AMY
(To CAROLINE) Sorry.

SIAN
Oh my god. Oh my god, you stole the hearse?

CAROLINE
And the casket!

SIAN
CASKET?!?

SHEP
Yeah dummies.

SIAN
(Screams) WHAT?!?

SHEP
Not ashes yet.

CAROLINE
(Screams) NANCY'S IN THERE!

SIAN
(Screams) NANCY?

CAROLINE
(Screams) HER BODY!

AMY
I may have had a lapse in judgment.

CAROLINE
NANCY'S IN THERE!

SIAN
NANCY?

CAROLINE
HER BODY! THE CASKET!

SHEP
I'm not looking so screwed up anymore, right?

SIAN
OH MY GOD!

AMY
Ok. Wait. I know this is bad.

CAROLINE
BAD?

SIAN
BAD?

SHEP
A lot worse than bad.

CAROLINE
THE HEARSE!

Amy
I know.

CAROLINE
THE HEARSE! NANCY?

SIAN
THE HEARSE? NANCY?

CAROLINE
THE HEARSE. NANCY?

SIAN
(Grabs AMY) WHAT DID YOU DO? WHAT DID YOU DO?

AMY
She's all there. She's ok. I wasn't thinking clearly. *(CAROLINE throws the funeral flag at AMY)* Ow!

SIAN
Care!

SHEP
Nancy's been out there baking in the sun.

AMY
It's not that hot.

CAROLINE
(Overlapping; to AMY) What did you do? What did you do?

AMY
I think it's kind of clear what I did--

SIAN
(Interrupting) Shut up.

CAROLINE
Yes, shut up. I went over there. Looking for your GODDAMN car and I see this thing, this, this, this

SHEP
The hearse

CAROLINE
This cannot be, I think. This cannot be... and I see the name of Lynch's funeral home on the side.

SIAN
Oh my god.

CAROLINE
And then I see the casket and I know. I know. I know exactly what you...

(SHEP sits on the kitchen counter, drinking her beer, and amused now. She starts documenting the conversation with video or pictures. AMY stands away from CAROLINE and SIAN)

(Overlapping dialogue)

CAROLINE
What the fuck were you thinking?

SIAN
(Yells to AMY) What are we going to do? Dave is gonna be so pissed.

CAROLINE
Pissed? Piseed? You think? How about the funeral home? Hell, what about us? We could all be arrested.

SHEP
What if that gun dude sees the hearse? We are in trouble.

CAROLINE
Oh shit. There's no we. This is her. ALL HER!

SIAN
We should call Dave.

CAROLINE
(To SIAN) Yes, call Dave. From the road. Let's leave her here to deal. –

SIAN
We need to move quick. He'll come back.

CAROLINE
--I don't want to help. She's a black hole drawing us in. Everything gone. Poof. Job. Poof. Friends--

SIAN
(Ovrlap. Notices Shep taking pics and video) What are you--? (Grabs the phone and smashes it)

SHEP
My phone.

CAROLINE
--Poof. Home. Poof. Life. Poof. Sucked into your blackhole disaster bullshit from hell.

SIAN
What about the police? Should we call them before Crazy comes back and...

CAROLINE
They've already been called; they are missing a damn hearse and body. I mean, maybe this could be fixable. Maybe. Maybe not. But maybe everyone is willing to negotiate. NANCY is out there. She's out there and...

AMY
You guys, deep breaths. Let's stop and talk this out. (Everyone stops and looks at her) I get that this is upsetting, but the--

CAROLINE
Upsetting?

SIAN
(To AMY, pointing) Sit there and say

nothing.

AMY
But...

SIAN
NOTHING!

(AMY sits and stays silent)

SHEP
Let's get rid of the evidence.

CAROLINE
(To SIAN) Here's the plan. We get the hell out of here, drive outta here with the... Nancy and call the funeral home from the road. I can try to explain without incriminating you or me—

SIAN
What about Amy?

SHEP
We dump the hearse.

CAROLINE
I don't know. I'll call a friend for some advice.

SIAN
(To CAROLINE) Maybe this isn't the first time that something like this has happened.

CAROLINE
It is. It abso-fucking-lutely is.

SHEP
You guys, you guys. I know people. People who can make this all disappear. The car. The body. The--

AMY
Let's take a minute. Let me explain.

SIAN
We don't have a minute.

CAROLINE
(To AMY) You've lost the right to talk.

AMY
No, I haven't.

SIAN
Amy, shut up.

AMY
This is what she wanted. This is what she made me promise her.

CAROLINE
I'm done. Done.

SIAN
Why not at least wait until... she wasn't a body?

AMY
Because... they were taking her away. And once that happened it out of my hands, my control So I tried. I pleaded with Dave after the service. I said, "please, Dave, you gotta let us take her up to the cottage. That's what she wanted. She asked me to make sure." And he grabbed my arm and told me to mind my own goddamn business and shut my mouth. So I knew. I knew it was over. That if they left with her... I thought I'd let her down. I would be letting her down.

SIAN
You should have talked to me

CAROLINE
(To SIAN) So Amy will drive the hearse back and we call them and say--

AMY
(Screams) You aren't taking her.

CAROLINE
--nothing's been touched or hurt. Apologize. Offer money.

AMY
You aren't taking her.

CAROLINE
You screwed up, Amy. I mean, royally screwed up.

AMY
We can't take her back. We'll never get to bring her here again.

CAROLINE
WE weren't involved with YOUR plan.

SIAN
We are trying to fix this, Amy. So say thank you, ok?

AMY
No.

CAROLINE
You need some serious help.

AMY
(Interrupting) Yes, this is a little messy, but I had a good reason.

CAROLINE
Hopefully it'll be court ordered help.

AMY
Nancy made me promise. She begged me and made me promise. She made me knee, G, double B.

(Everyone pauses)

SIAN
Knee, G, double B?

SHEP
What is that?

AMY
Yes.

CAROLINE
She did not.

AMY
Yes. She did.

SIAN
When?

CAROLINE
She literally uttered those words?

CAROLINE and AMY
(Together) Knee, G, double B?

AMY
Yes. She got up and we knee, G, double B'ed.

SIAN
When was this?

AMY
Two days before she…

SHEP
I don't get it. What are you talking about?

SIAN
(To SHEP) It's a thing.

SHEP
What thing?

CAROLINE
A thing from a long time ago that isn't your business.

SHEP
What's it mean?

CAROLINE
It means we were young and drunk.

AMY
Don't say that.

SHEP
It's like a code?

CAROLINE
She didn't mean it. She was doped up, right?

AMY
No. She was lucid. In pain, but meant it. Care, Sian, she meant it. You know when Nancy gets serious and she won't stop looking directly into you. Like she can see your insides. She's burning them. You

know what that is. You remember. It's unbreakable.

SHEP
What's unbreakable? Knee, G, Double B?

CAROLINE
Shep.

SHEP
I'm trying to understand.

CAROLINE
You haven't earned that right.

SIAN
(To AMY) You aren't lying? Swear you are not lying

AMY
Knee, G, double B, I am not.

CAROLINE
Stop saying that.

AMY
That's how serious I am. That's how you know I am not lying.

SIAN
I get it.

CAROLINE
Tell me again. Walk me through it. Nancy said...

AMY
I didn't make that up. I am realizing how this all looks. I get how crazy it is. I thought this would be easy. Get Dave to say okay and be done. But it got complicated really complicated and I didn't know what to do. What was I supposed to do?

SIAN
Tell us earlier.

AMY
I was worried you'd react badly.

CAROLINE
Good call.

SIAN
So now what?

SHEP
The boat's in.

CAROLINE
We have to go.

AMY
No, we have to honor her... together.

SHEP
Hell yes.

CAROLINE
Jesus Christ.

SIAN
Care.

CAROLINE
This is... This is... Nancy's in that hearse.

SIAN
I know.

CAROLINE
A hearse SHE stole.

SIAN
Correct.

CAROLINE
And now you both want to what? Leave her here?

AMY
Could we?

CAROLINE
People go to prison for this. I could get disbarred. You could get...

SHEP
Like what kind of sentence could we get? Do priors count?

AMY
It doesn't matter.

SIAN
Yes, it matters.

CAROLINE
Of course it matters.

SIAN
But Nance would have figured out a way.

CAROLINE
Would she?

SIAN
If she had Knee, G, doubled B'ed than yes.

CAROLINE
But she's not here anymore.

SIAN
I know.

SHEP
Listen, this is easy. We drive the hearse into the lake. Boom! Perfect. Let's get...

CAROLINE
Are you listening to yourself?

SHEP
Kind of.

SIAN
I'm wondering if there isn't some possible way to make this work.

CAROLINE
If we had more than five minutes, maybe.

AMY
This isn't how it was supposed to happen.

SIAN
You keep saying that. So do I. Nothing seems fair at the moment.

AMY
It's not fair.

SIAN
Nancy should have figured this out.

AMY
Sadly, she did with me. And I was not the right person for the job.

CAROLINE
No you weren't.

SHEP
It's life, man. You gotta roll with it.

CAROLINE
We could've planned this if you'd called me. Why didn't you call me?

SIAN
You keep thinking there was all this time. There was no time.

CAROLINE
I would've had a plan.

AMY
I wish I had called.

CAROLINE
Me too. Me too.

SIAN
Care, nobody could pause for a clear thought.

SHEP
Time was a real bastard.

SIAN
They couldn't even get her the good meds to make the pain stop.

AMY
She mainly kept wanting to talk in the last few days, not to anyone in particular, just talking.

SIAN
She was remembering stuff. "Rolodexing" as she called it.

(SHEP begins to eat the mac & cheese and listen)

AMY
Rolodexing, right. She was talking about you. Talking about you and laughing.

CAROLINE
Me?

AMY
Can't be a grouch at the cottage. You were lying in bed on a perfectly sunny day.

AMY & SIAN
"This is totally Bogue."

AMY
And she got up--

SIAN
Marched up. In that neon yellow and green bikini.

AMY
Oh yeah, that bikini. She found you on the bed.

SIAN
Pushed you off. And said "Enough."

AMY
And then she sat on you.

SIAN
Tickle torture began.

AMY & SIAN
Can't be a grouch at the cottage. Can't be a grouch at the cottage.

AMY
She loved your laugh.

SIAN
She did.

AMY
That's what she was thinking of. That's when she asked me to bring her back here.

CAROLINE
But she'd be disappointed because I'm... not that same person.

SIAN
Of course you are. Just older. Have more knowledge and sharp edges.

AMY
You still hate pointless conversations and meetings.

CAROLINE
Who doesn't?

SIAN
Hate doughnuts but love doughnut holes.

AMY
You stick a lot of things in you, but never a tampon.

SIAN
And when you are bored listening to someone talk, you start to think of old song lyrics.

CAROLINE
True.

SIAN
I might not know your day-to-day life anymore. I might not know what you'll say, but I know you.

CAROLINE
What do you know?

SIAN
You are uncomfortable. You think you might have been able to do something more, but you couldn't. Uncomfortable because you hate to mourn and be sad. You can be angry, you've got that down, but sadness is a different beast.

CAROLINE
You're still stoned.

AMY
Are you?

SIAN
A piece is missing. We are missing her. We are not the same. And I'm so… so… lost and--

AMY
You are the only ones that understand.

SIAN
(To CAROLINE) If you want to run from this, then run. I won't stop you. I won't. I promise. Because I have no idea what the heck we are gonna do. However, I hate you both as much as I love you. Always.

CAROLINE
Not always.

SIAN
Always.

CAROLINE
Can't be always. We used to be four, didn't we?

AMY
Yeah.

CAROLINE
And soon it'll be two and then one and then. At some point we're all alone.

SIAN
Then make sure you die next.

CAROLINE
Stop. It's easy for you. You've got your god and faith and comfort. I don't.

SIAN
Um, I mean it provides some comfort, but it doesn't help that fact that it's happening sooner than we thought. Not even Jesus was looking forward to it. But I can only really hope that when each of our time comes that my Rolodexing means laughing like that about this moment. I'm really hoping that this moment is one of the ones that make me laugh so hard my sides hurt. It's not funny now, but it will be. And you don't have to be there, Care. You don't either Amy. But just know, that that is what you've brought to my life. That is what I hope I go out thinking about and sharing with others. The gift you each have brought to me.

(Pause)

(The MAN walks back in)

MAN
Y'all makin yourself comfortable? Feeling at home? Move your asses on out.

SHEP
Lay off. We're having a moment.

MAN
You had your chance.

SIAN
Young man, we are trying to honor a friend. That's what we've been doing here. Albeit badly. But we are old friends who are grappling with some weighty…

MAN
So you're all friends?

AMY
(Pointing to herself, CAROLINE, and SIAN) Three of us are.

SHEP
Four.

AMY
Three.

SIAN
Over thirty years.

MAN
Uh huh.

AMY
We live in different parts of the...

MAN
I get it. Safe travels. Thanks for trashing the place.

SIAN
What's your name?

MAN
Mine?

SIAN
Yes.

MAN
Skip.

SIAN
Really?

MAN
Yes. Sometimes people call me Skipper.

SIAN
You don't look like a Skip.

AMY
He doesn't.

MAN
It's still Skip.

SIAN
I was wondering if... we just lost... our friend died.

MAN
Yeah.

SHEP
My sister, man.

SIAN
She was our best friend. And we came here all the time when we were younger. It was her favorite place.

CAROLINE
Ours too.

MAN
Uh huh.

SIAN
And her last request was to be brought here.

MAN
Huh.

SHEP
She made them promise to bring her here

MAN
A dying woman made you promise to break into my place?

CAROLINE
A miscommunication not a break in.

SIAN
Not exactly. She wanted to be here.

MAN
Let me guess, you wanna put her ashes here at the lake?

CAROLINE
Allegedly that is what we were considering.

MAN
Ok.

SHEP
Problem: she's not exactly in ash form.

AMY
Shep.

MAN
What?

SHEP
She's like Frank there.

CAROLINE
Shut up!

MAN
Frank?

SIAN
Let us explain.

MAN
What are you talking about? Frank is just a head.

SHEP
We've got the full body.

MAN
Why would you... What?

SIAN
Allow me to cut through this all. We all met our freshman year at college. We were all 18 and assigned to the dorms at...

CAROLINE
Sian! Listen, this is wrong, but here it goes. We currently have a hearse with our friend in it and I would like to know if you would consider letting us at some point leave her to eternal rest here.

MAN
Hearse?

CAROLINE
Hearse.

MAN
Is this a prank?

CAROLINE
Sadly no.

MAN
Is that illegal.

CAROLINE
Yes.

AMY
But it is what she wanted. She begged to be brought here and I jumped the gun but not really because her ex-husband was going to put her next to her grandmother whom she hated and would call her fat constantly and it seemed...

MAN
I come up here to get away from the crazies.

SIAN
Hear us out a little more. Nancy was our friend...

MAN
No. Crazy needs to check out of here. Bye-bye. Don't forget my shirt.

SIAN
Skip. Skipper. I know this sounds bizarre and...

MAN
OUT!

SIAN
Let's go.

AMY
But--

SIAN
Now.

CAROLINE
I could pay you.

MAN
Hell no. You don't have enough to cover this.

CAROLINE
Betcha I do.

MAN
I don't know what you did to this

person.

AMY
Nothing.

SIAN
She just died. Cancer.

MAN
I'm not gonna be a part of this. Get the hell out and expect a visit for your neighborhood boys in blue.

SHEP
Skippy, can you and I discuss a little business outside?

MAN
Not interested.

SHEP
I think we can make a trade.

MAN
I'm not interested in what you might think you've got.

SHEP
Take your gun if you're worried. I don't bite. Unless you're into that.

MAN
No.

SHEP
I wanna show you what I got.

SIAN
Shep. You sound desperate. Stop.

MAN
I've seen it. Saw it when I came in.

AMY
(To SIAN) Let her do it if she wants to whore herself out.

SHEP
Not that. Good god, look at him. No offense.

MAN
Then what is it?

SHEP
Come on... (She starts to walk and turns) Skippy, come on. (She continues to walk with SKIP following, gun out)

AMY
So that was... interesting.

CAROLINE
What is she doing?

SIAN
I think you could guess. You think his name is really Skip?

CAROLINE
What if she kills him?

AMY
She seems to be a little violent.

CAROLINE
Yep.

SIAN
She might have something up her sleeve. Maybe she will convince him.

CAROLINE
And then what? What's the plan now? Dig a hole and bury her...

AMY
That's what I thought. But we need shovels. Could we put her out in the lake, like a Viking Funeral?

SIAN
And set her on fire?

AMY
No.

CAROLINE
Is that what they did?

SIAN
Yes.

AMY
Yeah, maybe that's not a good idea.

CAROLINE
Agreed.

SIAN
So maybe we can… let her float on down to the bottom?

AMY
It is a deep lake. It's actually fitting.

SIAN
She'll sink in that heavy thing.

AMY
That could actually work.

SIAN
Really?

AMY
Yes. *(To CAROLINE)* What do you think?

CAROLINE
Me? Well, how do you plan on getting her all the way out there into the deepest part of the lake? *(Beat)* See.

AMY
I keep seeing Nancy here. I see her floating on her raft out there, remember. She'd become a dot on the lake as she went far out.

(We hear a car start and pull out of the driveway)

SIAN
She almost got hit by boats.

CAROLINE
She'd wave back at us and let the current carry her back in.

SIAN
Yeah.

AMY
She'd yell out "See you guys when I get back" as if she were really going away.

SIAN
She'd be out there for hours.

AMY
But she'd come back and say how she missed us all terribly.

CAROLINE
And she'd say that she got called by the sirens on the shore and saw the pirates and splashed with the mermaids.

SIAN
And then she'd say, "Well I'm off again."

(Car honks)

CAROLINE
Did Shep… did she leave?

AMY
What?

SIAN
She better not have…

(Door slams and in walks SHEP)

SHEP
Alright. Let's do this. What are we doing?

SIAN
Where's Skip?

AMY
What did you do?

SHEP
Nothing. We just made a deal.

CAROLINE
Deal?

SHEP
Yes. He's giving us the evening to do whatever we need to do.

SIAN
He is?

SHEP
Yep.

AMY
What'd you give him?

SHEP
It doesn't matter.

CAROLINE
Did you, you know?

SIAN
Blow him?

SHEP
Hell no. Dudes like that are my best customers, so I'll be providing him with some killer flower for the next six months. As long as I don't get busted.

SIAN
Weed.

AMY
You had more?

SHEP
A lot more. I told you about my grow room

CAROLINE
You solved something. Surprising, but...

SHEP
Hell yes I did. For Nancy. So let's do this.

(No one moves. Beat)

AMY
Are we?

SIAN
If Nancy wanted it then I think, well...

AMY
She did.

SIAN
Then yes?

CAROLINE
Grand theft auto. Desecration of a corpse.

SIAN
What?

CAROLINE
I'm thinking of the charges. Maybe mutilation of a corpse.

AMY
There's no mutilation. Come on.

SHEP
That doesn't carry a big sentence. *(They all look at her)* I know things.

CAROLINE
Definitely large fines for us all. And civil penalties as well as criminal.

SIAN
But we could fight any charges, right?

CAROLINE
You gonna lie, Sianny? In a court of law after swearing to God?

AMY
(To CAROLINE) So, you're out?

CAROLINE
You should know what you will be charged with.

AMY
So you're out.

SHEP
Who says we're gonna get caught?

SIAN
Let her process.

CAROLINE
I... I ...there are no pros to doing this. Only cons. Am I wrong?

(Pause)

AMY
No.

SIAN
No.

CAROLINE
If I could find a way around ...

SHEP
Are you all fucking kidding me? What have we been doing then? There's no pros or cons. There's right and wrong. And it's wrong for Nance not to get what she wanted... My sister deserves that. She has a right to that. She had to settle for lots. A shit marriage. A mother and father that didn't really care. A sister who... She gave up on a lot of her dreams. She'd never say that but we all know she did. She wanted to be a veterinarian. But then Emma came. And next Lucy. And Dave wanted her home. She thought there'd be time, but she pushed her wants aside. For her kids, husband, friends, family... she gave you all of her. So for her to ask for this last favor, I think you should all woman up, unclog your ovaries, and Knee, G, Double B this shit. For Nancy.

AMY
But how are we gonna get her...

SHEP
The boat. Skippy skipper's boat.

SIAN
The boat.

SHEP
Yep.

(Beat)

CAROLINE
We'll tie her up ...the casket. Get rope. Put it around the casket and drag it along side the boat to the middle and let her go.

AMY
Yes.

SIAN
So...

(Pause)

AMY
I'll get the car.

SIAN
Care?

CAROLINE
I've got the rope.

SHEP
Bet you wish you didn't break my pen.

CAROLINE
Let's go. Let's do this. Fast

(Everyone is off on their task and goes off-stage)

EPILOGUE

(A while later. They climb onto the dock with wet feet and hands. They watch the floating casket)

SIAN
Couldn't ask for a more beautiful evening.

AMY
No you couldn't.

CAROLINE
I forgot what a sunset looks like. Can't believe I've been missing out.

AMY
Ok. Put the beer down. We have to do it.

(The women perform Knee, G, Double B)

SHEP
Was that it? Was that the secret handshake? *(Pause)* Guys? *(Pause)* That was totally it, wasn't it?

CAROLINE
Shut up and grab your beer.

SHEP
Why?

SIAN
(Holds up her beer) To Nancy.

SHEP
To Nancy.

AMY
To Nancy.

CAROLINE
To Nancy.

(They all clink and drink. Silence. Watching. A few more seconds of silence and drinking)

SHEP
She was a lot heavier than I thought she'd be.

CAROLINE
The casket was.

AMY
No, she wasn't.

SHEP
You weren't holding the ropes, so easy for you to say.

(Silence)

AMY
Thank you.

SIAN
Who are you thanking?

AMY
You. All of you. I wouldn't have... couldn't have done this alone.

SHEP
Oh, I know.

CAROLINE
That was obvious.

AMY
Yes, but I know you have all risked a lot doing what we are doing and...

CAROLINE
Aim, we get it.

AMY
But what you did wasn't just for Nancy. It was for me too.

SIAN
Of course.

AMY
You... you saved me.

SIAN
Well.

CAROLINE
You'd do the same. Right?

AMY
Yes.

SIAN
Always, guys. Always.

SHEP
This is what I never got to have. You know with friends.

CAROLINE
You bear some of that blame.

SHEP
I know.

CAROLINE
But you've got it now.

SHEP
Not really. Gets harder as you get

older.

SIAN
Yes, but Care is saying you have it.

SHEP
She doesn't know that. Stoners are not great friends. Especially when--

AMY
(Interrupting) Us. Shep, Us!

SHEP
You guys? Oh really?

CAROLINE
Don't make me take it back.

SHEP
Ok. Ok. Thanks Wow. Really?

AMY/CAROLINE/SIAN
Yes.

SHEP
That's big.

(Silence)

AMY
Nance saw this.

SIAN
This?

AMY
"The sky will be purple and blue and pink and the sun will be deep orange and the clouds will seem like swirls."

CAROLINE
It is.

AMY
She said she'd be the sun bowing down in gratitude for her wonderful life.

(A beat as their faces change while watching the casket)

SHEP
Why's she still floating?

SIAN
Give it a second.

AMY
When is it going to sink?

CAROLINE
Give it time.

SIAN
It's bobbing.

AMY
Should we go out there again and…?

CAROLINE
No.

(Silence)

SHEP
Wait a second, you guys, don't caskets float?

(Lights out)

END OF PLAY

More Plays From SORDELET INK

Once A Ponzi Time
by Joe Foust

A Tale of Two Cities
by Christoper M Walsh
adapted from the novel by Charles Dickens

The Count of Monte Cristo
by Christoper M Walsh
adapted from the novel by Alexandre Dumas

The Moonstone
by Robert Kauzlaric
adapted from the novel by Wilkie Collins

Hound of the Baskervilles
by Althos Low
adapted from the novel by Sir Arthur Conan Doyle

Season on the Line
by Shawn Pfautsch
adapted from Herman Melville's Moby-Dick

My Italy Story & Long Gone Daddy
by Joseph Gallo

Eve of Ides
by David Blixt

Visit www.sordeletink.com for more!

Available Plays by Joseph Zettelmaier

It Came From Mars

Ebenezer - a Christmas Play

The Gravedigger - a Frankenstein play
adapted from the novel by Mary Shelly

The Scullery Maid

Dead Man's Shoes

Northern Aggression

All Childish Things

The Decade Dance

For information about production rights, visit:
www.jzettelmaier.com

NOVELS FROM
SORDELET INK

The Star-Cross'd Series
THE MASTER OF VERONA
VOICE OF THE FALCONER
FORTUNE'S FOOL
THE PRINCE'S DOOM
VARNISH'D FACES - STAR-CROSS'D SHORT STORIES

The Colossus Series
COLOSSUS: STONE & STEEL
COLOSSUS: THE FOUR EMPERORS

and coming 2016
COLOSSUS: WAIL OF THE FALLEN

HER MAJESTY'S WILL
a novel of Wit & Kit

All by bestselling author David Blixt!

THE DRAGONTAIL BUTTONHOLE
by Peter Curtis

VISIT WWW.SORDELETINK.COM FOR MORE!

www.ingramcontent.com/pod-product-compliance
Lightning Source LLC
Chambersburg PA
CBHW080723300426
44114CB00019B/2471